Nieuwe Zijde
Pages 72–87

Oude Zijde
Pages 58–71

Nieuwe
Zijde

Oude Zijde

Plantage

Eastern
Canal
Ring

Eastern Canal Ring
Page 116–125

Plantage
Pages 140–149

0 kilometres 500

0 miles 500

EYEWITNESS TRAVEL

AMSTERDAM

EYEWITNESS TRAVEL

AMSTERDAM

Main Contributors: **Robin Pascoe**
Christopher Catling

DK

DK

LONDON, NEW YORK,
MELBOURNE, MUNICH AND DELHI
www.dk.com

Project Editor Heather Jones
Art Editor Vanessa Hamilton
Editors Peter Adams, Sasha Heseltine,
Fiona Morgan, Alice Peebles, Nichola Tyrrell
US Editor Mary Sutherland
Designers Emma Hutton, Erika Lang, Malcolm Parchment

Contributors
Paul Andrews, Hedda Archbold, Marlene Edmunds,
Pip Farquharson, Adam Hopkins, Fred Mawer, Alison Melvin,
Kim Renfrew, Catherine Stebbings, Richard Widdows

Photographers
Max Alexander, Rupert Horrox, Kim Sayer

Illustrators
Nick Gibbard, Maltings Partnership,
Derrick Stone, Martin Woodward

Film outputting bureau Cooling Brown, London
Printed and bound in China

First American edition 1995

17 18 19 20 10 9 8 7 6 5 4 3 2

Published in the United States by DK Publishing,
345 Hudson Street, New York, New York 10014.

**Reprinted with revisions 1996, 1997, 1999, 2000, 2001,
2002, 2003, 2004, 2005, 2006, 2007, 2009, 2010, 2011, 2013, 2014, 2016**

Copyright 1995, 2016 © Dorling Kindersley Limited, London

A Penguin Random House Company

Published in the UK by Dorling Kindersley Limited.

A catalog record for this book is available from the Library of Congress.

ISSN 1542-1554

ISBN: 978-1-4654-3947-5

Throughout this book, floors are referred to in accordance with European usage;
i.e., the "first floor" is the floor above ground level.

MIX
Paper from
responsible sources
FSC
www.fsc.org   **FSC™ C018179**

**The information in this
DK Eyewitness Travel Guide is checked regularly.**
Every effort has been made to ensure that this book is as up-to-date as possible
at the time of going to press. Some details, however, such as telephone
numbers, opening hours, prices, gallery hanging arrangements and travel
information are liable to change. The publishers cannot accept responsibility for
any consequences arising from the use of this book, nor for any material on
third party websites, and cannot guarantee that any website address in this
book will be a suitable source of travel information. We value the views and
suggestions of our readers very highly. Please write to: Publisher, DK Eyewitness
Travel Guides, Dorling Kindersley, 80 Strand, London, WC2R 0RL, UK, or email:
travelguides@dk.com

Front cover main image: Achterburgwal Canal with Sint Nicolaasbasiliek

◀ Boats along the Canal Ring, at dusk

Contents

Model boat Scheepvaartmuseum

Introducing Amsterdam

Amsterdam Area by Area

Traditional lift bridge

Children in Dutch costume outside a church in the Zuiderzee Museum

Café terrace in Artis zoo

Survival Guide

Façade of the Rijksmuseum

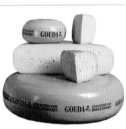
Wheels of Gouda cheese

Travellers' Needs

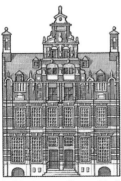

Dutch Renaissance canal house and details of cornices and gables

HOW TO USE THIS GUIDE

This guide helps you get the most from your stay in Amsterdam. It provides expert recommendations as well as detailed practical information. *Introducing Amsterdam* maps the city and sets it in its historical and cultural context. *Amsterdam Area by Area* describes the important sights, with maps, pictures and illustrations.

Further Afield looks at sights outside the city centre and *Beyond Amsterdam* explores other places near Amsterdam. Suggestions on food, drink, where to stay and what to do are made in *Travellers' Needs*, and *Survival Guide* has tips on everything from travel to Dutch telephones.

Amsterdam Area by Area

The centre of the city has been divided into seven sightseeing areas. Each area has its own chapter, which opens with a list of the sights described. All the sights are numbered and plotted on an Area Map. The detailed information for each sight is presented in numerical order, making it easy to locate within the chapter.

Sights at a Glance lists the chapter's sights by category: Churches, Museums and Galleries, Historic Buildings, Streets and Canals.

Each area of central Amsterdam has colour-coded thumb tabs.

A locator map shows where you are in relation to other areas of the city centre.

1 Area Map For easy reference, the sights are numbered and located on a map. The sights are also shown on the Amsterdam Street Finder on pages 280–87.

2 Street-by-Street Map This gives a bird's-eye view of the heart of each sightseeing area.

A suggested route for a walk covers the more interesting streets in the area.

Stars indicate the sights that no visitor should miss.

3 Detailed information on each sight All the sights in Amsterdam are described individually. Addresses and practical information are provided. The key to the symbols used in the information block is shown on the back flap.

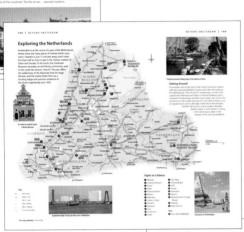

4 **Introduction to Beyond Amsterdam** Beyond Amsterdam has its own introduction, which provides an overview of the history and character of the region around Amsterdam and outlines what the region has to offer the visitor today. The area covered by this section is highlighted on the map of the Netherlands shown on page 167. It covers important cities, such as Den Haag, Haarlem and Rotterdam, as well as attractive towns and places of interest in the Dutch countryside.

5 **Regional Map** This gives an illustrated overview of the whole region. All the sights covered in this section are numbered, and the network of major roads is marked. There are also useful tips on getting around the region by bus and train.

6 **Detailed information on each sight** All the important cities, towns and other places to visit are described individually. They are listed in order, following the numbering given on the Regional Map. Within each town or city, there is detailed information on important buildings and other sights.

Stars indicate the best features and works of art.

The Visitors' Checklist provides a summary of the practical information you will need to plan your visit.

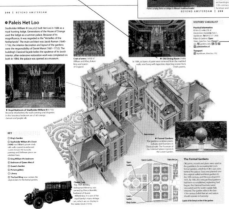

7 **The top sights** These are given two or more full pages. Historic buildings are dissected to reveal their interiors; museums and galleries have colour-coded floorplans to help you locate the most interesting exhibits.

INTRODUCING
AMSTERDAM

GREAT DAYS IN AMSTERDAM

Despite its compact size, Amsterdam has many different aspects and offers a range of attractions to suit all tastes and budgets. The city is home to some of the world's finest art galleries; there are bustling markets for those in search of street life; and for kids, there is a great choice of things to see and do. Over the following pages, you'll find itineraries for some of the best attractions Amsterdam has to offer, arranged first by theme and then by length of stay. Price guides include transport, meals and admission charges.

Rembrandt's studio in the Rembrandthuis

Two Great Artists

Two adults allow at least €100
- At home with Rembrandt
- Lunch by the Amstel river
- Van Gogh's greatest work

Morning
Of all the great painters that Amsterdam claims as its own, two stand head and shoulders above the rest: Rembrandt van Rijn and Vincent Van Gogh. Rembrandt's home from 1639 to 1658 is now the **Museum Het Rembrandthuis** *(see pp64–5)* and the house has been restored to look as it might have when he lived here, at the height of his wealth and fame. The atmosphere is such that one can clearly imagine the great artist and his family inhabiting these rooms. The museum houses an exhibition of Rembrandt's etchings and sketches, along with paintings by his contemporaries, notably his teacher Pieter Lastman. Equally interesting is the

recreation of the artist's studio, complete with chalks, charcoal, easels and brushes, not forgetting his wonderful "cabinet of curiosities" – a room cluttered with statues, stuffed birds and small beasts, arms and armour, all of which Rembrandt would have used as props in his portraits and still-lives. A great spot for lunch after the Rembrandthuis is Amstelhoeck, the café next to the **Nationale Opera & Ballet** *(see p244)*, just a minute's walk away. In summer its sunny terrace has a fine view of the Amstel, while in winter there is a cosy indoor restaurant.

Afternoon
The **Van Gogh Museum** *(see pp136–7)* houses the world's largest collection of the Dutch painter's work, with almost 800 paintings and drawings along with Van Gogh's own collection of glorious Japanese prints and an array of paintings by his contemporaries, including Paul Gauguin and Claude Monet. It is a dazzling collection, and you should allow 2–3 hours to take it in at leisure.

Hidden Histories

Two adults allow at least €120
- Explore life in hiding
- A vanished community
- Living history
- Secret church

Morning
The **Anne Frank House** *(see pp92–3)* receives up to 1,000 visitors a day, so try to get there early. In a tiny secret apartment above Otto Frank's warehouse, the Jewish Frank and van Pels families hid from the Nazis from 1942 until 1944, when they were betrayed and deported to concentration camps. The 13-year-old Anne Frank began recording life in hiding in her diary in July 1942 and it was published in 1947, two years after her death in Bergen-Belsen. There is a touching statue of Anne outside the **Westerkerk** *(see p92)*. Completed in 1631, the Westerkerk's tower is the tallest in the city at 85 m (278 ft) and

View of Prinsengracht from the tower of the Westerkerk

◀ *The Dutch Fleet of the India Company, 1675, by Ludolf Backhuysen* the climb to the top offers a breathtaking view. The Waterlooplein area was the heart of a Jewish community, who were drawn to the city in the 17th century because of its tolerance. The **Joods Historisch Museum** *(see pp66–7)* is housed in four former synagogues built in the 17th and 18th centuries and contains a collection of religious artifacts as well as documents relating to the Holocaust. The museum also has a great kosher café, which serves bagels, sandwiches and pastries.

Afternoon
A short walk away, the huge **Portuguese Synagogue** *(see p68)*, with its candlelit interiors, is still in use by the city's Sephardic Jews. Protestant Amsterdam in the 17th century, however, was less tolerant of Catholic worship. The **Museum Ons' Lieve Heer op Solder** *(see pp86–7)* is a perfectly restored "clandestine" church which was built at this time.

A Family Day

Family of four allow at least €140
- **Messing about in boats**
- **Ice cream, jugglers and fire-eaters**

Morning
Parental pedal-power provides the impetus for the first part of this day out. Amsterdam's **canal bikes** *(see p273)* are four-seater pedal boats that move at a gentle pace, passing old canalside houses, houseboats and nesting waterfowl. They can be rented in winter too, but for families this is really a summer activity. A good option is to pick up your vessel at the **Westerkerk** mooring and paddle around the picturesque Keizersgracht, before dropping it off at **Leidsestraat**. This excursion should take no more than an hour. Then stroll down to the bustling Leidseplein *(see p110)* with its many lively

Hands-on exhibits at the NEMO Science Center Amsterdam

outdoor cafés and street entertainers for a well-earned coffee and ice cream.

Afternoon
Take a tram to the **NEMO Science Center Amsterdam** *(see p152)*. This spectacular building looks like a giant, futuristic ship and is full of hands-on, state-of-the-art interactive exhibits for children of all ages. Allow at least a couple of hours to explore the possibilities of the themed technology, energy, science and humanity zones before heading for the centre's pleasant water-side terrace café-restaurant.

Colourful Markets

Two adults allow at least €50
- **Antiques and collectables**
- **Ethnic eating**
- **Vibrant street life**
- **Legendary nightlife**

Morning
You can buy just about anything in Amsterdam's markets. The **Waterlooplein** *(see p65)* open-air market still has the definite feel of the hippy era, with stalls selling tie-dyed clothing, exotic statuettes, vintage leather coats, army-surplus equipment and ceramics. Dive further into this open-air labyrinth to find 19th- and 20th-century collectables, from classic rock albums to psychedelic posters, pipes and cigarette holders, china,

glassware, and more. A short walk and tram ride from Waterlooplein, the **Albert Cuypmarkt** *(see p124)* is the heart and soul of De Pijp, the most cosmopolitan part of Amsterdam. It is an ideal place for lunch – there are many ethnic restaurants on and around Albert Cuypstraat, including Moroccan, Surinamese and Turkish.

Afternoon
There are more than 100 shops and 300 street stalls along Albert Cuypstraat, selling everything from exotic fruit and spices to Dutch cheese, chocolates, sausage and seafood, flowers, clothes and household goods. This is authentic Amsterdam street life at its best. You could easily spend an afternoon here, before taking a 10-minute stroll back to the **Leidseplein** *(see p110)* and a night out at one of its top night-time venues.

Eclectic stalls lining the length of the Albert Cuypmarkt

2 Days

Two adults allow at least €360

- Savour Amsterdam's distinguished history at the Koninklijk Paleis
- Stroll along the atmospheric canals of the delightful Grachtengordel
- Be moved by the Anne Frank House

Day 1

Morning Start the day in the **Dam** (see pp74–5), a bustling, busy square at the heart of the city. Dodging the trams, proceed to the **Nieuwe Kerk** (see pp76–7), one of Amsterdam's most impressive Gothic buildings. Afterwards, pop next door to explore the **Koninklijk Paleis** (Royal Palace) (see p78), built in the 17th century as the Stadhuis (town hall) when the city was at its richest. Inside, the highlight is a magnificent marble chamber, the Citizens' Hall.

Afternoon Take a stroll along the **Singel** (see pp100–102), the first of the four canals that make up the Grachtengordel, or "girdle of canals". This is Amsterdam at its most beguiling, its olive-green canals spanned by hump-backed bridges. Look out for the **Museum Van Loon** (see p124), an intriguing old canal house, and the **Westerkerk** (see p92), with its mighty spire. Next, head for the **Anne Frank House** (see pp92–3), where the teenage Jewish diarist Anne Frank listened to the church bells from her hiding place.

Day 2

Morning Spend a couple of hours at the **Rijksmuseum** (see pp130–33), Amsterdam's principal art museum, admiring its fabulous collection of Dutch paintings, especially the Rembrandts. Afterwards, spend some time in the **Van Gogh Museum** (see pp136–7), devoted to the greatest of all Dutch painters, and which contains the world's largest collection of his work.

Afternoon After some lunch, visit the city's third major museum, the **Stedelijk** (see pp138–9), a recently revamped gallery devoted to modern and contemporary art. Or, if museum fatigue is setting in, venture out from the tourist zone to explore the maze-like streets of the **Jordaan** (see pp89–95) or rest your legs on a **canal boat trip** (see p272).

3 Days

Two adults allow at least €510

- Explore the city's waterways on a boat trip
- Admire the superb artistry of Van Gogh at the Van Gogh Museum
- Shop till you drop in the bijou shops and stores of the Nine Streets

Day 1

Morning Begin in the charming **Museum Ons' Lieve Heer op Solder** (see pp86–7), where Catholics once held mass away from the prying eyes of the Protestants, and then proceed to the city's most atmospheric church, **Oude Kerk** (see pp70–71). Clearing the Red Light District, it's a pleasant stroll to the **Begijnhof** (see p79), a court-yard complex dating back hundreds of years, and the Spui, with its bevy of bookshops.

Afternoon People-watch at the city's main square, the **Dam** (see pp74–5), and pop into two

Tree-lined path in Vondelpark

of Amsterdam's proudest buildings, the **Koninklijk Paleis** (Royal Palace) (see p78), which started out as the Town Hall (Stadhuis) and the graceful **Nieuwe Kerk** (see pp76–7). Watch the sun set while relaxing on a **canal boat trip** (see p272).

Day 2

Morning Aim for the **Stedelijk Museum** (see pp138–9), which boasts a wonderful collection of modern and contemporary art. You can easily spend a whole morning here, but take a break by wandering the footpaths of the green and leafy **Vondelpark** (see pp134–5), home to a rowdy bunch of parakeets.

Afternoon Relish the superb artistic legacy of Van Gogh at the **Van Gogh Museum** (see pp136–7), which delves into the troubled life and times of this brilliant artist. Many of Van Gogh's key paintings are displayed here. Afterwards, be sure to pop into the **Rijksmuseum** (see pp130–3), the biggest museum in Amsterdam, which has an impressive collection of paintings from the city's Golden Age.

Day 3

Morning
Stroll the lynchpin of the **Grachtengordel** (see p89), the **Golden Bend** (Gouden Bocht; see p114), where opulent old mansions frame the Herengracht canal. Allow an hour to sample the architectural flavour of the area before visiting two hand-somely restored canal houses, the **Museum Willet-Holthuysen** (see pp122–3) and the **Museum Van Loon** (see p124). You should also drop by the **Bijbels Museum** (see pp114–15), which wins the quirkiness award for its assorted models of Jerusalem.

Afternoon Don't miss the **Anne Frank House** (see pp92–3), an evocative memorial to suffering and persecution in the building where Anne and a small group of Jews hid from the Germans in World War II. It is extremely popular – so arrive early. Then proceed to the **Westerkerk** (see p92), the city's most impressive and largest church, and stroll on to the chic designer and vintage shops of the cobbled **Nine Streets** neighbourhood *(see p235)*.

5 Days

Two adults allow at least €680

- **Enjoy fine Dutch paintings at the Rijksmuseum**
- **Sample the life of a rich Amsterdam merchant at the Van Loon Museum**
- **Wander the narrow streets of Marken beside the waters of the Markermeer**

Day 1
Morning Walk along the busy **Damrak**, once a canal crowded with merchant ships sailing into the heart of the city. The Damrak ends at the Dam square, and it's here you feel the beat of the city. Investigate two fascinating buildings beside the Dam, the **Koninklijk Paleis** (Royal Palace) *(see p78)* and **Nieuwe Kerk** *(see pp76–7)*, where the country's most famous admiral, de Ruyter, lies within the opulent tombs.

Afternoon Get the full flavour of 17th-century Amsterdam at the **Rembrandthuis** *(see pp64–5)*, where Rembrandt lived during the happiest years of his life, before bankruptcy overwhelmed him. Also in this corner of the city, drop by **Gassan Diamonds** *(see p238)*, one of the city's few remaining diamond factories complete with shop and showroom.

Day 2
Morning Begin the day with a visit to the **Anne Frank House** *(see pp92–3)*, the secret refuge of Anne Frank and several other Jews in World War II; arrive early to avoid the crowds. Afterwards, make the short walk along the canal to the **Westerkerk** *(see p92)*, where Rembrandt was buried. The church is a key sight in the **Grachtengordel** *(see p89)*, the canals encircling much of

One of the ornate bedrooms at Museum Van Loon

the city. Stop by the eccentric **Bijbels Museum** *(see pp114–15)* to see its antique bibles.

Afternoon Make a beeline for Herengracht's **Golden Bend** *(see p114)*, where a string of handsome merchants' houses comprise the prettiest part of the Grachtengordel. Be sure to visit two of them – the **Museum Willet-Holthuysen** *(see pp122–3)* and the **Museum Van Loon** *(see p124)*. Allow half an hour for each, followed by some perusing of the fancy shops of the so-called **Nine Streets** *(see p235)*.

Day 3
Morning If the weather is good, begin the day with an easy stroll round the leafy **Vondelpark** *(see pp134–5)*; if it's raining, see the city on an enclosed **canal boat trip** *(see p272)*. Afterwards, make your way to the outstanding **Van Gogh Museum** *(see pp136–7)*, devoted to the eponymous painter, who inspired many of the modern artists whose works are displayed at the adjacent **Stedelijk Museum** *(see pp138–9)*.

Afternoon Explore the oldest part of Amsterdam, beginning with the **Spui** *(see p74)*, one of the most vibrant squares in the city. Then proceed to the quiet charms of the convent-like **Begijnhof** *(see p79)* and the fascinating **Oude Kerk** *(see pp70–71)*, in the Red Light District. Wander along the canal from here and you will soon reach Amsterdam's quaintest museum, the historic **Museum Ons' Lieve Heer op Solder**

(see pp86–7), which is itself not far from bustling **Centraal Station** *(see p81)*.

Day 4
Morning Be sure to visit Amsterdam's best open-air market, the **Albert Cuypmarkt** *(see p124)*. To get from one end of the market to the other takes about 20 minutes, but allow longer if you are bargain hunting. Drop in at the **Heineken Experience** *(see p124)* to learn the legends and sample a drop or two of the namesake brew of the country's largest beer producer.

Afternoon If imbibing lager leaves you in a reflective mood, you can ponder the paintings of the **Rijksmuseum** *(see pp130–33)*, the city's premier and unmissable art gallery. Alternatively, elude the tourist crowds by delving into the cosy **Jordaan** and **Western Islands** areas *(see pp89–95)*.

Day 5
Escape the city by bike: catch a ferry across the River IJ from **Centraal Station** *(see p81)* and cycle across the pancake-flat landscape until you reach the coast. Then follow the cycle trail along the sea dyke as far as the inordinately pretty village of **Marken** *(see p174)*, about 25 km (16 miles) from Amsterdam. Allow time for a fishy lunch at one of the pretty cafés lining the waterfront. Alternatively, you can catch the bus straight to Marken from outside Centraal Station – saving your legs and allowing an extended lunch break.

Putting Amsterdam on the Map

Although the Netherlands' seat of government is at Den Haag, Amsterdam is the nominal capital. It is the country's largest city, with a population of around 811,000, and the most visited, receiving over 9.5 million foreign visitors a year. It stands on precariously low-lying ground at the confluence of the Amstel and IJ rivers near the IJsselmeer and, like much of the Netherlands, would flood frequently but for land reclamation and sea defences. This position places Amsterdam at the heart of the Randstad, a term used to describe the crescent-shaped conurbation covering much of the provinces of Noord Holland, Zuid Holland and Utrecht, and encompassing the cities of Utrecht, Rotterdam, Den Haag, Leiden and Haarlem.

Western Europe

NORWAY
SWEDEN
North Sea
DENMARK
REP. OF IRELAND
UNITED KINGDOM
NETHERLANDS ○ Amsterdam
GERMANY
BELGIUM
CZECH REPUBLIC
FRANCE
SWITZ. AUSTRIA
Atlantic Ocean
ITALY
SPAIN

Newcastle
See inset map below

Den Helder

NOORD HOLLAND
N9
N242 Enkhuizen
Hoorn
Alkmaar
IJsse
N30
Markermee
Leylst

AMSTERDAM

Schiphol ✈

Leiden
ZUID HOLLAND
Amersfoort
Den Haag
A44
Utrecht
UTRECH
A12
Gouda
Delft
Rotterdam ✈
Le
Le
Hoek van Holland
Rotterdam
A27
A2

Hull, Harwich

Barendrecht
Dordrecht
A15
A29
A16
's Hertogenbosch
N59
NOORD BRAB
Zierikzee
A17
A59
Hull
Breda
A27
Tilburg
ZEELAND
A58
Bergen op Zoom
A58
Eindhover
Middelburg

Ramsgate
Zeebrugge
A12
A1
Turnhout
N617
A21
Oostende
Antwerpen ✈
Albert Kanaal
Nieuwpoort
Brugge
Antwerpen
A14
A13
A10
A1
Mechelen
Demer
A17
Gent
BELGIUM
A2
Kortrijk
A14
A10
Hass
Ieper
A25
Brussels ✈
Leuven
Sint-Truiden
Bruxelles
A3
A22
Oudenaarde
A26
Tourcoing
A8
A7
A4

For map symbols *see back flap*

Norden

Wilhelmshaven

Bremerhaven

N210

EMS Jude Kanal

Emden

GRONINGEN

Leer

A28

Oldenburg

N355

Groningen

A7

Hunte

A28

Leeuwarden

Groningen ✈

Friesoythe

A29

A1

Assen

DRENTHE

Cloppenburg

Heerenveen

A28

Vechta

A32

69

Emmen

A37

Meppen

GERMANY

Meppel

N213

A1

Hoogeveen

A50

Vecht

Lingen

51

Zwolle

OVER IJSSEL

Nordhorn

Mittelland Kanal

A26

N35

Almelo

Osnabrück

NETHERLANDS

A1

Rheine

A30

A33

Deventer

70

Ems

A1

Apeldoorn

Enschede

✈ *Münster*

Berkel

A31

54

A50

GELDERLAND

Arnhem

IJssel

Coesfeld

megen

A43

N52

Rhein

A3

A31

A73

A57

Wesel

Recklinghausen

A2

Dortmund

Key

▫ Greater Amsterdam
▫ Area below sea level
▬ Motorway
▬ Major road
— Railway
- - - Country boundary

0 kilometres   20
0 miles   20

Helmond

hoven

A67

A40

A61

Blerick

Krefeld

LIMBURG

A73

Rur

Mönchengladbach

A2

A61

A44

57

✈ *Maastricht*

A4

Maastricht

A2

Aachen

A3

Liège

Amsterdam and Environs

Heemskerk

N244

N247

A9

N8

Markermeer

Purmerend

Beverwijk

A7

Volendam

IJmuiden

See next page

Haarlem

AMSTERDAM

Almere

Zandvoort

IJmeer

A6

Almere Haven

N201

A1

Hoofddorp

✈ *Schiphol*

Weesp

Hillegom

A4

Bussum

N206

N201

A1

Sassenheim

Uithoorn

A2

Hilversum

A44

A4

N201

Mijdrecht

Greater Amsterdam

Amsterdam retained its characteristic horseshoe shape within the Singelgracht until well into the 19th century. This pattern is still clearly visible in the network of streets and canals in the city centre. Since then the city has expanded dramatically in all directions. The whole of Greater Amsterdam enjoys first-class public transport (see Transport Map on inside back cover).

Key

- Central Amsterdam
- Greater Amsterdam
- Motorway
- Major road
- Railway

0 kilometres   2

0 miles   1

For map symbols see back flap

Central Amsterdam

This guide divides central Amsterdam into seven distinct areas, each of which has its own chapter. Most city sights are contained in these areas. The Oude Zijde and Nieuwe Zijde make up the two halves of medieval Amsterdam, while the Museum Quarter was developed in the 19th century and has the three most important national museums. In between lies the Canal Ring, which retains many fine buildings from Amsterdam's Golden Age, while the Plantage *(see pp140–49)*, once an area of green space outside the city, is today best known for the zoological and botanical gardens.

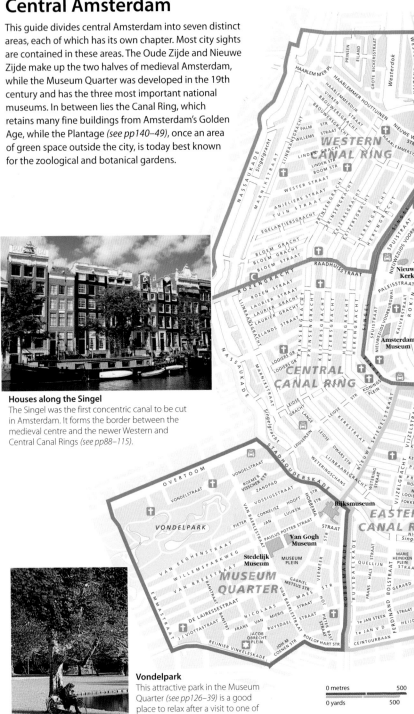

Houses along the Singel
The Singel was the first concentric canal to be cut in Amsterdam. It forms the border between the medieval centre and the newer Western and Central Canal Rings *(see pp88–115)*.

Vondelpark
This attractive park in the Museum Quarter *(see pp126–39)* is a good place to relax after a visit to one of Amsterdam's museums.

| 0 metres | 500 |
| 0 yards | 500 |

Spires of Nieuwe Kerk and the Magna Plaza
The Nieuwe Zijde's skyline *(see pp72–87)* is pierced by the Neo-Gothic spire of Magna Plaza (the former Postkantoor), the steeples of the Nieuwe Kerk and the statues on the Koninklijk Paleis.

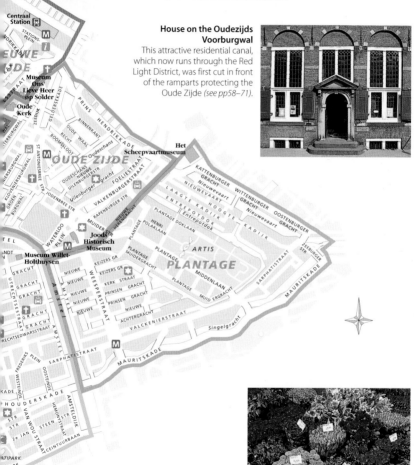

House on the Oudezijds Voorburgwal
This attractive residential canal, which now runs through the Red Light District, was first cut in front of the ramparts protecting the Oude Zijde *(see pp58–71)*.

Flowers at the Bloemenmarkt
A fragrant, floating flower market, the Bloemenmarkt is situated beside the Munttoren on the Singel in the Eastern Canal Ring *(see pp116–25)*.

Key

Major sight

THE HISTORY OF AMSTERDAM

Amsterdam, the greatest planned city of northern Europe, is today one in which beauty and serenity co-exist happily with a slightly seamy underside. Both parts of this split personality continue to draw visitors. Most of the racier aspects of Amsterdam spring directly from the city's long tradition of religious and political tolerance. The notion of individual freedom of conscience was fought for, long and hard, during the struggles against Spanish domination in the 16th century. This belief stands firm today, with the caveat that no one should be harmed by the actions of others – a factor that sparked off the riots involving squatters in the 1970s.

The city was founded as a small fishing village in an improbable position on marsh at the mouth of the Amstel river. The waters around the village were controlled by a system of dykes and polders, and the young township expanded prodigiously to become the chief trading city of northern Europe,

and ultimately, in the 17th century, the centre of a massive empire stretching across the world. The construction of the canals and gabled houses in the 16th and 17th centuries coincided with a period of fine domestic architecture. The result is a city centre of unusually consistent visual beauty. By the 18th century, Amsterdam was a major financial centre, but internal unrest and restrictions imposed under Napoleonic rule led to a decline in her fortunes.

The city quietly slipped into a period of obscurity, and industrialization came late. In the 20th century, however, the city entered the mainstream again. Now, well into the new millennium, ambitious architectural projects have given a new lease of life to former derelict areas, such as the Eastern Docklands and westwards along the banks of the IJ; Zuidas, the area south of the ring road also known as the "Financial Mile", is now a major business hub complemented by top-notch cultural facilities.

Plan of Amsterdam (c.1725) showing the Grachtengordel and Plantage *(see pp140–49)*

◀ *The Maid of Amsterdam Receiving the Homage of her People* (c.1685) by Gérard de Lairesse

The Origins of Amsterdam

Amsterdam emerged from the mists of the Low Countries in about 1200, on a watery site at the mouth of the Amstel river. It was a settlement of fisherfolk before turning to trade. The first permanent dwellings were built on terps, man-made mounds high enough to provide protection from flood water. As the settlement grew, it was fashioned by dynastic and religious combat, with feudal struggles between the lords van Amstel and the counts of Holland, who had the backing of the all-powerful bishops of Utrecht *(see p204)*. This rivalry continued into the next century.

Extent of the City
  1100   ☐ Today

Farming on polders
outside the village walls

Dam

Cooking Pot
Sturdy earthenware pots were used for cooking communal meals over an open fire in the kitchen area of 13th-century houses.

Wooden defence walls

Lord Gijsbrecht
The 19th-century etching shows Gijsbrecht van Amstel IV being marched into Utrecht as a prisoner by Guy of Hainaut, brother of the Count of Holland, in 1298.

The Village of Amsterdam in 1300

This medieval artist's impression shows the first tiny settlement on polders along the Damrak. The village was protected by wooden walls, and it is thought that the castle of the Van Amstels may have been located in the area around today's Dam square (see pp74–5).

Livestock grazed
on reclaimed land called polder.

1000 Fishermen float down Rhine in hollow pine logs

Small wooden cog ship used for fishing

| 1000 | 1050 | 1100 | 115 |

Primitive boat dating from c.6000 BC

1015 Local feudal leader repels attack by German tribes and declares himself Count of Holland

c.1125 Fishermen build huts at mouth of the Amstel river

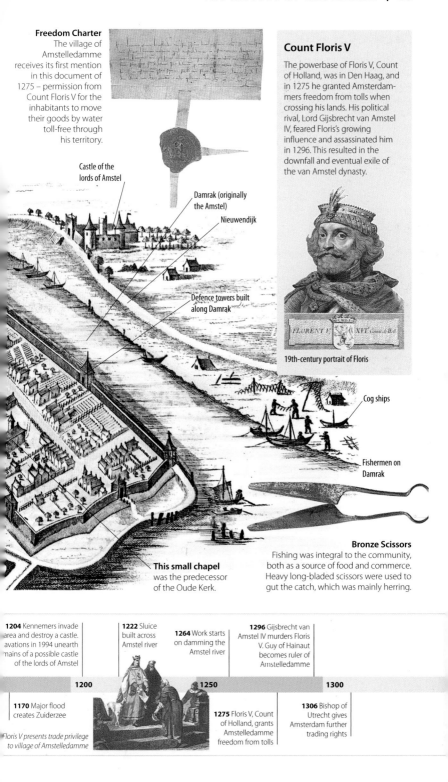

Freedom Charter
The village of Amstelledamme receives its first mention in this document of 1275 – permission from Count Floris V for the inhabitants to move their goods by water toll-free through his territory.

Count Floris V

The powerbase of Floris V, Count of Holland, was in Den Haag, and in 1275 he granted Amsterdammers freedom from tolls when crossing his lands. His political rival, Lord Gijsbrecht van Amstel IV, feared Floris's growing influence and assassinated him in 1296. This resulted in the downfall and eventual exile of the van Amstel dynasty.

FLORENT V XVI. Comte de Holl

19th-century portrait of Floris

Castle of the lords of Amstel

Damrak (originally the Amstel)

Nieuwendijk

Defence towers built along Damrak

Cog ships

Fishermen on Damrak

Bronze Scissors
Fishing was integral to the community, both as a source of food and commerce. Heavy long-bladed scissors were used to gut the catch, which was mainly herring.

This small chapel was the predecessor of the Oude Kerk.

1204 Kennemers invade area and destroy a castle. Excavations in 1994 unearth remains of a possible castle of the lords of Amstel

1222 Sluice built across Amstel river

1264 Work starts on damming the Amstel river

1296 Gijsbrecht van Amstel IV murders Floris V. Guy of Hainaut becomes ruler of Amstelledamme

1200

1250

1300

1170 Major flood creates Zuiderzee

Floris V presents trade privilege to village of Amstelledamme

1275 Floris V, Count of Holland, grants Amstelledamme freedom from tolls

1306 Bishop of Utrecht gives Amsterdam further trading rights

Medieval Amsterdam

The little town at the mouth of the Amstel fortified itself against both its enemies and the surrounding water. Amsterdam grew rich quickly after the discovery of a method of curing herring in 1385, which preserved the fish longer, enabling it to be exported. The town became a port for handling beer from Hamburg. Elaborate waterside houses with warehouses attached were used to service the trade. The Low Countries were under the rule of the dukes of Burgundy, and control passed by marriage to the Austrian Habsburgs.

Extent of the City

  1300   Today

Canalside House

Early canal houses were simple structures, built of wood with a thatched roof. From a single-storey design with the front and back on different levels, the layouts grew more complex. At the front, side rooms became separated off from the main room, and the back house was similarly divided up. The family slept on the first floor and goods were stored under the roof.

Miracle of Amsterdam
This tapestry cushion depicts a miraculous event. A dying man was given the Sacrament which he regurgitated. Thrown on the fire, the Host would not burn.

The wooden façades
had simple spout gables
(see pp98–9).

Flour, beer and other foodstuffs were stored under the sloping roof.

Philip of Burgundy and Isabella of Portugal
Philip was the ruler of the Low Countries after 1419. He married Isabella of Portugal in 1430.

Timber structure

1304 Lord Gijsbrecht van Amstel exiled

Early 1300s Work starts on Oude Kerk *(see pp70–71)*

Misericord in the Oude Kerk

c.1380 Work begins on Nieuwe Kerk *(see pp76–7)*

1385 Willem Beukelszoon discovers method of curing herring

1300	1325	1350	1375	140•

1301 Guy of Hainaut made Bishop of Utrecht

1323 Count of Holland designates Amsterdam a toll port for beer

1345 Miracle of Amsterdam

1350 Amsterdam becomes a beer and grain entrepôt

Stained-glass window in the Nieuwe Kerk

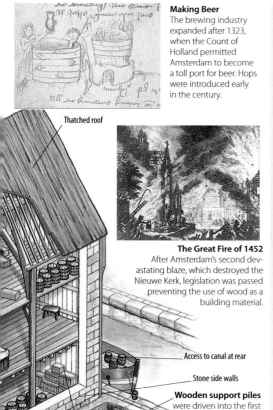

Making Beer
The brewing industry expanded after 1323, when the Count of Holland permitted Amsterdam to become a toll port for beer. Hops were introduced early in the century.

Thatched roof

The Great Fire of 1452
After Amsterdam's second devastating blaze, which destroyed the Nieuwe Kerk, legislation was passed preventing the use of wood as a building material.

Access to canal at rear

Stone side walls

Wooden support piles
were driven into the first stable layer of sand.

Warehouse space

Amsterdam's Seal
The seal shows the diagonal crosses of St Andrew, the coat of arms of the Habsburgs and the cog ship that brought wealth through trade.

Where to See Medieval Amsterdam

Few buildings remain from this period, as fire destroyed two-thirds of the city. The Oude Kerk (see pp70–71) dates from the early 14th century and the Nieuwe Kerk (pp76–7) from 1380. The Agnietenkapel (p63) was built in 1470 and is one of very few Gothic chapels to survive the Alteration of 1578 (pp26–7).

The Waag (p62)
Built in 1488, this was originally a gateway in the city wall.

No. 34 Begijnhof (p79)
Dating from the second half of the 15th century, this is one of the oldest wooden houses in the city.

Maximilian marries Maria of Burgundy

1477 Charles's daughter Maria marries Maximilian Habsburg of Austria

1452 Second Great Fire of Amsterdam

1480 Defensive walls built around Amsterdam

1494 Maximilian is Holy Roman Emperor. Power passes to his son, Philip, who marries the daughter of Isabella of Spain

1425

1450

1475

1500

1421 First Great Fire of Amsterdam

1419 Philip the Good of Burgundy begins to unify the Low Countries

1467 Charles the Bold succeeds Philip of Burgundy

Charles the Bold

1482 Maria dies and Maximilian Habsburg rules the Netherlands

1500 Birth of Philip's son, the future Emperor Charles V and king of Spain

The Age of Intolerance

By 1500, Amsterdam had outpaced rivals to become the main power in the province of Holland. Trade in the Baltic provided wealth and the city grew rapidly. Spain's Habsburg rulers tried to halt the Protestant Reformation sweeping northern Europe. Dutch resistance to Philip II of Spain resulted in 80 years of civil war and religious strife. Amsterdam sided with Spain but switched loyalties in 1578 – an event known as the Alteration – to become the fiercely Protestant capital of an infant Dutch Republic.

Extent of the City

▨ 1500   ▢ Today

Anabaptists' Uprising (1535)
An extremist Protestant cult of Anabaptists seized the Stadhuis. Many were executed after eviction.

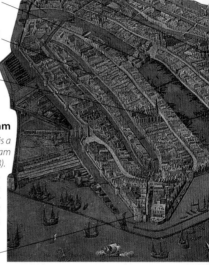

Nieuwe Kerk (1395)

Rokin

Dam square

Oudezijds Voorburgwal

Oude Kerk (1306)

Schreierstoren

Perspective of Amsterdam

This painted woodcut is a bird's-eye view of Amsterdam by Cornelis Anthonisz (1538). It is a critically important, detailed and precise map, heralding a centuries-long tradition of world-class map making in the city.

William of Orange
William, portrayed in 1555 by Anthonius Mor, led the Dutch against the Spanish until his assassination in Delft (see p197).

Much of the farmland in the Netherlands is below sea level.

1502 Population of Amsterdam 12,000

1516 Charles becomes king of Spain

1535 Anabaptists demonstrate on Dam square. Mass executions follow. Start of 40 years of religious strife

1550 Edict of Blood decrees death for Protestant heretics

1500	1510	1520	1530	1540

1506 Charles rules over the 17 provinces of the Netherlands

1519 Charles becomes Holy Roman Emperor, Charles V

Charles V, Holy Roman Emperor, king of Spain and ruler of the Netherlands

1543 Charles V unifies Low Countries

1551 Population of Amsterdam about 30,000

The Guild of St George (1533)
Guilds set up to keep order in the growing city later formed the Civic Guard *(see pp84–5)*. Map maker Cornelis Anthonisz painted this guild at supper.

Where to See 16th-Century Amsterdam

Few buildings of early 16th-century provenance remain, but No. 1 Zeedijk *(see p69)* was built mid-century as a hostel for sailors. The Civic Guards' Gallery at the Amsterdams Historisch Museum *(pp82–85)* contains a series of splendid group portraits of 16th-century militia companies and guilds.

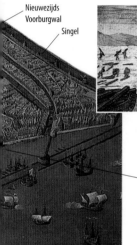

Nieuwezijds Voorburgwal

Singel

The Third Expedition
Gerrit de Veer's copper engraving (1597) shows Willem Barentsz on his search for a passage to the Arctic Sea.

Damrak

Montelbaanstoren
The lower section of the tower was built in 1512 *(see p68)*, forming part of the city defences.

Silver Drinking Horn
As the guilds grew richer, ceremony played a larger part in their lives. This ornate drinking horn shows St George defending the hapless maiden against the dragon.

Wind-powered pump

Sea

Draining the Polders
"Gangs" of windmills were built to drain the low-lying land. Each mill scooped water up, stage by stage, until it drained away into the sea *(see p175)*.

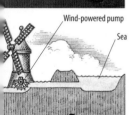

1555 Charles V abdicates. Philip II of Spain succeeds

Duke of Alva

1567 Duke of Alva introduces heavy taxation in Amsterdam

1578 Calvinists take civil power and expel Catholics from Amsterdam in the Alteration

1581 Philip II becomes king of Portugal

1596–7 Explorer Willem Barentsz finds route to Arctic Sea

1598 Philip II dies, unable to subdue Dutch Protestants

1560	1570	1580	1590	1600

1566 Calvinist iconoclasts demolish religious art in *Beeldenstorm*

c.1568 Beginning of Dutch Revolt under Protestant William of Orange

1579 Northern provinces sign Union of Utrecht

1584 William of Orange assassinated in Delft

1580 Spain absorbs Portugal, and Dutch establish new trade routes to the east

William was shot on the staircase of his headquarters in Delft in 1584 (see p197)

The Golden Age of Amsterdam

The 17th century was truly a Golden Age for Amsterdam. The population soared; three great canals, bordered by splendid houses, were built in a triple ring round the city; and scores of painters and architects were at work. Fortunes were made and lost, and this early capitalism produced paupers who were cared for by charitable institutions – a radical idea for the time. In 1648, an uneasy peace was formalized with Catholic Spain, causing tension between Amsterdam's Calvinist burgomasters and the less religious House of Orange, dominant elsewhere in the country.

Extent of the City
🟦 1600   ⬜ Today

Self-Portrait as the Apostle Paul (1661)
Rembrandt *(see p64)* was one of many artists working in Amsterdam in the mid-17th century.

Livestock and grain trading

Nieuwe Kerk (1395)

The new Stadhuis
(now the Koninklijk Paleis) was being constructed behind wooden scaffolding.

The Love Letter (1666)
Genre painting *(see p131)*, such as this calm domestic interior by Jan Vermeer, became popular as society grew more sophisticated.

Dam Square In 1656

Money poured into Amsterdam at this time of civic expansion. Jan Lingelbach (c. 1624–74) painted Dam square as a busy, thriving and cosmopolitan market, full of traders and wealthy merchants.

Delft Tiles
Delicate flower paintings were popular themes on 17th-century Delft tiles *(see p197)*, used as decoration in wealthy households.

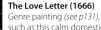

1625 Frederick Henry of Orange is stadholder. Plans to control navy from Den Haag fail

1642 Rembrandt paints *The Night Watch (see p131)*

Prince Frederick Henry of Orange

1614 Work finishes on Zuiderkerk *(see p64)*

1631 Rembrandt comes to live in Amsterdam *(see p64)*

1600	1610	1620	1630	1640

1609 Plan for triple ring of canals round heart of Amsterdam

1613 Work starts on first phase of canals

17th-century botanical drawing of a tulip

1634 Tulip mania begins

1637 The great tulip crash

Flora's Bandwagon (1636)
Many allegories were painted during "tulip mania". This satirical oil by HG Pot symbolizes the idiocy of investors who paid for rare bulbs with their weight in gold, forcing prices up until the market collapsed.

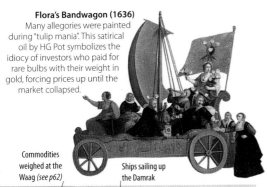

Commodities weighed at the Waag (see p62)

Ships sailing up the Damrak

Cargo unloaded by cranes

Turkish traders

Giving the Bread
The painting by Willem van Valckert shows the needy receiving alms. A rudimentary welfare system was introduced in the 1640s.

Where to See 17th-Century Amsterdam

Many public buildings sprang up as Amsterdam grew more wealthy. The Westerkerk (see p92) was designed by Hendrick de Keyser in 1620, the Lutherse Kerk (p80) by Adriaan Dortsman in 1671. Elias Bouman built the Portuguese Synagogue (p68) in 1675 for members of the immigrant Sephardic Jewish community (p66).

Apollo (c.1648)
Artus Quellien's statue is in the South Gallery of the Koninklijk Paleis (see p78).

Rembrandthuis (1606)
Jacob van Campen added the pediment in 1633 (see pp64–5).

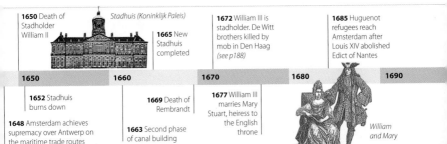

1650 Death of Stadholder William II

Stadhuis (Koninklijk Paleis)

1665 New Stadhuis completed

1672 William III is stadholder. De Witt brothers killed by mob in Den Haag (see p188)

1685 Huguenot refugees reach Amsterdam after Louis XIV abolished Edict of Nantes

1650 **1660** **1670** **1680** **1690**

1652 Stadhuis burns down

1669 Death of Rembrandt

1677 William III marries Mary Stuart, heiress to the English throne

William and Mary

1648 Amsterdam achieves supremacy over Antwerp on the maritime trade routes

1663 Second phase of canal building

The Golden Age Overseas

Supremacy in the Netherlands led to success overseas for Amsterdam. The Dutch colonized the Indonesian Archipelago, establishing a profitable empire based on spice trading in the East. The Dutch East India Company (VOC) thrived, using vast wooden ships called East Indiamen. In the New World, the Dutch ruled large parts of Brazil and bought Manhattan from its native owners, naming it New Amsterdam. However, war with England radically trimmed Dutch sea power by the end of the 17th century.

Purchase of Manhattan
In 1626, explorer Peter Minuit bought the island of Manhattan from the Native Americans for $24.

Salvaged Silverware
The *Batavia* sank off the coast of western Australia in 1629. This bed knob, ewer and plate were salvaged in 1972.

Main mast · Steering stand

Officers' cabin

Mizzen mast

Poop deck

World Map (1676)
Joan Blaeu's map charted the known world, with parts of Asia and Australia missing.

The Batavia

Owned by the VOC, the Batavia *was an East Indiaman, with three main masts. She was 45 m (148 ft) in length and carried a complement of about 350, including crew, soldiers and families.*

VOC logo

Peter Stuyvesant

1602 Dutch East India Company (VOC) founded

1620 Pilgrim Fathers depart for the New World *(see p187)*

1642 Abel Tasman discovers Tasmania

1600	1610	1620	1630	1640

1595 First voyage to Indonesia via Cape of Good Hope

1609 Hugo Grotius advocates freedom of trade at sea

1621 Dutch West India Company founded

1626 Peter Minuit buys Manhattan and founds New Amsterdam

Dutch Battle Ships (1683)
Ludolf Backhuysen (1631–1708) painted the
Dutch battle fleet routing the rival Portuguese
navy off the coast of northern Spain.

The Dutch East India Company

Founded in 1602, the VOC had a
monopoly on all profits from trade
east of the Cape of Good Hope. It
became a public company and
many a Dutch merchant's fortune
was made. By 1611, it was the
leading importer of spices into
Europe, with ships ranging as far
as China, Japan and Indonesia. For
nearly 200 years the VOC ran a
commercial empire more
powerful than some countries.

Het Scheepvaartmuseum (see
pp148–9) has a hall devoted to
the VOC. A replica of the East
Indiaman, the *Amsterdam*, is
moored outside.

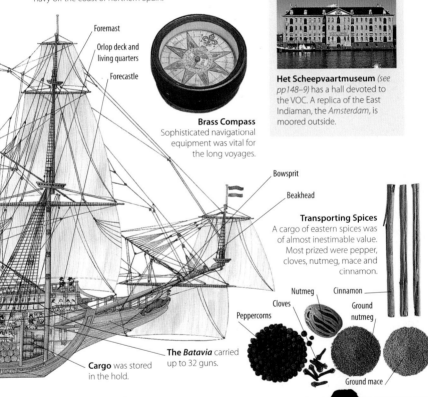

Foremast

Orlop deck and
living quarters

Forecastle

Brass Compass
Sophisticated navigational
equipment was vital for
the long voyages.

Bowsprit

Beakhead

Transporting Spices
A cargo of eastern spices was
of almost inestimable value.
Most prized were pepper,
cloves, nutmeg, mace and
cinnamon.

Nutmeg

Cinnamon

Cloves

Ground
nutmeg

Peppercorns

Ground mace

The *Batavia* carried
up to 32 guns.

Cargo was stored
in the hold.

| 1650 | 1660 | 1670 | 1680 | 1690 |

1647 Peter Stuyvesant made
governor of New Amsterdam

1648 Treaty of Munster ends
war with Spain. Dutch
Republic recognized

1664 British take
possession of New
Amsterdam

1665 Admiral de
Ruyter (see p77)
becomes
commander-in-
chief of the
Dutch navy

1672 *Rampjaar* (year of
disaster). France, under
Louis XIV, attacks Holland.
War with England breaks
out once more

King Louis XIV

1652 First
maritime war
with England

*Dutch fleet in river
Medway in 1667*

1667 Dutch sign
Breda Peace Treaty
with England

1666 Dutch navy wins
battle against British fleet

1688 William III (see p29),
invited to take over English
throne, becoming King
William III

The Age of Consolidation

Though the Dutch Empire declined, the Netherlands remained wealthy. Amsterdam's ships became commercial cargo carriers and by the mid-18th century, the city was the world's financial capital. Tolerance prevailed and the city was flooded with immigrants, including Jews from all across Europe. Dissatisfaction with the ruling House of Orange intensified; although Prussian troops crushed a Patriot uprising in 1787, the Patriots established a short-lived republic, with French backing, only to see Napoleon take over, making his brother Louis king of the Netherlands.

Extent of the City

1700   Today

Bathroom

Drying room with Japanese screen

Receiving Visitors (c.1713)
Amsterdam was cosmopolitan and decadent; in Cornelis Troost's satire, the ladies of a brothel parade before Prince Eugène of Savoy.

Wintertime in Amsterdam (c.1763)
Petrus Schenk's print shows people skating on the frozen canals. The icebreaking barges in the background are bringing fresh water to the city.

Drawing room

Dolls' House

Costly dolls' houses were designed for show rather than play, and are a fitting symbol of the extravagance of the age. This example is a miniature replica of the house of an Amsterdam merchant. Now in the Frans Hals Museum in Haarlem (see pp180–81), it was made around 1750 for Sara Rothé.

1702 Death of William III. Second stadholderless period begins in the Netherlands

1713 Treaty of Utrecht signed. Dutch Republic becomes isolated

French musketeer

1748 Tax collector riots

1744 France invades Southern Provinces

| 1700 | 1710 | 1720 | 1730 | 1740 | 1750 |

1697 Tsar Peter the Great of Russia visits Amsterdam to study shipbuilding

Portrait of Tsar Peter the Great (1727) on gold snuff box

1716 Second meeting of the Grand Assembly meets in Den Haag (see p188). Radical government reforms imposed

1747 Stadholdership becomes hereditary under William IV

1751 Death of William IV. Start of 40 years of political strife

Prussian Troops Enter Amsterdam (1787)
A lithograph by an unknown artist shows Prussian troops entering the city on 10 October 1787, coming to the aid of the House of Orange after pro-French Patriot upheavals.

Where to See 18th-Century Amsterdam

De Gooyer windmill (see p146) produced corn for the growing city from 1725. A clandestine church was opened in 1735 in today's Museum Ons' Lieve Heer op Solder (pp86–7), in response to the Alteration (pp26–7). Fine canal houses include No. 475 Herengracht (p114) built in 1730, and the Felix Meritis Building (p115), designed by Jacob Otten Husly in 1787. Museum Van Loon was renovated in 1752 (p124).

Pavilioned bed with green canopy

Florin (1781)
By 1750, Amsterdam possessed the most sophisticated and successful banking and brokering system in the world.

Lying-in room

Library

Museum Willet-Holthuysen
The elaborate, gilded staircase (see p123) was built in 1740.

Tax Collector Riots (1748)
This print by Simonsz Fokke shows an angry mob raiding the house of a tax collector in June 1748.

Ceramic Plate (c.1780)
The wealthy lived in great style, sparing no expense. This hand-painted plate is decorated with mythological figures and ornate gold leaf.

1795 Provinces unite briefly into republic, ruled jointly by Patriots and French

1763 Freezing winter

1791 VOC (see pp30–31) goes into liquidation

1806 Napoleon Bonaparte takes over republic

| 1760 | 1770 | 1780 | 1790 | 1800 | 1810 |

1766 William V comes of age

1780–84 War with England, whose navy destroys Dutch fleet

1768 William V marries Wilhelmina of Prussia

1787 Patriots' upheaval ends with Prussian army entering Amsterdam

Louis Napoleon (1778–1846)

1808 Louis Napoleon crowned king of the Netherlands

The Age of Industrialization

By the end of Louis Napoleon's rule, Amsterdam had stagnated. The decline continued, with little sign of enterprise and scant investment. Industrialization came late and attempts to revive the city's fortunes by digging a canal to the North Sea were less than effective. Politically, the country regrouped round the House of Orange, bringing the family back from exile and declaring a monarchy in 1813. The mid-century saw growth of the liberal constitution; by 1900 the Socialist tradition was well established.

Extent of the City

▨ 1800   ☐ Today

Centraal Station

The station (see p81) was completed in 1889. It became a symbol of the emergent industrial age – a sign that Amsterdam was finally moving towards the future rather than looking back to the Golden Age.

Cocoa Trading
Cocoa was one of Amsterdam's main exports in the 1890s.

Dutch Renaissance-style façade

The gilded "clock" shows the wind direction, acknowledging Amsterdam's earlier reliance on the wind to power her sailing ships.

Main concourse

The Sweatshop by H Wolter
As industrialization increased, sweatshops, with their attendant poverty, became commonplace.

Diamond Cutting
The diamond trade thrived in the late 19th century, when precious stones were imported from South Africa.

1813 House of Orange returns from exile

1824 Noordhollands-kanaal is dug but proves ineffective

1839 Amsterdam-to-Haarlem railway opens *(see p179)*

1845 Rioters in Amsterdam call for social reform

Johan Rudolf Thorbecke

1850 Population 245,000

1820   **1830**   **1840**   **1850**   **1860**

1815 William becomes king of the Netherlands

1831 Low Countries split into north and south. Southern provinces become Belgium

1840 William I abdicates. Succeeded by William II

King William I at Waterloo (1815)

1848 New constitution devised by Thorbecke

1860s Jews begin to arrive in Amsterdam from Antwerp

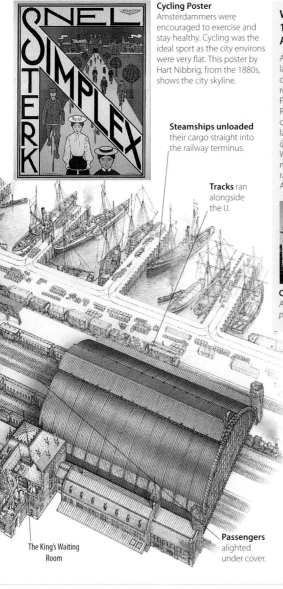

Cycling Poster
Amsterdammers were encouraged to exercise and stay healthy. Cycling was the ideal sport as the city environs were very flat. This poster by Hart Nibbrig, from the 1880s, shows the city skyline.

Steamships unloaded their cargo straight into the railway terminus.

Tracks ran alongside the IJ.

The King's Waiting Room

Passengers alighted under cover.

Where to See 19th-Century Amsterdam

An outburst of civic pride in the late 19th century led to the construction of some remarkable revivalist-style public buildings. PJH Cuypers' Neo-Renaissance Rijksmuseum (see pp130–3) opened in 1885, followed 10 years later by the Stedelijk Museum (pp138–9), the work of AW Weissman. HP Berlage's Beurs (p81) marked the beginning of the radical new style that led to the Amsterdam School (p99).

Concertgebouw (1888)
AL van Gendt's concert hall (see p134) is Neo-Renaissance in style.

The Jewish Quarter (1889)
The desperate conditions in the ghetto are shown in this painting by EA Hilverdink.

1874 Child Labour Act cuts working hours

1876 Noordzee-kanaal opened

1878 Willem Ansing founds the Social Democratic Association

1886 26 die in Palingoproer riots

1889 Cuypers finishes Centraal Station (see p81)

1902 Socialists win their first seat on city council

1909 Communists split from SDAP and become separate political force

1870	1880	1890	1900	1910

1883 World Exhibition draws a million visitors

Noordzee-kanaal

1894 Foundation of Social Democratic Workers' Party (SDAP)

1898 Wilhelmina ascends the throne

Queen Wilhelmina (c.1900) by Jean Veber

Amsterdam at War

The Netherlands remained neutral in World War I. After the war, political unrest was rife and the city council embarked on a programme of new housing projects and, in the 1930s, the Amsterdamse Bos was created to counter unemployment. When World War II broke out, the Netherlands again opted for neutrality – only to be invaded by Germany. The early 1940s were bitter years, and many died of starvation in the winter of 1944–5. During this time, most of the Jewish population was deported; many, like Anne Frank, tried to avoid detection by going into hiding.

Extent of the City
▨ 1945   ☐ Today

"Vote Red" Poster (1918)
The Social Democrats (Labour Party) were responsible for the introduction of a welfare state after World War II.

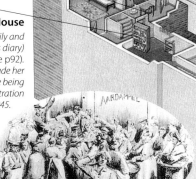

Attic

The van Pels' room

Anne's bedroom

The Franks' bedroom

Bathroom

Revolving bookcase (entrance to hideout)

Anne Frank's House

In July 1942, 13-year-old Anne Frank, her family and the van Pels (renamed van Daans in Anne's diary) went into hiding at the rear of this house (see p92). Anne had already begun her diary. She made her last entry in August 1944, three days before being arrested. She died in Bergen-Belsen concentration camp in March 1945.

Potato Riots (1917)
Daan Bout's drawing shows desperate women fighting for vegetables during World War I. Rioting followed and the army was brought in to quell the uprising.

1917 Potato riots in the Jordaan

1920 Air service from Schiphol to London inaugurated

Detail on façade of ABN Bank

1926 ABN Bank built on Vijzelstraat

1915 SDAP have majority on city council and shape housing policy

1910	1915		1920	1925

1914 World War I begins. Holland remains neutral

1928 Olympic Games held in Amsterdam

Cartoon satirizing the Netherlands' rejection of Germany's offer of friendship in 1915

1920s "Ring" built round southern part of the city. Many canals filled in but work is halted after considerable opposition

Het Schip by Michel de Klerk
At the end of World War I, Amsterdam School architects *(see p99)* designed new housing projects such as "the ship", to replace the slums in the west of the city.

Amsterdamse Bos
In 1930, as part of a job-creation scheme, 5,000 unemployed Dutch citizens were drafted in to help develop a woodland and leisure area to the southwest of the city.

Where to See Early-20th-Century Amsterdam

Innovative Amsterdam School architecture is found to the south of the city. HP Berlage, PL Kramer and Michel de Klerk collaborated on De Dageraad *(see p153)* and were largely responsible for the Nieuw Zuid *(p156)*. Much of this was built in the run up to the 1928 Olympics; it boasts spectacular housing developments and civic buildings.

Tuschinski Theater (1921)
The interior of this exotic complex is awash with colour.

Offices at the front of the building

Façade of No. 263 Prinsengracht

Dockworker Statue
The statue *(see p55)* by Mari Andriessen commemorates the February 1941 protest by dockers and transport workers against the Nazis' treatment of Jews.

The Deportation of Jews
Pamphlets were distributed by the Resistance vilifying those who stood by and let the Nazis round up the Jews.

NEDERLAND IN DEN OORLOG
ZOOALS HET WERKELIJK WAS

ONZE VERNEDERING II

1930 Population 750,000. Unemployment worsens. Work on public project of Amsterdamse Bos begins	**1939** Outbreak of World War II. The Netherlands chooses neutrality	**1940** Germany bombs Rotterdam. The Dutch surrender	**1945** Germany surrenders and western part of the Netherlands finally liberated
	1935 Work parties sent to Germany	**1942** Deportation of Jews begins	
1930	**1935**	**1940**	**1945**
	1934 Riots in Jordaan over reduction in social security. Seven die	**1944** D-Day Landings. "Hunger Winter"	
1932–7 Rise of Dutch Nazi Party under Anton Mussert	**1941** 450 Jews arrested. Dockworkers strike		

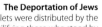

Yellow Star of David, which Jews had to wear during Nazi Occupation

Amsterdam Today

After World War II, Amsterdam suffered a series of social problems: its tolerance made it a haven for the 1960s hippy culture, it became a centre of drug use and trafficking, and the left-wing Provos challenged social order. In the 1970s, riots over the violent evictions of squatters and urban redevelopment led to measures that alleviated the social issues. Now Amsterdam is once again a tranquil, welcoming city for all to visit. Programmes of urban expansion and sympathetic architectural developments have combined to make the city an exciting hub of modernity.

Extent of the City
1950   Today

Football
The fans were ecstatic when the Dutch national team beat England 3:1 in 1988 in the European Championships.

Het Lieverdje
The statue of the *Little Urchin* by Carel Kneulman is in Spui. It became a symbol for the Provos in the 1960s.

The "normal water level" (NAP) of Amsterdam's canals

Lighthouse

Haarlem (*see pp176–81*)

Ringvaart Haarlemmer-meer

North Sea
Actual sea level

Sand dunes (7–20 m/ 23–65 ft in height)

Sand

Schiphol airport (*see pp262–3*)

30 km (19 miles) • AMSTERDAM

Locator Map

Bulbfields (*see pp182–3*)

Ringdijk

Haarlemmermeer (4.5 m/15 ft below sea level)

Normaal Amsterdams Peil
The city's water level (NAP), set in 1684, is on display near the Stopera (*see p65*).

Section of Noord Holland

This cross-section shows Holland's polders (see pp26–7) lying below sea level. Without the protection of dykes and tide barriers, Amsterdam would be inundated. Its buildings are supported by piles which pass through layers of clay and peat into firm sand.

1948 Queen Wilhelmina abdicates after 50 years. Juliana becomes queen

1957 The Netherlands signs Treaty of Rome, joining European Community

1965 Provos win seats on city council for first time

1963 The population peaks at 868,000

1966 Provos demonstrate at wedding of Princess Beatrix to German aristocrat Claus von Amsberg

1971 Ajax wins European Cup

1975 Nieuwmarkt riots erupt against destruction of Jewish Quarter

1981 Amsterdam is recognized as capital of Holland

| 1950 | 1955 | 1960 | 1965 | 1970 | 1975 | 1980 |

1967 Hippies arrive in Amsterdam

1952 Completion of the Amsterdam-Rhine Canal allows increased trade

1968 First residents move to the vast Bijlmermeer housing estate

1949 Indonesia officially independent from the Netherlands

Abdication speech by Queen Juliana

1980 Queen Juliana abdicates in favour of Beatrix

King Willem-Alexander

Born in 1967, he was crowned in the Nieuwe Kerk *(see pp76–7)* in 2013 following the abdication of his mother, Beatrix.

Where to See Modern Amsterdam

Amsterdam has many superb new buildings, particularly in the Eastern Docklands, along the banks of the IJ and along the Zuidas (South Axis). A striking 2012 addition to the northern IJ bank is the EYE Film Institute building *(see p153)*, designed by Vienna-based Delugan Meissl Associated Architects.

ING House *head office (2002) on the Zuidas was designed by Meyer & Van Schooten and is nicknamed "the ice-skate".*

House on the Singel

17th-century canal houses often subside, as their foundations are shallow. Traditionally they were propped up by wooden support beams, but now technology allows for the replacement of rotten support piles without demolition.

Headquarters of IBM West Amsterdam (2.1 m/7 ft below sea level)

Vondelpark *(see pp134–5)*

Central Amsterdam (2.1 m/7 ft above sea level)

Oude Kerk *(see pp70–71)*

Overground transport system

East Amsterdam (5.5 m/ 18 ft below sea level)

Rijnkanaal

Oranjesluizen tide barrier

Concrete piles

Layers of clay and peat

Wooden piles

Metro system

Frankendael *(see p152)*

IJmeer *(see p15)*

Hippies

In the late 1960s, Amsterdam was known for its tolerance of subcultures. It became a haven for hippies, who gathered in the Vondelpark *(see pp134–5)*.

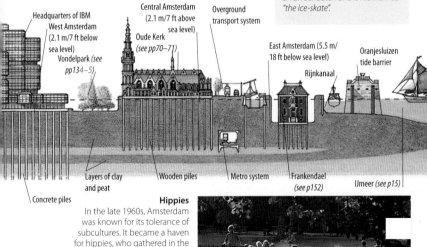

86 Opera House *(see p65)* opens in Stopera

1994 For first time since 1918, Christian Democrats do not form part of governing coalition

2000 Law passed legalizing euthanasia

2002 Death of Prince Claus, Beatrix's husband

2012 Stedelijk Museum *(see pp138–9)* reopens after an extensive renovation project

2013 Rijksmuseum reopens after a 10-year renovation.

	1990	1995	2000	2005	2010	2015	2020

1993 Schiphol Airport *(see pp262–3)* modernized

KLM – the Dutch national airline

2013 Queen Beatrix abdicates in favour of her son Willem-Alexander.

1989 Centre-right comes to power in Dutch Parliament

AMSTERDAM AT A GLANCE

There are more than 100 places of interest described in the *Area by Area* section of this book. The broad spectrum of entries covers recreational as well as cultural sights and ranges from sublime buildings, such as the Oude Kerk, to oddities like the Hash Marihuana & Hemp Museum *(see p63)*. The Golden Bend *(see p114)* and other impressive canalscapes also feature, along with suggested walks past some of Amsterdam's finest architecture and notable sights, such as Anne Frank House. To help you make the most of your stay, the following 10 pages are a time-saving guide to the best Amsterdam has to offer. Museums, canals, and cafés and bars all have their own sections. Below is a selection of attractions that no visitor should miss.

Amsterdam's Top 10 Attractions

Het Scheepvaartmuseum
See pp148–9

Van Gogh Museum
See pp136–7

Oude Kerk
See pp70–71

Begijnhof
See p79

Koninklijk Paleis
See p78

Rijksmuseum
See pp130–33

Stedelijk Museum
See pp138–9

Ons' Lieve Heer op Solder
See pp86–7

Magere Brug
See p121

Anne Frank House
See pp36–7 & 92–3

◄ Stern of replica ship of Dutch East India Company, East Indiaman, in Oosterdok

Amsterdam's Best: Museums

For a fairly small city, Amsterdam has a surprisingly large number of museums and galleries. The quality and variety of the collections are impressive and many are housed in buildings of historical or architectural interest. The Rijksmuseum, with its Gothic façade, is a city landmark, and Rembrandt's work is exhibited in his original home. For more information on museums see pp44–5.

Anne Frank House
This photo of the famous diarist is exhibited in the house where she hid during World War II.

Amsterdam Museum
A wealth of historical information is on display here. Once an orphanage, it is depicted in *Governesses at the Burgher Orphanage* (1683) by Amsterdam-born Adriaen Backer.

Western Canal Ring

Rijksmuseum
An extensive collection of more than 8,000 pieces, including paintings by Dutch masters, such as Jan van Huysum's *Still Life with Flowers and Fruit* (c.1730) *(see p133).*

Central Canal Ring

Museum Quarter

Van Gogh Museum
Van Gogh's *Self-Portrait with Straw Hat* (1870) hangs in this large, stark museum, built in 1973 to house the bulk of his work.

Stedelijk Museum
Gerrit Rietveld's simple Steltman chair (1963) is one of many exhibits at this ever-changing contemporary art museum.

Museum Ons' Lieve Heer op Solder
Three 17th-century merchant's houses conceal Amsterdam's only remaining clandestine church, restored as the Museum Ons' Lieve Heer op Solder (Our Lord in the Attic).

Het Scheepvaartmuseum
This national maritime museum is decorated with reliefs relating to the city's maritime history. Moored alongside is a replica of the East Indiaman *Amsterdam*.

Tropenmuseum
On display here are exhibits from former Dutch colonies in the tropics, including this wooden Nigerian fertility mask portraying a mother and twins.

Jwe de

Oude Zijde

Plantage

Eastern nal Ring

| 0 metres | 500 |
| 0 yards | 500 |

Museum Willet-Holthuysen
An impressive collection of furniture, silverware and paintings is housed in this beautifully preserved 17th-century canalside mansion.

Joods Historisch Museum
Four adjoining synagogues are linked to form this museum. The Holy Ark in the Grote Synagoge is the centrepiece of an exhibition on Judaism in the Netherlands.

Exploring Amsterdam's Museums

The richness of Amsterdam's history and culture is reflected by its wide range of museums, which cover everything from bibles, beer and African masks to shipbuilding and space travel. Its national art galleries house some of the world's most famous paintings, including Rembrandt's *The Night Watch*. Het Scheepvaartmuseum has the largest collection of model ships in the world, while the Anne Frank House is a stark reminder of the horrors of World War II.

View of a French-style garden from the Museum Van Loon

Painting and Decorative Arts

The world's most important collection of Dutch art is on display at the **Rijksmuseum**. This vast museum contains approximately 5,000 paintings, including works by Rembrandt, Vermeer, Frans Hals and Albert Cuyp as well as a significant collection of sculptures, prints, artifacts and Asiatic art. A 10-year renovation was completed in 2013.

A short stroll across Museumplein will bring you to the **Van Gogh Museum**. Besides a large collection of Van Gogh's paintings and drawings, which traces his entire career, you can see hundreds of his original letters to his brother Theo and the artist's private collection of Japanese prints. Works by other 19th-century Dutch painters are also displayed here.

Modern art is the focus of the **Stedelijk Museum**. While the collection features works by artists such as Henri Matisse and Vassily Kandinsky, the emphasis is on paintings, sculptures, drawings, graphics and photographs completed after 1945. Andy Warhol, Edward Kienholz and the Dutch Cobra artist Karel Appel are all represented.

The house where Rembrandt lived for 20 years opened as the **Museum Het Rembrandthuis** in 1911. As well as providing an insight into the artist's life, it contains an important collection of his work, including a series of self-portraits.

The **Museum Van Loon**, housed in a beautiful 17th-century mansion, is based on the outstanding private collections of the wealthy van Loon family.

Other wonderful collections of art can also be enjoyed by travelling from Amsterdam to the **Frans Hals Museum** in Haarlem, the **Mauritshuis** in Den Haag and the **Museum Boijmans Van Beuningen Rotterdam**.

Indonesian mask at the Tropenmuseum

History

Various aspects of Amsterdam's absorbing history are documented in several of the city's museums. The **Amsterdam Museum** covers the growth of Amsterdam from its origins as a fishing village in the 13th century, by means of an interactive display of maps, paintings and archaeological objects. The city's maritime history is recalled at the **Het Scheepvaartmuseum**, which has a vast collection of model ships. More modern boats are the focus of the **Museum 't Kromhout**, which is housed in one of the few working shipyards left in the city. In the **Museum Willet-Holthuysen**, the richly decorated rooms, Dutch paintings, Venetian glass, silverware and furniture reflect the wealth of Amsterdam in the Golden Age. Catholic ingenuity is revealed at the **Museum Ons' Lieve Heer op Solder**, where a secret church is preserved in the attic of a 17th-century merchant's home.

Jewish life in the city is remembered in the Jewish Cultural Quarter, a collaboration between the **Joods Historisch Museum**, the **Portuguese Synagogue** *(see p68)* and the **Hollandsche Schouwburg** *(see p144)*. A single ticket provides entry to all the three sites. The **Anne Frank House** provides a poignant reminder that

Rembrandt's *The Jewish Bride* (1663) in the Rijksmuseum

Amsterdam's Jewish community was almost wiped out in World War II, and its secret annexe shows what life in hiding was like. Displays on the activities of the Dutch Resistance at the **Verzetsmuseum Amsterdam** provide more fascinating insights on life in the Netherlands during the Nazi occupation.

Outside the city, the **Zuiderzeemuseum** recreates the life and traditions of the people who once fished these waters.

Specialist Museums

Mummies, sarcophagi and effigies of ancient Egyptian gods are just a few of the displays at the **Allard Pierson Museum**. The **Bijbels Museum**, in adjoining canal houses, also focuses on the archaeology of Egypt and the Middle East, and contains the oldest Bible ever printed in the Netherlands.

The **EYE Film Institute** screens more than 1,000 films a year, and **Foam** is a lively and welcoming photography museum, covering documentary, history and fashion.

The **Heineken Experience** offers a history of beer making as part of a tour of this former brewery and free samples at the end. More facts can be absorbed at the **Hash Marihuana & Hemp Museum**, which shows the many uses this product has had through the ages.

The **Tropenmuseum** is devoted to cultures from around the world and **Het Grachtenhuis** provides an insight into the creation of the triple canal ring.

The open-air reconstruction village at the Zuiderzeemuseum

Technology and Natural History

A hands-on approach is encouraged by **NEMO**, Holland's national science centre, to explain, for instance, how photography works or how computers process information. The centre is housed in a striking modern building.

Along with hundreds of live animals, the **Artis** complex (the oldest zoo in the Netherlands, founded in 1838) contains a variety of museums and some interesting examples of late 19th-century architecture. A fine example is the Aquarium, which also houses a small Zoological Museum displaying a collection of skulls and stuffed animals. The dome-shaped Planetarium takes visitors on a tour of the galaxy. The Hortus Botanicus is a tranquil botanical garden with a three-climate greenhouse and a stunning collection of trees.

Finding the Museums

Model showing the process of precipitation housed in the Artis complex

Amsterdam's Best: Canals and Waterways

From the grace and elegance of the waterside mansions along the Grachtengordel (Canal Ring) to the rows of converted warehouses on Brouwersgracht and the charming houses on Reguliersgracht, the city's canals and waterways embody the very spirit of Amsterdam. They are spanned by many beautiful bridges, including the famous Magere Brug *(see p121)*, a traditionally styled lift bridge. You can also relax at one of the many canalside cafés or bars and watch an array of boats float by.

Brouwersgracht
The banks of this charming canal are lined with houseboats, cosy cafés and warehouses.

Western Canal Ring

Bloemgracht
There is a great variety of architecture along this lovely, tree-lined canal in the Jordaan, including a row of houses with step gables *(see p93)*.

Central Canal Ring

Prinsengracht
The best way to see all the beautiful buildings along Amsterdam's longest 17th-century canal is by bicycle.

Museum Quarter

Leidsegracht
Relax at a pavement café along the exclusive Leidsegracht *(see p113)*.

Keizersgracht
A view of this canal can be had from any of its bridges.

Singel

The *Poezenboot*, a boat for stray cats, is just one of the many sights to be found along the Singel, whose distinctive, curved shape established the horseshoe contours of the Canal Ring.

Entrepotdok

The warehouses on the Entrepotdok *(see p146)* were redeveloped in the 1980s. The quayside is now lined in summer with lively café terraces that overlook an array of houseboats and pleasure craft.

0 metres	500
0 yards	500

Nieuwe Zijde

Oude Zijde

Plantage

Eastern Canal Ring

Herengracht

Known as "the twin brothers", these matching neck-gabled houses at Nos. 409–411 are two of the prettiest houses on the city's grandest canal.

Reguliersgracht

Many crooked, brick buildings line this pretty canal, which was cut in 1664. The statue of a stork, located at No. 92, is symbolic of parental responsibility and commemorates a 1571 bylaw protecting this bird.

Amstel

This river is still a busy commercial thoroughfare, with barges carrying grain and coal to the city's port.

Amsterdam's Best: Cafés and Bars

Amsterdam is a city of cafés and bars, about 1,500 in all. Each area has something to offer, from friendly and relaxed brown cafés to lively and crowded designer bars. The cafés and bars vary and each has some special attraction: a large range of beers, live music, canalside terraces, art exhibitions, board games and pool tables or simply a brand of *gezelligheid*, the unique Dutch concept of "cosiness". Further details of Amsterdam's cafés and bars are given on *pp50–51*. Addresses are given in the directory on *p233*.

De Tuin
This large brown café in the Jordaan is always crowded with regular customers, often local artists.

Van Puffelen
A smart and fashionable clientele is attracted to this intimate canalside café, with its impressive 19th-century interior, reading room and restaurant.

Het Blauwe Theehuis
Built in 1937, this architectural gem has a large, multi-layered terrace overlooking Vondelpark.

Wester Canal Ring

Central Canal Ring

Museum Quarter

Café Americain
The American Hotel's grand café has a beautiful Art Deco interior, and is the place to go to be seen.

Café Dulac
The interior of this quirky grand café, situated on Haarlemmerstraat, mixes Art Deco style with Gothic-kitsch fixtures and fittings.

In de Wildeman
There are more than 80 beers from around the world on offer at this modern *proeflokaal (see p50)*.

Nieuwe Zijde

Oude Zijde

Plantage

De Jaren
Popular with students, this trendy two-storey café has a superb view of the Amstel and a wide selection of newspapers.

Eastern Canal Ring

't Doktertje
This is the ultimate brown café, steeped in cobwebs and atmosphere. It is a dark, friendly and timeless place, tucked away in a tiny side street.

0 metres	500
0 yards	500

De Kroon
Tastefully restored, this grand café has DJs Thursday to Sunday.

Exploring Amsterdam's Cafés and Bars

Wherever you go in this vibrant city, you are never far from a café or bar. Amsterdammers are at their most friendly over a beer or a Dutch gin, so exploring the city's drinking establishments is an easy way to meet the locals. Table service is standard in most cafés and bars, though not universal. Instead of paying for each drink, bars keep a running total which you settle as you leave. The exception is outdoor terraces, where you pay as you order. Most places are open from about 11am (4pm for quite a few brown cafés) until 1am. Many Leidseplein and Rembrandtplein bars stay open until 4 or 5am at the weekends.

The cosy interior of De Tuin brown café in the Jordaan

Brown Cafés

The traditional Dutch "local pub", the brown café, is characterized by dark wooden panelling and furniture, low ceilings, dim lighting and a fog of tobacco smoke. It is a warm and friendly place and often a social focus for the neighbourhood. Some of the best brown cafés are found in old 17th-century canal houses or tucked away on side streets. The tiny and characterful **'t Doktertje**, just off the Kalverstraat shopping street, is worth a visit, as is the cheap and cheerful **Pieper**, close to Leidseplein. **De Tuin**, in the heart of the Jordaan, is popular with the local artistic community. Most brown cafés are more than just places to drink at and many serve good, reasonably priced food (see pp232–3).

Proeflokalen and Modern Tasting Bars

Literally meaning "tasting houses", proeflokalen go back to the Dutch Golden Age of the 17th century. In order to increase sales, wine and spirit importers would invite merchants to taste their wares. Today, proeflokalen denote bars specializing in either wine, spirits or beer. One of the oldest tasting bars, **De Drie Fleschjes**, dates from 1650, and jenever (Dutch gin) is its speciality. **Mulliner's** offers a superb range of vintage wines and ports, while **In de Wildeman** serves beers from around the world, many of them on draught. See the directory on p233 for other good proeflokalen.

Sampling the wide range of beers in one of Amsterdam's many tasting bars

What to Drink

The Dutch national drink is beer. A standard pils (a lager-like beer) is served in bars and cafés – the main brands are Heineken and Grolsch. Darker beers like De Koninck have a stronger flavour, and the wheat-brewed witbiers like Hoegaarden are white and cloudy. Beers from Amsterdam's 't IJ brewery, such as Columbus, are widely available. The most popular spirit, jenever, is the slightly oily Dutch gin. There is either the sharp-tasting jonge (young), or the smoother oude (old) variety. For the complete Dutch experience, drink jenever in a single gulp or order a refreshing pils with a jenever chaser.

Bottle of jonge jenever

Traditional oude jenever

Hoegaarden, brewed in Belgium

Tarwebok, a strong type of Heineken

Grand Cafés and Designer Bars

Grand cafés first emerged in the 19th century. Today, these large and opulent venues are the haunts of the upwardly mobile and fashion-conscious. **Café Luxembourg** has a street terrace for people-watching, while **Café Schiller** is more intimate and has a beautiful Art Deco interior. Designer bars cater for a similar clientele, but they are modern, stark and bright in style. Some of the best are the chic **Het Land Van Walem**, **De Balie** and the trendy **De Jaren**.

Café Schiller, one of Amsterdam's Art Deco grand cafés

Smoking Coffeeshops

Smoking coffeeshops are ones where cannabis is openly sold and smoked. Although technically illegal, the sale of soft drugs is tolerated by the Dutch authorities if it remains discreet *(see p257)*. Many of these cafés are recognizable by their loud music and often

The beautifully restored De Jaren

psychedelic decor. Smoking coffeeshops appeal to a surprising range of people – old and young alike (under 16s are not permitted) from every social and professional background. **Rusland** and **Siberië** are two of the smaller, more relaxed places, while **The Bulldog Palace** is commercial and tourist-filled. As well as coffee, soft drinks and snacks are generally available. **Abraxas** has a psychedelically colourful interior. If tempted to smoke in a coffeeshop, ask for the menu listing what is on sale. The cannabis is strong, especially the local "skunk". Be wary of hash cakes and cookies as there is no way to gauge their strength. See the directory on page 233 for other good smoking coffeeshops.

Coffeeshops and Salons De Thé

The more conventional type of coffeeshop is where well-to-do ladies go for a chat over coffee and cake. A number of these places use the Dutch spelling, *koffieshop*, or the French *salons de thé* to distinguish themselves from the many smoking coffeeshops, although the differences are obvious. Many, such as **Arnold Cornelis** and **Pompadour**, are attached to confectioners, patisseries or delicatessens, and have a tempting range of cakes and sweets on offer. Several of the city's

larger stores and hotels also have tearooms, ideal places to sit down in comfort and relax after a busy day sightseeing or shopping. **De Laatste Kruimel** offers a delicious array of home-baked goods such as scones, fruit tarts and savoury quiches. A canalside experience not to be missed is **Tazzina**, which serves excellent coffee, Italian sandwiches and sweets. For something slightly different, try **Taart van m'n Tante**, a kitsch café serving scrumptious treats that are baked on the premises.

Where to Find the Best Cafés

All the cafés and bars described on these pages are listed in the directory on page 233. The best, as shown on pages 48–9, are also listed below.

Café Americain
American Hotel, Leidsekade 97.
Map 4 E2.
Tel 556 3010.

Het Blauwe Theehuis
Vondelpark 5.
Map 3 C3.
Tel 662 0254.

't Doktertje
Rozenboomsteeg 4. **Map** 7 B4.
Tel 626 4427.

Café Dulac
Haarlemmerstraat 118. **Map** 1 C3.
Tel 624 4265.

In de Wildeman
Kolksteeg 3. **Map** 7 C1.
Tel 638 2348.

De Jaren
Nieuwe Doelenstraat 20.
Map 7 C4.
Tel 625 5771.

De Kroon
Rembrandtplein 17. **Map** 7 C5.
Tel 625 2011.

De Tuin
2e Tuindwarsstraat 13 (near Anjeliersstraat). **Map** 1 B3.
Tel 624 4559.

Van Puffelen
Prinsengracht 377. **Map** 1 B5.
Tel 624 6270.

De Koninck, a dark Belgian beer

Amstel Bock-bier, a dark winter beer

Columbus, brewed in Amsterdam

AMSTERDAM THROUGH THE YEAR

Although there is no guarantee of good weather in Amsterdam, the cosmopolitan ambience of this 700-year-old city and the congeniality of the Dutch make it an appealing place to visit whatever time of year you go. Most tourists flock into the city from April to September, when temperatures are mild. Amsterdammers, however, are undaunted by the weather and maintain an active programme of festivals and outdoor pursuits throughout the year. Crisp autumn days invite long walks along the city's stately canals, followed by a cosy chat in one of Amsterdam's brown cafés. About twice a decade, the winter temperatures drop so low that the canals freeze over. When this occurs a skating race is held between 11 Dutch cities.

Spring

Spring begins in late March when daffodils and crocuses blossom overnight all over the city. Flower lovers descend on Amsterdam, using it as a base for day trips to Keukenhof, the Netherlands' 28-hectare (69-acre) showcase for Dutch bulb growers (see pp182–3).

March

Stille Omgang (second or third Sat), Rokin. Silent night-time procession celebrating the Miracle of Amsterdam (see p24).
Opening of Keukenhof (late Mar). One of the world's largest flower gardens (see p183).

April

National Museum Weekend (second weekend of Apr). Cut-price or free admission to many state-run museums.
Bloemencorso (third weekend). The highlight of the bulb season is a flower parade of colourful floats between Noordwijk and Haarlem.
Koningsdag (27 Apr). The city becomes the world's biggest flea market-cum-street party on King Willem-Alexander's official birthday. Transport grinds to a

Revellers celebrating in the streets to commemorate Koninginnedag

halt as people throng the streets during the day and dance the night away.
World Press Photo (end Apr–early Jun), Oude Kerk. Exhibits the very best press photographs from around the world.

May

Herdenkingsdag (4 May). Commemorations throughout the city for the victims of World War II. Largest in Dam square.
Bevrijdingsdag (5 May). Concerts and speeches around the city celebrate the end of the German occupation.
Kunst RAI (mid May). A large exhibition of contemporary art, held at Amsterdam RAI.
Nationale Molendag (second Sat). Windmills all over the country open to the public.
Boeken op de Dam (every third or fourth Sun, May–September): Dam square fills with book stalls, and sometimes along the Amstel at Nationale Opera & Ballet (see p65) – Boeken aan de Amstel.

Tulip fields in bloom near Alkmaar

Average Daily Hours of Sunshine

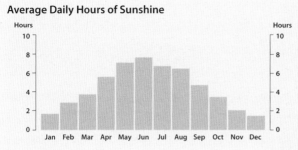

Hours

| | | | | | | | | | | | |
|Jan|Feb|Mar|Apr|May|Jun|Jul|Aug|Sep|Oct|Nov|Dec|

Sunshine Chart
The summer months are the sunniest, but this is no guarantee of good weather. Amsterdammers will often carry an umbrella even on the hottest of July days as summer rain in the morning often precedes the arrival of bright sunshine later.

Summer

Summer, which starts with the three-week-long Holland Festival, is a hectic cultural roller-coaster ride. As well as the events listed below, classic European drama is staged in the Amsterdamse Bos (p157), and open-air concerts are held in the Vondelpark (pp134–5). This is the best time for people-watching in one of Amsterdam's street-side cafés and bars.

Japanese band Asakusa Jinta performing at the Amsterdam Roots Festival

June

Open Garden Days (third weekend in Jun). For one weekend, Amsterdam's most elegant private gardens open their gates to the public. Visit www.canalmuseums.nl for more information.

Open Air Theatre in Vondelpark (early Jun–end Aug). Theatre, music and children's shows (see p135).

Holland Festival (3 weeks in June). In venues throughout Amsterdam and in other major cities in the Netherlands, a varied programme of concerts, plays, operas and ballets.

Amsterdam Roots Festival (late June), De Melkweg (pp112–13), Oosterpark, and Concertgebouw (p134). An ethnic programme of music, dance, film and theatre from Africa and other non-Western countries.

July

North Sea Jazz Festival (mid-Jul), the Ahoy Exhibition Centre. Weekend of jazz ranging from Dixieland to jazz rock a short train ride away in Rotterdam.

Summer Concerts (Jul–Aug), Concertgebouw (see p134). Annual showcase of classical music.

Orchestral performance at the Prinsengracht Concert

August

Uitmarkt (mid-Aug). A weekend of music and theatre performances at Leidseplein and Museumplein launches the start of the cultural season.

Grachtenfestival (Wed–Sun, around third Sat). Classical concerts on Herengracht, Keizersgracht and Prinsengracht. The main concert is on Saturday on a barge in front of the Hotel Pulitzer (see p218).

Café-goers relaxing and soaking up the sun at de Jaren Terrace

Average Monthly Rainfall

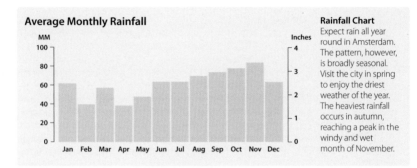

Rainfall Chart

Expect rain all year round in Amsterdam. The pattern, however, is broadly seasonal. Visit the city in spring to enjoy the driest weather of the year. The heaviest rainfall occurs in autumn, reaching a peak in the windy and wet month of November.

Autumn

Temperatures drop quickly at the end of August, but the cultural heat is maintained with the diary of music, dance, opera and drama promoted in the Uitmarkt *(see p53)*. The Autumn is also a busy time for more sporting types. There is a range of spectator sports to watch, and it is a good time of year to enjoy brisk walks in one of the city's many parks or along the Amstel. By November, many Amsterdammers retreat indoors on rainy evenings to cafés like Schaakcafé Het Hok in the Lange Leidsedwarsstraat.

September

Open Monumentendagen *(first or second weekend)*. A chance to see inside some historic, listed buildings which are normally closed to the public. **Jordaan Festival** *(third weekend, including Fri)*. Festivals are held near Westerkerk and elsewhere in this picturesque district, with fairs, street parties, talent contests and music. **Amsterdam Fringe Festival** *(10 days in September)*. A festival of theatre and dance, with performances by national and international companies. **Dam tot Damloop** *(third Sun)*. The biggest running event in the Netherlands, with around 30,000 athletes taking part. The 16-km (10-mile) course starts in Amsterdam and ends on the Dam in Zaandam. There's also a mini event in Zaandam for children.

Barges moored along an Amsterdam waterfront in autumn

October

Grachtenrace *(second Sat)*, Oosterdok. One of many rowing competitions. **TCS Amsterdam Marathon** *(third Sun)*. Some 1,500 runners circle the city before converging on the Olympic stadium in this 42-km (26-mile) run. A further 10,000 people join in for a 10-km (6-mile) stretch of the race. **Camping and Caravan RAI** *(end Oct)*, Amsterdam RAI. Annual fair for open-air holiday enthusiasts.

November

PAN *(Nov–Dec)*. Art and antiques fair in RAI. **Museumnacht** *(first Sat)*. Many museums stay open during the night. There are often theatrical and musical events, too, as well as a special guided tour. **Sinterklaas' Parade** *(second or third Sat)*. The Dutch equivalent of Santa Claus arrives by boat near St Nicolaasbasiliek *(see p81)* accompanied by Zwarte Piet (Black Peter) and distributes sweets to Amsterdam's waiting children.

Sinterklaas parading through Amsterdam

Average Monthly Temperature

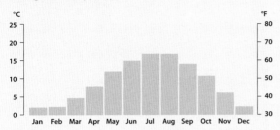

Temperature Chart
The chart shows the average temperature for each month in Amsterdam. Summer is often cooled by the North Sea wind, both spring and autumn can be chilly, and temperatures in winter are frequently freezing.

Winter

Christmas is a busy tourist season, with visitors and residents thronging to watch Christmas trees being hawked from barges on the main canals. Barrows throughout the city tantalize passers-by with the smell of freshly fried *oliebollen* and *appelflappen*, sugary treats not to be missed. After Christmas, if it is cold enough for skating on the canals to be permitted, which is rare, large crowds turn out to skate under the stars.

Amsterdammers ice skating on the Prinsengracht

December

Sinterklaasavond *(5 Dec)*. The traditional Dutch gift-giving day when Sinterklaas and his Moorish helpers visit children to leave a sack of presents. Friends give poems caricaturing each other.
Christmas Day *(25 Dec)*. Increasingly accepted as the main gift-giving day.
New Year's Eve *(31 Dec)*. Firework celebrations through-

The Dokwerker Monument in JD Meijerplein

out the city with an organized display over the Amstel.
Amsterdam Light Festival *(Dec–mid-Jan)*. Winter evenings are illuminated by light sculptures along the Amstel, from Amstel Hotel towards Centraal Station.

January

Jumping Amsterdam *(Jan–Feb)*, Amsterdam RAI. International indoor showjumping competitions.
Chinese New Year *(Jan or Feb)*, Nieuwmarkt. Traditional lion dance, fireworks, Chinese exhibitions and stage art.

February

Februaristaking *(25 Feb)*, JD Meijerplein. Commemoration of dockworkers' action against the deportation of Jewish residents by the Nazis during World War II.

Public Holidays

New Year's Day (1 Jan)
Tweede Paasdag (Easter Monday) *
Koningsdag (27 April)
Bevrijdingsdag (5 May)
Hemelvaartsdag (Ascension Day) *
Pinksteren (Whitsun) *
Eerste Kerstdag (Christmas Day) (25 Dec)
Tweede Kerstdag (26 Dec)
*Dates change in accordance with church calendar.

Aerial shot of Amsterdam city centre ▶

AMSTERDAM AREA BY AREA

OUDE ZIJDE

The eastern half of Amsterdam became known as the Oude Zijde (Old Side). Originally it occupied a narrow strip on the east bank of the Amstel river, running between Damrak and the Oudezijds Voorburgwal *(see pp46–7)*. At its heart was built the Oude Kerk, the oldest church in the city. In the early 1400s the Oude Zijde began an eastward expansion which continued into the 17th century. This growth was fuelled by an influx of Jewish refugees from Portugal. The oldest of the four synagogues, now containing the Joods Historisch Museum, dates from this period. These were central to Jewish life in the city for centuries. During the Golden Age *(see pp28–30)*, the Oude Zijde was an important commercial centre. Boats could sail up the Geldersekade to Nieuwmarkt, where goods were weighed at the Waag before being sold at the market.

Sights at a Glance

Historic Buildings and Monuments
2 Waag
5 Agnietenkapel
6 Oudemanhuispoort
7 Oostindisch Huis
8 Trippenhuis
16 Pintohuis
17 Montelbaanstoren
18 Scheepvaarthuis
19 Schreierstoren

Opera Houses
11 Stadhuis-Nationale Opera & Ballet

Museums
4 Hash Marihuana & Hemp Museum
10 Museum Het Rembrandthuis
14 Joods Historisch Museum *pp66–7*

Churches and Synagogues
9 Zuiderkerk
13 Mozes en Aäronkerk
15 Portuguese Synagogue
21 Oude Kerk *pp70–71*

Streets and Markets
1 Red Light District
3 Nieuwmarkt
12 Waterlooplein
20 Zeedijk

▢ Restaurants *pp224–5*
1 A-Fusion
2 De Bakkerswinkel
3 Bird
4 Blauw aan de Wal
5 Bridges (Grand Hotel)
6 Café Bern
7 Café de Engelbewaarder
8 Café de Jaren
9 Éénvistwéévis
10 Ganesha Indian Restaurant
11 Geisha
12 Golden Chopsticks
13 Greetje
14 Hemelse Modder
15 In De Waag
16 Kilimanjaro
17 Latei
18 Looks
19 Me Naam Naan
20 Olijfje
21 Oriental City

See also Street Finder pp274–87

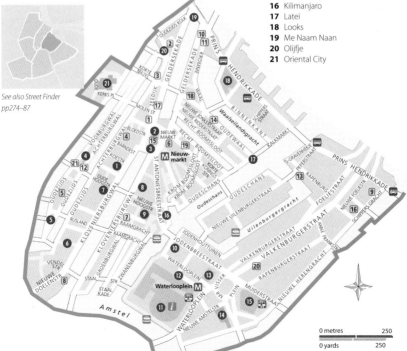

◀ The magnificent 18th-century organ in Oude Kerk

For map symbols *see back flap*

Street-by-Street: University District

The University of Amsterdam, founded in 1877, is predominantly located in the peaceful, southwestern part of the Oude Zijde. The university's roots lie in the former Atheneum Illustre, which was founded in 1632 in the Agnietenkapel. Beyond Damstraat, the bustling Red Light District meets the Nieuwmarkt, where the 15th-century Waag evokes a medieval air. South of the Nieuwmarkt, Museum Het Rembrandthuis gives a fascinating insight into the life of the city's most famous artist.

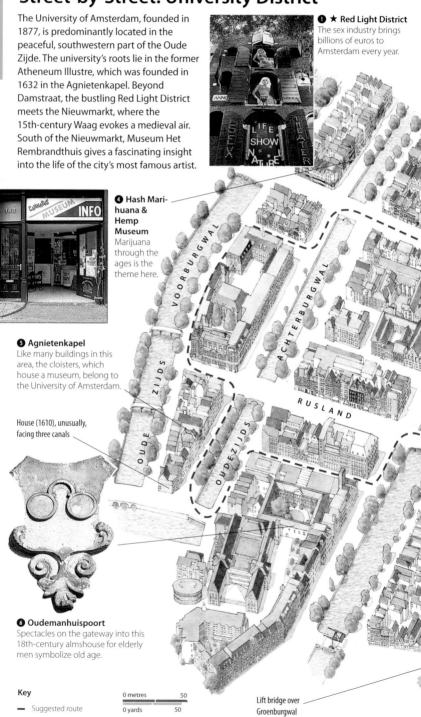

❶ ★ Red Light District
The sex industry brings billions of euros to Amsterdam every year.

❹ Hash Mari-huana & Hemp Museum
Marijuana through the ages is the theme here.

❺ Agnietenkapel
Like many buildings in this area, the cloisters, which house a museum, belong to the University of Amsterdam.

House (1610), unusually, facing three canals

VOORBURGWAL

ACHTERBURGWAL

OUDE ZIJDS

RUSLAND

OUDEZIJDS

❻ Oudemanhuispoort
Spectacles on the gateway into this 18th-century almshouse for elderly men symbolize old age.

Key

— Suggested route

0 metres   50
0 yards   50

Lift bridge over Groenburgwal

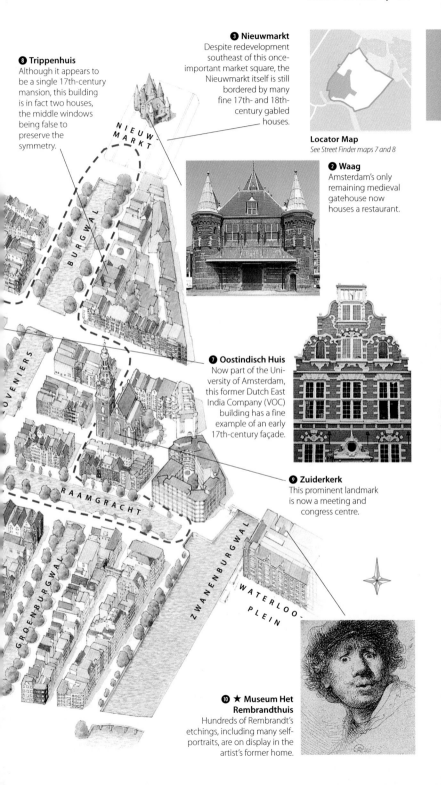

❽ Trippenhuis
Although it appears to be a single 17th-century mansion, this building is in fact two houses, the middle windows being false to preserve the symmetry.

❸ Nieuwmarkt
Despite redevelopment southeast of this once-important market square, the Nieuwmarkt itself is still bordered by many fine 17th- and 18th-century gabled houses.

Locator Map
See Street Finder maps 7 and 8

❷ Waag
Amsterdam's only remaining medieval gatehouse now houses a restaurant.

❼ Oostindisch Huis
Now part of the University of Amsterdam, this former Dutch East India Company (VOC) building has a fine example of an early 17th-century façade.

❾ Zuiderkerk
This prominent landmark is now a meeting and congress centre.

❿ ★ Museum Het Rembrandthuis
Hundreds of Rembrandt's etchings, including many self-portraits, are on display in the artist's former home.

❶ Red Light District

Map 8 D2. 🚋 4, 9, 14, 16, 24.

Barely clad prostitutes bathed in a red neon glow and touting for business at their windows is one of the defining images of modern Amsterdam. The city's Red Light District, referred to locally as de Walletjes (the little walls), is concentrated on the Oude Kerk *(see pp70–71)*, although it extends as far as Warmoesstraat to the west, the Zeedijk to the north, the Kloveniersburgwal to the east and then along the line of Damstraat to the south.

Prostitution in Amsterdam dates back to the city's emergence as a port in the 13th century. By 1478, prostitution had become so widespread, with increasing numbers of sea-weary sailors flooding into the city, that attempts were made to contain it. Prostitutes straying outside their designated area were marched back to the sound of pipe and drum.

A century later, following the Alteration *(see pp26–7)*, the Calvinists tried to outlaw prostitution altogether. Their attempts were half-hearted, and by the mid-17th century prostitution was openly tolerated. In 1850, Amsterdam

Entrance to one of the clubs in the Red Light District

had a population of 200,000, and more than 200 brothels. The most famous of these, like the luxurious Madame Traese's, catered for rich clients.

Today, the area is criss-crossed by a network of narrow lanes. By day, hordes of visitors crowding in generate a festive buzz, and among the sleaze there are interesting cafés, bars, restaurants and beautiful canalside houses. The city council is trying to make this area more culturally attractive by reducing the number of window-prostitutes, closing the seediest clubs and encouraging entrepreneurs outside the sex industry to open up shops here.

❷ Waag

Nieuwmarkt 4. **Map** 8 D3. **Tel** 422 7772. 🚋 9, 14. Ⓜ Nieuwmarkt. **Closed** upper rooms closed to the public.

The multi-turreted Waag is Amsterdam's oldest surviving gatehouse. Built in 1488, it was then, and often still is, called St Antoniespoort. Public executions were held here, and prisoners awaited their fate in the "little gallows room". In 1617, the building became the public weigh house *(waaggebouw)*. Peasants had their produce weighed here and paid tax accordingly. Various guilds moved into the upper rooms of each tower. From 1619 the Guild of Surgeons had their meeting room and anatomy theatre here. They added the central octagonal tower in 1691. Rembrandt's *Anatomy Lesson of Dr Tulp*, now in the Mauritshuis *(see pp190–91)*, and *The Anatomy Lesson of Dr Jan Deijman*, in the Amsterdams Historisch Museum *(see pp82–3)*, were commissioned by the guild and hung here.

After the weigh house closed in the early 1800s, the Waag served as a fire station and two city museums. It is now home to the café-restaurant In de Waag *(see p224)*.

The imposing 15th-century Waag on Nieuwmarkt

Part of the commemorative photo display in Nieuwmarkt metro

❸ Nieuwmarkt

Map 8 D3. 🚊 9, 14. Ⓜ Nieuwmarkt. Antiques market: **Open** May–Sep: 9am–5pm Sun. Organic market: **Open** 9am–4pm Sat.

An open, paved square, the Nieuwmarkt is flanked to the west by the Red Light District. With the top end of the Gelderseкаde, it forms Amsterdam's Chinatown. The Waag dominates the square, and construction of this gateway led to the site's development in the 15th century as a marketplace. When the city expanded in the 17th century (see pp28–9), the square took on its present dimensions and was called the Nieuwmarkt. It retains an array of 17th- and 18th-century gabled houses. True to tradition, an antiques market is held on Sundays during the summer.

The old Jewish Quarter leads off the square down St Antoniesbreestraat. In the 1970s, many houses were demolished to make way for the metro, sparking off clashes between protesters and police. The action of conservationists persuaded the city council to renovate rather than redevelop old buildings. In tribute to them, photographs of their protests decorate the metro.

❹ Hash Marihuana & Hemp Museum

Oudezijds Achterburgwal 148. **Map** 7 C3. **Tel** 624 8926. 🚊 4, 9, 14, 16, 24. Ⓜ Nieuwmarkt. **Open** 10am–10pm daily. **Closed** 27 Apr. 🅿 🏠 🌐 **hashmuseum.com**

This museum charts the history of hemp (marihuana). Exhibits refer back 8,000 years to early Asiatic civilizations, which used the plant for medicines and clothing. It was first used in the Netherlands, according to a herbal manual of 1554, as a cure for earache.

Until the late 19th century, however, hemp was the main source of fibre for rope, and was therefore important in the Dutch shipping industry. Other exhibits relate to the psychoactive properties of this plant. They include an intriguing array of pipes and bongs (smoking devices), along with displays that explain smuggling methods. The museum also has a small cultivation area where plants are grown under artificial light. Police sometimes raid the museum and take away exhibits, so there may be occasional gaps in displays.

❺ Agnietenkapel

Oudezijds Voorburgwal 231. **Map** 7 C4. 🚊 4, 9, 14, 16, 24. **Closed** to the public.

Previously home to the University Museum, the Agnietenkapel was part of the convent of St Agnes until 1578, when it was closed after the Alteration (see pp26–7). In 1632, the Athenaeum Illustre, the precursor of the University of Amsterdam, took it over and by the mid-17th century it was a centre of scientific learning. It also housed the municipal library until the 1830s.

The Agnietenkapel, dating from 1470, is one of the few Gothic chapels to have survived the Alteration. During restoration from 1919 to 1921, elements of Amsterdam School architecture were introduced (see p99). Despite these changes and long periods of secular use, the building still has the feel of a Franciscan chapel.

The large auditorium on the first floor is the city's oldest, and is used for university lectures. It has a lovely ceiling, painted with Renaissance motifs and a portrait of Minerva, the Roman goddess of wisdom and the arts. A series of portraits of scholars – a gift from local merchant Gerardus van Papenbroeck in 1743 – also adorns the walls.

The chapel is currently used as a conference centre and is not open to the public.

Entrance to Agnietenkapel, part of the University of Amsterdam

❻ Oudemanhuis-poort

Between Oudezijds Achterburgwal and Kloveniersburgwal. **Map** 7 C4. 🚊 4, 9, 14, 16, 24. Book market: **Open** 10am–6pm Mon–Sat.

The Oudemanhuispoort was once the entrance to old men's almshouses (Oudemannenhuis), built in 1754. Today the building is part of the University of Amsterdam. The pediment over the gateway in the Oudezijds Achterburgwal features a pair of spectacles, a symbol of old age. Trading inside this covered walkway dates from 1757 and today there is a market for second-hand books. Although the building is closed to the public, visitors may enter the 18th-century courtyard via the arcade.

Crest of Amsterdam, Oudemanhuispoort

The spire of the Zuiderkerk, a prominent city landmark

❼ Oostindisch Huis

Oude Hoogstraat 24 (entrance on Kloveniersburgwal 48). **Map** 7 C3. **Tel** 525 2258. 🚊 4, 9, 14, 16, 24. Ⓜ Nieuwmarkt. **Open** phone for opening times of VOC room.

The Oostindisch Huis, former headquarters of the Dutch East India Company or VOC (see pp30–31), is now part of the University of Amsterdam. Built in 1605, it is attributed to Hendrick de Keyser (see p92). The premises have been expanded several times, in 1606, 1634 and 1661, to house spices, pepper, porcelain and silk from the East Indies.

The VOC was dissolved in 1800 (see p33), and for a while the Oostindisch Huis was taken over by the customs authorities. Later, the state tax offices also moved in, and the VOC medallion carved in the stone gate was replaced with a lion, the traditional heraldic symbol of the Netherlands.

Major restyling in the 1890s destroyed much of the interior decoration, but the façade has remained largely intact, and the former meeting room of the VOC lords has been restored to its 17th-century state.

❽ Trippenhuis

Kloveniersburgwal 29. **Map** 8 D3. 🚊 4, 9, 14, 16, 24. Ⓜ Nieuwmarkt. **Closed** to the public.

Justus Vingboons designed this ornate Classical mansion, completed in 1662. It appears to be one house: it is in fact two. The façade, outlined by eight Corinthian columns, features false middle windows. The house was designed for the wealthy arms merchants Lodewijk and Hendrick Trip, and hence the chimneys look like cannons. The city's art collection

Ornate balustrade of the Oostindisch Huis

was housed here from 1817 to 1885, when it moved to the Rijksmuseum (see pp130–3). The Trippenhuis now houses the Dutch Academy. Opposite at No. 26 is the Kleine Trippenhuis, built in 1698. It is only 2.5 m (8 ft) wide and has very detailed cornicing, which includes two carved sphinxes.

❾ Zuiderkerk

Zuiderkerkhof 72. **Map** 8 D4. 🚊 9, 14. Ⓜ Nieuwmarkt. **Closed** to the public. 🚹 Tower: **Closed** for renovation until 2017. 🖥 **westertorenamsterdam.nl**

Designed by Hendrick de Keyser in 1603, the Renaissance-style Zuiderkerk was the first Calvinist church in Amsterdam after the Alteration (see pp26–7). The spire, with its columns, decorative clocks and onion dome, is a prominent city landmark. The tower will re-open in 2017 for private tours after renovation.

The Zuiderkerk ceased to function as a church in 1929. Restored in 1988, it is now a meeting and congress centre. The surrounding houses include Theo Bosch's modern apartment building, the "Pentagon".

❿ Museum Het Rembrandthuis

Jodenbreestraat 4. **Map** 8 D4. **Tel** 520 0400. 🚊 9, 14. Ⓜ Nieuwmarkt. **Open** 10am–6pm daily. **Closed** 1 Jan, 27 Apr, 25 Dec. 🅿 🏠 🖥 ♿ 🖥 **rembrandthuis.nl**

Rembrandt worked and taught here from 1639 until 1656. He lived in the ground-floor rooms with his wife, Saskia, who died here in 1642, leaving the artist with a baby son, Titus (see p202).

Many of Rembrandt's most famous paintings were created in the first-floor studio. A fine collection of Rembrandt's drawings includes self-portraits in different moods and guises. The interior has been restored to its former glory, and furnished with objects and art works using the original inventory drawn up when

Façade of Museum Het Rembrandthuis

Rembrandt sold the house in 1656. Printing and paint-making demonstrations take place regularly, as do temporary exhibitions.

⓫ Stadhuis-Nationale Opera & Ballet

Waterlooplein 22. **Map** 8 D4. 🚇 9, 14. Ⓜ Waterlooplein. Stadhuis: **Tel** 14020. **Open** offices: 8:30am–4pm Mon–Wed & Fri, 1–8pm Thu. Nationale Opera & Ballet: **Tel** 625 5455. Free concerts Sep–May: 12:30pm Tue. *See Entertainment: pp242–7.* 🚹 🔗 🔲 **operaballet.nl**

Few buildings in Amsterdam caused as much controversy as the Stadhuis (town hall) and Nationale Opera & Ballet (opera house). Nicknamed the "Stopera" by protesters, the scheme required the destruction of dozens of medieval houses, which were virtually all that remained of the original Jewish quarter. This led to running battles between squatters and police *(see pp38–9)*.
  The building was completed in 1988, a massive confection of red brick, marble and glass. A mural illustrating the Normaal Amsterdams Peil *(see pp38–9)* is shown on the arcade linking the two parts of the complex. The Nationale Opera & Ballet has the largest auditorium in the country, with a seating capacity for 1,689 people, and it is home to the Netherlands' national opera and

ballet companies. There are guided backstage tours.

⓬ Waterlooplein

Map 8 D5. 🚇 9, 14. Ⓜ Waterlooplein. Market: **Open** 9am–5pm Mon–Fri, 8:30am–5pm Sat.

The Waterlooplein dates from 1882, when two canals were filled in to create a large market square in the heart of the Jewish quarter. The site was originally known as Vlooyenburg, an artificial island built in the 17th century to house the Jewish settlers *(see p66)*.
  The original market disappeared during World War II when most of the Jewish residents of Amsterdam were transported by the Nazis to concentration camps *(see pp36–7)*. After the war, a popular flea market grew up in its place.
  Despite encroachment by the Stadhuis-Nationale Opera & Ballet, the northern end of the Waterlooplein still operates a

lively and interesting market, selling anything from bric-a-brac and army-surplus clothing to Balinese carvings.

⓭ Mozes en Aäronkerk

Waterlooplein 205. **Map** 8 E4. **Tel** 622 1305. 🚇 9, 14. Ⓜ Waterlooplein. **Open** prayer services: 8pm Tue & Fri; Holy Mass: 5pm Sun. 🔲 **santegidio.nl**.

Designed by the Flemish architect T Suys the Elder in 1841, Mozes en Aäronkerk was built on the site of a hidden Catholic church. The later church took its name from the Old Testament figures of Moses and Aaron depicted on the gable stones of the original building. These are now set into the rear wall.
  The church was restored in 1990, when its twin wooden towers were painted to look like sandstone. After years of hosting exhibitions and concerts, it is again a place of worship.

Bric-a-brac on display at the flea market in Waterlooplein

⓮ Joods Historisch Museum

This remarkable museum of Jewish heritage is housed in four monumental synagogues near Waterlooplein, in the heart of the old Jewish quarter. Three permanent multimedia exhibitions present the history and culture of the Jewish people in the Netherlands through paintings, drawings, artifacts, photographs, films and 3D displays. In addition there are temporary exhibitions as well as a Children's Museum.

Galleries of the Nieuwe Synagoge
The side galleries of the Nieuwe Synagoge house part of the permanent collection, while the downstairs area hosts regular temporary exhibitions.

★ Festival Prayer Book
Presented to Amsterdam's Jewish community by printer Uri Phoebus ha-Levi in 1669, this Festival Prayer Book was one of the few to survive the late Middle Ages.

KEY

① **The Nieuwe Synagoge** was built in 1752.

② **Obbene Shul (1685)
(Children's Museum)**

③ **Café**.

④ **Dritt Shul (1778)**

⑤ **The *mikveh***, or bath for ritual purification.

Jews in Amsterdam

The first Jew to gain Dutch citizenship was a member of the Portuguese Sephardic community in 1597. The Ashkenazi Jews from eastern Europe came to Amsterdam later, in the 1630s. They were restricted to working in certain trades, but were granted full civil equality in 1796. With the rise of Zionism in the 19th century, Jewish identity re-emerged, but the Nazi occupation decimated the community (*see pp36–7*).

18th-century Torah scroll finial in the shape of the Westerkerk tower

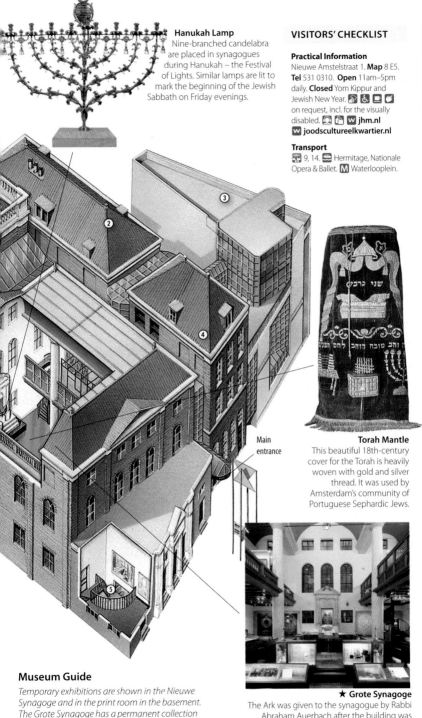

Hanukah Lamp
Nine-branched candelabra are placed in synagogues during Hanukah – the Festival of Lights. Similar lamps are lit to mark the beginning of the Jewish Sabbath on Friday evenings.

VISITORS' CHECKLIST

Practical Information
Nieuwe Amstelstraat 1. **Map** 8 E5.
Tel 531 0310. **Open** 11am–5pm daily. **Closed** Yom Kippur and Jewish New Year. 🚻 🚭 📷 🎧 on request, incl. for the visually disabled. 🚌 📷 **w jhm.nl**
w joodscultureelkwartier.nl

Transport
🚊 9, 14. 🚌 Hermitage, Nationale Opera & Ballet. M Waterlooplein.

Torah Mantle
This beautiful 18th-century cover for the Torah is heavily woven with gold and silver thread. It was used by Amsterdam's community of Portuguese Sephardic Jews.

Main entrance

★ **Grote Synagoge**
The Ark was given to the synagogue by Rabbi Abraham Auerbach after the building was completed in 1671, to a design by Elias Bouman (*see p68*). The Neo-Classical entrance was added during renovations in 1822–3.

Museum Guide

Temporary exhibitions are shown in the Nieuwe Synagoge and in the print room in the basement. The Grote Synagoge has a permanent collection illustrating the religion, culture and history of the Jews in the Netherlands. Younger visitors will enjoy exploring the Children's Museum.

⑮ Portuguese Synagogue

Mr Visserplein 3. **Map** 8 E5.
Tel 531 0380. 🚋 9, 14.
Ⓜ Waterlooplein. **Open** 10am–
5pm Sun–Thu (to 4pm Dec & Jan),
10am–4pm Fri (to 2pm Nov–Feb).
Closed Jewish hols. 🈯 ♿ 📷
🌐 portugesesynagoge.nl

Elias Bouman's design for this
synagogue was inspired by the
architecture of the Temple of
Solomon in Jerusalem. Built for
the Portuguese Sephardic
community of Amsterdam (see
p66) and inaugurated in 1675,
the huge building has a
rectangular ground plan with
the Holy Ark in the southeast
corner facing Jerusalem, and
the tebah (the podium from
which the service is led) at the
opposite end.

The wooden, barrel-vaulted
ceiling is supported by four
Ionic columns. The interior of
the Synagogue is illuminated by
more than 1,000 candles.

Treasure chambers in the
basement contain a sumptuous
collection of ceremonial objects
made of silver, gold and silk
brocades, and rare manuscripts.

Italianate façade of the 17th-century
Pintohuis

⑯ Pintohuis

Sint Antoniesbreestraat 69.
Map 8 D4. **Tel** 370 0210. 🚋 9, 14.
Ⓜ Nieuwmarkt. **Open** 10:30am–
5:30pm Mon–Fri, noon–4:30pm Sat.
🌐 huisdepinto.nl

Isaac de Pinto, a wealthy
Portuguese merchant, bought
the Pintohuis in 1651 for the
then enormous sum of 30,000

guilders. He had it remodelled
over the next decades to a design
by Elias Bouman, and it is one of
the few private residences in
Amsterdam to follow an Italianate
style. The exterior design was
reworked from 1675 to 1680. Six
imposing pilasters break up the
severe, cream façade into five
recessed sections, and the
cornice is topped by a blind
balustrade concealing the roof.

In the 1970s, the house was
scheduled for demolition
because it stood in the way
of a newly planned main road.
However, concerted protest
saved the building, and a
branch of the public library
opened here. The library has
since moved and the building is
now a literary and cultural salon.

⑰ Montel-baanstoren

Oude Waal/Oudeschans 2. **Map** 8 E3.
🚋 9, 14. Ⓜ Nieuwmarkt. **Closed** to
the public.

The lower portion of the
Montelbaanstoren was built in
1512 and formed part of
Amsterdam's medieval fortifications. It lay just beyond the city
wall, protecting the city's wharves
on the newly built St Antoniesdijk
(now the Oudeschans) from the
neighbouring Gelderlanders.

The octagonal structure and
open-work timber steeple were
both added by Hendrick de
Keyser (see p92) in 1606. His
decorative addition bears a close
resemblance to the spire of the
Oude Kerk, designed by Joost
Bilhamer, which was built 40
years earlier (see pp70–71). In
1611, the tower began to list,
prompting Amsterdammers to
attach ropes to the top and pull
it right again.

Sailors from the VOC (see
pp30–31) would gather at the
Montelbaanstoren before being
ferried in small boats down the IJ
to the massive East Indies-bound
sailing ships, anchored further
out in deep water to the north.

The building, now housing
Amsterdam's water authority
offices, appears in a number of
Rembrandt etchings, and is still a
popular subject for artists.

One of many stone carvings on the
Scheepvaarthuis façade

⑱ Scheepvaarthuis

Prins Hendrikkade 108. **Map** 8 E2.
Tel 552 0000 (Hotel Amrâth). 🚋 1, 2,
4, 5, 9, 13, 16, 17, 24. 🚌 22, 59.
Ⓜ Centraal Station.
🌐 amrathamsterdam.com

Built as an office complex in
1916, the Scheepvaarthuis
(Shipping House) is regarded as
the first true example of
Amsterdam School architecture
(see p99). It was designed by Piet
Kramer (1881–1961), Johan van
der May (1878–1949) and
Michel de Klerk (1884–1923) for
a group of shipping companies,
which no longer wanted to
conduct business on the quay.

The imposing triangular
building has a prow-like front
and is crowned by a statue of
Neptune, his wife and four
female figures representing the
four points of the compass. No

The medieval Montelbaanstoren, with its
decorative timber steeple

expense was spared on the construction and internal decoration of the building, and local dock workers came to regard the building as a symbol of capitalism. The doors, stairs, window frames and interior walls are festooned with nautical images, such as dolphins and anchors. Beautiful stained-glass skylights are also decorated with images of sailing ships and compasses.

The Scheepvaarthuis is now a luxury hotel, the Grand Hotel Amrâth *(see p218)*, with a magnificent hallway and an impressive marble staircase spanning four floors.

⓳ Schreierstoren

Prins Hendrikkade 94–95. **Map** 8 E1.
🚊 1, 2, 4, 5, 9, 13, 16, 17, 24.
Ⓜ Centraal Station. **Closed** to the public. VOC Café: **Tel** 428 8291. **Open** 10am–11pm.

The Schreierstoren (Weepers' Tower) was a defensive structure forming part of the medieval city walls, and dates from 1480. It was one of the few fortifications not to be demolished as the city expanded beyond its medieval boundaries in the 17th century. The building now houses a nautical equipment shop.

Popular legend states that the tower derived its name from the weeping (*schreien* in the original Dutch) of women who came here to wave their men off to sea. It is more likely, however, that the title has a less romantic origin and comes from the tower's position on a sharp (*screye* or *scherpe*), 90-degree bend in the old town walls. The earliest of four wall plaques, dated 1569, adds considerably to the confusion by depicting a weeping woman alongside the inscription *scrayer hovck*, which means sharp corner.

In 1609, Henry Hudson set sail from here in an attempt to discover a new and faster trading route to the East Indies. Instead, he unintentionally "discovered" the river in North America which bears his name. A bronze plaque, laid in 1927, commemorates his voyage.

The Schreierstoren, part of the original city fortifications

⓴ Zeedijk

Map 8 D2. 🚊 1, 2, 4, 5, 9, 13, 16, 17, 24. Ⓜ Centraal Station, Nieuwmarkt.

Along with the Nieuwendijk and the Haarlemmerdijk, the Zeedijk (sea dyke) formed part of Amsterdam's original fortifications. Built in the early 1300s, some 30 years after Amsterdam had been granted its city charter, these defences took the form of a canal moat with piled-earth ramparts reinforced by wooden palisades. As the city grew and the

Plaque on the Café 't Mandje (Little Basket), a gay bar at No. 63 Zeedijk

boundaries expanded, the canals were filled in and the dykes became obsolete. The paths that ran alongside them became the streets and alleys which bear their names today.

One of the two remaining wooden-fronted houses in Amsterdam can be found at No. 1. It was built in the mid-16th century as a hostel for sailors and now houses Café In 't Aepjen (Tel 626 8401). Opposite is St Olofskapel, built in 1445 and named after the first Christian king of Norway and Denmark.

By the 1600s, the Zeedijk had become a slum. The area is on the edge of the city's Red Light District, and in the 1960s and 1970s it became notorious as a centre for drug-dealing and street crime. Following a clean-up campaign in the 1980s, the Zeedijk is now much improved.

Plaques on the gables of some of the street's cafés reveal their former use – the red boot at No. 17 indicates that it was once a cobbler's.

㉑ Oude Kerk

The Oude Kerk dates from the early 13th century, when a wooden church was built in a burial ground on a sand bank *(see pp22–3)*. The present Gothic structure is 14th-century and has grown from a single-aisled church into a basilica. As it expanded, it became a gathering place for traders and a refuge for the poor. Its paintings and statuary were destroyed after the Alteration *(see pp26–7)* in 1578, but the gilded ceiling and stained-glass windows were undamaged. The Great Organ was added in 1724. The church floor consists of around 2,500 tombstones.

The Oude Kerk Today
The old church, in the heart of the frenetic Red Light District, juxtaposes contemporary art within its medieval interior.

★ Great Organ (1724)
Christian Vater's oak-encased organ has eight bellows and 4,000 pipes. Marbled-wood statues of biblical figures surround it.

KEY

① **Tomb of Admiral Abraham van der Hulst**

② **Christening Chapel**

③ **The spire** of the bell tower was built by Joost Bilhamer in 1565. François Hemony added the 47-bell carillon in 1658.

④ **Tomb of Saskia, wife of Rembrandt** *(see pp64–5)*

⑤ **Tomb of Admiral Jacob van Heemskerk (1567–1607)**

⑥ **17th- and 18th-century houses**

⑦ **Former sacristy**

The Red Door
The inscription on the lintel above the door into the former sacristy warns those about to enter: "Marry in haste, repent at leisure."

★ **Gilded Ceiling**
The delicate 15th-century vault paintings have a gilded background. They were hidden with layers of blue paint in 1755 and not revealed until 1955.

VISITORS' CHECKLIST

Practical Information
Oudekerksplein. **Map** 7 C2.
Tel 625 8284. **Open** 10am–5:30pm Mon–Sat, 1–5pm Sun.
🕙 11am Sun. ♿ ♿
Tower: 📷 call 689 2565.
Closed 1 Jan, 30 Apr, 25 Dec.
W oudekerk.nl

Transport
🚊 4, 9, 16, 24.

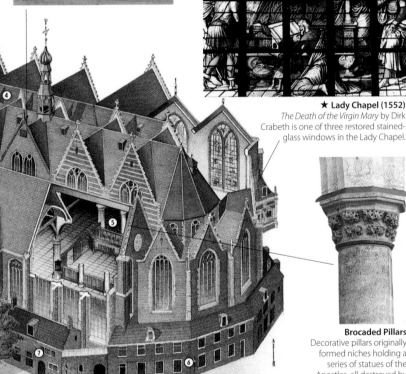

★ **Lady Chapel (1552)**
The Death of the Virgin Mary by Dirk Crabeth is one of three restored stained-glass windows in the Lady Chapel.

Brocaded Pillars
Decorative pillars originally formed niches holding a series of statues of the Apostles, all destroyed by the iconoclasts in 1578.

1412 North transept completed		**1462** First side chapel demolished to build south transept		**1658** Carillon installed		**1979** Church reopens to public
1330 Church consecrated to St Nicholas			**1552** Lady Chapel added		**1724** Great Organ installed	**1951** Church closes
1300	**1400**	**1500**	**1600**	**1700**	**1800**	**1900**
1300 Small stone church built	**1500** Side chapels added		**1578** Calvinists triumph in the Alteration		**1912–14** Partial restoration of northwest corner	
1390 Pseudo-basilica replaced by three-nave hall	**1565** Spire added to 13th-century tower	*Stained-glass coats of arms in Lady Chapel*		**1955** Restoration of church begins	
1250 First wooden chapel						

NIEUWE ZIJDE

The western side of medieval Amsterdam was known as the Nieuwe Zijde (New Side). Together with the Oude Zijde it formed the heart of the early maritime settlement. Nieuwendijk, now a busy shopping street, was originally one of the earliest sea defences. As Amsterdam grew, it expanded eastwards, leaving large sections of the Nieuwe Zijde, to the west, neglected and in decline. With its many wooden houses, the city was prone to fires and in 1452 much of the area was burnt down. During rebuilding, a broad moat, the Singel, was cut, along which warehouses, rich merchants' homes

and fine quays sprang up. The Amsterdams Historisch Museum, which is now housed in a splendid, converted orphanage, has scores of maps and paintings charting the growth of the city from these times to the present day. One room is devoted to the Miracle of Amsterdam *(see p24)*, which made the city a place of pilgrimage, and brought commerce to the Nieuwe Zijde. Nearby lies Kalverstraat, Amsterdam's main shopping street, and also the secluded Begijnhof. This pretty courtyard is mostly fringed by narrow 17th-century houses, but it also contains the city's oldest surviving wooden house.

Sights at a Glance

Historic Buildings, Monuments and Bridges
❷ Koninklijk Paleis
❹ Nationaal Monument
❾ Torensluis
❿ Magna Plaza
⓬ Centraal Station
⓯ Beurs van Berlage

Streets and Squares
❺ Nes
❼ Begijnhof

Churches
❶ *Nieuwe Kerk pp76–7*
⓭ Lutherse Kerk
⓭ St Nicolaasbasiliek

Museums
❸ Madame Tussauds Scenerama
❻ *Amsterdam Museum pp82–5*
❽ Allard Pierson Museum
⓮ *Museum Ons' Lieve Heer op Solder pp86–7*

See also Street Finder pp274–87

0 metres   250
0 yards   250

Restaurants *pp225–6*
1 1e Klas
2 Barco
3 Brasserie Harkema
4 Català
5 De Compagnon
6 Côte Ouest
7 Getto Food & Drink
8 Greenwoods
9 Kam Yin
10 Kapitein Zeppos
11 Moti Mahal
12 Supperclub
13 Sushi
14 Tibet
15 Trattoria Caprese
16 Van Kerkwijk
17 Vermeer
18 D'Vijff Vlieghen
19 Visrestaurant Lucius

◀ Weather vane adorning the façade of the Centraal Station

For map symbols *see back flap*

Street-by-Street: Nieuwe Zijde

Although much of the medieval Nieuwe Zijde has disappeared, the area is still rich in buildings that relate to the city's past. The Dam, dominated by the Koninklijk Paleis and Nieuwe Kerk, provides examples of architecture from the 15th to the 20th century. Around Kalverstraat, the narrow streets and alleys follow the course of some of the earliest dykes and footpaths. Here, most of the traditional gabled houses have been turned into bustling shops and cafés. Streets such as Rokin and Nes are now home to financial institutions, attracted by the nearby stock and options exchanges. Nes is also known for its venues which feature alternative theatre.

❻ ★ **Amsterdam Museum**
Wall plaques and maps showing the walled medieval city are on display in this converted orphanage that dates from the 16th century.

Kalverstraat, now a busy tourist shopping area, took its name from the livestock market which was regularly held here during the 15th century.

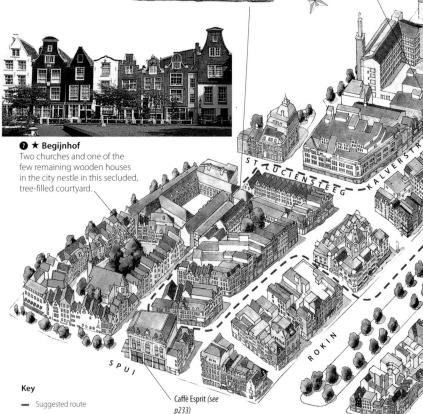

❼ ★ **Begijnhof**
Two churches and one of the few remaining wooden houses in the city nestle in this secluded, tree-filled courtyard.

Key

— Suggested route

Caffè Esprit (see p233)

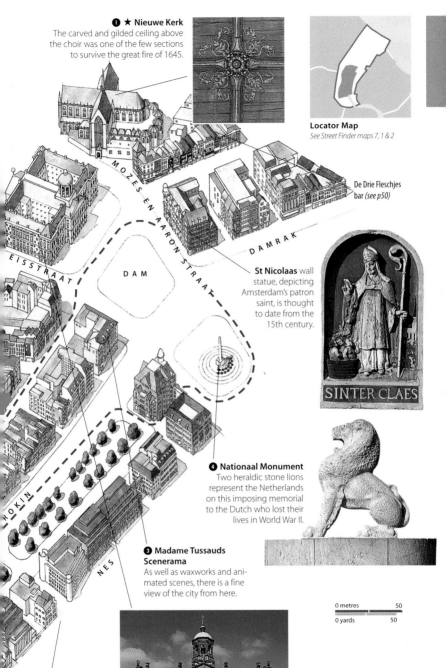

❶ ★ Nieuwe Kerk
The carved and gilded ceiling above the choir was one of the few sections to survive the great fire of 1645.

Locator Map
See Street Finder maps 7, 1 & 2

De Drie Fleschjes
bar *(see p50)*

St Nicolaas wall statue, depicting Amsterdam's patron saint, is thought to date from the 15th century.

SINTER CLAES

❹ Nationaal Monument
Two heraldic stone lions represent the Netherlands on this imposing memorial to the Dutch who lost their lives in World War II.

❸ Madame Tussauds Scenerama
As well as waxworks and animated scenes, there is a fine view of the city from here.

0 metres   50
0 yards   50

❺ Nes
This street is one of Amsterdam's oldest and has been a centre for theatre for 150 years.

❷ Koninklijk Paleis
Built as the town hall, the building's Classical façade and fine sculptures were intended to glorify the city and its government.

❶ Nieuwe Kerk

Dating from the 14th century, Amsterdam's second parish church was built as the population outgrew the Oude Kerk *(see pp70–71)*. During its turbulent history, the church has been destroyed several times by fire, rebuilt and then stripped of its finery after the Alteration *(see pp26–7)*. It reached its present size in the 1650s. Since 1814 all the Dutch monarchs have been crowned here. A cultural centre hosts impressive exhibitions.

★ Great Organ (1645)
Marbled-wood cherubs and angels adorn the elaborate gilded casing of the Great Organ, which was designed by Jacob van Campen.

The New Stadhuis, Dam Square
The Nieuwe Kerk is in the background, at the corner of Dam square, in this painting by Jan van der Heyden (1637–1712). It shows the newly completed Stadhuis, which is now the Koninklijk Paleis *(see p78)*.

Gilded Cherubs
Grimacing gilded cherubs struggle to support the corners of the wooden barrel vault above the transept crossing.

KEY

① Ornate blind windows

② Box pews around the carved pulpit

③ Baptistry

④ Rood screen by Johannes Lutma (c.1650)

⑤ Orphans' Gallery

⑥ Apse

⑦ Mason's Chapel

★ Carved Pulpit (1664)
It took Albert Vinckenbrinck 15 years to carve the pulpit, which is unusually flamboyant for a Dutch Protestant church.

Stained-Glass Windows
The lower-right section of the colourful arched window in the south transept was designed by Otto Mengelberg in 1898. It depicts Queen Wilhelmina *(see p35)* surrounded by courtiers at her coronation.

Brass Candelabra
Magnificent three-tiered brass candelabra were hung from the ceilings of the nave and transepts during restoration work following the fire of 1645.

Main entrance

★ Tomb of Michiel de Ruyter (1607–76)
Rombout Verhulst's memorial to De Ruyter is in the apse. The admiral, greatly revered by the Dutch, died at sea in battle against the French at Messina.

1421 Fire destroys much of original building	**1452** Damaged in the Great Fire	*Goblet commemorating beginning of renovation of the church (1647)*		**1841** First royal investiture in Nieuwe Kerk		
	1540 North transept razed		**1653** Work on tower halted, reason unclear	**1847** Gothic structure built to replace tower		
1350	**1450**	**1550**	**1650**	**1750**	**1850**	**1950**
1380 Estimated date of earliest church on site	**1578** Church plundered following the Alteration *(see pp26–7)*	**1646** Work begins on construction of Jacob van Campen's tower		**1907** Large-scale restoration		
	1645 Fire destroys all but façade and walls	**1783** Part of tower torn down		**1959** Restoration begins and lasts 20 years		

The vast marble-floored Burgerzaal in the Koninklijk Paleis

❶ Koninklijk Paleis

Dam. **Map** 7 B2. 🚋 1, 2, 4, 5, 9, 13, 14, 16, 17, 24. **Open** Usual hours are Jul–Aug: 10am–5pm daily; Sep–Jun: 10am–5pm Tue–Sun: check website for up-to-date info. 🚼 🅿 ♿ 🏠 📷 (**Tel** 620 4060 to reserve a private group tour). 🆆 **paleisamsterdam.nl**

The Koninklijk Paleis, still used occasionally by the Dutch royal family for official functions, was built as the Stadhuis (town hall). Work began in 1648, after the end of the 80 Years War with Spain (see pp30–31). It dominated its surroundings and more than 13,600 piles were driven into the ground for the foundations. The Classically inspired design by Jacob van Campen (1595–1657) reflects Amsterdam's mood of confidence after the Dutch victory. Civic pride is also shown in the allegorical sculptures by Artus Quellien (1609–68), which decorate the pediments, and in François Hemony's statues and carillon. The full magnificence of the architecture is best seen in the vast Burgerzaal (citizens' hall).

Based on the assembly halls of ancient Rome, this 30-m- (95-ft-) high room runs the length of the building. It boasts a marble floor inlaid with maps of the eastern and western hemispheres, as well as epic sculptures by Quellien.

Most of the furniture on display, including the chandeliers, dates from 1808, when Louis Napoleon declared the building his royal palace (see pp32–3).

❸ Madame Tussauds Scenerama

Peek & Cloppenburg Building, Dam 20. **Map** 7 B3. **Tel** 523 0623. 🚋 4, 9, 14, 16, 24. **Open** Jul–Aug: 10am–9pm daily; Sep–Jun: 10am–7pm daily (last adm 1 hr before closing). **Closed** 27 Apr. 🚼 ♿ 🏠 🆆 **madametussauds.nl**

Located above the Peek & Cloppenburg department store, Madame Tussauds offers thematic and interactive displays featuring royalty, sporting heroes, popular musicians, film stars and Dutch celebrities. Visitors can paint with Rembrandt, have a photograph taken with James Bond or work out with David Beckham.

❹ Nationaal Monument

Dam. **Map** 7 B3. 🚋 4, 9, 14, 16, 24.

Sculpted by John Raedecker and designed by architect JJP Oud, the 22-m (70-ft) obelisk in the Dam commemorates Dutch World War II casualties. It was unveiled in 1956, and is fronted by two lions, heraldic symbols of the Netherlands. Embedded in the wall behind are urns containing earth from all the Dutch provinces and the former colonies of Indonesia, the Antilles and Surinam.

❺ Nes

Map 7 B3 & B4. 🚋 4, 9, 14, 16, 24.

This quiet, narrow street is home to several theatres. In 1614, Amsterdam's first bank was opened in a pawnshop at No. 57. A wall plaque marks the site, and pawned goods still clutter the shop window. At night, Nes can be dangerous for the unguarded visitor.

De Engelenbak, one of several theatres located along Nes

❻ Amsterdam Museum

See pp82–5.

❼ Begijnhof

Spui (entrance at Gedempte Begijnensloot). **Map** 7 B4. 🚊 1, 2, 5, 9, 14, 16, 24. Gates: **Open** 9am–5pm daily.

The Begijnhof was originally built in 1346 as a sanctuary for the Begijntjes, a lay Catholic sisterhood who lived like nuns, although they took no monastic vows. In return for lodgings within the complex, these worthy women undertook to educate the poor and look after the sick. Nothing survives of the earliest dwellings, but the Begijnhof still retains a sanctified atmosphere. The rows of beautiful houses that overlook its well-kept green include Amsterdam's oldest surviving house at No. 34. On the adjoining wall, there is a fascinating collection of wall plaques with a biblical theme taken from the houses.

The southern fringe of the square is dominated by the Engelse Kerk (English Church), which dates from the 15th century. Directly west stands the Begijnhof Chapel, a clandestine church in which the Begijntjes and other Catholics worshipped in secret until religious tolerance was restored in 1795. It once housed relics of the Miracle of Amsterdam *(see pp24–5)*. Four splendid stained-glass windows and paintings depict scenes of the Miracle.

The occupants request that noise be kept to a minimum and no tour groups are allowed.

Plaque on the Engelse Kerk

The Begijnhof Chapel, a clandestine church (Nos. 29–30), was completed in 1680. It contains many reminders of Amsterdam's Catholic past.

No. 19 has a plaque depicting the exodus of the Jews from Egypt.

Houses in the Begijnhof are still occupied by single women.

Biblical plaques cover the wall behind No. 34.

Spui entrance

Main entrance from Gedempte Begijnensloot

Het Houten Huis at No. 34 is one of Amsterdam's oldest houses, dating from the second half of the 15th century. It is one of only two wooden-fronted houses in the city, as timber houses were banned in 1521 after a series of catastrophic fires. Most of the houses in the Begijnhof were not built until after the 16th century.

Engelse Kerk was built around 1419 for the Begijntjes. The church was confiscated after the Alteration *(see pp26–7)* and rented to a group of English and Scottish Presbyterians in 1607. The Pilgrim Fathers *(see p187)* may have worshipped here.

8 Allard Pierson Museum

Oude Turfmarkt 127. **Map** 7 B4.
Tel 525 2556. 🚃 4, 9, 14, 16, 24.
Open 10am–5pm daily.
Closed 1 Jan, 27 Apr, 25 Dec.
🖼 ♿ 🎦 🅆 **allardpierson museum.nl**

Detail of the Allard Pierson Museum's
Neo-Classical stone façade

Amsterdam's only specialist archaeological collection is named after Allard Pierson (1831–96), a humanist and scholar. The museum contains Cypriot, Greek, Egyptian, Roman, Etruscan and Coptic artifacts. Look out for a case of rather gruesome Egyptian mummy remains, a computer that enables you to write your name in hieroglyphics, a jointed Greek doll from 300 BC and some fine Roman jewellery. Next door is Amsterdam University's special collections department.

9 Torensluis

Singel between Torensteeg and Oude Leliestraat. **Map** 7 B2. 🚃 1, 2, 5, 13, 14, 17.

The Torensluis is one of the widest bridges in Amsterdam. It was built on the site of a 17th-century sluice gate and took its name from a tower that stood on the bridge until demolished in 1829 (its outline is marked in the pavement). A jail was built in its foundations.

In summer, visitors can sit out at café tables on the bridge and enjoy pleasant views down the Singel. The statue dominating the bridge is of Multatuli, the 19th-century Dutch writer who wrote the well-known book *Max Havelaar*.

10 Magna Plaza

Nieuwezijds Voorburgwal 182. **Map** 7 B2. **Tel** 626 9199. 🚃 1, 2, 5, 13, 14, 17. **Open** 11am–7pm Mon, 10am–7pm Tue, Wed, Fri, Sat, 10am–9pm Thu, noon–7pm Sun. **Closed** 1 Jan, 27 Apr, 25 & 26 Dec. ♿ 🅆 **magnaplaza.nl**

A post office building has been sited here since 1748. A wall panel on the current building's façade depicts the original office, which was taken out of service in 1854. The present building was completed in 1899. CH Peters, the architect, was ridiculed for the extravagance of its Neo-Gothic design. Critics dubbed the Postkantoor's elaborately decorated style and spindly towers "post-office Gothic". It has been redeveloped, and is now a shopping mall, the Magna Plaza. The grand dimensions of Peters' design have been well preserved.

11 Lutherse Kerk

Kattengat 2. **Map** 7 C1. 🚃 1, 2, 5, 13, 17. **Closed** to the public.

The Lutherse Kerk was designed by Adriaan Dortsman (1625–82) and opened in 1671. It is sometimes known as the Ronde Lutherse Kerk, being the first Dutch Reformed church to feature a circular ground plan and two upper galleries, giving the whole congregation a clear view of the pulpit.

In 1882 a fire started by careless plumbers destroyed everything except the exterior walls. When the interior and entrance were rebuilt in 1883, they were made squarer and more ornate, in keeping with church architectural style of that

An outdoor café on the Torensluis bridge overlooking the Singel canal

time. A vaulted copper dome replaced the earlier ribbed version.

Falling attendances led to the closure and deconsecration of the church in 1935. The building is now used by the Renaissance Amsterdam Hotel (*see p216*) as a conference centre and banqueting chamber.

⑫ Centraal Station

Stationsplein. **Map** 8 D1. **Tel** 0900 9292. 🚊 1, 2, 4, 5, 9, 11, 13, 16, 17, 24. Ⓜ Centraal Station. **Open** 6am–midnight Mon–Fri, 7am–midnight Sat, Sun & public hols. ♿

When the Centraal Station opened in 1889, it replaced the old harbour as the symbolic focal point of the city (*see pp34–5*) and effectively curtained Amsterdam off from the sea. The Neo-Renaissance red-brick railway terminus was designed by PJH Cuypers, who was also responsible for the Rijks-museum (*see pp130–33*), and AL van Gendt, who designed the Concertgebouw (*see p134*).

Three artificial islands were created, using 8,600 wooden piles to support the structure. In the design of the station's twin towers and imposing central section there are archi-tectural echoes of a triumphal arch. The imposing façade is adorned with elaborate gold and coloured decoration showing allegories of maritime trade – a tribute to the city's past. Today it is a major

Weather vane on Centraal Station

Decorative brickwork on the façade of the Beurs van Berlage

meeting point as well as the transport hub of the capital, with 1,400 trains operating daily (*see p264*), and buses and trams terminating here. The station is currently undergoing major renovation.

⑬ Sint Nicolaasbasiliek

Prins Hendrikkade 73. **Map** 8 D1. **Tel** 624 8749. 🚊 1, 2, 4, 5, 9,13, 16, 17, 24. Ⓜ Centraal Station. **Open** noon–3pm Mon & Sat, 11am–4pm Tue–Fri. ✝ 12:30pm Mon–Sat (Tue in English, Fri in Spanish); 10:30am, 1pm (in Spanish) Sun. Ⓦ **nicolaas-parochie.nl**

Sint Nicolaas, the patron saint of seafarers, is an important icon in Holland. Many churches are named after him, and the Netherlands' principal day for the giving of presents, 5 December, is known as Sinterklaasavond (*see p55*).

The Sint Nicolaasbasiliek was designed by AC Bleys (1842–1912), and completed in 1887. It replaced some clandestine Catholic churches set up in the city when Amsterdam was officially Protestant (*see p86*).

The exterior is rather grim and forbidding, its twin towers dominating the skyline. The colourful interior is enlivened by stained-glass windows in the dome.

⑭ Museum Ons' Lieve Heer op Solder

See pp86–7.

⑮ Beurs van Berlage

Damrak 2. **Map** 7 C2. **Tel** 530 4141. 🚊 4, 9, 16, 24. **Open** only during exhibitions. **Closed** 1 Jan. 🚫 ♿ 📷 11am Sat. 🛗 Ⓦ **beursvanberlage.nl**

Hendrik Berlage's stock exchange was completed in 1903. Its clean, functional appearance marked a departure from late 19th-century Revivalist architecture. Many of its design features were adopted by the Amsterdam School (*see p99*). It has an impressive frieze show-ing the evolution of man from Adam to stockbroker. Now used as a conference venue, it also hosts a variety of changing exhibitions and concerts.

Neo-Renaissance façade of the Sint Nicolaasbasiliek

❻ Amsterdam Museum

The Convent of St Lucien was turned into a civic orphanage two years after the Alteration of 1578 *(see pp26–7)*. The original red brick convent has been enlarged over the years, with new wings added in the 17th century by Hendrick de Keyser *(see p92)* and Jacob van Campen *(see p78)*. The present building is largely as it was in the 18th century. Since 1975 the complex has housed the city's historical museum.

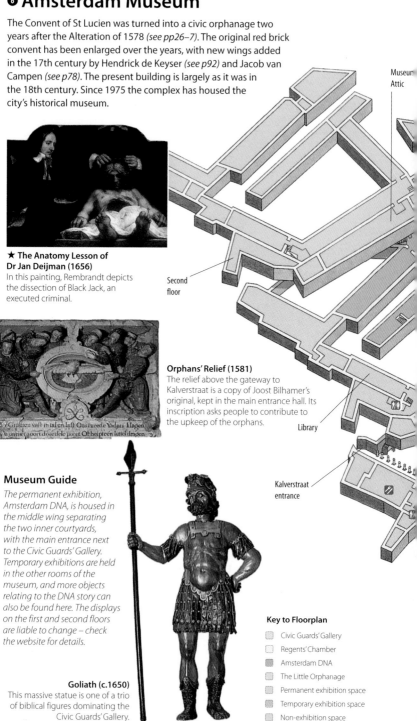

★ The Anatomy Lesson of Dr Jan Deijman (1656)
In this painting, Rembrandt depicts the dissection of Black Jack, an executed criminal.

Orphans' Relief (1581)
The relief above the gateway to Kalverstraat is a copy of Joost Bilhamer's original, kept in the main entrance hall. Its inscription asks people to contribute to the upkeep of the orphans.

Museum Attic

Second floor

Library

Kalverstraat entrance

Museum Guide
The permanent exhibition, Amsterdam DNA, is housed in the middle wing separating the two inner courtyards, with the main entrance next to the Civic Guards' Gallery. Temporary exhibitions are held in the other rooms of the museum, and more objects relating to the DNA story can also be found here. The displays on the first and second floors are liable to change – check the website for details.

Goliath (c.1650)
This massive statue is one of a trio of biblical figures dominating the Civic Guards' Gallery.

Key to Floorplan
- Civic Guards' Gallery
- Regents' Chamber
- Amsterdam DNA
- The Little Orphanage
- Permanent exhibition space
- Temporary exhibition space
- Non-exhibition space

★ **The Flower Market and the Town Hall (1673)**
This scene by Gerrit Berckheijde (1638–98) shows the city's original flower market on the Nieuwezijds Voorburgwal, which was filled in in the late 1800s. In the background is the Koninklijk Paleis *(see p78)*.

VISITORS' CHECKLIST

Practical Information
Kalverstraat 92, St Luciensteeg 27.
Map 1 C5. **Tel** 523 1822. **Open** 10am–5pm daily. **Closed** 1 Jan, 27 Apr, 25 Dec.
w amsterdammuseum.nl

Transport
1, 2, 4, 5, 9, 13, 14, 16, 17, 24.

Gilded Silver City Keys (1810)
These two silver keys were presented to Napoleon upon his entry into Amsterdam on 9 October 1811 *(see p33)*.

First floor

★ **The Governesses (seated) and two Wardresses of the Spinhuis**
This was painted in 1638 by DD Santvoort.

Ground floor

Main entrance

17th-century red-brick façade

St Luciensteeg entrance

Hunting Day (1926)
Johan Braakensiek's illustration shows the lively carnival atmosphere in Zeedijk during the celebrations for this two-day event, which took place on the third Monday of August.

Exploring the Amsterdam Museum

At the museum's heart is the Amsterdam DNA exhibition, which offers a multimedia introduction to the development of Amsterdam from its humble origins as a small fishing village at the mouth of the Amstel in the Middle Ages to today's cosmopolitan city. Visitors can then explore the other rooms, where aspects of Amsterdam's history are dealt with in more detail, including the city's Golden Age in the 17th century *(see pp28–9)*. A series of Civic Guard group portraits are a highlight of the collection. At "The Little Orphanage" children discover what life was like in the 17th century.

Civic Guards' Gallery

This covered walkway is accessible to all during museum hours and it is free to enter. Queen Juliana *(see pp38)* opened the Civic Guards' Gallery in 1975 to house the group portraits which were popular during the 16th century.

The Civic Guard, or town watch, comprised three guilds of marksmen, which merged in 1580. The Guard held an annual banquet, which became a popular setting for the group portrait. For posterity the Guard were usually depicted in their Sunday best as opposed to their guard dress.

This is a rare collection as few portraits were commissioned after 1650. Best-known are Rembrandt's works; highlights are by Dirck Barendsz and Cornelis Anthonisz, such as *The Meal of the 17 Guardsmen of Company H* (1533). These 15 large and imposing works are juxtaposed with contemporary portraits of Amsterdam citizens and celebrities on the opposing wall.

Regents' Chamber

Built in 1634, this room was the meeting place of the orphanage's directors (regents). Its fine ceiling, added in 1656, shows the orphans receiving charity. Portraits of the regents hang on the walls alongside Abraham de Verwer's two paintings of *The Battle of Slaak* (1633). The long table and cabinets are 17th-century.

Amsterdam DNA

The Amsterdam DNA exhibition, the heart and soul of the museum, is a 45-minute, historical tour of the city. The exhibition explores Amsterdam's main cultural characteristics, including the spirit of enterprise, freedom of thought, civic virtue and creativity. Key moments are examined chronologically via touch-sensitive screens and archival film footage, in a variety of different languages.

The exhibition begins by explaining how the past and present have influenced each other. This is followed by a

Terrestrial globe by cartographer Willem Blaeu on display at the museum

chronological history of the city, beginning in the year 1000 when the first settlement was built. These initial inhabitants constructed a dam across the river Amstel and the village slowly grew, thanks to trade and shipping brought alongside the dam. The city also became a popular destination for pilgrims who were inspired by the Miracle of Amsterdam in 1345; a dying man was given the Sacrament, which he regurgitated, but when thrown on the fire the Host would not burn. A woman reached into the fire and retrieved the Sacramental bread without being burned by the flames. Many churches were built in response, including one on the very spot where the miracle had taken place, and thousands of pilgrims flocked to the city.

Between 1500 and 1560 the city's population tripled. The Civic Guard became defenders of law and order in the over-crowded city and a display of its armour and weaponry is shown in the exhibition. There is also an opportunity for visitors to have their photo taken posing with the armour. Cornelis Anthonisz's bird's-eye view of Amsterdam *(see pp26–7)* is the oldest city plan to survive, and is also on display here.

The evolution of Amsterdam continues through the turbulent revolt against Spain and Catholicism in the second half of the 16th century.

Regents' Chamber, furnished with 17th-century pieces and oil paintings

The Gouden Leeuw on the IJ at Amsterdam by Willem van de Velde (1665)

During the Alteration, in 1578, Protestants took control of the city and many churches were plundered. The city became a haven for Protestant refugees from the Southern Netherlands. With the influx of fleeing tradesmen and artisans, Amsterdam prospered, and this became known as the city's Golden Age *(see pp28–9)*.

Amsterdam DNA emphasises the importance of overseas trade and colonial expansion and includes the iconic globe of the famous cartographer Willem Blaeu. Portraits and busts of dignitaries and governors of Amsterdam's poor houses emphasize the great discrepancy between the rich and poorer inhabitants of the city. The patronage of art flourished in the city's Golden Age and artists flooded into the city. Contemporary paintings, often allegorical in nature, portray rich families, such as Jacob de Wit's *Maid of Amsterdam* (1741). These artworks by great masters, such as Pieter de Hooch and Rembrandt, are just a few of the superlative exhibits bringing the rich and varied history of Amsterdam to life.

The exhibition further highlights changes to the city during the 18th, 19th and 20th centuries, beginning with French troops entering the city in 1795. The republic of the Netherlands became a kingdom in 1806, when Napoleon appointed his brother Louis Bonaparte as the country's ruling monarch. Amsterdam fell into a steady decline, as Great Britain became the principal maritime power.

During the latter half of the 19th century, the Dutch economy began to flourish again, thanks to its colonies, and the city of Amsterdam grew dramatically. Socialists campaigned for housing of the poorer classes to improve and art of the day reflected the city's social problems. Works by George Hendrik Breitner *(see p133)* and sombre black-and-white photographs depict this less salubrious side of the city.

Amsterdam DNA touches on the further hardship and famine experienced during World War II *(see pp36–7)*. The round-up and deportation of Jews led to a mass strike in the city. By the war's conclusion, in 1945, some 60,000 Amsterdam Jews had perished in Nazi concentration camps.

The exhibition concludes with a celebration of multicultural Amsterdam and its role as a 21st-century capital of freedom – a "thousand-year-old city on the water" that was founded on, and continues to hold dear and vehemently protect, the values of free enterprise and freedom of speech, religion and self-expression.

The Little Orphanage

This exhibition gives children and parents the opportunity to experience life in a 17th-century orphanage. The museum relocated from the Waag building *(see p62)* to this large premesis 15 years after the orphanage's closure, and retains many indications of the building's original purpose. This, combined with interactive exhibits and hands-on activities, gives families a real taste of the orphanage's place in Amsterdam 400 years ago.

Along with authentically arranged classrooms, kitchens and animal sheds for children to explore are talking exhibits and pop up characters to guide visitors through life in the orphanage. Children also have the opportunity to dress up, milk cows and practice their calligraphy.

The Old Orphanage

Orphan Girls Going to Church (c.1880) by Nicolaas van der Waaij

The orphanage moved to St Lucien's convent in 1580. It was open only to the children of burghers, excluding the poorest children. As the city grew, so did the number of orphans. In the 17th century, two wings were built to accommodate more children, and a separate entrance for girls was added on St Luciensteeg. The building was used as an orphanage until 1960, but the formal uniform was abandoned in 1919.

⓮ Museum Ons' Lieve Heer op Solder

Tucked away on the edge of the Red Light District is a restored 17th-century canal house, with two smaller houses to the rear. The upper storeys conceal a secret Catholic church known as Our Lord in the Attic (Ons' Lieve Heer op Solder), originally built in 1663. After the Alteration *(see pp26–7)*, when Amsterdam officially became Protestant, many hidden churches were built throughout the city. The building became a museum in 1888, and has fine church silver, religious artifacts and paintings. The church has been restored to its original state and modernized. Next door to the church is an exhibition space, café and shop.

Museum Façade
The house on the canal has a simple spout gable and includes the two smaller houses behind. It was built by bourgeois merchant Jan Hartman in 1661.

Main entrance

KEY

① House on the canal

② **A chaplain's** tiny box bedroom is hidden off a bend in the stairs. There was a resident chaplain in the church from 1663.

③ **Wooden viewing gallery of church**

④ **Sacristy**

⑤ **Rear house**

⑥ **Middle house**

Canal Room
Located on the first floor, at the front of the house, the canal room is where 17th-century residents would have spent the day.

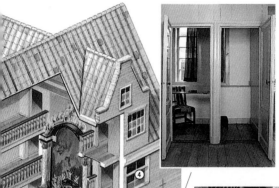

VISITORS' CHECKLIST

Practical Information
Oudezijds Voorburgwal 40.
Map 8 D2. **Tel** 624 6604. **Open**
10am–5pm Mon–Sat, 1–5pm Sun
and public hols. **Closed** 27 Apr.
 w opsolder.nl

Transport
4, 9, 16, 24.

Confessional
The landing where the tiny wooden confessional stands was formerly the living room of the rear house.

★ Our Lord in the Attic
The original hidden church was extended in c.1735 to create more seating space. It served the Catholic community until St Nicolaasbasiliek (see p81) was finished in 1887.

17th-Century Kitchen
The kitchen was originally part of the priest's living quarters. The Delft tiles, fireplace and black-and-white floor are all original.

★ The Parlour
Restored to its former opulence, the parlour is an unusually fine example of a living room decorated and furnished in the Dutch Classical style of the 17th century.

WESTERN CANAL RING

At the start of the 17th century, construction of the Grachtengordel began here, just west of the Singel. At the same time, city planner Hendrick Staets laid out the marshy area beyond these fashionable canals as an area for workers whose industries were banned from the town centre. Its network of narrow streets and oblique canals followed the course of old paths and drainage ditches. Immigrants fleeing religious persecution also settled here. It is thought that Huguenot refugees called the district *jardin* (garden), later corrupted to "Jordaan". Historically a poor area, it is famous for its almshouses (*hofjes*), and the Claes Claeszhofje is a fine early example. The Jordaan now has a more bohemian air. Further north are the characterful Western Islands, created in the mid-17th century to meet the demand for warehouses.

Sights at a Glance

Historic Buildings and Monuments
❶ Homomonument
❹ Huis met de Hoofden
⓭ Haarlemmerpoort

Museums
❸ Anne Frank House
⓫ Pianola en Piano Museum

Canals and Islands
❺ Egelantiersgracht
❻ Bloemgracht
⓬ Brouwersgracht
⓮ Western Islands

Churches
❷ Westerkerk
❾ Noorderkerk

Markets
❿ Noordermarkt

Hofjes
❼ Claes Claeszhofje
❽ De Star and Zon's Hofje

Restaurants pp226–7
1 Black and Blue
2 De Bolhoed
3 Bordewijk
4 Chez Georges
5 Daalder
6 Lof
7 Mantoe
8 Pancake Bakery
9 Piqniq
10 Semhar
11 Stout!

See also Street Finder pp274–87

Street-by-Street: Around the Jordaan

West of the Grachtengordel, the Jordaan still retains a network of narrow, characterful streets and delightful canals. Among the 17th-century workers' houses are dozens of quirky shops, which are well worth a browse, selling anything from designer clothes to old sinks, and lively brown cafés and bars, which spill on to the pavements in summer. A stroll along the Grachtengordel provides a glimpse into some of the city's grandest canal houses, including Huis met de Hoofden.

❸ ★ Anne Frank House
For two years, the Frank family and four others lived in a small upstairs apartment that was hidden behind a revolving bookcase.

❻ Bloemgracht
This quiet, pretty canal was once a centre for makers of paint and dye.

❷ ★ Westerkerk
Hendrick de Keyser's church is the site of Rembrandt's unmarked grave, and was the setting for the wedding of Queen Beatrix and Prince Claus in 1966.

❺ Egelantiersgracht
This charming tree-lined Jordaan canal is overlooked by an interesting mixture of old and new architecture. Pretty views are provided from its numerous bridges.

❹ Huis met de Hoofden
The name "House with the Heads"
refers to the six Classical busts at
the entrance, depicting Apollo,
Ceres, Mars, Minerva,
Bacchus and Diana.

Locator Map
See Street Finder maps 1 & 7

PRINSENGRACHT

KEIZERSGRACHT

KEIZERSGRACHT

LELIEGRACHT

KEIZERSGRACHT

**The Eerste Hollandsche
Levensverzekeringsbank building**, with its
fine façade, is a rare example of Dutch Art
Nouveau, designed by Gerrit van Arkel in 1905.

Key

— Suggested route

0 metres   75
0 yards   75

❶ Homomonument
The pink triangle used to
"brand" homosexual men
during World War II influenced
the design of this memorial to
oppressed gay men and
women everywhere. It was
unveiled in September 1987.

❶ Homomonument

Westermarkt (between Westerkerk and Keizersgracht). **Map** 1 B4. 🚊 13, 14, 17. 🚏 Keizersgracht.
W homomonument.nl

This monument to the homosexual men and women who lost their lives during World War II provides a quiet place of contemplation amid the bustle of the Westermarkt.

The pink triangular badge which gay men were forced to wear in Nazi concentration camps later became an emblem of gay pride, and provided the inspiration for Karin Daan's 1987 design. The monument consists of three large pink granite triangles, one of which bears an engraving from a poem by Jacob Israël de Haan (1881–1924).

❷ Westerkerk

Prinsengracht 281. **Map** 1 B4. **Tel** 624 7766. 🚊 13, 14, 17. **Open** 10am–5pm Mon–Fri, 11am–3pm Sat. 🚏 629 7766. **Tower: Open** Apr & Oct: 10am–6pm Mon–Sat; May–Sep: 10am–8pm Mon–Sat. 🎫 📷 **W** westerkerk.nl

Built as part of the development of the Canal Ring (see pp46–7), this church has the tallest tower in the city at 85 m (272 ft), and the largest nave of any Dutch Protestant church. It was

Re-creation of Otto Frank's office in the Anne Frank House

designed by Hendrick de Keyser, who died in 1621, a year after work began.

Rembrandt was buried here though his grave has never been found. The shutters of the huge organ (1686) were painted, by Gérard de Lairesse, with scenes showing King David, the Queen of Sheba and the Evangelists.

The spire of the Westerkerk, which is built in tapering sections, is topped by the Imperial Crown of Maximilian (see pp24–5). The panoramic views of Amsterdam from the top of the tower justify the rather gruelling climb.

The church is undergoing restoration and sections may be out of bounds during this time.

❸ Anne Frank House

Prinsengracht 267. **Map** 1 B4.
Tel 556 7105. 🚊 13, 14, 17.
🚏 Prinsengracht. **Open** Apr–Jun & Sep–Oct: 9am–9pm Sun–Fri, 9am–10pm Sat; Jul–Aug: 9am–10pm daily; Nov–Mar: 9am–7pm daily (to 9pm Sat); 1 Jan: noon–7pm; 4 May: 9am–7pm; 25 Dec: noon–5pm; 31 Dec: 9am–5pm. **Closed** Yom Kippur.
📷 📧 🚫 🎫 **W** annefrank.org

For two years during World War II, the Frank and van Pels families, both Jewish, hid here until their betrayal to the Nazis. In 1957, the Anne Frank Stichting (foundation) took over the house, to carry out

The Westerkerk in the 18th century, a view by Jan Ekels

"the ideals set down in the *Diary of Anne Frank*." The 13-year-old Anne began her now-famous diary in July 1942. It gives a unique account of growing up under persecution, and of life in confinement *(see pp36–7)*. It was first published in 1947 as *Het Achterhuis (The Annexe)*.

Visitors to the Anne Frank House enter the annexe via the revolving bookcase that hid its entrance. Its rooms are now empty, except for the film-star pin-ups in Anne's room, and Otto Frank's model of the annexe as it was during the occupation. Otto Frank's office has been re-created using period furniture. Original documents concerning the Frank family are on display. Get here early or late in the day – with nearly one million visitors a year, the museum gets very crowded. Avoid queues by ordering tickets online. Last admittance is half an hour before closing.

❹ Huis met de Hoofden

Keizersgracht 123. **Map** 7 A1. 🚋 13, 14, 17. **Closed** to the public.

Built in 1622, the Huis met de Hoofden (house with the heads) is one of the largest double houses of the period. It has a fine step gable and takes its name from the six heads placed on pilasters along the façade. Legend has it that they commemorate a housemaid who, when left alone in the house, surprised six burglars and cut off their heads. The sculptures are in fact portrayals of six Classical deities (from left to right): Apollo, Ceres, Mars, Minerva, Bacchus and Diana.

The design of the building is sometimes attributed to Pieter de Keyser (1595–1676), the son of Hendrick de Keyser.

Bikes and boats along the tranquil Bloemgracht

Head of Apollo on the Huis met de Hoofden

❺ Egelantiersgracht

Map 1 B4. 🚋 13, 14, 17.

Many canals in the Jordaan were named after trees or flowers, and this includes the Egelantiersgracht (sweetbrier or eglantine). The canal was cut in the 17th century along a drainage ditch. The houses in this area, built for artisans, are on a more intimate scale than the grand mansions along Herengracht, Keizersgracht and Prinsengracht. As a result, demand for canalside residences in the Jordaan has boomed. Despite some development, the Egelantiersgracht retains much of its original character and one of the most charming spots along the canal is the St Andrieshofje at Nos. 107–114. This *hofje* was built in 1617, and the passage through to its courtyard is decorated with splendid blue-and-white tiles.

❻ Bloemgracht

Map 1 B4. 🚋 13, 14, 17.

The Bloemgracht (flower canal) was a centre for dye and paint manufacture in the 17th century. Today, only one paint maker remains, and this quiet canal is called the Herengracht (gentlemen's canal) of the Jordaan, because of the fine gable houses along its banks.

The most beautiful are the three houses at Nos. 87 to 91. Built in 1642 in the traditional "burgher" style of the period, they feature stepped gables and a strong use of glass. Their gable stones, which served as house names until numbering was introduced in the 19th century, depict a farmer, a townsman and a seaman.

Stone plaque on the *hofje* founded in 1616 by the merchant Anslo

❼ Claes Claeszhofje

1e Egelantiersdwarsstraat. **Map** 1 B3.
🚋 3, 10, 13, 14, 17. **Open** on & off.

This is a group of *hofjes*, the earliest of which was founded in 1616 by a textile merchant, Claes Claesz Anslo. They were renovated by the Stichting Diogenes, a foundation which now rents out the houses to art students.

One of the oldest and most distinctive is the "Huis met de Schrijvende Hand" (house with the writing hand), Egelantiersstraat 52. Once the home of a teacher, it dates from the 1630s.

❽ De Star Hofje and Zon's Hofje

De Star Hofje: Prinsengracht 89–133; Zon's Hofje: Prinsengracht 159–171. **Map** 1 C3. 🚋 3, 10, 13, 14, 17. Star: **Open** 6am–6pm Mon–Fri, 6am–2pm Sat. Zon: **Open** 10am–5pm Mon–Fri.

These two charming *hofjes* are within a short walk of each other. De Star was built on the site of the Star Brewery in 1804

and is officially known as Van Brienen *hofje*. Legend has it that a merchant, Jan van Brienen, founded this almshouse in gratitude for his release from a vault in which he had been accidentally imprisoned. The peaceful courtyard has a lovely flower garden.

Zon's *hofje* was built on the site of a clandestine church, known as Noah's Ark, now indicated by a plaque in the courtyard. The church's original name of Kleine Zon (Little Sun) gave the *hofje* its name.

❾ Noorderkerk

Noordermarkt 44–48. **Map** 1 C3.
Tel 626 6436. 🚋 3, 10, 13, 14, 17.
Open 10:30am–12:30pm Mon, 11am–1pm Sat. 🕙 10am & 6:30pm Sun. 🌐 noorderkerk.nl

Built for poor settlers in the Jordaan, the North Church was the first in Amsterdam to be constructed in the shape of a Greek cross. Its layout around a central pulpit allowed all in the encircling pews to see and hear well.

The church was designed by Hendrick de Keyser (*see p92*), who died in 1621, a year after building began. It was completed in 1623. The church is still well attended by a Calvinist congregation, and bears many reminders of the working-class origins of the Jordaan. By the entrance is a sculpture of three

bound figures, inscribed: "Unity is Strength". It commemorates the Jordaanoproer (Jordaan Riot) of 1934 (*see pp36–7*). On the south façade is a plaque recalling the strike of February 1941, a protest at the Nazis' deportation of Jews.

There are regular concerts on Saturday afternoons.

Visitors to the Saturday morning fair in Noordermarkt

❿ Noordermarkt

Map 1 C3. 🚋 3, 10, 13, 14, 17. General Market: **Open** 9am–1pm Mon. Boerenmarkt (organic fruit and vegetables): **Open** 9am–5pm Sat.

Since 1627, the square that surrounds the Noorderkerk has been a market site. At that time, it sold pots and pans and *vodden* (old clothes), a tradition that continues today with a flea market. Since the 18th century, the area has been a centre for bed shops and bedding, curtains and fabrics are still sold on Monday morning along the Westerstraat. On Saturday mornings, the *vogeltjes* (small birds) market sells various birds and rabbits. Around 10am, the *boerenmarkt* takes over, selling health foods, ethnic crafts and candles.

⓫ Pianola en Piano Museum

Westerstraat 106. **Map** 1 B3.
Tel 627 9624. 🚋 3, 10, 13, 14, 17.
Open 2–5pm Sun & for concerts.
📷 🎫 🌐 pianola.nl

Fifteen instruments and some 15,000 piano rolls are on show here, celebrating the automatic pianos that were introduced in 1900. There are regular performances often with live pianists.

The lush garden in the courtyard of De Star *hofje*

A flower-filled houseboat on Brouwersgracht

⑫ Brouwersgracht

Map 1 B2. 🚋 3.

Brouwersgracht (brewers' canal) was named after the breweries established here in the 17th and 18th centuries. Leather, spices, coffee and sugar were also processed and stored here. Today, most of the warehouses are smart residences that look out on an array of houseboats moored between the canal's picturesque hump-backed bridges.

Prime examples of these functional buildings, with their spout gables (see pp98–9) and shutters, can be seen at Nos. 188 to 194. The last distillery in the area, the Ooievaar, is just off Brouwersgracht on Driehoekstraat (Triangle street). The Dutch gin, *jenever*, has been made here since 1782. Visit one of the many *proeflokalen* or tasting houses (see p50) around the city to sample it.

⑬ Haarlemmerpoort

Haarlemmerplein 50. **Map** 1 B1. 🚋 3. **Closed** to the public.

Originally a defended gateway into Amsterdam, the Haarlemmerpoort marked the beginning of the busy route to Haarlem. The original gateway, dating from 1840, was built for King William II's triumphal entry into the city (see pp34–5) and officially named Willemspoort. However, as the third gateway to be built on or close to this site, it is still referred to as the Haarlemmerpoort by Amsterdammers.

Designed by Cornelis Alewijn (1788–1839), the Neo-Classical gatehouse was used as tax offices in the 19th century and was made into flats in 1986. Traffic no longer goes through the gate, since a bridge has been built over the adjoining Westerkanaal. Beyond the Haarlemmerpoort is the peaceful Westerpark (see p153), a pleasant retreat.

Plaque with shipping motif on a house in Zandhoek, Realeneiland

⑭ Western Islands

Map 1 C1. 🚋 3.

This district comprises three islands built on the IJ in the early 17th century to provide space for warehouses and shipyards. Some of these are still in use and many of the period houses have survived.

Bickerseiland was bought in 1631 by the merchant Jan Bicker, who then developed it. Today, the island is residential with a mix of colourful apartment blocks on one side of its walkway and a jumble of tugs and houseboats on the other.

Photogenic Realeneiland has one of the city's prettiest spots, the waterside street of Zandhoek. Here, a row of 17th-century houses built by the island's founder, Jacobsz Reaal, overlook the sailboats moored along Westerdok.

Prinseneiland, the smallest island, is dominated by characterful warehouses, many of which are now apartments. The walk on pages 160–61 explores the area in more detail.

The "house with the writing hand" (c.1630) in Claes Claeszhofje

Dutch Hofjes

Before the Alteration (see pp26–7), the Catholic Church usually provided subsidized housing for the poor and elderly, particularly women. During the 17th and 18th centuries, rich merchants and Protestant organizations took on this charitable role and built hundreds of alms-house complexes, which were planned around courtyards and known as *hofjes*. Behind their street façades lie pretty houses and serene gardens. Visitors are admitted to some but are asked to respect the residents' privacy. Many *hofjes* are found in the Jordaan and some still serve their original purpose (see p99).

A CANAL WALK AND GUIDE TO ARCHITECTURE

With the increase in wealth and civic pride in Amsterdam during the 17th century, an ambitious plan was formed to build a splendid ring of canals round the city *(see pp28–9)*. Conceived in 1609, and added to in 1664 by Daniel Stalpaert, the scheme grew to encompass wide canals lined with opulent town houses in a variety of architectural styles *(see pp98–9)*. The houses on the canals of Singel, Keizersgracht, Herengracht, Reguliersgracht and Prinsengracht, illustrated on pp100–107, form a fascinating walk through Golden Age Amsterdam.

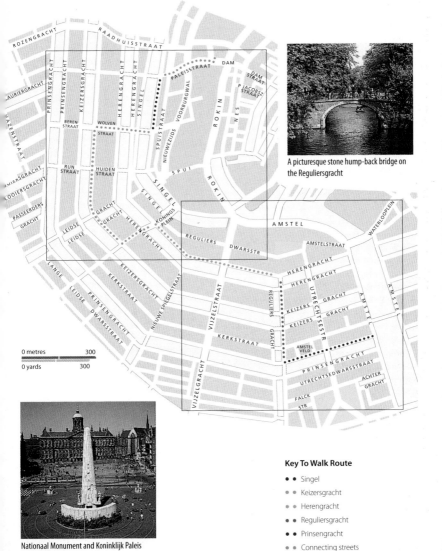

A picturesque stone hump-back bridge on the Reguliersgracht

0 metres 300
0 yards 300

Nationaal Monument and Koninklijk Paleis in Dam square

◀ Typical Amsterdam houses on the Damrak canal

Key To Walk Route
- ● ● Singel
- ● ● Keizersgracht
- ● ● Herengracht
- ● ● Reguliersgracht
- ● ● Prinsengracht
- ● ● Connecting streets

A Guide to Canal House Architecture

Amsterdam has been called a city of "well-mannered" architecture because its charms lie in intimate details rather than in grand effects. From the 15th century on, planning laws, plot sizes and the instability of the topsoil dictated that façades were largely uniform in size and built of lightweight brick or sandstone, with large windows to reduce the weight. Canal house owners stamped their own individuality on the buildings, mainly through the use of decorative gables and cornices, ornate doorcases and varying window shapes.

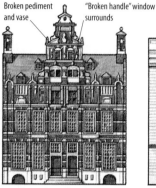

Broken pediment and vase

"Broken handle" window surrounds

Pediment carvings symbolize the arts and sciences.

Bartolotti House (1617)
The contrasting brick and stone, flamboyant step gable, with its marble obelisk and scrolls, is typical of the Dutch Renaissance style of Hendrick de Keyser.

Felix Meritis Building (1778)
The Corinthian columns and triangular pediment are influenced by Classical architecture. This marks the building *(see p115)* by Jacob Otten Husly as Dutch Classical in style.

Ground Plans
Taxes were levied according to width of façade, so canal houses were often long and narrow, with an *achterhuis* (back annexe) used for offices and storage.

Cornices

Decorative top mouldings, called cornices, became popular from 1690 onwards when the fashion for gables declined. By the 19th century, they had become unadorned.

Louis XV-style with Rococo balustrade (1739)

19th-century cornice with mansard roof

19th-century dentil (tooth-shaped) cornice

Gables

The term gable refers to the front apex of a roof. It disguised the steepness of the roof under which goods were stored (see pp24–5). In time, gables became decorated with scrolls, crests, and even coats of arms.

Simple tri-angular gable

No. 34 Begijnhof (late 15th century) is one of few surviving timber houses *(see pp24–5)*.

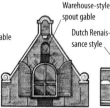

Warehouse-style spout gable

Dutch Renaissance style

The style of gable on No. 213 Leliegracht (c.1620) was used for warehouses.

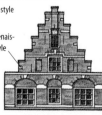

Step gables like the one on No. 2 Brouwersgracht were in vogue between 1600 and 1665.

Leaning Façades

Canal houses were often built with a deliberate tilt, allowing goods to be winched up to the attic without crashing against the windows. A law dating from 1565 restricted this lean to 1:25, to limit the risk of buildings collapsing into the streets.

Amsterdam School Architecture

Members of the Amsterdam School, a loose grouping of like-minded and idealistic architects, built many distinctive housing estates between 1911 and 1923 (see p153). They believed in the ability of unusual architecture to enhance residents' lives, many of whom were rehoused from appalling slums. Michel de Klerk's development, Het Schip (1921), is on the corner of Zaanstraat Spaarndammerplantsoen in northwest Amsterdam (www.hetschip.nl). It is typical of the lively style of the Amsterdam School.

Michel de Klerk (1884–1923)

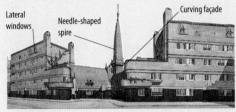

Het Schip (the ship), built to resemble an ocean-going liner

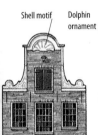

Dutch Hofjes

Almshouses (hofjes) were built throughout the Netherlands by rich benefactors in the 17th and 18th centuries. By providing accommodation for the elderly and infirm (see p95), the hofjes marked the beginning of the Dutch welfare system.

Sign of a sailor's hostel

Noah's Ark – a refuge for the poor

Symbol of a dairyman

Wall Plaques

Carved and painted stones were used to identify houses before street numbering was introduced in the 19th century. Many reflect the owner's occupation.

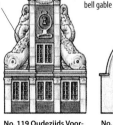

Shell motif   Dolphin ornament

No. 419 Singel has a neck gable, a common feature from 1640 to around 1840.

No. 119 Oudezijds Voorburgwal has an ornate 17th-century neck gable.

Unadorned bell gable

No. 57 Leliegracht has a plain bell gable, popular from the late 17th century.

Stonework with cornucopia decoration

No. 298 Oudezijds Voorburgwal has a bell gable dating from the 18th century.

Dam Square to Herengracht 487

The walk along Amsterdam's finest canals begins in Dam square. Following the grey dots on the map, leave the square past the Koninklijk Paleis *(see p78)*, cross Nieuwezijds Voorburgwal and Spuistraat down Paleisstraat, and turn left along the left bank of Singel, marked by purple dots. Further directions are incorporated into the route below.

Locator Map

Singel

No. 239 Singel
AL van Gendt *(see p134)* designed this massive stone office block for trader Julius Carle Bunge. Known as the Bungehuis, it was completed in 1934.

The double-fronted 17th-century canal house at No. 265 Singel has been rebuilt several times since it was first constructed.

The step gable at No. 279 Singel dates from the 19th century – most along this canal were built between 1600–65 *(see p98)*.

The three neck gables on Nos. 353–7 Keizersgracht date from the early 18th century *(see pp98–9)*.

Huidenstraat

No. 345a Keizersgracht is a narrow house sharing a cornice with its neighbour.

In 1708, No. 333 Keizersgracht was rebuilt for tax collector Jacob de Wilde. It has been converted into apartments.

The Sower at Arles (1888)
In March 1878, Vincent van Gogh *(see pp136–7)* visited his uncle, who ran a bookshop and art dealership at No. 453 Keizersgracht.

Nos. 289–293 Singel
These houses stand on an alley once called Schoorsteenvegersteeg (chimney sweeps' lane), home to immigrant chimney sweeps.

Yab Yum Brothel
This famous former brothel, with its opulent interior, was located at No. 295 Singel.

The doorway of No. 365 Keizersgracht was taken from an almshouse on Oudezijds Voorburgwal in the 19th century.

Jacob de Wit
The artist *(see p124)* bought Nos. 383 and 385 Keizersgracht, living in No. 385 until his death in 1754.

Metz & Co department store used to occupy this elegant corner building. It now houses Abercrombie & Fitch *(see p114)*.

Gerrit Rietveld
Rietveld *(see p138)* designed the cupola on the then Metz & Co building, and a line of plain, inexpensive furniture for the store.

De Vergulde Ster (gilded star), at No. 387 Keizersgracht, was built in 1668 by the municipal stonemasons' yard. It has an elongated neck gable *(see p98–9)* and narrow windows.

Directions to Herengracht

Turn left on to Leidse-straat, and walk to Koningsplein, then take the left bank of the Herengracht eastwards towards Thorbeckeplein.

Herengracht

Tsar Peter (see p103) stayed at No. 527 Herengracht, home of the Russian ambassador, after a night of drunken revelry at No. 317 Keizersgracht in 1716.

Herengracht (1790)
A delicate watercolour by J Prins shows the "gentlemen's canal" from Koningsplein.

The asymmetrical building at Nos. 533–7 Herengracht was built in 1910 on the site of four former houses. From 1968–88 it was the Registry of Births, Marriages and Deaths.

The façades of Nos. 37 and 39 Reguliersgracht lean towards the water, showing the danger caused by subsidence when building on marshland.

Reguliersgracht Bridge
Seven arched stone bridges cross the canal, which was originally designed to be a street.

Keizersgracht

Nos. 1059 and 1061 Prinsengracht
have tiny basement entrances, rare amid the splendour of the *Grachtengordel*, where the height of the steps was considered an indication of wealth.

My Domestic Companions
Society portraitist Thérèse van Duyl Schwartze painted this picture in 1916. She owned Nos. 1087, 1089 and 1091 Prinsengracht, a handsome row of houses where she lived with her extended family.

The sober spout-gabled building at No. 1075 Prinsengracht was built as a warehouse in 1690.

Keizersgracht

This photograph of the "emperor's canal" is taken at dusk, from the corner of Leidsegracht. The Westerkerk *(see p92)* is in the distance.

Behind the contrasting 18th-century façades at Nos. 317 and 319 Singel are two second-hand bookshops, which are well worth browsing through.

Directions to Keizersgracht

At Raamsteeg, cross the bridge, take the Oude Spiegelstraat, cross Herengracht and walk along Wolvenstraat to the left bank of Keizersgracht.

Keizersgracht

No. 399 Keizersgracht

dates from 1665, but the façade was rebuilt in the 18th century. Its *achterhuis (see p98)* has been perfectly preserved.

No. 409 Keizersgracht

Built in 1671 on a triangular piece of land, this house contains a newly discovered, highly decorated wooden ceiling.

No. 401 Keizersgracht houses a museum of photography known as Huis Marseille.

No. 469 Herengracht

The modern office block by KL Sijmons replaced the original 18th-century houses in 1971.

The plain, spout-gabled building *(see pp98–9)* at No. 403 Keizersgracht was originally a warehouse – a rarity in this predominantly residential area.

Jan Six II
The façade of No. 495 Herengracht was rebuilt and a balcony added by Jean Coulon in 1739 for burgomaster and art expert Jan Six.

Riots in 1696
No. 507 Herengracht was home of mayor Jacob Boreel. His house was looted in retaliation for the burial tax he introduced into the city.

Vijzelstraat

Three houses boasting typical neck gables, at Nos. 17, 19 and 21 Reguliersgracht, are now much sought after as prestigious addresses.

The Nieuwe Amsterdammer
A weekly magazine aimed at Amsterdam's Bolshevik intelligentsia was published at No. 19 Reguliersgracht from 1914–20.

The spout-gabled
(see pp98–9) 16th-century warehouses at Nos. 11 and 13 Reguliersgracht are called the Sun and the Moon.

Café Marcella, at No. 1047a Prinsengracht, is a typical local bar which has seating outside in summer.

Houseboats on Prinsengracht
All registered houseboats have postal addresses and are connected to the electricity mains.

Utrechtsestraat

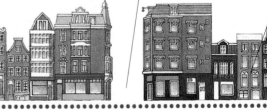

The unusual office block at No. 313 Keizersgracht was built in 1914 by CN van Goor.

No. 319 Keizersgracht was built by the architect Philips Vingboons (1608–78) in 1639. It has a rare, highly decorated façade covered with scrolls, vases and garlands.

Peter the Great *(1716)* The Russian tsar sailed up Keizersgracht to No. 317, the home of his friend Christoffel Brants. Legend says the tsar got drunk and kept the mayor waiting while at a civic reception.

Leidsegracht This canal marked the end of Daniel Stalpaert's city expansion plan of 1664 *(see p28)*. It has a mixture of fine 17th- and 18th-century canal houses.

The Louis XIV-style house at No. 323 Keizersgracht was built in 1728. It has a raised cornice embellished with two hoisting beams, one functional and the other to provide symmetry.

Art patron Jan Gildemester bought No. 475 Herengracht in 1792. Attributed to Jacob Otten Husly *(see p115)*, it has a stuccoed entrance hall.

Jan Corver Burgomaster of Amsterdam 19 times, Corver built No. 479 Herengracht in 1665.

Turn over to continue walk at top of page 104

❾ Herengracht 48 to the Amstel

The second half of the walk takes you along Herengracht, winding past grand, wide-fronted mansions. It then follows Reguliersgracht and Prinsengracht down to the Amstel. Many of the fine houses have recently been converted into banks, offices and exclusive apartment blocks.

Locator Map

Herengracht

The house at No. 491 Herengracht was built in 1671. The façade, rebuilt in the 18th century, is decorated with scrolls, vases and coats of arms.

No. 493 Herengracht
This 17th-century house was given a Louis XV-style façade in 1767 by Anthony van Hemert.

The Kattenkabinet at No. 497 Herengracht was created by financier B Meijer in 1984. It is devoted to exhibits featuring the cat in art.

Directions to Reguliersgracht

At Thorbeckeplein, take the bridge to the right, which marks the beginning of Reguliersgracht. Follow the left bank.

Reguliersgracht

Amstelveld in the 17th Century
This etching shows the construction of a wooden church at Amstelveld, with sheep grazing in front of it.

Restaurant Janvier
The Amstelkerk (see p121) now contains a restaurant and offices, while the square itself is a popular play area for local children.

Directions to Prinsengracht

Turn left by the church, take the left bank of Prinsengracht and walk to the Amstel river.

Prinsengracht

Herengracht (c.1670)
GA Berckheijde's etching shows one side of the canal bare of trees. Elms were later planted, binding the topsoil, to strengthen the buildings' foundations.

No. 543 Herengracht was built in 1743 under the supervision of owner Sibout Bollard. It has a double-fronted façade with an ornate balustrade and decorated balcony.

The small houses at the corner of Herengracht and Thorbeckeplein contrast with the grand neighbouring buildings.

Isaac Gosschalk
The architect designed Nos. 57, 59 and 63 Reguliersgracht in 1879. They have ornate stone, brick and woodwork façades.

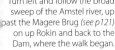

Reguliers Monastery
This engraving by J Wagenaar (1760) shows the monastery that once stood on the canal.

The Amstel
Turn left and follow the broad sweep of the Amstel river, up past the Magere Brug (see p121) on up Rokin and back to the Dam, where the walk began.

CENTRAL CANAL RING

The extension of Amsterdam's three major canals continued from the early 17th century (see pp28–9), as the merchant classes sought to escape the overcrowding and industrial squalor in the old city, around the Amstel. They bought plots of land along the new extensions to the Herengracht, Keizersgracht and Prinsengracht, and in the 1660s the wealthiest built opulent houses on a stretch of Herengracht known as the Golden Bend. Designed and decorated by the best architects of the day, such as Philips Vingboons (see p103), the mansions built here were often twice the width of standard canal houses (see p98). Today, many of these grand buildings are owned by institutions. Other architectural landmarks include the Neo-Gothic Krijtberg, with its soaring steeples, the imposing Former City Orphanage and the Art Nouveau American Hotel overlooking the busy Leidseplein.

Sights at a Glance

Historic Buildings and Monuments
2 American Hotel
5 Former City Orphanage

Museums
9 Het Grachtenhuis
10 Bijbels Museum
13 Houseboat Museum

Churches
8 De Krijtberg

Markets
11 Antiekcentrum Amsterdam

Clubs and Theatres
3 De Melkweg
4 Stadsschouwburg
12 Felix Meritis Building

Canals and Squares
1 Leidseplein
6 Leidsegracht
7 Golden Bend

Restaurants pp227–8
1 Akitsu
2 Aphrodite
3 Bagels and Beans
4 Balthazar's Keuken
5 Blue Pepper
6 Brix
7 Fou Fow Ramen
8 Goodies
9 Hosokawa
10 Nomads
11 Pancake Corner
12 Pancakes! Amsterdam
13 Los Pilones
14 Proeverij 274
15 Puri Mas
16 Restaurant Portugália
17 Restaurant Vinkeles
18 Stoop en Stoop
19 Struisvogel

See also Street Finder pp274–87

0 metres   250
0 yards   250

◀ Picturesque view of Leidsegracht canal

For map symbols see back flap

Street-by-Street: Leidsebuurt

The area around Leidseplein is one of Amsterdam's busiest nightspots. There are various films to be seen at the many cinemas, plays at the Stadsschouwburg and lively programmes of music at De Melkweg. In contrast, there is fine architecture to admire around the Canal Ring, such as the Former City Orphanage on Prinsengracht, the lavish De Krijtberg on the Singel and scores of grand houses on the Golden Bend.

⑩ Bijbels Museum
In addition to bibles, there are several archaeological finds from Egypt and the Middle East on display here.

⑥ Leidsegracht
Cut in 1664, this canal was the main waterway for barges heading for Leiden.

④ Stadsschouwburg
This historic theatre, built in 1894, is the venue for Amsterdam's Holland Festival in June (see p53).

② ★ American Hotel
The hotel's Café Americain has a fine Art Deco interior and is a popular place to while away an afternoon (see p112).

③ De Melkweg
This converted milk-processing factory and former hippy hangout survives as one of Amsterdam's key venues for alternative entertainment.

① Leidseplein
Young people flock to this square to watch street performances and enjoy the vibrant nightlife.

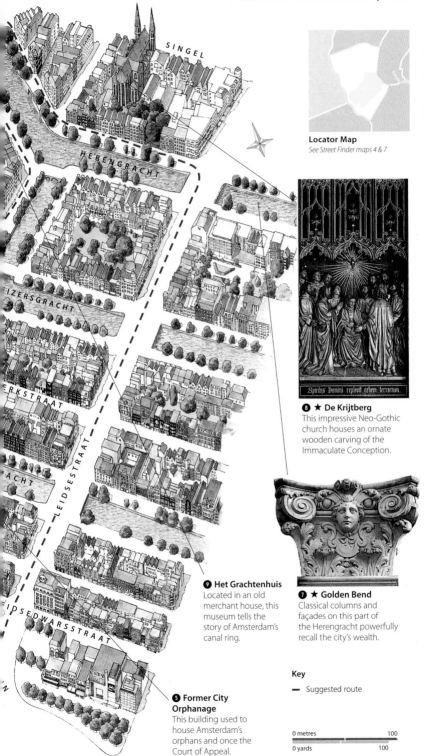

SINGEL

HERENGRACHT

EIZERSGRACHT

ERKSTRAAT

LEIDSESTRAAT

ACHT

IDSEDWARSSTRAAT

N

Locator Map
See Street Finder maps 4 & 7

❽ ★ **De Krijtberg**
This impressive Neo-Gothic church houses an ornate wooden carving of the Immaculate Conception.

❼ ★ **Golden Bend**
Classical columns and façades on this part of the Herengracht powerfully recall the city's wealth.

❾ **Het Grachtenhuis**
Located in an old merchant house, this museum tells the story of Amsterdam's canal ring.

❺ **Former City Orphanage**
This building used to house Amsterdam's orphans and once the Court of Appeal.

Key
— Suggested route

0 metres		100
0 yards		100

Spiritus Domini replevit orbem terrarum.

❶ Leidseplein

Map 4 E2. 🚋 1, 2, 5, 7, 10.

Amsterdam's liveliest square, Leidseplein is also a busy tram intersection and centre of night-time transport.

The square developed in the 17th century as a wagon park on the outskirts of the city – farmers and peasants would leave their carts here before entering the centre. It takes its name from the Leidsepoort, the massive city gate demolished in 1862, which marked the beginning of the route out to Leiden.

During the day, the square is buzzing with fire-eaters, buskers and other street performers playing to café audiences. It is also popular with pickpockets. At night, it is the focal point for the city's youth, who hang out in the many bars, cafés, restaurants, nightclubs and cinemas in and around the square.

Street performer in Leidseplein

❷ American Hotel

Leidsekade 97. **Map** 4 E2. **Tel** 556 3000. 🚋 1, 2, 5, 7, 10. 🖥 🖋

Leidseplein was fast becoming a fashionable entertainment area when the American Hotel was built overlooking it in 1882. The hotel got its name because its architect, W Steinigeweg, studied hotel design in the United States, and adorned his Neo-Gothic creation with a bronze eagle, wooden figures of native Indians and murals of American landscapes. Within 20 years it was deemed passé and the hotel was demolished. The present building is by Willem Kromhout (1864–1940) and was completed in 1902. His design marked a radical departure, interpreting the Art Nouveau style in an angular Dutch fashion. The building's turreted exterior and elaborate brickwork anticipated the progressive Amsterdam School *(see p99)*. A carved stone plaque on the Leidseplein side of the hotel shows the original building.

The Café Americain *(see p48)*, decorated in Art Deco style, remains one of the most elegant in Amsterdam. It retains its period furnishings and stained-glass windows. The rest of the hotel was redecorated in the 1980s. Samples of the original furnishings are in the Rijksmuseum *(see pp130–33)*.

❸ De Melkweg

Lijnbaansgracht 234a. **Map** 4 E2. **Tel** 531 8181. 🚋 1, 2, 5, 7, 10. Box office: **Open** from noon Mon–Fri; from 4:30pm Sat & Sun. Performances: 8:30pm approx. 🎭 *See Entertainment p245*. 🌐 **melkweg.nl**

De Melkweg (Milky Way) is a multimedia centre situated in a former dairy behind the Stadsschouwburg. It opened in 1970 and soon gained a dazzling reputation as an alternative cultural meeting place. Nowadays, it offers a wide range of entertainment, including live music, film, video, theatre, dance and a

The American Hotel seen from Singelgracht

photographic gallery. The theatre has a stage for new international acts, and De Melkweg's annual Amsterdam Roots Festival *(see p53)* promotes the latest in world music and film.

De Melkweg's star-lit façade

❹ Stadsschouw- burg

Leidseplein 26. **Map** 4 E2. **Tel** 624 2311. 🚊 1, 2, 5, 7, 10. Box Office: **Open** noon–6pm Mon–Sat; two hours before performance Sun. *See Entertainment p242.* 🅿 🖂 ♿ 🌐 ssba.nl

This Neo-Renaissance building is the most recent of three successive municipal theatres in the city, its predecessors having burned down. The theatre was designed by Jan Springer, whose other credits include the Frascati building on Oxford Street in London, and AL van Gendt, who was also responsible for the Concertgebouw *(see p134)* and for part of the Centraal Station *(see p81)*. The planned ornamentation of the theatre's red-brick exterior was never carried out because of budget cuts. This, combined with a hostile public reaction to his theatre, forced a disillusioned Springer into virtual retirement. Public

disgust was due, however, to the theatre management's policy of restricting use of the front door to patrons who had bought expensive tickets. The whole building has been given a face-lift.

Until the Nationale Opera & Ballet was completed in 1986 *(see p65)*, the Stadsschouwburg was home to the Dutch national ballet and opera companies. Today, the theatre stages plays by local groups such as the resident Toneelgroep Amsterdam, and international companies, including some English-language productions.

An auditorium, which is located between the Melkweg and the Stadsschouwburg, is used by both centres for concerts and dance performances.

❺ Former City Orphanage

Prinsengracht 434–436. **Map** 4 E1. 🚊 1, 2, 5, 7, 10. **Closed** to the public.

The orphanage opened in 1666 with space for 800 children. By 1811, the building housed more than 2,000 children, over half of the city's orphans. To control their rising numbers, a royal decree was passed permitting the relocation of orphans to other towns. When this act was implemented in 1822, there was widespread protest from local people and accusations that the authorities had stolen children. Once all the children were relocated, the orphanage was closed.

Conversion of the former city orphanage into the Empire-style Palace of Justice, designed by the city architect Jan de Greef, was completed in 1829. Balustrades run along the roofline and the monotony of the imposing Neo-Classical façade is broken up by Corinthian pilasters. The building once housed the Court of Appeal, but since the Court moved to new premises in 2013, it sits empty awaiting new owners.

No. 39 Leidsegracht, on the right

❻ Leidsegracht

Map 4 E1. 🚊 1, 2, 5, 7, 10.

The Leidsegracht was for a few years the main route for barges from Amsterdam to Leiden. It was cut in 1664 to a plan by city architect Daniel Stalpaert, and is now one of the city's smartest addresses.

Cornelis Lely, who drew up the original plans for draining the Zuiderzee *(see p167)*, was born at No. 39 in 1854. A wall plaque shows Lely poised between the Zuiderzee and the newly created IJsselmeer.

The elongated Neo-Classical façade of the former city orphanage

Boats moored along the Golden Bend

❼ Golden Bend

Map 7 A5. 1, 2, 4, 5, 9, 14, 16, 24, 25. Kattenkabinet: Herengracht 497. **Tel** 626 5378. **Open** 10am–5pm Mon–Fri, noon–5pm Sat & Sun. **Closed** 1 Jan, 27 Apr, 25 Dec.

The stretch of the Herengracht between Leidsestraat and Vijzelstraat was first called the Golden Bend in the 17th century, because of the great wealth of the shipbuilders, merchants and politicians who originally lived along here. Most of the mansions have been converted into offices or banks, but their former elegance remains. The majority of the buildings are faced with sandstone, which was more expensive than brick and had to be imported. The earliest mansions date from the 1660s. One very fine and largely untouched example of the Classicist style, designed by Philips Vingboons in 1664, stands at No. 412. Building continued into the 18th century, with the Louis XIV style predominating. No. 475 is typical of this trend. Built in 1730, it is often called the jewel of canal houses. Two sculpted female figures over the front door adorn its monumental sandstone façade. The ornate mansion at No. 452 is a good example of a 19th-century conversion. The Kattenkabinet (Cat Museum) at No. 497 Herengracht is one of the few houses on the Golden Bend which is accessible to the public. The museum is well worth visiting for its interesting collection of feline artifacts.

❽ De Krijtberg

Singel 448. **Map** 7 A4. **Tel** 623 1923. 1, 2, 5. **Open** half an hour before the services; 1–5pm Tue–Thu, Sat & Sun. 12:30pm, 5:45pm Mon–Fri; 12:30pm, 5:15pm, Sat; 9:30am, 11am, 12:30pm, 5:15pm Sun. **krijtberg.nl**

An impressive Neo-Gothic church, the Krijtberg (or chalk hill) replaced a clandestine Jesuit chapel *(see p86–7)* in 1884. It is officially known as Franciscus Xaveriuskerk, after St Francis Xavier, one of the founding Jesuit priests.

Designed by Alfred Tepe, the church was constructed on the site of three houses; the presbytery beside the church is on the site of two other houses, one of which had belonged to a chalk merchant – hence the church's nickname. The back of the church is wider than the front. The narrowness of the façade is redeemed by its two magnificent, steepled towers.

The twin-steepled façade of the Neo-Gothic Krijtberg

The ornate interior of the building contains some good examples of Neo-Gothic design. The stained-glass windows, walls painted in bright colours and liberal use of gold are in striking contrast to the city's austere Protestant churches. A statue of St Francis Xavier stands in front and to the left of the high altar; one of St Ignatius, founder of the Jesuits, stands to the right.

❾ Het Grachtenhuis

Herengracht 386. **Map** 7 A4. 1, 2, 5. **Open** 10am–5pm Tue–Sun (daily Jun–Aug). **Closed** 27 Apr, 25 Dec. **hetgrachtenhuis.nl**

This ornate canal house was designed in 1663–5 by Philips Vingboons, who was also the architect of the Bijbels Museum *(see below)*.

Once the home of merchants and bankers, the house is now a museum, telling the story of town planning and engineering for the creation of Amsterdam's triple canal ring. The ground floor has been restored to its 18th-century splendour, complete with original wall paintings. The upper rooms showcase detailed models, films and 3D animation on the construction of the canals, along with the stately mansions that line the route.

❿ Bijbels Museum

Herengracht 366–368. **Map** 7 A4. **Tel** 624 2436. 1, 2, 5. Herengracht/Leidsegracht. **Open** 10am–5pm Tue–Sun & public hols. **Closed** 1 Jan, 27 Apr. **bijbelsmuseum.nl**

Reverend Leendert Schouten founded the Bijbels Museum in 1860, when he first put his private collection of biblical artifacts on public display. In 1975, the museum moved to its present site, two 17th-century houses in a group of four designed by Philips Vingboons, known as the Cromhout Houses, after the original owners.

The Bible Museum is packed with artifacts that aim to give historical weight to Bible stories. Displays feature models of historical sites, and archaeological finds from Egypt and the Middle East. Highlights include a copy of the Book of Isaiah from the Dead Sea Scrolls, and the Delft Bible, dating from 1477. The museum also has a beautiful garden, two ceiling paintings by Jacob de Wit and two well-preserved 17th-century kitchens.

⓫ Antiekcentrum Amsterdam

Elandsgracht 109. **Map** 4 D1.
Tel 624 9038. 🚊 7, 10, 13, 14, 17.
Open 11am–6pm Mon & Wed–Fri, 11am–5pm Sat & Sun.
Closed Tue, public hols. 🖂 ♿
W antiekcentrumamsterdam.nl

A vast network of ground-floor rooms in a block of houses has been turned into the Amsterdam Antiques Centre. The market, which covers an area between the Elandsgracht and the Looiersgracht, boasts the largest collection of art and antiques in the Netherlands.

Around 100 stalls sell everything from glassware to dolls. On Wednesdays, Saturdays, and Sundays anyone can rent a stall here. In one corner, a café serves lunch and dinner.

The Palladian façade of the 18th-century Felix Meritis Building

⓬ Felix Meritis Building

Keizersgracht 324. **Map** 1 B5.
Tel 627 9477. 🚊 1, 2, 5, 10, 13, 14, 17. **Closed** for renovation until late 2017 🖉 🖂 ♿
W felixmeritis.nl

This Neo-Classical building is best viewed from the opposite side of the canal (see p98). Designed by Jacob Otten Husly, it opened in 1787 as a science and arts centre set up by the Felix Meritis society. The name means " happiness through merit". An association of wealthy citizens, the society was founded by watchmaker Willem Writs in 1777, at the time of the Dutch Enlightenment (see pp32–3).

Five reliefs on the façade proclaim the society's interest in natural science and art. The building was fitted out with an observatory, library, laboratories and a small concert hall. Mozart, Edvard Grieg, Johannes Brahms and Saint-Saëns are among the distinguished musicians who have given performances here.

In the 19th century, it became Amsterdam's main cultural centre, and its concert hall inspired the design of the Concertgebouw (see p134).

The Dutch Communist Party (CPN) occupied the premises from 1946, but cultural prominence was restored in the 1970s when the Shaffy Theatre Company used the building as a theatre and won acclaim for its avant-garde productions.

In 1988 the building housed the European Centre for Arts and Sciences. It is undergoing extensive renovation and will re-open once more as a cultural centre in 2017.

⓭ Houseboat Museum

Prinsengracht, opposite no. 296. **Map** 1 B5. **Tel** 427 0750. 🚊 1, 2, 5, 7, 10, 13, 14, 17. **Open** Mar–Jun & Sep–Oct: 10am–5pm Tue–Sun; Jul & Aug: 10am–5pm daily; Nov–Feb: 10am–5pm Fri–Sun. **Closed** Jan, 27 Apr, 25 & 26 Dec. 🖉 **W** houseboatmuseum.nl

Moored on the Prinsengracht canal on the edge of the Jordaan, the *Hendrika Maria* is a showcase of life aboard an Amsterdam houseboat. Built in 1914, it served as a barge and transported coal, sand and gravel until the 1960s when it was converted into a houseboat. Coffee is served in the spacious living room.

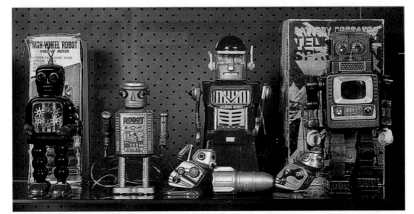

Vintage robots on sale at the Antiekcentrum Amsterdam

EASTERN CANAL RING

Stretching south from Muntturen, part of a former city gate, this area lies wholly beyond the line of the medieval city wall. From the 1660s, the Grachtengordel was extended further east towards the Amstel. One of Amsterdam's prettiest canals, Reguliersgracht with its seven bridges, was cut at this time. Today, houses on the major Canal Ring, such as the Museum Van Loon, with its grand façade and fine interior, convey a sense of life in the Golden Age *(see pp28–31)*. Beyond is the 19th-century De Pijp, a working-class district built to relieve the overcrowded Jordaan. De Pijp is now a lively multicultural area, and home to the Albert Cuypmarkt, the city's biggest street market.

Sights at a Glance

Historic Buildings and Bridges
3 Blauwbrug
5 Stadsarchief Amsterdam
6 Magere Brug
7 Amstelkerk
12 Muntturen

Squares and Markets
1 Rembrandtplein
8 Albert Cuypmarkt
13 Bloemenmarkt

Cinema
11 Tuschinski Theater

Museums
2 *Museum Willet-Holthuysen pp122–3*
4 Foam Museum
9 Heineken Experience
10 Museum Van Loon

Restaurants *pp228–9*
1 Azmarino
2 Bazar
3 Bouchon du Centre
4 Buffet van Odette
5 Coffee & Jazz
6 Dik & Cunningham
7 Golden Temple
8 Hans & Grietje
9 Kingfisher
10 Rose's Cantina
11 Sluizer
12 Take Thai
13 Utrechtsedwarstafel
14 Vamos A Ver
15 Village Bagels
16 De Waaghals
17 Le Zinc...et les Autres
18 Zushi

See also Street Finder pp274–87

0 metres   250
0 yards   250

◄ Blue Drawing Room in the Museum Van Loon

For map symbols *see back flap*

Street-by-Street: Amstelveld

The eastern end of the Grachtengordel is quiet and largely residential, especially around the Amstelveld, with its pretty wooden church and houseboats. A short walk will take you past shops and numerous cafés, particularly on the bustling Rembrandtplein. As you wander down the broad sweep of the Amstel river, Amsterdam suddenly loses its village atmosphere and begins to feel like a city.

❶ ★ Rembrandtplein
Looking on to the former Botermarkt (butter market) and the cast-iron statue of Rembrandt, there are dozens of cafés dating from the 19th century, including the De Kroon at No. 17 *(see p49)*.

Café Schiller
(see p51)

❷ ★ Museum Willet-Holthuysen
This double canal house contains a number of period rooms, including this fine Blue Room hung with heavy blue damask, and a magnificent 18th-century staircase.

❼ Amstelkerk
This wooden church was meant to be a temporary structure while money was raised to build a big new church on Rembrandtplein, but the grand scheme fell through. Today, the church houses offices and a restaurant *(see p121)*.

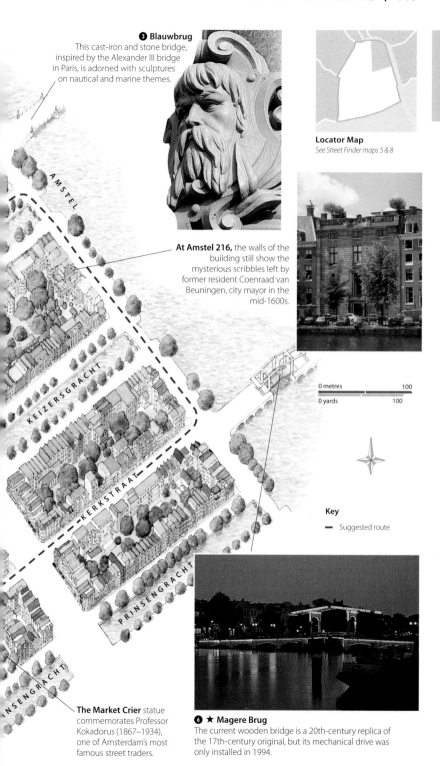

❸ Blauwbrug

This cast-iron and stone bridge, inspired by the Alexander III bridge in Paris, is adorned with sculptures on nautical and marine themes.

Locator Map
See Street Finder maps 5 & 8

At Amstel 216, the walls of the building still show the mysterious scribbles left by former resident Coenraad van Beuningen, city mayor in the mid-1600s.

0 metres 100
0 yards 100

Key

— Suggested route

The Market Crier statue commemorates Professor Kokadorus (1867–1934), one of Amsterdam's most famous street traders.

❻ ★ Magere Brug

The current wooden bridge is a 20th-century replica of the 17th-century original, but its mechanical drive was only installed in 1994.

❶ Rembrandtplein

Map 7 C5. ❏ 4, 9, 14.

Formerly called the Botermarkt, after the butter market held here until the mid-19th century, this square acquired its present name when the statue of Rembrandt was erected in 1876.
Soon afterwards, Rembrandtplein developed into a centre for nightlife with the opening of various hotels and cafés. The Mast (renamed the Mille Colonnes Hotel) dates from 1889, and the NH Schiller hotel *(see p219)* and the Café Schiller *(see p51)* both opened in 1892. De Kroon *(see p49)*, which epitomizes a typical grand café, dates from 1898. The popularity of Rembrandtplein has persevered, and the café terraces are packed during summer with people enjoying a pleasant drink and watching the world go by.

❷ Museum Willet-Holthuysen

See pp122–3.

❸ Blauwbrug

Amstel. **Map** 8 D5. ❏ 9, 14.
Ⓜ Waterlooplein.

The Blauwbrug (Blue Bridge) is thought to have taken its name from the colour of the wooden bridge that originally crossed this particular stretch of the Amstel in the 17th century. The present bridge is made of stone. It was built in

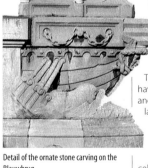

Detail of the ornate stone carving on the Blauwbrug

Outdoor café on Rembrandtplein

preparation for the World Exhibition, which attracted thousands of visitors to Amsterdam in 1883.
The Blauwbrug is decorated with sculptures of medieval boats, fish and the imperial crown of Amsterdam and is surmounted by ornate lamps. The design was inspired by the plans for the elaborate Alexander III bridge in Paris.

❹ Foam Museum

Keizersgracht 609. **Map** 5 A3.
Tel 551 6500. ❏ 16, 24.
Open 10am–6pm Sat–Wed, 10am–9pm Thu & Fri.
Closed 27 Apr. ♿ ▣ ▢
▣ Ⓦ **foam.org**

Three elegant canal houses have been joined together and renovated to create a labyrinth of modern rooms filled with photographs. Foam (Fotografiemuseum Amsterdam) is dedicated to exhibiting and celebrating every form of

photography, from historical to journalistic, to cutting-edge and artistic.
The museum holds four major exhibitions a year and 15 smaller ones, showcasing both established figures of the art form and emerging local talent. Some of the most recent exhibitions at Foam have included Annie Leibovitz's "American Music", a retrospective on Henri Cartier-Bresson and "50 Years of World Press Photo".
More than just a museum, though, Foam prides itself for being an interactive centre for photography, a place where amateurs can learn more about the art by meeting professionals, attending lectures and taking part in discussion evenings, or just stop for a coffee and a browse of the well-stocked bookshop.

❺ Stadsarchief Amsterdam

Vijzelstraat 32. **Map** 4 F2. **Tel** 251 1511.
❏ 16, 24. **Open** 10am–5pm Tue–Fri, noon–5pm Sat & Sun. **Closed** public hols. ♿ (with permission).
▣ 2pm Sat & Sun. ▣ ▢
Ⓦ **stadsarchief.amsterdam.nl**

The Stadsarchief, which houses the city's municipal archives, has moved from its former location in Amsteldijk to this monumental building. Designed by KPC de Bazel, one of the principal representatives of the Amsterdam school of architecture, the edifice was completed in 1926 for the Netherlands Trading Company. In spite of much renovation work at the end of World War II and in the 1970s, the building retains many attractive original features, such as the colourful floor mosaics (designed by de Bazel himself) and the wooden panelling in the boardrooms on the second floor. There is a permanent display of treasures from the archives in the monumental vaults.
In 1991 the building, affectionately known as "The Bazel", was declared a national monument.

⑥ Magere Brug

Amstel. **Map** 5 B3. 🚊 4.

Of Amsterdam's 1,400 or so bridges, the Magere Brug (Skinny Bridge) is undoubtedly the city's best-known, instantly associated with Amsterdam. The original drawbridge was constructed in about 1670. The traditional story has it that it was named after two sisters called Mager, who lived on either side of the Amstel. However, it appears more likely that the bridge acquired the name from its narrow *(mager)* design. At night many lights illuminate the bridge.

The drawbridge was widened in 1871 and most recently renovated in 2010, though it still conforms to the traditional double-leaf style. Since 2003 traffic has been limited to bicycles and pedestrians. The bridge is made from African azobe wood, and was intended to last for at least 50 years. Several times a day, the bridge master lets boats through, then jumps on his bicycle and opens up the Nieuwe Herengracht bridge.

The Amstelkerk, built as a temporary church in the 17th century

⑦ Amstelkerk

Amstelveld 10. **Map** 5 A3. **Tel** 520 0060. 🚊 4. **Open** 9am–5pm Mon–Fri. **Closed** public hols.

Designed by Daniel Stalpaert in 1668, the wooden Amstelkerk was originally intended to be only a temporary structure, while in the meantime money was going to be raised for a large new church on the Botermarkt (now Rembrandtplein). Unfortunately, the necessary funds for the grand scheme were never forthcoming, and so the temporary Amstelkerk had to be kept and maintained. In 1825, the Protestant church authorities attempted to raise money to renovate the Amstelkerk's plain interior in a Neo-Gothic style. It was not until 1840, however, when Frederica Elisabeth Cramer donated 25,000 guilders to the project, that work could begin. The interior walls, pulpit, pews and organ, which was made by Jonathan Batz, all date from this period. The windows, however, are older and date from 1821.

During the late 1980s, the Amstelkerk underwent a substantial and radical conversion, which cost some 4 million guilders. Glass-walled offices were installed inside the building. However, concerts are still held in the nave, which was preserved in all its Neo-Gothic magnificence. The excellent top-class café-restaurant Nel is housed in a side building.

Magere Brug, a traditional double-leaf Dutch drawbridge

How the Magere Brug Works

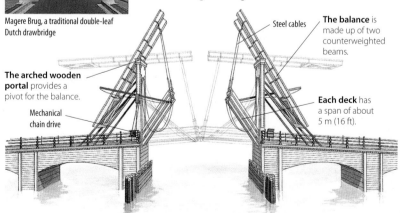

The balance is made up of two counterweighted beams.

Steel cables

The arched wooden portal provides a pivot for the balance.

Mechanical chain drive

Each deck has a span of about 5 m (16 ft).

❷ Museum Willet-Holthuysen

Named after its last residents, the museum allows the visitor a glimpse into the lives of the merchant class who lived in luxury along the Grachtengordel (Canal Ring). The house was built in 1685 and became the property of coal magnate Pieter Holthuysen (1788–1858) in 1855. It passed to his daughter Louisa (1824–95) and her husband, Abraham Willet (1825–88), both fervent collectors of paintings, glass, silver and ceramics. When Louisa died childless and a widow in 1895, the house and its many treasures were left to the city. Room by room, the house is being restored and brought back to the time Abraham and Louisa lived here.

KEY

① Ticket office

② Front room

③ Ballroom

④ Bedroom

⑤ Hall

⑥ **The Blue Room** porcelain collection includes Chinese vases made during the Kangxi dynasty (1662–1722).

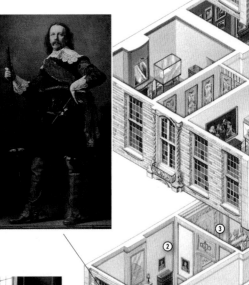

Portrait of Abraham Willet
Painted in 1877 by André Mniszech, a Polish artist, this full-length portrait shows the master of the house dressed in a traditional 17th-century costume.

★ **Blue Room**
Hung with heavy blue damask, the room boasts a chimney piece by Jacob de Wit, and was the exclusive preserve of the men of the house.

Entrance

Collector's Room
Abraham Willet called this small, low-ceilinged room his antique room. Decorated in dark red velvet, it was used to entertain guests at informal gatherings.

Staircase
The staircase was built in 1740 and has an elaborate gilded balustrade. The upper walls are painted to look like marble.

★ Dining Room
The wallpaper is a careful copy of the 18th-century silk original. The elaborate 275-piece Meissen dinner service provided up to 24 places.

Kitchen
The 18th-century kitchen has been restored using items salvaged from similar houses, including the sink and pump.

❽ Albert Cuypmarkt

Albert Cuypstraat. **Map** 5 A5. 🚋 4, 16, 24. **Open** 9:30am–5pm Mon–Sat.

The market running along Albert Cuypstraat began trading in 1904, shortly after the expansion of the city was completed. The wide street, once a canal, is named after the Dutch landscape painter Albert Cuyp (1620–91). It is located in the Pijp district, originally built for workers.

Described by the stallholders as "the best-known market in Europe", it attracts some 20,000 visitors on weekdays and often twice as many on Saturdays. The goods on sale at the 325 stalls range from fish, poultry, cheese, fruit and vegetables to clothes, and prices are among the cheapest in Amsterdam.

Smoked fish in Albert Cuypmarkt

❾ Heineken Experience

Stadhouderskade 78. **Map** 4 F3. 🚋 7, 10, 16, 24. **Open** Sep–Jun: 10:30am–7:30pm Mon–Thu, to 8:30pm Fri–Sun; Jul & Aug: 10:30am–9pm daily; last tickets 2 hours before closing. 🅰 Ⓦ heinekenexperience.com

Gerard Adriaan Heineken founded the Heineken company in 1864 when he bought the 16th-century Hooi-berg (haystack) brewery on the Nieuwezijds Voorburgwal.

Formal rose garden at Museum Van Loon

The original Stadhouderskade building was erected in 1867. His readiness to adapt to new methods and bring in foreign brewers established him as a major force in Amsterdam's profitable beer industry.

In 1988, the company finally stopped producing beer in its massive brick brewery on Stadhoudersskade, as it was unable to keep up with the demand. Production is now concentrated in two breweries, one in Zoeterwoude, near Den Haag, another in Den Bosch. Today, Heineken produces around half of the beer sold in Amsterdam, has production facilities in dozens of countries and exports all over the world.

The Stadhouderskade build-ing now houses the Heineken Experience, where visitors can learn about the history of the company and beer-making in general. Extensive renovations accommodate the increasing number of visitors. There is also a tasting bar, mini brewery and a "stable walk", offering the opportunity to view Heineken's splendid dray horses. Visitors under the age of 18 must be accompanied by an adult.

❿ Museum Van Loon

Keizersgracht 672. **Map** 5 A3. **Tel** 624 5255. 🚋 16, 24. **Open** 11am–5pm daily. **Closed** 1 Jan, 27 Apr, 25 Dec. 🅰 🗐 🗐 Ⓦ museumvanloon.nl

Van Loon was the name of one of Amsterdam's foremost families in the 17th century. They did not move into this house on the Keizersgracht, however, until 1884. Designed by Adriaan Dortsman, No. 672 is one of a pair of symmetrical houses built in 1672 for the Flemish merchant Jeremias van Raey. It was redecorated in 1752 when Dr Abraham van Hagen and his wife Catharina Elisabeth Trip moved in.

The house was opened as a museum in 1973, after many years of restoration. It is now a delightful canalside museum, retaining the original charming character of the house. It con-tains a collection of Van Loon family portraits, stretching back to the early 1600s. The period rooms are adorned with fine pieces of furniture, porcelain and sculpture. Some of the upstairs rooms contain sumptuous illusionistic wall paintings, popular in the 17th and 18th centuries. Four were painted by the classicist artist Gérard de Lairesse (1641–1711). Outside, in the formal rose garden, is the original 18th-century coach house, now restored and housing the Van Loon family coaches and livery worn by the servants.

Dray horse and beer wagon at the Heineken Experience

⓫ Tuschinski Theater

Reguliersbreestraat 26–28. **Map** 7 C5.
Tel 0900 1458. 🚊 4, 9, 14. Box office:
Open 12:15–10pm. 🎦 🎦 🎦

Abraham Tuschinski's cinema
and variety theatre caused a
sensation when it opened in
1921. Until then, Amsterdam's
cinemas had been sombre
places, but this was an exotic
blend of Art Deco and Amsterdam School architecture (see
pp98–9). Its twin towers are 26 m
(85 ft) in height. Built in a slum
area known as the Duivelshoek
(Devil's Corner), it was designed
by Heyman Louis de Jong and
decorated by Chris Bartels, Jaap
Gidding and Pieter den Besten. In
its heyday, Marlene Dietrich and
Judy Garland performed here.

Now converted into a six-
screen cinema, the building has
been meticulously restored,
both inside and out. The carpet
in the entrance hall, replaced in
1984, is an
exact copy of
the original.
Visitors may
take a guided
tour, but the
best way to
appreciate the
opulence of
the Tuschinski
Theater is to
go and see a

Detail of Tuschinski Theater façade

film. For just a
few extra
euros, you
can take a seat in one of
the exotic boxes that make
up the back row of the huge
semi-circular, 1,472-seater
main auditorium.

The Munttoren at the base of Muntplein

⓬ Munttoren

Muntplein. **Map** 7 B5. 🚊 4, 9, 14, 16,
24. Tower **Closed** to the public. Shop:
Open 9:30am–6pm Mon–Sat,
11am–6pm Sun.

The polygonal base of the
Munttoren (mint tower) formed
part of the Regulierspoort, a
gate in Amsterdam's medieval
city wall. The gate was
destroyed by fire in 1618, but
the base survived. In the
following year, Hendrick de
Keyser (see p92) added the clock
tower, capped with a steeple
and openwork orb. The carillon
was designed by François
Hemony (see p70) in 1699,
and rings every 15 minutes.
The tower acquired its name
in 1673, during the French
occupation, when the city
mint was temporarily housed
here. A shop in the tower
sells delftware.

⓭ Bloemenmarkt

Singel. **Map** 7 B5. 🚊 1, 2, 4, 5, 9, 14,
16, 24. **Open** 9:30am–5pm daily.

On the Singel, west of Muntplein, is the last of the city's
floating markets. In the past,
nurserymen sailed up the
Amstel from their smallholdings
and moored here to sell cut
flowers and plants directly
from their boats. Today, the
stalls are still floating but are
permanent. Despite the sellers'
tendency to cater purely for
tourists, the displays of fragrant
seasonal flowers and bright
spring bedding plants are
always beautiful to look at.

Florist arranging his display at the Bloemenmarkt

MUSEUM QUARTER

Until the late 1800s, the Museum Quarter was little more than an area of farms and smallholdings. At this time, the city council designated it an area of art and culture and plans were conceived for constructing Amsterdam's great cultural monuments: the Rijksmuseum, the Stedelijk Museum and the Concertgebouw. The Van Gogh Museum followed in 1973, its striking extension being added in 1999. The Museumplein has two memorials to the victims of World War II. The *plein* is still used as a site for political demonstrations. To the north and south are turn-of-the-century houses, where the streets are named after artists and intellectuals, such as the 17th-century poet Roemer Visscher. To the west, the Vondelpark offers a pleasant, fresh-air break from all the museums.

Sights at a Glance

Museums and Workshops

1. Rijksmuseum pp130–33
2. Coster Diamonds
3. Van Gogh Museum pp136–7
4. Stedelijk Museum pp138–9

Concert Halls

5. Concertgebouw

Historic Buildings

7. Hollandsche Manege
8. Vondelkerk

Parks

6. Vondelpark
9. VondelCS

See also Street Finder pp274–87

0 metres 250
0 yards 250

◀ Beautiful setting of the VondelCS, Vondelpark

For map symbols see back flap

Street-by-Street: Museum Quarter

The green expanse of Museumplein was once
bisected by a busy main road known locally as the
"shortest motorway in Europe". But dramatic
renovation between 1996 and 1999 has transformed
it into a stately park, fringed by Amsterdam's major
cultural centres. The district is one of the wealthiest in
the city, with wide streets lined with grand houses.
After the heady delights of the museums, it is
possible to window-shop at the up-market boutiques
along the exclusive PC Hooftstraat and Van
Baerlestraat, or watch the diamond polishers at
work in Coster Diamonds.

❸ ★ Van Gogh Museum
This wing of the museum, an elegant
oval shape, was designed by Kisho
Kurokawa and opened in 1999. It was
enlarged in 2015 to create more space
for temporary exhibitions.

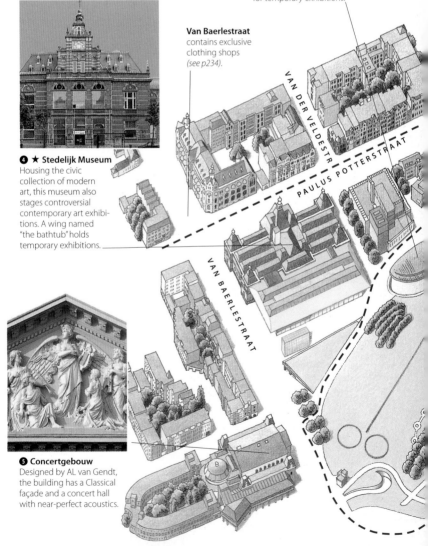

Van Baerlestraat
contains exclusive
clothing shops
(see p234).

❹ ★ Stedelijk Museum
Housing the civic
collection of modern
art, this museum also
stages controversial
contemporary art exhibi-
tions. A wing named
"the bathtub" holds
temporary exhibitions.

VAN DER VELDESTR

PAULUS POTTERSTRAAT

VAN BAERLESTRAAT

❺ Concertgebouw
Designed by AL van Gendt,
the building has a Classical
façade and a concert hall
with near-perfect acoustics.

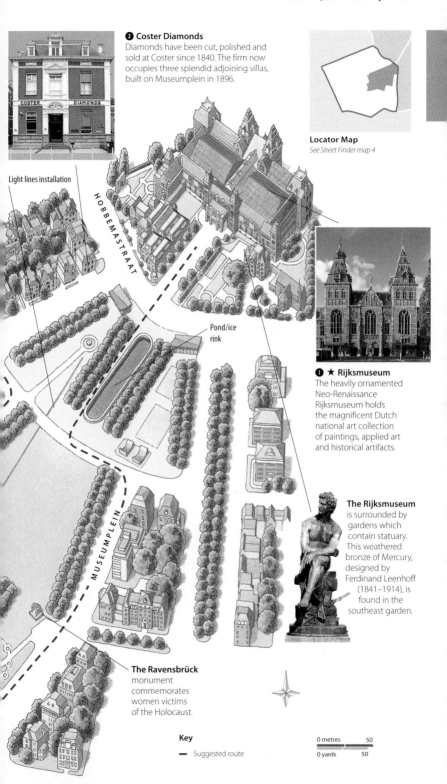

❷ Coster Diamonds
Diamonds have been cut, polished and sold at Coster since 1840. The firm now occupies three splendid adjoining villas, built on Museumplein in 1896.

Locator Map
See Street Finder map 4

Light lines installation

HOBBEMASTRAAT

Pond/ice rink

❶ ★ Rijksmuseum
The heavily ornamented Neo-Renaissance Rijksmuseum holds the magnificent Dutch national art collection of paintings, applied art and historical artifacts.

The Rijksmuseum
is surrounded by gardens which contain statuary. This weathered bronze of Mercury, designed by Ferdinand Leenhoff (1841–1914), is found in the southeast garden.

MUSEUMPLEIN

The Ravensbrück
monument commemorates women victims of the Holocaust.

Key

— Suggested route

| 0 metres | 50 |
| 0 yards | 50 |

❶ Rijksmuseum

The Rijksmuseum is a familiar Amsterdam landmark and possesses an unrivalled collection of Dutch art, begun in the early 19th century. The museum opened in 1885 to criticism, most vehemently from Amsterdam's Protestant community for its Catholic Neo-Renaissance style. The main building, designed by PJH Cuypers, underwent extensive renovation for 10 years, reopening in 2013.
The collection has over a million pieces, 8,000 of which are on display.

Second floor

Winter Landscape with Skaters (1618)
Painter Hendrick Avercamp specialized in intricate icy winter scenes.

★ The Kitchen Maid (1658)
The light falling through the window and the stillness of this scene are typical of Jan Vermeer *(see p196)*.

First floor

The Neo-Renaissance façade of PJH Cuypers' building is made of red brick with elaborate decoration, including coloured tiles.

Entrance

Gallery Guide

The entrance to the main building is through the atrium. Around 8,000 artworks are on display, chronologically telling the story of 800 years of Dutch history. Paintings, sculpture, historical objects and applied arts are shown side by side, emphasising contrasts and connections. A pavilion between the main building and the Philips Wing houses the Asiatic Collection.

Key to Floorplan

- Special collections
- Medieval and Renaissance art
- Golden Age
- 18th-century art
- 19th-century art
- 20th-century art
- Asian Pavilion
- Non-exhibition space

★ St Elizabeth's Day Flood (1500)
An unknown artist painted this altarpiece, showing a disastrous flood in 1421. The dykes protecting Dordrecht were breached, and 22 villages were swept away by the flood water.

Entrance

VISITORS' CHECKLIST

Practical Information
Museumstraat 1.
Map 4 E3. **Tel** 674 7000.
Open 9am–5pm daily (garden,
shop and café to 6pm).

w rijksmuseum.nl

Transport
2, 5, 7, 10. Stadhouderskade.

★ The Night Watch (1642)
The showpiece of Dutch
17th-century art, this vast canvas was
commissioned as a group portrait of
an Amsterdam militia company.

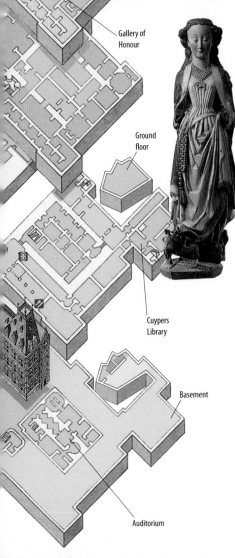

Gallery of
Honour

Ground
floor

Cuypers
Library

Basement

Auditorium

St Catherine (c.1465)
This sculpture by the Master of
Koudewater shows the saint stamping on
Emperor Maxentius, who allegedly killed
her with his sword.

Jan Steen's *Woman at her Toilet* was painted in
about 1660

Genre Painting

For the contemporaries of Jan Steen
(1625–79), this cosy everyday scene was full
of symbols that are obscure to the modern
viewer. The dog on the pillow may represent
fidelity, and the red stockings the woman's
sexuality; she is probably a prostitute.
Such genre paintings were often raunchy,
but nearly always had a moral twist
(see p191) – domestic scenes by artists such
as ter Borch and Honthorst were symbolic
of brothels, while other works illustrated
proverbs. Symbols like candles or skulls
indicated mortality.

Exploring the Rijksmuseum

The Rijksmuseum is almost too vast to be seen in a single visit, with its 80 galleries and 8,000 works of art and historical objects. It is famous for owning arguably the best collection of Dutch art in the world, from early religious works to the masterpieces of the Golden Age. Paintings, applied arts, furniture and sculpture are displayed side-by-side, and the Asiatic collection has its own pavilion. If time is short, visit the 1600–1700 floor, taking in Frans Hals, Vermeer and scores of other Old Masters, to finally arrive at Rembrandt's *The Night Watch* at the centre of the building.

Feeding the Hungry (1504) from a series of seven panels by the Master of Alkmaar

1100–1600

Alongside a small collection of Flemish and Italian art, including portraits by Piero di Cosimo (1462–1521), are the first specifically "Dutch" paintings. These works are mostly religious, such as *The Seven Works of Charity* (1504) by the Master of Alkmaar, Jan van Scorel's quasi-Mannerist *Mary Magdalene* (1528) and Lucas van Leyden's triptych, *Adoration of the Golden Calf* (1530). As the 16th century progressed, religious themes were superseded by pastoral subjects; by 1552, paintings like Pieter Aertsen's *The Egg Dance* were full of realism, the keystone of Dutch art during this period.

A collection of religious sculpture and liturgical objects includes *Our Lady of Sorrows* (1500–1510) a terracotta bust of the Virgin Mary in mourning.

1600–1700

During this century the Netherlands developed into a wealthy and powerful nation, with the arts profiting from the prosperous climate. By the Alteration in 1578 *(see pp26–7)*, Dutch art had moved away completely from religious to secular themes. Artists turned to realistic portraiture, landscapes, still lifes, seascapes, domestic interiors, including genre work *(see p131)*, and animal portraits. Rembrandt *(see pp64–5)* is one of the most famous artists who lived and worked around Amsterdam at this time. Rembrandt's works can be found in the Gallery of Honour, including *Portrait of Titus in a Monk's Habit* (1660), *Self Portrait as the Apostle Paul* (1661), *The Jewish Bride (see p44)* and the incredible *The Night Watch (see p131)*. Look out too for the work of his pupils, who included Nicolaes Maes and Ferdinand Bol. Don't miss Jan Vermeer's (1632–75) serenely light-filled interiors including *The Kitchen Maid (see p130)* and *The Woman Reading a Letter* (1662). Of several portraits by Frans Hals *(see pp180–81)*, the best known are *The Wedding Portrait* and *The Merry Drinker* (1630). *The Windmill at Wijk* by Jacob van Ruisdael (1628–82) is a landscape by an artist at the very height of his power. Other artists who feature in the collection include Pieter Saenredam, Jan van de Capelle, Jan Steen *(see p131)* and Gerard ter Borch.

1700–1800

Exhibits from the 18th century deal with the impact of revolutionary France on Amsterdam, ending in 1815 after the Napoleonic Wars. In many ways, Dutch painting continued the themes and quality of 17th-century portraiture and still lifes, with the evocative *Still Life with Flowers and Fruit* by Jan van Huysum (1682–1749) standing out. A trend developed later for elegant "conversation pieces" by artists such as Adriaan van der Werff (1659–1722) and Cornelis Troost (1696–1750). Most had

The Wedding Portrait (c.1622) by Frans Hals

satirical undertones, like *The Art Gallery of Jan Gildemeester Jansz* (1794) by Adriaan de Lelie (1755–1820), showing an 18th-century salon whose walls are crowded with 17th-century masterpieces. Another highlight is the mahogany-panelled reception room from Matthijs Beuning's Keizersgracht mansion, complete with stuccoed ceiling, and chimney painting by Jacob de Wit.

1800–1900

The early 19th century is represented by the Dutch romantics, who all reinterpreted the art of landscape painting but in contrasting styles. Artists such as Johannes Tavenraat and Wijnand Nuijen excelled in painting stormy and dramatic scenes, while Andreas Schelfhout preferred to paint more temperate and serene landscapes, lit by golden sunsets. The so-called Hague School was made up of a group of Dutch artists who came together around 1870 in Den Haag. Their landscape work captures the atmospheric quality of subdued Dutch sunlight. One of the prizes of the 19th-century collection is *Morning Ride on the Beach* (1876) by Anton Mauve (1838–88), painted in soft pearly colours, which hangs alongside the beautiful polder landscape, *View near the Geestbrug* by Hendrik Weissenbruch (1824–1903). In contrast, the Dutch Impressionists, closely linked to the French Impressionists, preferred active subjects shown in *The Bridge over the Singel at Paleisstraat, Amsterdam* (1890) by George Hendrik Breitner (1857–1923).

1900–2000

A small collection of 20th-century works under the museum's roof completes the tour. Along with clothing, photography and sculpture, works by artists le Corbusier and Karel Appel are on display. The FK 23 "Bantam" biplane, designed by Frederick

Still Life with Flowers and Fruit (c. 1730) by artist Jan van Huysum (1682–1749), one of many still lifes exhibited in the Rijksmuseum

Koolhoven for the British Aerial Transport Company in 1918 is a highlight of this section.

Asiatic Art

Rewards of the Dutch imperial trading past are on show in the pavilion between the main building and the Philips Wing. Some of the earliest artifacts are the most unusual: tiny bronze Tang dynasty figurines from 7th-century China and gritty, granite rock carvings from Java (c.8th century). Later exhibits include a lovely – and extremely explicit – Hindu statue entitled *Heavenly Beauty*, inlaid Korean boxes and Vietnamese dishes painted with curly-tailed fish and a superbly modelled bronze *Shiva Nataraja* (Dancing Shiva). This veritable

Late 7th-century Cambodian Head of Buddha

hoard of delights is testament to the sophistication and skill of artists and artisans in early Eastern cultures.

Special Collections, Philips Wing and the Gardens

The Special Collections gallery in the basement is a treasure trove of glassware, costumes, naval models, delftware, porcelain and much more. Temporary exhibitions are held on the upper floor of the Philips Wing. The ground floor houses a restaurant. The gardens, regularly the backdrop for sculpture exhibitions, have been redesigned using Cuypers' original plan and adding elements like a children's playground.

❷ Coster Diamonds

Paulus Potterstraat 2–6.
Map 4 E3. **Tel** 305 5555. 🚊 2, 5.
Open 9am–5pm daily. 🅿️ 📷
🅦 costerdiamonds.com

Coster was founded in 1840. Twelve years later, Queen Victoria's consort, Prince Albert, honoured the company by giving them the task of repolishing the enormous *Koh-i-Noor* (mountain of light) diamond. This blue-white stone is one of the treasures of the British crown jewels and weighs in at 108.8 carats. A replica of the coronation crown, with a copy of the fabulous stone, is found in Coster's entrance hall.

More than 6,000 people visit the factory each week to witness the processes of grading, cutting and polishing the stones. Goldsmiths and diamond-cutters work together to produce customized items of jewellery, which are available over the counter. For serious diamond-buyers, such as the jewellers who come to Amsterdam from all over the world, there is a series of private sales rooms where discretion is assured. A few doors down is a small museum, in which the history of the diamond is traced.

The stately façade of the Coster Diamonds factory and showrooms

❸ Van Gogh Museum

See pp136–7.

❹ Stedelijk Museum

See pp138–9.

Façade of the award-winning Concertgebouw (1881) by AL van Gendt

❺ Concertgebouw

Concertgebouwplein 10. **Map** 4 D4.
Tel 0900 671 8345. 🚊 2, 3, 5, 12, 16, 24. Box office **Open** 1–7pm Mon–Fri, 10am–7pm Sat & Sun. 🎭 Mon 5pm, Sun 12:15pm. 🅿️ 📷
🅦 concertgebouw.nl

Following an open architectural competition held in 1881, AL van Gendt (1835–1901) was chosen to design a vast new concert hall for Amsterdam. The resulting Neo-Renaissance building boasts an elaborate pediment and colonnaded façade, and houses two concert halls. Despite Van Gendt's lack of musical knowledge, he managed to produce near-perfect acoustics in the Grote Zaal (main concert hall), which is renowned the world over.

The inaugural concert at the Concertgebouw was held on 11 April 1888, complete with an orchestra of 120 musicians and a choir of 600.

The building has been renovated several times over the years, most recently in 1983, when some serious subsidence threatened the building's foundation. To remedy this, the whole superstructure had to be lifted up off the ground while the original supporting piles, which rested on sand 13 m (43 ft) underground, were removed and replaced by concrete piles sunk into the ground to a depth of 18 m (59 ft). A glass extension and new entrance were added by Pi de Bruijn in 1988. The original entrance was relocated round to the side of the building. Though primarily designed to hold concerts, the Concertgebouw has become multifunctional; it has played host to business meetings, exhibitions, conferences, political meetings and occasional boxing matches.

Bandstand in Vondelpark

❻ Vondelpark

Stadhouderskade. **Map** 4 E2. 🚊 1, 2, 3, 5, 12. Park **Open** 24hrs daily. Open-air theatre: **Open** Jun–last week Aug: Wed–Sun.

In 1864, a group consisting of prominent Amsterdammers formed a committee with the aim of founding a public park, and they raised enough money to buy 8 hectares (20 acres) of land. JD and LP Zocher, a father-and-son team of landscape architects, were then commissioned to design the park in typical English landscape style. They used vistas, pathways and ponds to create the illusion of a large natural area, which was opened to the public on 15 June 1865, as the Nieuwe Park. The park's present name was adopted in 1867, when a statue of Dutch poet Joost van den Vondel (1587–1679) was erected in the grounds. The committee soon began to raise money to enlarge the park, and by June 1877 it had reached its current dimensions of 47 hectares (116 acres). The park now supports around 100 plant species and 127 types of tree. Squirrels, hedgehogs, ducks and garden birds mix with a huge colony of greedy, bright green parakeets, which gather in front of the pavilion every morning to be fed. Herds of cows, sheep, goats and even a lone llama graze in the pastures.

Vondelpark welcomes more than ten million visitors a year, and is popular with the locals for dog-walking, jogging, or just for the view. Free concerts are given at the *openluchttheater* (open-air theatre) or at the bandstand in the summer.

❼ Hollandsche Manege

Vondelstraat 140. **Map** 3 C2. **Tel** 618 0942. 🚊 1. **Open** 10am–5pm daily. ♿ 🌐 **levendpaardenmuseum.nl**

The Dutch Riding School was originally situated on the Leidsegracht *(see p113)*, but in 1882 a new building was opened, designed by AL van Gendt and based on the Spanish Riding School in Vienna. The riding school was threatened with demolition in the 1980s, but was saved after a public outcry. Reopened in 1986 by Prince Bernhard, it has been

Façade of the Hollandsche Manege

restored to its former glory. The Neo-Classical indoor arena boasts gilded mirrors and moulded horses' heads on its elaborate plasterwork walls. Some of the wrought-iron stalls remain and sound is muffled by sawdust. At the top of the staircase, one door leads to a balcony overlooking the arena, another to the café.

❽ Vondelkerk

Vondelstraat 120. **Map** 3 C2. 🚊 1, 3, 12. **Closed** to the public.

The Vondelkerk was the largest church designed by PJH Cuypers, architect of the Centraal Station *(see pp34–5)*. Work began on the building in 1872, but funds ran out by the following year. Money gathered from public donations and lotteries allowed the building

to be completed by 1880. When fire broke out in November 1904, firefighters saved the nave of the church by forcing the burning tower to fall away into Vondelpark. A new tower was added later by the architect's son, JT Cuypers. The church was deconsecrated in 1979 and converted into offices in 1985.

❾ VondelCS

Vondelpark 3. **Map** 4 D2. 🚊 1, 3, 12.

Vondelpark's pavilion, which was commissioned by the committee that founded the Vondelpark, opened in 1881 as a café and restaurant. A flamboyant, Neo-Renaissance style building, the pavilion was the favourite haunt of Amsterdam's bohemian crowd, and its salons often featured contemporary art exhibitions. After World War II, the pavilion reopened as a cultural centre and from 1972 it was the home of the Filmmuseum. Renamed EYE Film Institute *(see p153)*, the museum moved to a new location on the Badhuisweg across the IJ, behind Centraal Station.

The pavilion, now VondelCS, is home to AVROTROS, one of Netherlands' public broadcasting corporations. It hosts talk shows, concerts and debates on culture and current affairs. The ground floor of the pavilion is occupied by a café-restaurant, Vondelpark3.

The fairy-tale Vondelkerk, at the edge of the Vondelpark

❸ Van Gogh Museum

The Van Gogh Museum is based on a design by De Stijl architect Gerrit Rietveld (1888–1965) *(see p138)*. The building was completed after Rietveld's death and opened in 1973. A freestanding wing, designed by Kisho Kurokawa, was added in 1999. When Van Gogh died in 1890, he was on the verge of being acclaimed. His brother Theo, an art dealer, amassed a collection of 200 of his paintings and 500 drawings. These, with around 850 letters by Van Gogh, and selected works by his contemporaries, form the core of the collection.

Key to Floorplan

- ☐ Works by Van Gogh
- ☐ Study collection & print room
- ☐ Other 19th-century paintings
- ☐ Temporary exhibitions

★ **Vincent's Bedroom in Arles (1888)**
One of Van Gogh's best-known works, this was painted to celebrate his achievement of domestic stability at the Yellow House in Arles. He was so delighted with the colourful painting that he did it twice.

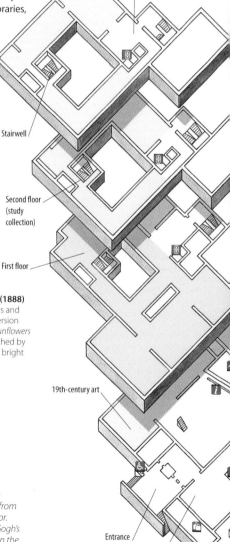

Third floor

Stairwell

Second floor (study collection)

First floor

19th-century art

Entrance

Ground floor

★ **Sunflowers (1888)**
The vivid yellows and greens in this version of Van Gogh's *Sunflowers* have been enriched by broad streaks of bright mauve and red.

Museum Guide

The museum owns the world's largest Van Gogh collection. Paintings from his Dutch period and from his time in Paris and Provence are on the first floor. The study collection, occasional exhibits of Van Gogh's drawings and other temporary exhibitions are on the second floor. Works by other 19th-century artists are on the ground floor and third floor. The main entrance is through the Exhibition Wing, which houses temporary exhibitions. Every Friday night the central hall is turned into a bar with lounge chairs and DJs.

An Artist's Life

Vincent Van Gogh (1853–90), born in Zundert, began painting in 1880. He worked in the Netherlands for five years before moving to Paris, later settling at Arles in the south of France. After a fierce argument with Gauguin, he cut off part of his own ear and his mental instability forced him into an asylum in Saint-Rémy. He sought help in Auvers, where he shot himself, dying two days later.

Van Gogh in 1871

VISITORS' CHECKLIST

Practical Information
Museumplein. **Map** 4 E3.
Tel 570 5200. **Open** Jan–Jun, Sep, Nov & Dec: 9am–5pm Sat–Thu (to 6pm Mar–Jun), 9am–10pm Fri; Jul, Aug & Oct: 9am–6pm Sun–Thu, 9am–10pm Fri & Sat. 🗓 🚺 🔲
♿ 🖥 🛍 🖼
w **vangoghmuseum.com**

Transport
🚊 2, 3, 5, 12.

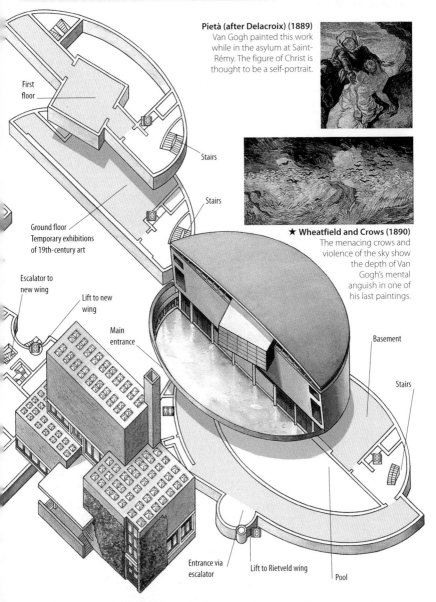

Pietà (after Delacroix) (1889)
Van Gogh painted this work while in the asylum at Saint-Rémy. The figure of Christ is thought to be a self-portrait.

First floor

Stairs

Stairs

Ground floor
Temporary exhibitions of 19th-century art

★ **Wheatfield and Crows (1890)**
The menacing crows and violence of the sky show the depth of Van Gogh's mental anguish in one of his last paintings.

Escalator to new wing

Lift to new wing

Main entrance

Basement

Stairs

Entrance via escalator

Lift to Rietveld wing

Pool

❹ Stedelijk Museum

Built to house a collection left to the city by Sophia de Bruyn in 1890, the Stedelijk Museum became the national museum of modern art and design in 1938, displaying works by artists such as Picasso, Matisse, Mondriaan, Chagall and Cézanne, and designers like Rietveld, Wirkkala and Sottsass. The renovated museum and its spectacular new wing (nicknamed the "bathtub") holds collections from present-day artists in a larger exhibition space, with a café-restaurant and a terrace overlooking Museumplein.

Portrait of the Artist with Seven Fingers (1912)
Marc Chagall's self-portrait is heavily autobiographical; the seven fingers of the title allude to the seven days of Creation and the artist's Jewish origins. Paris and Rome, the cities Chagall lived in, are inscribed in Hebrew above his head.

Bathtub
The Stedelijk's modern addition, the giant "bathtub", appears to float given its continuous glass walls at ground level; it remains a love-it-or-loathe-it addition to the city's architecture.

The Museum Building
The Neo-Renaissance building was designed by AW Weissman (1858–1923) in 1895. The façade is adorned with turrets and gables and with niches containing statues of artists and architects. Inside, it is ultramodern. The museum also stages performances, film screenings and large-scale events.

Hendrick de Keyser (1565–1621)

Jacob Cornelisz van Oostsanen (1470–1533)

Pieter Aertsen (1509–75)

Joost Jansz Bilhamer (1541–90)

Gerrit Rietveld's *Red Blue Chair* (1918)

De Stijl Movement

The Dutch artistic movement known as De Stijl (The Style) produced startlingly simple designs which have become icons of 20th-century abstract art. These include Gerrit Rietveld's famous *Red Blue Chair* and Pieter Mondriaan's *Composition in Red, Black, Blue, Yellow and Grey* (1920). The movement was formed in 1917 by a group of artists who espoused clarity in their work, which embraced the mediums of painting, architecture, sculpture, poetry and furniture design. Many De Stijl artists, like Theo van Doesburg, split from the founding group in the 1920s, and their legacy can be seen in the work of the Bauhaus and Modernist schools which followed.

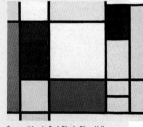

Composition in Red, Black, Blue, Yellow and Grey by Mondriaan

Dancing Woman (1911)
Ernst Ludwig Kirchner (1880–1938) was inspired by the primitive art of African and Asian cultures, and by the natural qualities of the materials he worked with.

Man and Animals (1949)
Karel Appel (born 1921) was a member of the short-lived, experimental Cobra movement. The human figure, dog, fish and mythical creature are painted in the naive style of a child.

Permanent Artists

Works by Dutch American Willem de Kooning, Russian artist Kazimir Malevich and sculptor Jean Tinguely are usually on show in the museum.

Willem de Kooning's (1904–97) work was abstract expressionist, often focussing on the female figure.

Elaborate bell tower

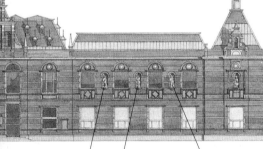

Jan van der Heyden (1637–1712)

Thomas de Keyser (1596–1667)

Jacob van Campen (1595–1657)

Kazimir Malevich (1878–1935) founded Suprematism, an abstract movement which experimented with colour.

Untitled (1965)
Jasper Johns (born 1930) believed viewers should draw their own conclusions from his work. This huge canvas, with its bold rainbow (red, blue and yellow streaks and slabs), invites the viewer to think about the symbolism of colour.

Jean Tinguely (1925–1991) created humorous, moving sculptures, welded together from junk and recycled metal.

PLANTAGE

Known as the "plantation", this area was once green parkland beyond the city wall, where 17th-century Amsterdammers spent their leisure time. From about 1848, it became one of Amsterdam's first suburbs. The tree-lined streets around Artis and Hortus Botanicus are still popular places to live. In the 19th century, many middle-class Jews prospered in the area, mainly in the diamond-cutting industry. They formed a large part of the Diamond Workers' Union, whose headquarters were housed in De Burcht. From the Museum 't Kromhout, once a thriving shipyard, there is a fine view of De Gooyer Windmill, one of the few in Amsterdam to survive. The national maritime collection is kept at Het Scheepvaartmuseum, a former naval storehouse.

Sights at a Glance

Museums
2 De Burcht
3 Hollandsche Schouwburg
11 Museum 't Kromhout
12 *Het Scheepvaartmuseum pp148–9*
15 Verzetsmuseum
16 Hermitage Amsterdam

Historic Buildings and Structures
8 Entrepotdok
9 Muiderpoort
10 De Gooyer Windmill
14 Amstelsluizen

Sights of Scientific Interest
4 Artis
5 Planetarium
6 Micropia
7 Aquarium

Botanical Gardens
1 Hortus Botanicus Amsterdam

Theatres
13 Koninklijk Theater Carré

Restaurants *pp230–31*
1 Aguada
2 Amstelhaven
3 Bloem
4 Café Kadijk
5 Elkaar
6 Neva
7 Paerz
8 Palorma
9 De Pizzabakkers
10 La Rive (Amstel Hotel)
11 Tempura

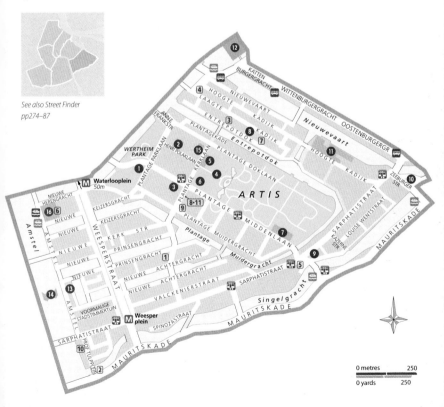

See also Street Finder pp274–87

0 metres 250
0 yards 250

◀ Exterior of Het Scheepvaartmuseum, housed in the 17th-century former arsenal of the navy   **For map symbols** *see back flap*

Street-by-Street: Plantage

With its wide, tree-lined streets and painted, sandstone buildings, the Plantage is a graceful and often overlooked part of the city. Though it seems like a quiet part of town, there is a lot to see and do. The area is dominated by the Artis complex. It has a diverse range of popular attractions which can get very busy on sunny days. The area has a strong Jewish tradition, and several monuments commemorate Jewish history in Amsterdam, including a basalt memorial in the Hollandsche Schouwburg. The cafés of the Entrepotdok offer a pleasant setting for a relaxing coffee, within earshot of the zoo.

❾ Entrepotdok
This was the largest warehouse development in Europe during the 19th century. It has been redeveloped and transformed into an attractive quayside housing, office and leisure complex.

❷ De Burcht
Inspired by an Italian palazzo, this was the headquarters of the Dutch Diamond Workers' Union.

❺ Planetarium
Part of the Artis complex, the domed Planetarium explores man's relationship with the stars. Interactive displays show the positions of the planets.

PLANTAGE PARKLAAN

PLANTAGE KERKLAAN

Moederhuis, Aldo van Eyck's refuge for pregnant women, has a colourful, modern façade intended to draw people inside.

❻ Micropia
Part of the Artis zoo complex, Micropia is the world's first museum dedicated to microbes and microorganisms, with cutting-edge displays.

❶ ★ Hortus Botanicus Amsterdam
The old glasshouses have been restored, and this new one put up to hold tropical and desert plants.

❸ ★ Hollandsche Schouwburg
Little remains of this former theatre, now a sombre monument to the deported Jews of World War II.

❹ ★ Artis
More than 900 species, including a pride of
lions, live in the zoo complex, which occupies
a beautifully laid out garden site.

Locator Map
See Street Finder maps 5 & 6

❼ Aquarium
The fine Neo-Classical
building is home to
thousands of aquatic species,
ranging from tiny, fluorescent
tropical fish to gigantic,
European moray eels.

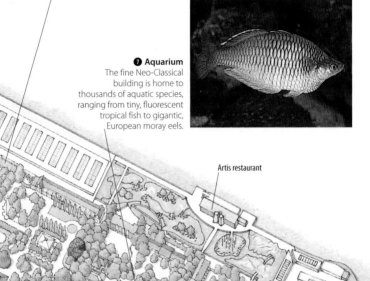

Artis restaurant

ANTAGE MIDDENLAAN

St Jacob's incorporates
the stone portal from
an old peoples' home
formerly on this site.

0 metres   100
0 yards   100

Tropical plants in the Hortus Botanicus

❶ Hortus Botanicus Amsterdam

Plantage Middenlaan 2. **Map** 5 C2. **Tel** 625 9021. 🚊 9, 14. Ⓜ Waterlooplein. **Open** 10am–5pm daily. **Closed** 1 Jan, 25 Dec. 🅿 ♿ 🎥 in English by arrangement. 🖥 📷 🆆 **dehortus.nl**

This botanical garden began as a small apothecaries' herb garden in 1682, and now boasts one of the world's largest botanical collections. Its range of flora expanded when tropical plants were brought back by the Dutch East India Company (see pp30–31). In 1706, it became the first place outside Arabia to succeed in cultivating the coffee plant.

The glass-domed Palm House, built in 1912, contains an exceptional collection of palms, conservatory plants and cycads, including one that is more than 400 years old. The restored Orangery has a café and terrace, where art shows with a botanical theme are held.

A modern glass and aluminium construction, designed by Moshé Zwarts and Rein Jansma, was opened in 1993 to make room for the tropical, subtropical and desert plants. There is also a butterfly house.

❷ De Burcht

Henri Polaklaan 9. **Map** 5 C2. **Tel** 624 1166. 🚊 9, 14. **Open** for guided tours in Dutch only, one Sun each month. Reservations essential; book by phone or via website. 🎥 ♿ 🆆 **deburcht.nl**

This red-brick crenellated building, known locally as "the castle", was designed by HP Berlage (see p81) in 1899. It housed the head-quarters of the General Dutch Diamond Workers'

Union (ANDB). Founded in 1894, the ANDB was the first, largest and wealthiest union in the Netherlands.

The building has a beautiful interior, with murals by the socialist artist Richard Ronald Holst of the Amsterdam School (see p99), and a spectacular arched foyer. It has been restored and now houses the research and conference centre for the Dutch Trade Unions. The building can only be visited by booking a tour.

❸ Hollandsche Schouwburg

Plantage Middenlaan 24. **Map** 5 C2. **Tel** 531 0310. 🚊 9, 14. **Open** 11am–5pm daily. **Closed** 27 Apr, Rosh Hashanah (Jewish New Year), Yom Kippur. ♿ 🆆 **hollandscheschouwburg.nl**

Part of the Jewish Historical Quarter (see p44), this former theatre is now a memorial to the 104,000 Dutch Jewish victims of World War II. Thousands were detained here before deportation to concentration camps. Post war, the building was abandoned until 1962. A basalt column with a base in the shape of the Star of David

now stands on the site of the stage. Written behind it is: "To the memory of those taken from here".

Following its restoration in 1993, the Hollandsche Schouwburg became an education centre. On the ground floor, a candle illuminates the names of the war victims. Upstairs, there is a permanent exhibition on the persecution of the Jews in the Netherlands from 1940 to 1945.

❹ Artis

Plantage Kerklaan 38–40. **Map** 6 D2. **Tel** 0900 278 4796. 🚊 9, 14. Artis: **Open** 9am–5pm daily (Apr–Sep: to 6pm, Jun–Aug: till sunset Sat). 🅿 ♿ 🎦 📷 🎥 11am Sat & Sun. Artisplein: **Open** 9am–10:30pm daily 🆆 **artis.nl**

Artis (Natura Artis Magistra, to give the zoo its full name) is the oldest surviving zoological complex in the Netherlands. Since its inception in 1838, its aim has been to promote the knowledge of natural history, and since it opened, the general public have been allowed in to admire the collection of plants, trees and animals.

The complex has more than 900 animal species, as well as three greenhouses, the Planetarium, Aquarium,

Decorative tiles on the staircase of the De Burcht building

Lush greenery and colourful butterflies inside the Artis Butterfly Pavilion

Amfibarium, Insectarium and Zoölogisch Museum.

The zoo's attractions include big cats, giraffes, penguins, gorillas, hippos and seals. In the Insectarium, displays explain the versatility and adaptability of these creatures. The Butterfly Pavilion, which is the largest of its kind in the Netherlands, houses thousands of butterflies in a large greenhouse filled with vegetation.

Over the coming years, Artis is expanding. The Groote Museum, a natural history museum currently in disrepair, is being restored. A public square has been created between Artis and Micropia, the Artisplein, which serves as a terrace for the adjacent Plantage café.

❺ Planetarium

Plantage Kerklaan 38–40. **Map** 6 D2. **Tel** 0900 278 4796. 🚃 9, 14. **Open** 9am–5pm daily (Apr–Sep: to 6pm, Jun–Aug: till sunset Sat); shows every hour. 👇 📷

Budding astronomers should not miss the show at the Planetarium, which takes place on the hour every hour. In this large, domed building a powerful projector shows films on several themes. One film is *Spacetrip*, which takes visitors on a journey through the galaxy and beyond, travelling at speeds even faster than the speed of light. Other films concentrate on the life of an astronaut or the magical world

of the coral reefs. Although the commentary is in Dutch, just watching the beautiful images is still an enjoyable experience.

Around the edge of the Planetarium, stellar and planetary systems are mapped out using models, photographs, videos and pushbutton exhibits. There are also educational computer games and displays on exploration and astronomy.

❻ Micropia

Plantage Kerklaan 38–40. **Map** 5 C2. **Tel** 0900 278 4796. 🚃 9, 14. **Open** 9am–6pm Sun–Wed, 9am–8pm Thu–Sat. 📷 👇 🌐 **micropia.nl**

More like a laboratory than a museum, at Micropia, the world's first microbe museum, the mysterious realm of micro-organisms is made visible. Through its unique interactive displays and cleverly lit models, visitors can learn about the vast diversity of these minuscule creatures and their important role in life on earth.

❼ Aquarium

Plantage Kerklaan 38–40. **Map** 6 D3. **Tel** 0900 278 4796. 🚃 9, 14. Aquarium **Open** 9am–5pm daily (Apr–Sep: to 6pm, Jun–Aug: till sunset Sat). Zoölogisch Museum: **Open** as above. 👇 📷

Perhaps the best feature of the Artis complex is its Aquarium, which opened in 1882 in a

grand Neo-Classical building. Mainly housed on the first floor, there are now four separate aquatic systems: one freshwater and three saltwater. Together they hold almost a million litres (220,000 gallons) of water. These tanks, each kept at a different temperature, contain almost 500 species of fish and marine animals that can be viewed at close quarters. They range from simple invertebrates to piranhas, sharks and massive marine turtles. Look out especially for the vivid coral fish and charming sea horses housed at the far end of the gallery.

The basement has four large tanks accommodating different biotypes. Among the various waterscapes, visitors can see life in the Amazon, a coral reef and even fish in a recreated Amsterdam canal. Also in the basement is the Amfibarium. This hall contains a substantial collection of frogs, toads and salamanders in all shapes, sizes and colours.

Tropical fish at the Aquarium, home to almost 500 marine species

Spout-gable façades of former warehouses along Entrepotdok

🎱 Entrepotdok

Map 6 D2. 🚃 9, 14, 22.

The redevelopment of the old VOC *(see pp30–31)* warehouses at Entrepotdok has revitalized this dockland area. It was once the greatest warehouse area in Europe during the mid-19th century, being a customs-free zone for goods in transit. The quayside buildings of Entrepotdok are now a lively complex of offices, homes and eating places. Some of the original façades of the warehouses have been preserved, unlike the interiors, which have been opened up to provide an attractive inner courtyard. Café tables are often set out alongside the canal. On the other side, brightly coloured houseboats are moored side by side, and herons doze at the water's edge.

🎱 Muiderpoort

Alexanderplein. **Map** 6 E3. 🚃 9, 10, 14. **Closed** to the public.

Formerly a city gate, the Muiderpoort was designed by Cornelis Rauws in about 1770. The central archway of this Classical structure is topped with a dome and clock tower. Napoleon entered the city through this gate in 1811 and, according to legend, forced the citizens to feed and house his ragged troops.

🎱 De Gooyer Windmill

Funenkade 5. **Map** 6 F2. 🚃 10. 🚌 22. **Closed** to the public.

Of the six remaining windmills within the city's boundaries, De Gooyer, also known as the Funenmolen, is the most central. Dominating the view down the Nieuwevaart, the mill was built around 1725, and was the first cornmill in the Netherlands to use streamlined sails.

It first stood to the west of its present site, but the Oranje Nassau barracks, built in 1814,

The grand dome and clock tower of the Muiderpoort

acted as a windbreak, and the mill was then moved piece by piece to the Funenkade. The octagonal wooden structure was rebuilt on the stone foot of an earlier water-pumping mill, demolished in 1812.

By 1925, De Gooyer was in a very poor state of repair and was bought by the city council, which fully restored it. Since then, the lower part of the mill, with its neat thatched roof and tiny windows, has been a private home, though its massive sails still creak into action sometimes. Next to the mill is the IJ brewery *(see p50)*, one of two independent breweries in the city.

🎱 Museum 't Kromhout

Hoogte Kadijk 147. **Map** 6 E2. **Tel** 627 6777. 🚃 9, 10, 14. 🚌 22. 🚢 Scheepvaartmuseum. **Open** 10am–3pm Tue (May–Sep: noon–4pm & 1st and 3rd Sun of month). 🟡 **kromhoutmuseum.nl**

The Museum 't Kromhout is one of the oldest working shipyards in Amsterdam, and is also a museum. Ships were built here as early as 1757. In the second half of the 19th century, production changed from sailing ships to steamships. As ocean-going ships got bigger, the yard, due to its small size, turned to building lighter craft for inland waterways. It is now used only for restoration and repair work. The museum is largely dedicated to the history of marine engineering, with engines, maritime photographs and a well-equipped forge. Work is carried out at the shipyard.

Museum 't Kromhout and its working shipyard

⑫ Het Scheepvaart-museum

See pp148–9.

⑬ Koninklijk Theater Carré

Amstel 115–125. **Map** 5 B3. **Tel** 0900 252 5255. 🚋 4, 7, 9, 10, 14. Ⓜ Weesperplein. Box office **Open** 4–8pm daily. *See Entertainment p242.* 📷 11am Sat (phone in advance). ✉ ♿ ⊘ 🌐 carre.nl

During the 19th century, the annual visit of the Circus Carré was a popular event. In 1868, Oscar Carré built wooden premises for the circus on the banks of the Amstel river. The city council considered the structure a fire hazard, so Carré persuaded them to accept a permanent building modelled on his other circus in Cologne. Built in 1887, the new structure included both a circus ring and a stage. The Classical façade is richly decorated with sculpted heads of dancers, jesters and clowns.

The Christmas circus is still one of the annual highlights at the theatre, but for much of the year the enlarged stage is taken over by concerts and big-show musicals, such as *The Sound of Music*, *Chicago* and *Mamma Mia*.

⑭ Amstelsluizen

Map 5 B3. 🚋 4, 7, 9, 10, 14. Ⓜ Weesperplein.

The Amstelsluizen, a row of sturdy wooden sluice gates spanning the Amstel river, form part of a complex system of sluices and pumping stations that ensure Amsterdam's canals do not stagnate. Four times a week in summer the sluices are closed while fresh water from large lakes north of the city is allowed to flow into Amsterdam's canals. Sluices to the west of the city are left open, allowing the old water to flow, or be pumped, into the sea.

The Amstelsluizen date from the 18th century, and were operated manually until 1994, when they were mechanized.

⑮ Verzetsmuseum

Plantage Kerklaan 61. **Map** 6 D2. **Tel** 620 2535. 🚋 9, 14. **Open** 10am–5pm Tue–Fri, 11am–5pm Sat–Mon & public hols. **Closed** 1 Jan, 27 Apr, 25 Dec. 🅿 ♿ ⊘ ⊡ ⊘ 🌐 verzetsmuseum.org

Carving on façade of Koninklijk Theater Carré

Located in a building that used to be the home of a Jewish choral society, the Resistance Museum holds a fascinating collection of memorabilia recording the activities of Dutch Resistance workers in World War II. It focuses on the courage of the 25,000 people actively involved in the movement. On display are false documents, film clips, slide shows, photographs, weaponry and equipment. By 1945 there were 300,000 people in hiding in the Netherlands, including Jews and

anti-Nazi Dutch. Subsequent events organized by the Resistance, like the February Strike against deportation of the Jews *(see p37)*, are brought to life by exhibits showing where the refugees hid and how food was smuggled in. The museum includes a special children's wing, Verzetsmuseum Junior, in which the real-life war-time experiences of children are told.

⑯ Hermitage Amsterdam

Amstel 51. **Map** 8 E5. **Tel** 0900 437 648 243. 🚋 4, 9, 14. Ⓜ Waterlooplein. 🚌 City Hall. **Open** 10am–5pm daily. **Closed** 27 Apr, 25 Dec. ♿ ⊘ ⊡ 🔳 🌐 hermitage.nl

The State Hermitage Museum in St Petersburg decided upon Amsterdam as the ideal city to open a branch of the Russian museum. This satellite museum would display rotating temporary exhibitions drawn from the Hermitage's rich collection.

The Hermitage Amsterdam opened in early 2004, in a side wing of the Amstelhof (a former old people's home), with a spectacular exhibition of fine Greek gold jewellery from the 6th to the 2nd century BC. Other exhibitions have included the collection of the last Tsars Nicholas and Alexandra. The Amstelhof building has been fully restored and the Hermitage now occupies the whole complex, with two exhibition wings, an auditorium and a special children's wing that encourages children to discover their own creative talents.

The Hermitage Amsterdam, housed in the former Amstelhof, overlooking the Amstel river

⑫ Het Scheepvaartmuseum

Once the arsenal of the Dutch Navy, this vast Classical sandstone building was built by Daniel Stalpaert in 1656 round a massive courtyard. It was supported by 2,300 piles driven into the bed of the Oosterdok. The navy stayed in residence until 1973, when the building was converted into the Maritime Museum. A renovation project has returned the building to its former glory, and the former artillery courtyard now has a stunning glass roof. Visitors of all ages enjoy the museum's interactive exhibitions and displays of maritime objects.

★ Tale of the Whale
This exhibition tells the story of the whale, starting with the first whaling exhibitions in the 16th century, when whales were thought to be fearsome sea monsters. It covers the current efforts to preserve them from extinction.

First floor

Yacht Models
The museum has a fine collection of beautifully decorated model boats. It features examples of pleasure craft through the ages, from the 17th century to the present day. Each one is a work of art with exquisitely painted details.

Classical sandstone façade

Main entrance

Open Courtyard
The navy used to store its artillery in the arsenal's internal courtyard. The design of its modern glass roof is inspired by navigational lines on antique nautical maps.

Second floor

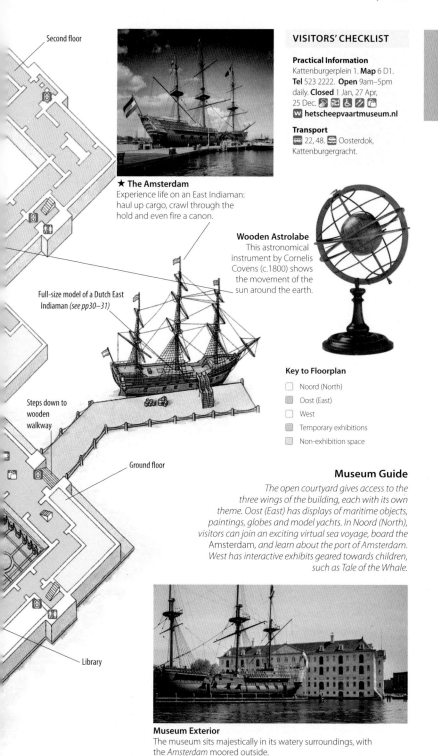

★ The Amsterdam
Experience life on an East Indiaman:
haul up cargo, crawl through the
hold and even fire a canon.

Wooden Astrolabe
This astronomical
instrument by Cornelis
Covens (c.1800) shows
the movement of the
sun around the earth.

Full-size model of a Dutch East
Indiaman *(see pp30–31)*

Steps down to
wooden
walkway

Key to Floorplan

☐ Noord (North)
▨ Oost (East)
☐ West
▨ Temporary exhibitions
▨ Non-exhibition space

Ground floor

Museum Guide

*The open courtyard gives access to the
three wings of the building, each with its own
theme. Oost (East) has displays of maritime objects,
paintings, globes and model yachts. In Noord (North),
visitors can join an exciting virtual sea voyage, board the*
Amsterdam, *and learn about the port of Amsterdam.
West has interactive exhibits geared towards children,
such as Tale of the Whale.*

Library

Museum Exterior
The museum sits majestically in its watery surroundings, with
the *Amsterdam* moored outside.

FURTHER AFIELD

Great architecture and good town planning are not confined to central Amsterdam. Parts of the Nieuw Zuid (New South) bear testament to the imagination of the innovative Amsterdam School architects *(see p99)* under the auspices of the Municipal Councils. Many fine buildings can be found in De Dageraad housing complex and the streets around the Olympic Quarter. If you are seeking old-world charm, the historic small town of Ouderkerk aan de Amstel, nestling on the southern fringes of the city,

prides itself on being older than Amsterdam. There are also fine parks just a short tram ride from the city centre, which offer a whole host of leisure activities. Visitors can view the lakes, woods and parkland of the Amsterdamse Bos *(see pp36–7)* from the deck of an antique tram which tours the park from the Electrische Museumtramlijn. The more formal horticulture of the Amstelpark can be viewed aboard a miniature train. There is also a clutch of instructive museums to be found in the suburbs of Amsterdam.

Sights at a Glance

Historic Monuments, Buildings and Districts
❶ Frankendael
❻ De Dageraad Housing
❽ Ouderkerk aan de Amstel
❾ Olympic Quarter

Museums and Exhibition Halls
❷ *Tropenmuseum see pp154–5*
❸ NEMO Science Center Amsterdam
❹ EYE Film Institute
❿ Electrische Museumtramlijn
⓬ Schiphol Airport

Parks and Gardens
❺ Westerpark
❼ Amstelpark
⓫ Amsterdamse Bos

Key
▢ Central Amsterdam
▢ Greater Amsterdam
═ Major road
═ Minor road

0 kilometres   2
0 miles   2

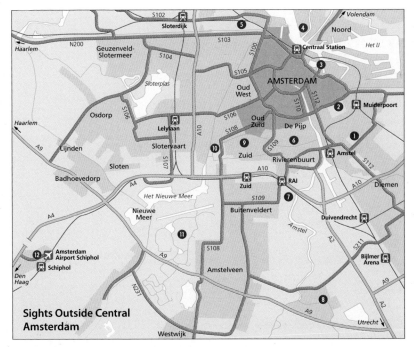

Sights Outside Central Amsterdam

For additional map symbols *see back flap*

The back of the Frankendael, with its well-tended formal gardens

❶ Frankendael

Middenweg 72. **Map** 6 F5. 🚊 9.
🚌 41. Restaurant: **Tel** 665 0880.
Open dawn–dusk.

During the early part of the 18th century, many of Amsterdam's wealthier citizens built country retreats south of Plantage Middenlaan on reclaimed land called the Watergraafsmeer. The elegant Louis XIV-style Frankendael is the last survivor; the best views of the ornamented façade are from Middenweg. This is also the best place to view the fountain made by Ignatius van Logteren in 1714, complete with reclining river gods, in the front garden.

The formal gardens at the back of the Frankendael are open to the public. They have been painstakingly reconstructed over the past few years and now offer a peaceful refuge of shrubs and ancient trees. The coach house has a café-restaurant, Merkelbach.

Ignatius van Logteren's fountain in the grounds of the Frankendael

❷ Tropenmuseum

See pp154–5.

❸ NEMO Science Center Amsterdam

Oosterdok 2. **Map** 2 F4. **Tel** 531 3233.
🚌 22, 48. **Open** 10am–5:30pm Tue–Sun (daily during school hols).
Closed 1 Jan, 27 Apr, 25 Dec. 🅿 🔲
♿ ✍ 🏠 🅦 e-nemo.nl

In June 1997 Holland's national science centre moved to this dazzling curved building which protrudes 30 m (98 ft) over water. NEMO is the largest science centre in the Netherlands and presents technological innovations in a manner which allows visitors' creativity full expression. You can interact with virtual reality, operate the latest industrial equipment under expert supervision and harness science to produce your own art. The Centre is divided into seven themed zones (Sound, Brain, Energy, Senses, Construction, Electricity and Mathematics), each of which is revamped every three years to keep pace with scientific evolution. Visitors – who in this setting might equally be termed explorers – can participate in experiments, demonstrations, games and workshops or take in lectures, films and even educational stage shows.

NEMO Science Center has the largest roof terrace in Amsterdam (closed in winter), with great views of the city. Access to the roof is by lift or stairs and is free. Check the website for special events held in summer.

Striking architecture of NEMO Science Center

The sleek, modern interior of the EYE Film Institute

❹ EYE Film Institute

IJpromenade 1. **Map** 2 E2.
🚋 Buiksloterweg. **Tel** 589 1400.
Ticket office: **Open** 10am–10pm daily (to 11pm Fri & Sat). Exhibitions: **Open** 11am–5pm daily. 🎫 card payments only. Basement: **Open** 10am–6pm daily. ♿ 🖥 📷 ∅
🔲 eyefilm.nl/en

Located on the northern bank of the river IJ, the EYE Film Institute is a merger between the Filmmuseum and several other cinematic organizations. For almost 40 years the Filmmuseum was housed in the Vondelpark Pavilljoen *(see p131)*. The Institute's film collection tells the story of the Netherlands film industry, from silent films at the end of the 19th century to digital technology and 3D cinema. There is also a wide display of film memorabilia, including photographs, posters, soundtracks and technical equipment.

Housed in a sleek, modern, building the EYE Film Institute has four cinemas, an exhibition space and a café-restaurant with a waterside terrace. In the basement, visitors can view films for free; watching clips or complete films in specially designed viewing cabins, each with a cinemascope screen and a small sofa. EYE's information specialists can be found on the basement level on weekdays to answer questions about the collections and film history.

❺ Westerpark

Polonceaukade. 🚋 10. 🚌 21, 22. Westergasfabriek **Tel** 586 0710. Museum Het Schip Spaarndammerplantsoen 140. **Map** 1 B1. **Tel** 686 8595. **Open** 11am–5pm Tue–Sun. 🎫 🕐 hourly. 🖥 🔲 **westergasfabriek. com** 🔲 hetschip.nl

The wasteland around Amsterdam's former gasworks (Westergasfabriek) was transformed into a 14-ha (35-acre) park in the early 2000s. Facilities in this green area include playgrounds, bars, restaurants and several performance spaces.

The gasworks itself has been redeveloped and is being rented out to various associations that organize festivals, performances and exhibitions. The Westergasfabriek is now one of the city's foremost cultural destinations.

Nearby is Het Schip (The Ship), one of the most iconic buildings by the Amsterdam School *(see p99)*. Designed by Michel de

Klerk in 1919, this apartment block contains 102 homes and the Museum Het Schip, displaying a restored working-class house.

❻ De Dageraad Housing

Pieter Lodewijk Takstraat. 🚋 4, 12. **Open** 11am–5pm Fri–Sun. 🎫 tours depart from Burgemeester Tellegenstraat 128; call 686 8595 to book.
🔲 hetschip.nl

One of the best examples of Amsterdam School architecture *(see p99)*, De Dageraad housing project was developed for poorer families following the revolutionary Housing Act of 1901 by which the city council was forced to condemn slums and rethink housing policy in Amsterdam.

Socialist architect HP Berlage *(see p81)* drew up ingenious plans for the suburbs, aiming to integrate rich and poor by juxtaposing their housing. After Berlage's death, Piet Kramer and Michel de Klerk of the Amsterdam School adopted his ideas. Between 1918 and 1923, they designed this complex for a housing association known as De Dageraad (the Dawn). They used a technique called "apron architecture" in which an underlayer of concrete allows for tucks, folds and rolls in the subtly coloured brick exterior, which was then interspersed with decorative doors and windows. Each house mirrors the one opposite and there is a corner tower at the end of every block.

Het Schip, a standard of the Amsterdam School

❷ Tropenmuseum

Built to house the Dutch Colonial Institute, this vast complex was finished in 1926 by architects MA and JJ Nieukerken. The exterior of what is one of the city's finest historic buildings is decorated with symbols of imperialism, such as stone friezes of peasants planting rice. When the building's renovation was completed in 1978, the Royal Tropical Institute opened this fascinating ethnographic museum. The displays of art objects, photographs and film focus on widely different cultures in the tropics and subtropics. Children will enjoy participating in the interactive exhibition in Tropenmuseum Junior.

Plaster Figure of Iemanja
In Afro-Brazilian religion, Iemanja is the goddess of the ocean and patron deity of fishermen.

★ **Pustaha – Book of Divinations**
Made of wood and tree bark, this volume contains prescriptions applied by the village healer-priest.

Great Hall

★ **Bisj Poles**
The roots of massive mangrove trees were used to make these exotic, painted ritual totem poles from New Guinea.

Gallery Guide

Temporary exhibitions are held in the North Wing on the ground floor and the Park Hall on the second floor. On the upper floors, the permanent exhibitions combine static and interactive displays covering diverse topics. Displays are liable to change during renovation work over the next few years – check the website for the latest details. The shop on the ground floor has a wide range of gifts and there is a café-restaurant as well.

Main entrance

Basement

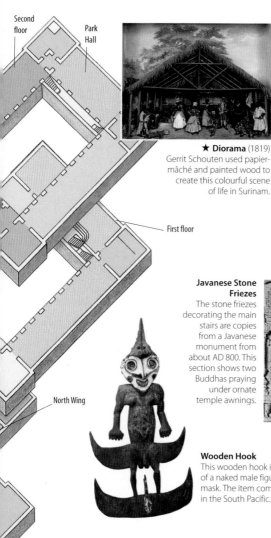

Second floor

Park Hall

First floor

North Wing

★ **Diorama** (1819)
Gerrit Schouten used papier-mâché and painted wood to create this colourful scene of life in Surinam.

Javanese Stone Friezes
The stone friezes decorating the main stairs are copies from a Javanese monument from about AD 800. This section shows two Buddhas praying under ornate temple awnings.

Wooden Hook
This wooden hook is carved in the shape of a naked male figure wearing a tribal mask. The item comes from New Guinea, in the South Pacific.

Key to Floorplan
- SE Asia
- W Asia & N Africa
- Latin America & the Caribbean
- Music, Dance & Theatre
- Africa
- Dutch Colonialism
- Dutch New Guinea
- Tropenmuseum Junior
- Temporary exhibition space
- Non-exhibition space

Jeepney
Old army trucks left behind by the Americans after World War II are used as taxibuses, or jeepneys, in Manila, in the Philippines. The one housed here is a typically colourful example.

Amstelpark's Rieker windmill

⑦ Amstelpark

Europaboulevard. 🚋 4. Ⓜ 🚆 RAI. 🚌 62. **Open** dawn–dusk.

Situated in the suburb of Buitenveldert, southwest of Amsterdam, this large park was created in 1972. Among its attractions are a rose garden, rhododendron walk and model garden with nursery.

The park offers good facilities for children, including a playground, pony rides, minigolf and mini-football. The well-preserved Rieker windmill (1636) stands at the southern tip of the park, and art exhibitions are held in the Glazen Huis (Glass House) and the Papillon Gallery. From Easter to October, you can tour the park in a miniature train.

⑧ Ouderkerk aan de Amstel

Ⓜ 🚆 Bijlmer. 🚌 175 & 300 from Bijlmer station. Wester Amstel Garden **Open** 9am–4:30pm Mon–Fri, (also mid-Apr–Oct: noon–4:30pm Sat & Sun).

This pretty village at the junction of the Amstel and the Bullewijk rivers has been a favourite with Amsterdammers since the Middle Ages. They had no church of their own until 1330 *(see pp70–71)*, and worshippers had to travel to the 11th-century Ouderkerk that gave the village its name. The Old Church was destroyed in a tremendous storm in 1674, and a fine 18th-century church now stands on its site. Opposite is the Beth Haim Jewish cemetery, where more than 27,000 Jews from Amsterdam have been buried since 1615. The elders of the Jewish community bought this land to use as a burial ground because Jews were forbidden to bury their dead inside the city.

Today Ouderkerk aan de Amstel is popular with cyclists who come to enjoy the ambience of its waterfront cafés and restaurants. The skyline is dominated by the 50-m (160-ft) spire of the Urbanuskerk, a Catholic church designed by PJH Cuypers *(see pp34–5)* and consecrated in 1867. A short walk upriver along Amsteldijk, there are two 18th-century country houses. There is no access to the first, but the wooded garden of the second, Wester Amstel (built in 1720), is open to the public.

⑨ Olympic Quarter

🚋 16, 24. 🚌 15, 62, 142, 170, 172, 174, 197.

Development of the western side of the Nieuw Zuid (New South) began during the run up to the Olympic Games, held here in 1928. Many of the streets and squares were given Grecian names, like Olympiaplein and Herculesstraat.

The Stadium was designed by J Wils and C van Eesteren. Its stark vertical lines and soaring torch tower recall the work of the American architect Frank Lloyd Wright. Once threatened with demolition, it is now a sports venue.

The sturdy bridge across the Noorder Amstelkanaal at Olympiaplein is typical Amsterdam School design. It is the work of PL Kramer and the sculptor H Krop. Beyond the bridge, the Amsterdams Lyceum (a secondary school) shows the style at its best.

The peaceful waterfront at Oudekerk aan de Amstel, south of Amsterdam

Pedalos on a lake in the Amsterdamse Bos

⑩ Electrische Museumtramlijn

Amstelveenseweg 264. **Tel** 673 7538.
🚋 16. 🚌 15, 62, 142, 170, 172, 174,
197. **Open** Easter–Oct: 11am–5:30pm
Sun. 🅿 **W** **museumtramlijn.org**

Not a museum, as the name
suggests, but a tram ride that
operates from Haarlemmer-
meerstation and the southern tip
of the Amster-
damse Bos.
The tramcars,
which date
from 1910 to
1950, come
from all over
the Netherlands,
Vienna, Prague and
Berlin. The fleet is run by a group
of enthusiasts along traditional
lines and cars depart regularly
from either terminus. A one-
way journey takes about 20
minutes and provides a good
view of the Olympic Stadium.

Classic tram from the
Museumtramlijn

⑪ Amsterdamse Bos

Amstelveenseweg corner Van
Nijenrodeweg. 🚋 Electrische
Museumtramlijn (see entry 10).
🚌 142, 170, 172, 174. Theatre
Tel 643 3286. **W** **amsterdamsebos.nl**

This woodland park is the
largest recreational area in
Amsterdam. It was laid out in
the 1930s in a bid to reduce
unemployment in the city
(see p37). Extensive wooded
areas, interspersed with grassy
meadows, lakes, waterways and
even a hill, were created on
reclaimed land that lies 3 m

(10 ft) below sea level. The park
was enlarged periodically until
1967, when it reached its present
size of 1,000 ha (2,471 acres).
Today, the marshy areas
around Nieuwe Meer and the
lakes at Amstelveense Poel and
Kleine Poel are nature reserves.
Other highlights include an
animal enclosure, a goat farm
and the Vogeleiland botanical
garden. Among
the facilities are
an extensive
network of
planned walks,
cycle paths and
bridle ways, as
well as water
sports and an
open-air theatre (see p241)
during the summer. A map
of the park which includes
hiking and cycling trails is
available at the information
centre near the entrance.

⑫ Schiphol Airport

Evert van de Beekstraat 202.
Tel 0900 0141. 🚉 Schiphol Airport.
W **schiphol.nl**

Attracting over 140,000 people
each day, this modern, forward-
thinking airport (official name:
Amsterdam Airport Schiphol)
is one of the world's most
efficient and user-friendly, with
different colour-coded signs to
help visitors navigate around
this huge area (see pp262–3).
The airport has a wide variety
of exciting extras to help pass
the time while waiting for a
flight. The Rijksmuseum has a
small selection of classic works
of art for the public to view,
located on Holland Boulevard.
The museum is situated
beyond passport control, and
entrance is free to everyone
with a boarding pass.
The airport also boasts a
small casino between gates E
and F (open from 6:30am to
7:30pm) to help pass the time,
as well as a haven for the sore
and weary traveller in the form
of a chair massage.
The "Silence Centre", is open
between 9am and 5pm. This
is a place of worship for all
religions, or simply a place
for quiet contemplation.
In addition to the vast
number of shops, bars and
restaurants at the airport,
there is also a Panorama
Terrace offering great views
of the aircraft.

The entrance to Amsterdam's modern Schiphol Airport

TWO GUIDED WALKS

Many of Amsterdam's most important historical landmarks, and several fine examples of 16th- and 17th-century architecture, can be enjoyed on both of these walks. The first takes the visitor through the streets of the Jordaan, a peaceful quarter known for its narrow, pretty canals, houseboats and traditional architecture. The route winds through to the man-made Western Islands of Bickerseiland, Realeneiland and Prinseneiland, built in the 17th century to accommodate the expansion in Amsterdam's overseas trade. The area, with its rows of warehouses and wharves, is a reminder of the city's erstwhile supremacy at sea. The city's maritime heritage is also evident on the second walk, which starts off from the Schreierstoren, where women waved their husbands off to sea in the 17th century, and finishes at the Nederlands Scheepvaart Museum. On the way, the walk passes the original city boundaries, countless converted warehouses and along streets named after the spices brought in by the East India Company (VOC). On any weekday, there is also the opportunity to spend a few pleasurable hours browsing round the Waterlooplein flea market.

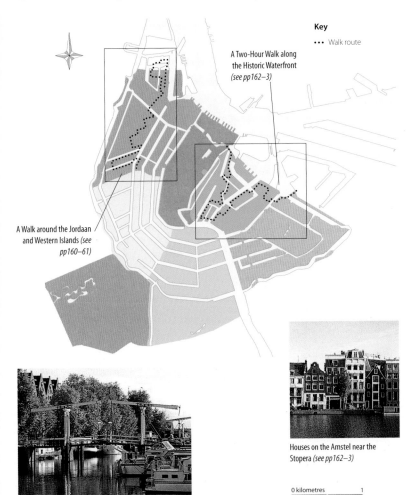

Key

••• Walk route

A Two-Hour Walk along the Historic Waterfront *(see pp162–3)*

A Walk around the Jordaan and Western Islands *(see pp160–61)*

Houses on the Amstel near the Stopera *(see pp162–3)*

0 kilometres 1

0 miles 0.5

The Drieharingenbrug across Prinsengracht *(see pp160–61)*

◄ Westerkerk overlooking the Prinsengracht canal

A Walk around the Jordaan and Western Islands

The Jordaan is a tranquil part of the city, crammed with canal houses, old and new galleries, restaurants, craft shops and pavement cafés. The walk route meanders through narrow streets and along enchanting canals. It starts from the Westerkerk and continues past Brouwersgracht, up to the IJ river and on to the Western Islands. These islands have now been adopted by the bohemian artistic community as a fashionable area in which to live and work.

Plaque on No. 8 Zandhoek, a former sailors' hostel

Prinsengracht to Westerstraat

Outside Hendrick de Keyser's Westerkerk ① *(see p92)* turn left up Prinsengracht, past the Anne Frank House ② *(see p92)*, and cross over the canal. Turn left down the opposite side of Prinsengracht and walk along Bloemgracht – the prettiest canal in the Jordaan. Before crossing the second bridge, look out for the three identical canal houses called the Drie Hendricken (the three Henrys) ③ *(see p93)*. Continue up 3e Leliedwarsstraat, lined with an eclectic mix of old and modern gables, turn right and walk past the St Andrieshofje ④, one of the numerous well-preserved almshouses in the city. It is worth pausing to take a look across Egelantiersgracht at No. 360, a rare example of an Art Nouveau canal house.

Follow the bank to the end, turn left on to Prinsengracht, passing the Café 't Smalle, and turn left into Egelantiersstraat. In 1e Egelantiersdwarsstraat can be

Ornate step gables (1642) at Nos. 89 and 91 Bloemgracht

found a group of 17th-century almshouses, known as the Claes Claeszhofje ⑤ *(see p94)*. Follow this tiny street past several cafés as well as many unusual shops selling clothes, bric-a-brac, pottery and paintings, to Westerstraat.

Simple wooden gable with hoisting hook on Westerstraat

Westerstraat to Bickerseiland

Cross the street – Westerstraat originally bordered a canal, now filled in – and turn right. The gabled houses are typical of the late-17th-century style of the Jordaan. Walk along for one block and take the first left into 1e Boomdwarsstraat, then right to the Noorderkerk ⑥ *(see p94)*. Each Monday morning, a lively flea market takes place in the Noordermarkt *(see p94)*. Continue on to the south side

of the Lindengracht. To the left, at Nos. 149–163, is the Suyckerhofje ⑦, a former refuge for abandoned women. Turn right and you will pass a wall plaque on No. 55 Lindengracht depicting fish swimming in trees and echoing an inverted view of houses reflected in the city's canals. The statue on Lindengracht is of the writer and educationalist, Theo Thijssen. Turn left down Brouwersgracht *(see p95)*, which is lined with colourful houseboats. Cross the first lift bridge and go into Binnen Oranjestraat, then under the railway bridge on to Bickerseiland, which is named after one of the city's most wealthy 17th-century families.

Key

• • • Walk route

0 metres 200
0 yards 200

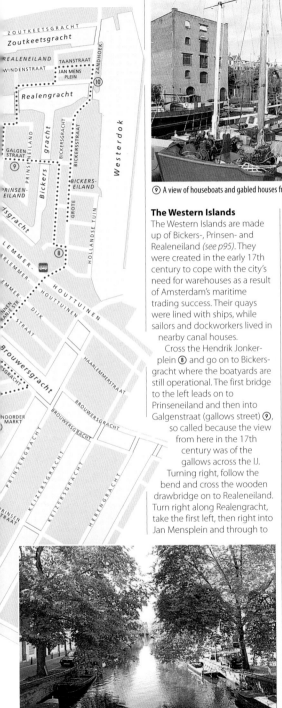

⑨ A view of houseboats and gabled houses from Galgenstraat

The Western Islands

The Western Islands are made up of Bickers-, Prinsen- and Realeneiland *(see p95)*. They were created in the early 17th century to cope with the city's need for warehouses as a result of Amsterdam's maritime trading success. Their quays were lined with ships, while sailors and dockworkers lived in nearby canal houses.

Cross the Hendrik Jonker-plein **⑧** and go on to Bickersgracht where the boatyards are still operational. The first bridge to the left leads on to Prinseneiland and then into Galgenstraat (gallows street) **⑨**, so called because the view from here in the 17th century was of the gallows across the IJ. Turning right, follow the bend and cross the wooden drawbridge on to Realeneiland. Turn right along Realengracht, take the first left, then right into Jan Mensplein and through to

Taanstraat, first looking back along Vierwindenstraat where there stands a series of sombre old warehouses, once used for storing grain, hemp and flax. At the end, turn right down Zandhoek (sand corner) **⑩** *(see p95)*, with its rows of charming 17th-century houses. The name originates from the sand market which once took place here.

Follow Zandhoek and cross the wooden bridge (a 1983 replica of the original). Stay on the canal and follow the footpath that runs along Bickersgracht. Keep your eyes on the water and you might see a blue-grey heron looking for fish. Walk along Grote Bickersstraat and you will find yourself back where you started, at the bridge leading on to Prinseneiland. To leave the islands and return to the city centre, retrace your steps to Haarlemerdijk and turn left.

Tips for Walkers

Starting point: Outside the Westerkerk on the Prinsengracht.
Length: 4.5 km (2.8 miles).
Duration: One and a half hours.
Getting there: Buses 142, 144, 170 and 172. Trams 13 and 17 from Centraal Station.
Stopping-off points: The Jordaan is packed with cafés and bars. On the Egelantiersgracht, 't Smalle is particularly atmospheric and there are bars in Noordermarkt, Haarlemmerdijk and Hendrik Jonkerplein. De Gouden Reael in Zandhoek is ideal to rest in before the trip home.

The tranquil, tree-lined Egelantiersgracht

A Two-Hour Walk along the Historic Waterfront

Begin the walk at the Schreierstoren *(see p69)*, once a defence tower in the medieval town wall. The route follows the development of Amsterdam as a great trading city, as wharves, warehouses and houses were built to accommodate the boom in overseas trade and in population. The city's expansion was carefully planned; as existing waterfronts became overcrowded, more islands were created to the east, slowly reclaiming the surrounding marshy countryside. The walk takes in a number of reminders of the Dutch East India Company (VOC) *(see pp30–31)*, such as the streets named after spices, and ends up at the imposing Het Scheepvaartmuseum.

① 16th-century stone tablet near the main door, Schreierstoren

Gables and façades along the right bank of Kromme Waal

Schreierstoren to St Antoniesbreestraat

From the Schreierstoren ①, walk along Prins Hendrikkade, turning at Kromme Waal and following the right bank, with its series of rich façades and gables, to Lastageweg ②. Lastage is an area which was developed for trade after the fire of 1452 *(see p25)*. The expansion which followed in the 16th century *(see p27)* brought Lastage within the city walls.

Continue to Recht Boomssloot and turn right and keep going until you reach Geldersekade, one of the town boundaries in the 15th century. Follow along Recht Boomssloot, then along the side of Krom Boomssloot, until you see the Schottenburch warehouses ③ at Nos. 18–20. Built in 1636, these are among the oldest in the city and are now converted into apartments. Next door is an Armenian church, converted from a warehouse in the mid-18th century. Then follow Snoekjesgracht, turning left into St Antoniesbreestraat ④.

St Antoniesbreestraat to Uilenburg Island

On St Antoniesbreestraat, cross the road at Elias Bouwman's Pintohuis ⑤ *(see p68)*, the only surviving building from the original street. Enter the Zuiderkerk ⑥ yard opposite through its skull-adorned gateway. The church was built by Hendrick de Keyser *(see p92)* in 1603 and now hosts a permanent exhibition on various aspects of urban renewal. Cross the

Lift bridge on Staalstraat, crossing Groenburgwal

| 0 metres | | 200 |
| 0 yards | | 200 |

Key

••• Walk route

square and continue to Zandstraat. Continue on to Kloveniersburgwal and turn left along the canal on to Staalstraat, where another left turn takes you past the Saaihal ⑦ (the draper's hall), with its unusual trapezoid gable. The first bridge crosses the Groenburgwal, with splendid views of the Amstel to the right and Zuiderkerk to the left. The next bridge leads to the Stopera ⑧ *(see p65)*, and Waterlooplein flea market ⑨ *(see p65)*. Follow the market stalls and half way along turn left towards

Wall plaque at Museum Het Rembrandthuis

Jodenbreestraat, transformed since it was the heart of Jewish Amsterdam. To the left on Jodenbreestraat is the Museum Het Rembrandthuis ⑩ *(see p64)*. Cross the road and continue on to Nieuwe Uilenburgerstraat and on to the island of Uilenburg, built in the late 16th century to provide housing for the poor. On the right can be seen the vast Gassan Diamonds factory ⑪, with two synagogues in the yard, a reminder of the time when diamond polishing was one of the few trades open to Jews.

Uilenburg to the Eastern Islands

Turn left into Nieuwe Batavierstraat and then right at Oude Schans, a broad canal with former warehouses and quays full of eccentric-looking houseboats. On

⑫ The 16th-century Montelbaanstoren, part of the city defences

streets on these man-made islands, Peperstraat was named after a commodity imported by the VOC *(see pp30–31)* in the 17th century. From here, turn right onto the main road of Prins Hendrikkade and then into Nieuwe Foeliestraat. Turn left onto Rapenburg, then left again onto Rapenburger Plein. Take the bridge across Nieuwe Herengracht to the gateway of the Entrepotdok ⑬ *(see p146)*. Turn left into Kadijksplein, continue along Prins Hendrikkade and across the Nieuwevaart bridge from which you can see Daniel Stalpaert's Oosterkerk. Continue on to the Eastern Islands, built in 1658 to create more shipyards. Het Scheepvaartmuseum ⑭ *(see pp148–9)* dominates the Oosterdok to the left. To return to the centre, follow Prins Hendrikkade westwards.

Oosterdok

Oosterdok

the opposite bank of the canal is the Montelbaanstoren ⑫ *(see p68)*, an old defence tower. At the bend, cross over the Rapenburgwal bridge until you reach Peperstraat. Like other

Tips for Walkers

Starting point: The Schreierstoren on Prins Hendrikkade.
Length: 6 km (4 miles).
Duration: 2 hours.
Getting there: Some buses go along Prins Hendrikkade, but it is easier to take a tram to Centraal Station *(see p81)* and walk along the IJ. To pick up the walk halfway, trams 9 and 14 go to Waterlooplein.
Stopping-off points: There are brown cafés *(see pp50 and 232)* along the start of the walk and at the Stopera *(see p65)*. There are also bars on Schippersgracht and within the Entrepotdok.

⑨ Antiques and bric-a-brac at Waterlooplein flea market

Flowering bulbs, Keukenhof Gardens ▶

BEYOND AMSTERDAM

Amsterdam is at the heart of a region known as the Randstad, the economic powerhouse of the Netherlands. The city is a haven for tourists; within easy reach are the ancient towns of Leiden and Utrecht, as well as Den Haag and Haarlem with their exceptional galleries and museums. The Randstad extends south as far as Rotterdam, a thriving modern city full of avant-garde architecture.

Much of the land comprising the Randstad has been reclaimed from the sea during the last 300 years, and the fertile soil is farmed intensively. Production is centred around early season greenhouse crops, like tomatoes and cucumbers and the incomparable Dutch bulbs. Spreading to the southwest in spring, dazzling colours carpet the fields, and the exquisite gardens at Keukenhof (see p183) are the showcase of the bulb industry.

Reclamation continues apace, and Flevoland, the Netherlands' newest province, consists entirely of polder. This flat marshy land, interspersed with drainage channels, has been created since 1950 by draining 1,800 sq km (695 sq miles) of the IJsselmeer. The

flat terrain provides shelter for wild birds such as herons, swans and grebes, which nest along the reed-fringed canals. The area beyond Utrecht, to the east of Amsterdam, is much less populated than the Randstad, with vast tracts of unspoilt forest, moorland and peat bog, home to red deer and wild boar.

North of Amsterdam, the traditional fishing communities that depended on the Zuiderzee before it was closed off from the sea in 1932 (see p172–3), have now turned to tourism for their income.

The coast round Zandvoort, lying to the west of Amsterdam, takes the full brunt of vicious North Sea storms in winter, but maritime vegetation and wild birds find shelter among the sandbanks of the exposed coastline.

Lift bridge and canalside café at Enkhuizen – a popular haunt for visitors to the Zuiderzee Museum

◀ A windmill near Alkmaar, north west of Amsterdam

Exploring the Netherlands

Amsterdam is at the centre of a part of the Netherlands where there are many places of interest within easy reach. Haarlem is just 15 minutes away, and it takes less than half an hour to get to the cheese markets of Edam and Gouda. To the north, the Zuiderzee Museum recreates an old fishing community, and to the south lies historic Utrecht. The east offers the wilderness of the Nationale Park De Hoge Veluwe, and the stately Paleis Het Loo, a hunting lodge and summer residence of the Dutch royal family since 1692.

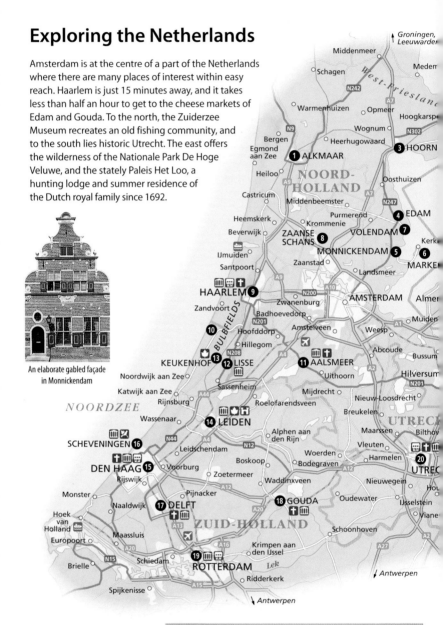

An elaborate gabled façade
in Monnickendam

Suspension bridge crossing the Maas river at Rotterdam

Key

≡ Motorway
▬ Major road
∷∷ Minor road
·▬· Main railway
— Minor railway
≡ Provincial border

For map symbols *see back flap*

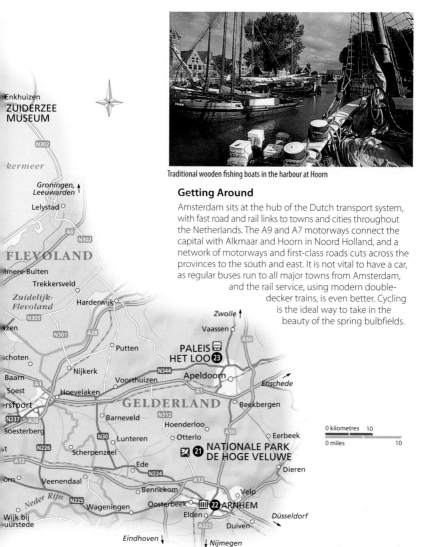

Traditional wooden fishing boats in the harbour at Hoorn

Getting Around

Amsterdam sits at the hub of the Dutch transport system, with fast road and rail links to towns and cities throughout the Netherlands. The A9 and A7 motorways connect the capital with Alkmaar and Hoorn in Noord Holland, and a network of motorways and first-class roads cuts across the provinces to the south and east. It is not vital to have a car, as regular buses run to all major towns from Amsterdam, and the rail service, using modern double-decker trains, is even better. Cycling is the ideal way to take in the beauty of the spring bulbfields.

Catamarans at Scheveningen

Sights at a Glance

Renaissance façade and bell tower of
Alkmaar's Waaggebouw (1582)

❶ Alkmaar

40 km (25 miles) NW of Amsterdam.
🚗 94,000. 🚉 ℹ️ Waaggebouw,
Waagplein 2–3. (072) 511 4284. 📷
🧀 cheese market: Apr–1st Fri in Sep:
10am–12:30pm Fri; main market: Sat.
🌐 vvvhartvannoordholland.nl

Alkmaar is an attractive old town
with tree-lined canals and an
historic centre, scene of an
unsuccessful siege by the
Spanish in 1573. It is one of the
few Dutch towns to maintain its
traditional cheese market, held
every Friday in summer. Local
producers lay out Gouda cheeses
and some rounds of Edam in
the Waagplein, and from here
porters take them off on sledges
for weighing. The porters, who
sport colourful straw hats,
belong to an ancient guild and
indulge in good-natured rivalry.

The streets around the
Waagplein are packed with stalls
that sell everything from cheese
to locally made pottery.

🏛 Waaggebouw
Waagplein 2. **Tel** (072) 515 5516.
Hollands Kaasmuseum: **Open** Apr–
Oct: 10am–4pm Mon–Sat; Nov–Mar:
10am–4pm Sat. **Closed** 27 Apr.
♿ 🌐 kaasmuseum.nl

The focal point of the cheese
market is the imposing Waaggebouw (weigh house), which was
altered in 1576 from a 14th-
century chapel. It now
contains the Hollandse
Kaasmuseum, where
local cheese-making
techniques are revealed. On
the hour, mechanical knights,
under the clock of the Waaggebouw, stage a jousting
tournament, as a clarion
blower sounds his trumpet.

🏛 Grote Kerk
Kerkplein, Koorstraat 2.
Tel (072) 514 0707.
Open mid-Apr–May:
10am–4pm Thu–Sat; Jun–
Aug: 10am–4pm Tue–Sun.
🌐 grotekerk-alkmaar.nl

This imposing Gothic church
contains the tomb of Floris V (see
p23), whose body was exhumed
and brought here when the
building was completed in 1520.
The 17th-century organ, built
after designs by Jacob van
Campen (see p76) and painted
by Cesar van Everdingen,
dominates the Grote Kerk's nave.

Painted unicorn,
Westfries Museum

❷ Zuiderzee Museum

See pp172–3.

❸ Hoorn

40 km (25 miles) N of Amsterdam.
🚗 68,000. 🚉 ℹ️ Roode Steen 1.
(072) 511 4284. 🧀 Sat; mid-Jun–Aug:
Wed (for tourists). 🌐 vvvhoorn.nl

Hoorn was the capital of the
ancient province of West Friesland and one of the great
seafaring towns of the
Golden Age (see pp28–31).
The collection of ornate
patrician houses
around Roode Steen,
Hoorn's main square,
attests to the town's
prosperous history.
Several famous
maritime heroes were
born here, including
Willem Schouten
(1580–1625), who
named the tip of
South America
Cape Horn after his
birthplace, and Abel
Tasman (see pp30–31). A statue
in Roode Steen commemorates
Jan Pietersz Coen (1587–1629),
a famous explorer who went on
to found Batavia, now known as
Jakarta, the capital of Indonesia
(see pp30–31).

🏛 Westfries Museum
Roode Steen 1. **Tel** (0229) 280 022.
Open 11am–5pm Tue–Fri (also Mon
Apr–Oct), 1–5pm Sat & Sun.
Closed 1 Jan, 27 Apr, 3rd Mon in Aug,
25 Dec. ♿ 🌐 wfm.nl

The Westfries Museum, in the
beautiful Statencollege (1632),
was built to house an assembly
of representatives of the seven
principal towns of West
Friesland. The richly adorned
17th-century façade bears the
regional coats of arms.
  Within the imposing halls,
intimate chambers, cellars and
loft with prison cells, Hoorn's
rich past is detailed by a series
of themed rooms, each one
highlighting a star exhibit. There
is much to enjoy here, from
archaeological displays to
17th-century rooms filled with
furniture and antique clocks.

Porters carrying cheese on sledges in Alkmaar's traditional market

Wooden clogs outside a restored fisherman's cottage in Monnickendam

❹ Edam

22 km (14 miles) N of Amsterdam.
🏠 7,200. 🚌 *i* Damplein 1. (0299)
315 125. 🧀 cheese market: Jul–mid-Aug: 10:30am–12:30pm Wed; general market: every Wed. 🔳 **vvv-edam.nl**

The name of Edam is known throughout the world for its ball-shaped cheeses wrapped in wax – red for export, and yellow for local consumption. In the summer, cheese lovers should head for the *kaasmarkt* (cheese market), held in the main square, which is called Jan van Nieuwenhuizenplein. The *kaasmarkt's* single-gabled weigh house dates from 1592 and has a gaudy painted façade. Cheese-making is now an automated process and some factories around the outskirts of the town offer guided tours for visitors.

Edam itself is exceptionally pretty, full of narrow canals bordered by elegant, gabled Golden Age canal houses and crossed by wooden lift bridges. The imposing Grote Kerk is noted both for its 16th-century carillon, and its outstandingly beautiful stained-glass windows (1606–24). The harbour to the east of the town was built in the 17th century, in the days when Edam was a prominent whaling centre.

🏛 Edams Museum

Damplein 8. **Tel** (0299) 372 644.
Open Apr–Oct: 10am–4:30pm Tue–Sat, noon–4:30pm Sun. **Closed** 27 Apr. 🅿 🔳 **edamsmuseum.nl**

The former town hall (1737) and a nearby merchant's house (1530) are home to the eclectic collection of the Edams Museum. The house, with its steep stairs and half-timbered interior, is said to have been built for a retired sea captain who could not bear sleeping on dry land. The unusual floating cellar has a floor that rises and falls with fluctuations in the water table. Just as strange are the 17th-century portraits of odd-looking locals, such as Trijntje Keever, who was said to be almost 2.8 m (9 ft) tall.

❺ Monnickendam

16 km (10 miles) N of Amsterdam.
🏠 10,000. 🚌 *i* Zuideinde 2. (0299) 820 046. 🧀 Sat. 🔳 **vvv-waterland.nl**

Visitors flock to this beautifully preserved port to admire the gabled houses and the renovated fishermen's cottages in the narrow streets around the harbour. Freshly smoked local eel can be bought here, and the fish restaurants are a popular draw for tourists.

The **Waterlandsmuseum de Speeltoren** is dedicated to the history of Monnickendam. It is housed in the clock tower of the Stadhuis, with its ornate 15th-century carillon. When bells chime the hour, the clockwork knights in armour parade around the tower.

🏛 Waterlandsmuseum de Speeltoren

Noordeinde 4. **Tel** (0299) 652 203.
Open Apr–Oct: 11am–5pm Tue–Sat; Nov–Mar: 11am–5pm Sat & Sun.
🅿 🔳 **despeeltoren.nl**

Lift bridge on one of the canals at Edam

❷ Zuiderzeemuseum

Enkhuizen was one of several villages around the edge of the Zuiderzee whose fishing-based economy was devastated when access to the North Sea was blocked by construction of the Afsluitdijk in 1932 *(see p167)*. The village's fortunes were revived with the opening of this museum complex. The binnenmuseum (indoor museum) focuses on the Zuiderzee history, including an impressive display of historic boats. The buitenmuseum (open-air museum) consists of rescued buildings, reconstructed to create a typical Zuiderzee village, with demonstrations of local crafts.

★ **Houses from Urk**
Buildings from the little island of Urk have been rebuilt in the open-air museum. Daily life on the island in 1905 is recreated by actors in role play.

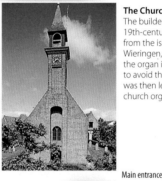

The Church
The builders of this late 19th-century church, from the island of Wieringen, disguised the organ in a cupboard to avoid the tax that was then levied on church organs.

★ **Marine Hall**
Housed in an old warehouse of the Dutch East India Company *(see pp30–31)*, the indoor museum's Marine Hall contains sailing and fishing boats. A small pleasure boat is rigged up for children to play in.

Main entrance

Lime Kilns
Bottle-shaped kilns were used to burn shells dredged from the sea bed. The resulting quicklime was used as an ingredient in mortar for bricklaying. These kilns are from Akersloot in Noord Holland.

★ **Contemporary Delft blue design**
Modern Dutch culture is presented on traditional Delft blue tiles in this installation by Hugo Kaagman. Icons such as the Internet Explorer sign are scattered throughout the piece.

VISITORS' CHECKLIST

Practical Information
Wierdijk, Enkhuizen; 50 km (31 miles) NE of Amsterdam. **Tel** (0228) 351 111. Indoor museum: **Open** 10am–5pm daily. **Closed** 25 Dec. Open-air museum: **Open** Apr–Oct: 10am–5pm daily. **Closed** Nov–Mar. 🅿️ ♿ 🚻 📷 **w** zuiderzeemuseum.nl.

Transport
🚉 Enkhuizen. 🚌 leaves from behind train station.

Fish Smoking
Herrings, the main catch of the former Zuiderzee, are preserved by smoking them over smouldering woodchips. They are then ready for visitors to eat.

0 metres 50
0 yards 50

KEY

① **Barges** carry visitors to the open-air museum.

② **Smoke-houses from Monnickendam**

③ **Reconstruction of Marken harbour**

④ **Shed for refitting barges**

⑤ **A working windmill** shows how excess water was cleared from the dykes to create polders (see pp26–7).

⑥ **Houses brought from the nearby island of Urk**

⑦ **Houses in this area** are from Zoutkamp, a fishing village once on the Zuiderzee.

Keeping House in 1930
In this interactive exhibition, a 1930s "housewife" sits down with visitors and describes her daily life over a cup of tea.

⑥ Marken

16 km (10 miles) NE of Amsterdam.
🏘 2,000. 🚌 🚢 𝒊 (0299) 820 046.
🛒 Sat. **W** vvv-waterland.nl

Marken was once an island fishing community that had changed very little over 200 years. However, the construction of a causeway link between the village and the mainland in 1957 brought an abrupt end to its isolation.

The village is popular with tourists, who are drawn here by its old-world character. The locals sometimes wear traditional dress, and the gabled timber houses are painted in shades of black and green.

Marken's transition from fishing community to tourist centre is neatly symbolized by the **Marker Museum**, which consists of six historical houses, one of which is furnished as a traditional fisherman's abode.

🏛 Marker Museum
Kerkbuurt 44. **Tel** (0299) 601 904.
Open Apr–Sep: 10am–5pm daily (from noon Sun); Oct: 11am–4pm Mon–Sat, noon–5pm Sun. 🦽

Yachts and pleasure boats in Volendam's marina

⑦ Volendam

18 km (11 miles) NE of Amsterdam.
🏘 21,000. 🚌 𝒊 Zeestraat 37.
(0299) 363 747. 🛒 Sat.
W vvv-volendam.nl

The harbour in Volendam is overrun with tourists, but the village is still worth exploring for the narrow canals and streets behind the main dykes, an area known as the Doolhof. The residents wear traditional costume: tight bodices, winged lace caps and striped aprons for the women; baggy trousers and jerseys for the men.

Artists flocked to Volendam in the late 19th century to paint views of this pretty town. Many stayed at the Spaander Hotel at No. 15 Haven, and the walls of the hotel's café are covered with paintings accepted by the owners in lieu of payment.

⑧ Zaanse Schans

Schansend 7, Zaandam 13 km (8 miles) N of Amsterdam. 🚉 Koog-Zaandijk. 🚌 391 (Centraal Station).
🏘 50. 𝒊 Zaandam. **Tel** (075) 681 0000. **Open** 9am–5pm daily. **Closed** 1 Jan, 25 Dec. 🦽 for some buildings and parking. **W** zaanseschans.nl

Part of the town of Zaandam, Zaanse Schans was created in 1960 as a monument to village life in the 17th century. Shops, cottages, windmills, houses and historic buildings from all over the Zaan region have been relocated here to create a museum village in which people can live and work.

The local community is dedicated to preserving the traditional Dutch way of life, and Zaanse Schans is run as a piece of living history. The inhabitants operate the carefully restored windmills themselves. Of the 1,000 windmills found in the region, 13 have been preserved and ten are found on the Zaanse Schans. These include a mustard mill, an oil mill and a mill for sawing logs for building timber.

In summer, cruises can be taken in open-topped boats along the surrounding dykes. They depart on the hour from next to the mustard mill and take around 50 minutes.

A typical 17th-century gabled timber house in Marken

Windmill Technology

Windmills have been a familiar feature of the Dutch landscape since the 13th century. They had many uses, including grinding corn, crushing seed to make oil and driving sawmills. However, as much of the Netherlands lies below sea level, their most vital function was to drain the land of lakes and marshes, and extend the shoreline to create fertile farmland called polder. Subsequently, the windmills have had to cope with the constant threat of flooding. To help prevent this, canals were dug to drain water from the soil; the mills then pumped excess water via a series of stepped canals until it drained into the main river system. Today, most land drainage is carried out by electric pumps driven by wind turbines. Of the thousands of windmills that once dotted the Dutch countryside, about 950 survive, many preserved in working order.

Modern aerogenerators, or wind turbines, are widely used in the Netherlands. They harness strong gusts of wind to create electricity without the pollution caused by burning fossil fuels such as gas or coal.

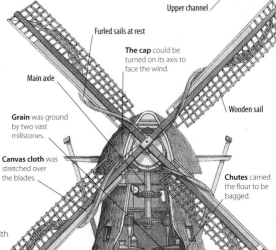

Trelliswork and canvas sail

Smock mills, shaped like peasants' smocks, were drainage mills used, from the 17th century, in groups known as gangs. The Archimedes' screw rotated to force the water upwards.

Drive shaft

Archimedes' screw

Upper channel

Furled sails at rest

The cap could be turned on its axis to face the wind.

Main axle

Wooden sail

Grain was ground by two vast millstones.

Canvas cloth was stretched over the blades.

Chutes carried the flour to be bagged.

The sails of this traditional windmill transmit power via mechanical gears. A rotating cog operates an adjacent wheel to drive the water pump.

Flour mills, thatched with reeds and shaped like giant pepperpots, were vital to Dutch daily life. Sophisticated internal mechanisms were used to grind the wheat, barley and oats which formed the basis of the community's diet.

⑨ Street-by-Street: Haarlem

Haarlem is the commercial capital of Noord Holland province and the eighth largest city in the Netherlands. It is the centre of the Dutch printing, pharmaceutical and bulb-growing industries, but there is little sign of this in the delightful pedestrianized streets of the historic heart of the city. Most of the sites of interest are within easy walking distance of the Grote Markt, a lively square packed with ancient buildings, cafés and restaurants. Old bookshops, antique dealers and traditional food shops are all to be discovered in nearby streets.

Statue of Laurens Coster
According to local legend, Haarlem-born Laurens Jansz Coster (1370–1440) invented printing in 1423, 16 years before Gutenberg. The 19th-century statue in the Grote Markt celebrates the claim.

No. 31 Nieuwe Groenmarkt is a quaint restaurant called "Ma Brown".

The Hoofd-wacht is a 17th-century, former guard house.

SMEDESTRAAT

BARTELJORISSTRAAT

KONINGSTRAAT

G R O T E
M A R K T

GR. HOUTSTR.

LEPELSTRAAT

Stadhuis
Lieven de Key's allegorical figure of *Justice* (1622) stands above the main entrance. She carries a sword and the scales of justice.

Vleeshal (1603)
The old meat market is part of the Frans Hals Museum *(see pp180–81)*.

Grote Markt
The tree-lined market square is bordered with busy pavement restaurants and cafés. It has been the meeting point for the townspeople for centuries.

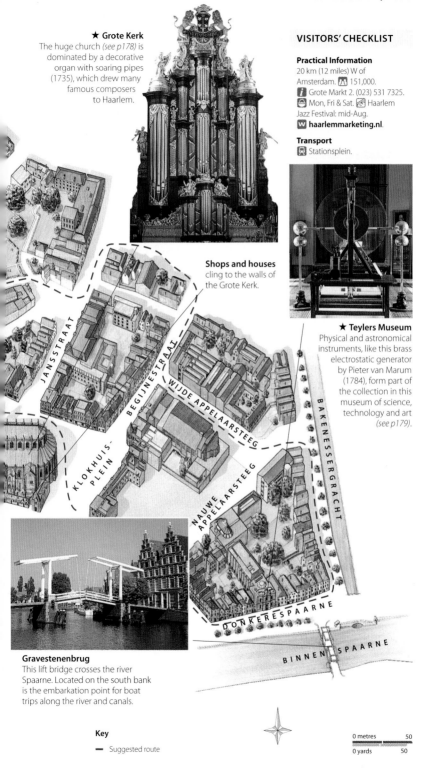

★ Grote Kerk
The huge church *(see p178)* is dominated by a decorative organ with soaring pipes (1735), which drew many famous composers to Haarlem.

Shops and houses cling to the walls of the Grote Kerk.

VISITORS' CHECKLIST

Practical Information
20 km (12 miles) W of Amsterdam. 🅼 151,000.
ℹ️ Grote Markt 2. (023) 531 7325.
🗓️ Mon, Fri & Sat. 🎷 Haarlem Jazz Festival: mid-Aug.
🆆 haarlemmarketing.nl.

Transport
🚉 Stationsplein.

★ Teylers Museum
Physical and astronomical instruments, like this brass electrostatic generator by Pieter van Marum (1784), form part of the collection in this museum of science, technology and art *(see p179)*.

JANSSTRAAT

BEGIJNESTRAAT

WIJDE APPELAARSTEEG

KLOKHUIS-PLEIN

NAUWE APPELAARSTEEG

BAKENESSERGRACHT

DONKERESPAARNE

BINNEN SPAARNE

Gravestenenbrug
This lift bridge crosses the river Spaarne. Located on the south bank is the embarkation point for boat trips along the river and canals.

Key

— Suggested route

| 0 metres | 50 |
| 0 yards | 50 |

Exploring Haarlem

Haarlem became a city in 1245, and had grown into a thriving cloth-making centre by the 15th century. But in the Spanish siege of 1572–3 the city was sacked, and a series of fires wreaked further destruction in 1576. The town's fortunes changed in the 17th century, when industrial expansion ushered in a period of prosperity lasting throughout the Golden Age *(see pp28–31)*. The centre was largely rebuilt by Lieven de Key (1560–1627) and still retains much of its character. The Grote Kerk continues to overlook the city's *hofjes* (almshouses), and the brick-paved lanes around the Grote Markt are little changed.

Grote Markt, Haarlem (c.1668) by Berckheyde, showing the Grote Kerk

🏛 Frans Hals Museum
See pp180–81.

⛪ Grote Kerk
Grote Markt 22. **Tel** (023) 553 2040. **Open** 10am–4pm Mon–Sat (Apr–Sep: to 5pm). **Closed** 25 Dec–2 Jan, Easter, Whitsun, 5 May, 27 Apr. 🚻 ♿
W bavo.nl

The enormous Gothic edifice of Sint Bavo's great church, often referred to simply as the Grote Kerk, was a favourite subject of the 17th-century Haarlem School artists Pieter Saenredam (1597–1665) and Gerrit Berckheyde (1639–98). Built between 1400 and 1550, the church and its ornate bell tower dominate the market square. The construction of a stone tower commenced in 1502, but the pillars started to subside and the tower was demolished. A new wooden tower, covered in lead, was erected and finished in 1520. Clinging on to the exterior of the south wall is a jumble of 17th-century shops and houses. The rents raised from them helped to maintain the church.

The church has a high, delicately patterned, vaulted cedarwood ceiling, white upper walls, and 28 supporting columns. The intricate choir screen, like the magnificent brass lectern in the shape of a preening eagle, was made by master metal worker Jan Fyerens in about 1510. The choirstalls (1512) are painted with coats of arms, and the armrests and misericords are carved with caricatures of animals and human heads. Not far away is the simple stone slab covering the grave of Haarlem's most famous artist, Frans Hals.

The Grote Kerk boasts one of Europe's finest and most flamboyant organs, built in 1738 by Christiaan Müller. In 1740 Handel tried the organ and pronounced it excellent. It found favour with the infant prodigy Mozart, who shouted for joy when he gave a recital on it in 1766. The organ is still used for concerts, recordings and teaching.

🏛 Stadhuis
Grote Markt 2. **Tel** (023) 511 5115. **Open** by appt only. ♿

Haarlem's Stadhuis (town hall) has grown rather haphazardly over the centuries and is an odd mixture of architectural styles dating from 1250. The oldest part of the building is the beamed medieval banqueting hall of the counts of Holland *(see p23)*, originally known as the Gravenzaal. Much of this was destroyed in two great fires in 1347 and 1351, but the 15th-century panel portraits of the counts of Holland can still be seen.

The wing of the town hall bordering the Grote Markt was designed by Lieven de Key in 1622. It is typical of Dutch Renaissance architecture, combining elaborate gables, ornate painted detail and Classical features, such as pediments over the windows.

In a niche above the main entrance is a plump allegorical figure of Justice, bearing a sword in one hand and scales in the other as she smiles benignly upon the pavement cafés in the market below. To the left, in Koningstraat, an archway leads to the university buildings behind the Stadhuis, where there is a 13th-century cloister and library.

🏛 De Hallen Haarlem (Vleeshal and Verweyhal)
Grote Markt 16. **Tel** (023) 511 5775. **Open** as Frans Hals Museum *(p181)*. **Closed** 1 Jan, 25 Dec. 🚻
W dehallen.nl

De Hallen Haarlem (the halls) is the collective name for two buildings in the Grote Markt which are part of the Frans Hals Museum *(see pp180–81)*. The Verweyhal accommodates exhibitions of Dutch Expressionism, the Cobra School, Impressionism and contemporary works. It is named after the painter Kees Verwey, whose Impressionist still lifes are an

Detail on Vleeshal façade by Lieven de Key

The west gate of the Amsterdamse Poort (1355)

important feature of the collection. The heavily ornamented Vleeshal (meat market) is situated just to the west of the church and houses temporary exhibitions of modern art. It was built in 1602 by the city surveyor, Lieven de Key, and has a steep step gable which disguises the roof line. The extravagantly over-decorated miniature gables above each dormer window bristle with pinnacles. A giant painted ox's head on the building's façade signifies its original function.

🎭 Amsterdamse Poort

Nr Amsterdamsevaart. **Closed** to public.

The imposing medieval gateway that once helped protect Haarlem lies close to the west bank of the river Spaarne.

The Amsterdamse Poort was one of a complex of 12 gates guarding strategic transport routes in and out of Haarlem. The gate was built in 1355, though much of the elaborate brickwork and tiled gables date from the late 15th century.

The city defences were severely tested in 1573, when the Spanish, led by Frederick of Toledo, besieged Haarlem for seven months during the Dutch Revolt *(see pp26–7)*. The city fathers agreed to surrender the town on terms that included a general amnesty for all its citizens. The Spanish appeared to accept, but once inside they slaughtered nearly 2,000 people – almost the entire population of the city.

🏛 Teylers Museum

Spaarne 16. **Tel** (023) 516 0960. **Open** 10am–5pm Tue–Sat, noon–5pm Sun & holidays. **Closed** 1 Jan, 25 Dec. ♿ 🚻 📷 🆆 **teylersmuseum.eu**

This was the first major public museum to be founded in the Netherlands. It was established in 1778 by the silk merchant Pieter Teyler van der Hulst to encourage the study of science and art. The museum's eccentric collection of fossils, drawings and scientific paraphernalia is displayed in Neo-Classical splendour in a series of 18th-century rooms. The two-storey Oval Hall was added in 1779, and contains bizarre glass cabinets full of minerals and cases of intimidating medical instruments. A significant collection of sketches by Dutch and Italian masters are shown a

few at a time. There is also a multimedia room.

🏛 Museum Haarlem

Groot Heiligland 47. **Tel** (023) 542 2427. **Open** 11am–5pm Tue–Sat, noon–5pm Sun. **Closed** 1 Jan, Easter, Whitsun, 25 Dec. 🆆 **museumhaarlem.nl**

St Elisabeth's Gasthuis was built in 1610, around a pretty courtyard in one of Haarlem's most picturesque streets. A stone plaque carved above the main doorway in 1612 depicts an invalid being carried off to hospital. After extensive restoration, this almshouse was opened as Haarlem's principal historical museum.

Museum Haarlem is an inspiring museum focusing on the history of the city and its environs. Changing exhibitions connect the past with the present day making the museum the perfect starting point for exploring the city. The museum organizes walking tours too.

🚉 Haarlem Station

Stationsplein. **Tel** 0900 9292.

The first railway line in the Netherlands opened in 1839 and ran between Haarlem and Amsterdam *(see pp34–5)*. The original station, built in 1842, was reworked in Art Nouveau style between 1905–8. It is a grandiose brick building with an arched façade and square towers. The green and beige interior is decorated with brightly coloured tiles depicting modes of transport. Other highlights include the timberwork of the offices.

17th- and 18th-century gabled houses along the river Spaarne in Haarlem

Frans Hals Museum

Hailed as the first "modern" artist, Frans Hals (c.1582–1666) introduced a new realism into painting. While contemporary painters aimed for an exact likeness, Hals captured the character of his sitters through a more impressionistic technique. In his eighties, he still painted passionate portraits, such as *The Governesses of the Old Men's Home* (1664). The Old Men's Home, one of many in Haarlem, became the Frans Hals Museum in 1913. Besides his work, there is a selection of paintings and applied art from the 16th and 17th centuries by other Haarlem artists.

★ **Banquet of the Officers of the Civic Guard of St George (1616)**
The characteristics of each of the 12 Civic Guards and the opulence of their banqueting hall are superbly portrayed in this formal group portrait by Frans Hals.

The Market Square at Haarlem with the Great or St Bavo's Church, the Meat Market and the Fish Market (1696)
This painting by Gerrit Adriaensz Berckheyde depicts the old Vleeshal (meat market) and the fish market; both buildings date from 1603.

Hals's Civic Guard portraits

18th-century doll's house

★ **Still Life (1613)**
Precise attention to detail and texture was the hallmark of Floris van Dijck (1575–1651). The damask tablecloth shown in the painting was a product of Haarlem's thriving linen industry.

Key to Floorplan

- ☐ Works by Frans Hals
- ☐ Renaissance Gallery
- ▨ Old Masters
- ☐ The Hals Phenomenon
- ▣ Frans Hals' Workshop
- ▨ Non-exhibition space

Doll's House (c.1750)
This 11-room house, which belonged to Sara Rothé, is made to a scale of 1:10. Its representation is so realistic that it offers a good view into what it was like inside an 18th-century canalside mansion (see pp32–3).

VISITORS' CHECKLIST

Practical Information
Groot Heiligland 62, Haarlem.
Tel (023) 511 5775. **Open**
11am–5pm Tue–Sat; noon–5pm
Sun & public hols. **Closed** 1 Jan,
25 Dec. 🖼 🚻 🎫 📷 🏛 📷
W franshalsmuseum.nl

Transport
🚊 Haarlem.

★ Mercury (1611)
Hendrick Goltzius (1558–1617) painted a lot of biblical and mythological scenes. This canvas was commissioned by a wealthy Haarlem burgomaster as one of a series of three.

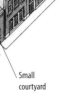

Small
courtyard

Main entrance

Museum Guide
The entrance leads into a modern wing with a museum shop. The best route is anti-clockwise; displays of Frans Hals' work, other portraits, still lifes and many other paintings are usually reordered each year. Exhibits of modern art are held in De Hallen Haarlem (Vleeshal and Verweyhal) which are in the Grote Markt (see p178).

Portrait of Cornelia Claesdr Vooght (1631)
Frans Hals's portrait of the wife of Nicolaes van der Meer, sheriff and officer of the civic guard, is painted in classic Baroque style. The prominent Haarlem couple are depicted in separate paintings, both of which can be seen here.

An Allegory on Tulip Mania (c. 1640)
Jan Breughel II's painting ridicules the obsession with tulips that was gripping Holland at the time.

⑩ A Tour of the Bulbfields

Occupying a 30-km (19-mile) strip between Haarlem and Leiden, the Bloembollenstreek is the main bulb-growing area in the Netherlands. From late January, the polders bloom with a series of vividly coloured bulbs, beginning with early crocuses and building to a climax around mid-April when the tulips flower. These are followed by late-blooming flowers like lilies, which extend the season into late May. If you don't have a car, the I amsterdam Visitor Centre *(see p255)* has details on a variety of tours. You can also hire a bicycle at Haarlem railway station, cycle to Leiden and take the bike back to Haarlem on the train.

Tips for Drivers

Starting point: Haarlem.
Length: Approx 30 km (19 miles).
Stopping-off points: In addition to the places named below, all of which have a selection of restaurants, cafés and bars, it is worth diverting to Noordwijk aan Zee. This lively seaside town, with its lovely dune-backed beach, is a perfect picnic spot. Good viewpoints en route are marked on the map.

Sand dunes lining the coast

③ Vogelenzang
The first nurseries in Vogelenzang were established in 1789 – the Frans Rozen nurseries (sadly they recently went bankrupt).

④ Keukenhof
Visitors to this park are greeted by the heady scents and brilliant colours of millions of bulbs in bloom.

① De Cruquius Museum
The museum contains exhibits that explain how polders and dams work and how they have kept sea and flood water at bay.

② Linnaeushof
Named after an 18th-century botanist, this huge park contains one of Europe's largest adventure playgrounds.

⑤ Lisse
There is a small bulb museum in Lisse and boat trips are available on Kager Plassen lake, nearby.

0 kilometres		5
0 miles	2.5	

Key

⸺ Tour route

⸱⸱⸱ Roads

⑦ Katwijk
A rare, early-17th-century lighthouse is situated just to the north of this seaside town, which stands at the mouth of the Oude Rijn.

⑥ Sassenheim
West of the town lie the remains of Burcht Teylingen, an 11th-century castle where Jacoba of Bavaria, the deposed Countess of Holland, died in 1436.

A tulip field in the Bloembollenstreek

Dutch Bulbs

The most cultivated bulbs in the Netherlands include gladioli, lilies, daffodils, hyacinths, irises, crocuses and dahlias. Tulips, however, are still far and away the country's most cultivated flower. Originally from Turkey, the tulip was first grown in Dutch soil by Carolus Clusius in 1593.

Aladdin tulips

China pink tulips

Tahiti daffodils

Minnow daffodils

Blue jacket hyacinths

An array of bulbs in flower in the wooded Keukenhof park

⓫ Aalsmeer

10 km (6 miles) south of Amsterdam.
🏠 23,000. 🚌 ℹ Zijdstraat 12. (0297) 324 454. 🚆 Tue. 🆆 **vvvaalsmeer.nl**

Aalsmeer is home to the world's largest flower auction, the Bloemenveiling FloraHolland (see www.floraholland.nl). Visitors can watch the proceedings from a viewing gallery above the trading floors. As the 3.5 billion cut flowers and 400 million pot plants sold here annually all have a short shelf life, speed is of the essence. A reverse auction is held. The price lowers as the big-screen auction clock counts down. Buyers can stop the clock at any price point and state the quantity they want. The price continues to drop until the entire lot is sold.

⓬ Lisse

35 km (22 miles) west of Amsterdam.
🏠 22,000. 🚌 ℹ Grachtweg 53. (0252) 414 262. 🆆 **vvvlisse.nl**

The best time to visit Lisse is at the end of April, when the Bloemencorso flower parade passes through the town.

The **Museum de Zwarte Tulp** (Black Tulip Museum) has displays on the history and life cycle of bulbs. Imported from Turkey in the early 17th century, by the mid-1630s "tulip mania" gripped the nation (see pp28–9). At the height of the boom, rare bulbs were sold for their weight in gold. By February 1637 however, the market had collapsed.

🏛 **Museum de Zwarte Tulp**
Grachtweg 2a. **Tel** (0252) 417 900.
Open 1–5pm Tue–Sun. **Closed** 1 Jan, Easter Sun, 27 Apr, Whitsun, last Thu in Sep, 5 Dec, 15 Dec–15 Jan. 🎟
🆆 **museumdezwartetulp.nl**

⓭ Keukenhof

Stationsweg, Lisse. **Tel** (0252) 465 555.
🚌 854 (Leiden Centraal Station) or 858 (from Schiphol airport). **Open** late Mar–mid-May: 8am–7:30pm daily (last adm 6pm). 🎟 combined ticket including bus fare available through website. 🆆 **keukenhof.nl**

Situated on the outskirts of Lisse, this flower garden was set up in 1949 as a showcase for Dutch bulb growers and is now planted with some 7 million bulbs. It is at its most spectacular from late March to late May, when drifts of daffodils, hyacinths or tulips are in bloom. The flowers are complemented by the snowy blossom of Japanese cherry trees early in the season, and by splashes of azaleas and rhododendrons later in the year.

⓮ Street-by-Street: Leiden

Leiden is a prosperous university town, with its origins in Roman times. It grew due to its position on a branch of the Rijn (Rhine) and is still an important commercial crossroads. During term-time, the streets are crowded with students cycling between lectures or packing the cafés and bookshops. A number of exceptional museums document Leiden's turbulent history, including the Golden Age, when the town was a centre for worldwide trade *(see pp30–31)*. The wall plaque on the façade of Rembrandt's house in Weddesteeg marks his birthplace in June 1606 *(see p64)*.

★ **Rijksmuseum van Oudheden**
This squat statue of a kneeling treasury scribe is among the many Egyptian artifacts in the museum.

John Robinson
(see p187) lived in the Jan Pesijnshofje.

★ **Hortus Botanicus**
The botanical gardens *(see p186)* are owned by Leiden University, and were laid out initially as a study aid for botany students in 1590.

LANGEBRUG

PAPENGRACHT

SCHOOLSTEEG

GERECHT

RAPENBURG

HOUTSTRAAT

KLOKSTEEG

Oude Rijn
Many of the gabled houses along Leiden's canals have shops and cafés on the ground floor.

NONNENSTRAAT

Neo-Classical houses on Rapenburg

University library

Het Gravensteen
The university's law faculty lies behind the Classical façade of this complex of buildings, which grew up between the 13th and 17th centuries.

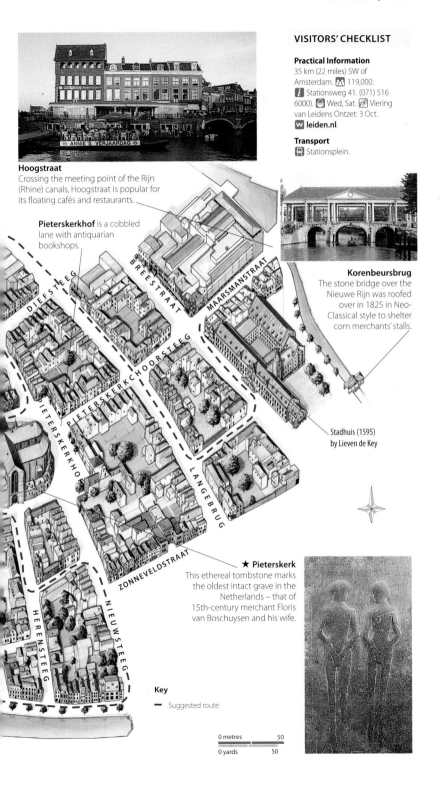

VISITORS' CHECKLIST

Practical Information
35 km (22 miles) SW of
Amsterdam. 🚇 119,000.
ℹ️ Stationsweg 41. (071) 516
6000). 🛍️ Wed, Sat. 🎏 Viering
van Leidens Ontzet: 3 Oct.
🆆 **leiden.nl**.

Transport
🚇 Stationsplein.

Hoogstraat
Crossing the meeting point of the Rijn
(Rhine) canals, Hoogstraat is popular for
its floating cafés and restaurants.

Pieterskerkhof is a cobbled
lane with antiquarian
bookshops.

Korenbeursbrug
The stone bridge over the
Nieuwe Rijn was roofed
over in 1825 in Neo-
Classical style to shelter
corn merchants' stalls.

Stadhuis (1595)
by Lieven de Key

★ Pieterskerk
This ethereal tombstone marks
the oldest intact grave in the
Netherlands – that of
15th-century merchant Floris
van Boschuysen and his wife.

Key

— Suggested route

| 0 metres | 50 |
| 0 yards | 50 |

Exploring Leiden

Leiden is famous for its university, the oldest and most prestigious in the Netherlands. It was founded in 1575 by William of Orange, a year after he relieved the town from a year-long siege by the Spanish *(see pp26–7)*. As a reward for their endurance, William offered the citizens of Leiden a choice of the building of a university or the abolition of tax. They chose wisely, and the city's reputation as a centre of intellectual and religious tolerance was firmly established. English Puritan dissidents, victims of persecution in their homeland, were able to settle here in the 17th century before undertaking their epic voyage to the New World.

Arched gazebo within the Clusiustuin in the Hortus Botanicus

🏛 Stedelijk Museum De Lakenhal

Oude Singel 28–32. **Tel** (071) 516 5360. **Open** 10am–5pm Tue–Fri, noon–5pm Sat & Sun (renovation under way until spring 2018 so check website for opening times). **Closed** 1 Jan, 25 Dec. 🅿 ♿ 🖥 📷 🗗 🌐 **lakenhal.nl**

The Lakenhal (cloth hall) was the 17th-century headquarters of Leiden's cloth trade. Built in 1640 in Dutch Classical style by Arent van 's-Gravesande, it houses the municipal museum, with temporary exhibitions of modern art and furniture from the 16th century onwards.

The pride of the collection is Lucas van Leyden's Renaissance triptych of *The Last Judgment* (1526–7), rescued from the Pieterskerk during the religious struggles of 1566 *(see pp26–7)*. A wing built in the 1920s offers a silver collection, furniture and exhibits covering the local

weaving industry. Not to be missed is a big bronze *hutspot*, or cauldron, allegedly left behind by the Spanish when William of Orange broke the siege in 1574. The cauldron contained a spicy stew which the starving people ate. This meal is now cooked every year on 3 October, to commemorate Dutch victory over the Spanish.

🌿 Hortus Botanicus Leiden

Rapenburg 73. **Tel** (071) 527 7249. **Open** Apr–Nov: 10am–6pm daily; Dec–Mar: 10–4pm Tue–Sun. **Closed** 3 Oct, 24 Dec–1 Jan. 🅿 ♿ partial. 🖥 📷 🌐 **hortusleiden.nl**

Leiden's botanical garden was founded in 1590 as part of the university. The varied trees and shrubs include a 350- year-old laburnum. Carolus Clusius, who was responsible for introducing the tulip to the Netherlands in 1593 *(see pp28–9)*,

became the first professor of botany at Leiden University. Today the Hortus Botanicus contains a modern reconstruction of his original walled garden, called the Clusiustuin. Other delights include hothouses full of exotic orchids, rose gardens and an exquisite Japanese garden.

🏛 Museum Boerhaave

Lange St Agnietenstraat 10. **Tel** (071) 521 4224. **Open** 10am–5pm Tue–Sun, pub hols (open daily mid-Jul–Aug). **Closed** 1 Jan, 27 Apr, 3 Oct, 25 Dec. 🅿 ♿ 🖥 🌐 **museumboerhaave.nl**

This museum is named after the great Dutch professor of medicine, botany and chemistry, Herman Boerhaave (1668–1738). Its collections reflect the development of mathematics, astronomy, physics, chemistry and medicine. They range in time from a magnificent 15th-century astrolabe to the electron-microscope and the surgeon's equipment of yesteryear. It is located in the former Caecilia Hospital.

🏛 Museum Volkenkunde

Steenstraat 1. **Tel** (071) 516 8800. **Open** 10am–5pm Tue–Sun. **Closed** 1 Jan, 27 Apr, 5 May, 3 Oct, 25 Dec. 🅿 ♿ 🖥 🗗 🌐 **volkenkunde.nl**

This outstanding ethnological museum, founded in 1837, houses collections from non-western cultures. Individual displays are linked together to create

Lucas van Leyden's triptych of *The Last Judgment* in the Stedelijk Museum de Lakenhal

a worldwide cultural journey that shows both the differences and connections between cultures. Temporary exhibitions feature living conditions across the world, from the Arctic wastes to the hills of China, adding to this eclectic museum's wide appeal to people of all age groups.

🏛 Stedelijk Molenmuseum de Valk

2e Binnenvestgracht 1. **Tel** (071) 516 5353. **Open** 10am–5pm Tue–Sat, 1–5pm Sun. **Closed** 1 Jan, 27 Apr, 2 & 3 Oct, 25 Dec. 🅿 ⬛
W **molenmuseumdevalk.nl**

This towering grain mill, built in 1743, is Leiden's last remaining mill. It is an imposing seven storeys high, and now restored to its original working state. A tour takes in the living quarters on the ground floor, the repair workshop and a retrospective exhibition on the history of Dutch windmills.

🏛 Pieterskerk

Pieterskerkhof 1a. **Tel** (071) 512 4319. **Open** 11am–6pm daily, unless special events are taking place. Check website for details, or phone. **Closed** 3 Oct, 31 Dec. 🅿 ⬛ **W** **pieterskerk.com**

The magnificent Gothic church was built in the 15th century in rose-pink brick, and stands in a leafy square surrounded by elegant houses. Now a community centre, the church is worth visiting for its austere interior and its organ, built by the Hagenbeer brothers in 1642 and

enclosed in gilded woodwork. The floor of the nave is covered with worn slabs marking the burial places of 17th-century intellectuals like Puritan leader John Robinson and Golden Age artist Jan Steen *(see p135)*.

🏛 De Burcht

Nieuwe Rijn. Battlements. **Open** daily.
De Burcht is an odd 12th-century fortress with crenellated battlements. It sits between two channels of the Rijn (Rhine) atop a grassy, man-made mound, which is thought to be of Saxon origin. The top of the citadel offers superb views over Leiden.

🏛 Rijksmuseum van Oudheden

Rapenburg 28. **Tel** (071) 516 3163. **Open** 10am–5pm Tue–Sun. **Closed** 1 Jan, 27 Apr, 3 Oct, 25 Dec. 🅿 ♿ 🖼 📷 **W** **rmo.nl**

The Dutch museum of antiquities, established in 1818, is Leiden's main attraction. The centrepiece of the collection is the Egyptian Temple of Taffeh, reassembled in the main exhibition hall in 1978. It dates from the 1st century AD, and was dedicated to Isis, Egyptian goddess of fertility, from the 4th century AD.

The museum's rich collection of Egyptian artifacts occupies the first two floors. There are also impressive displays of musical instruments, textiles and shoes, expressive Etruscan bronze work and fragments of Roman mosaic and frescoes.

The presentation has been designed with children in mind with interactive exhibits and multimedia reconstructing daily life in ancient Egypt, Greece and Rome.

A lift bridge across the Oude Rijn in Leiden

⑮ Den Haag

Den Haag ('s-Gravenhage or The Hague) is the political capital of the Netherlands, home to prestigious institutions such as the Dutch Parliament and International Court of Justice, located in the Vredespaleis *(see p192)*. When Den Haag became the seat of government in 1586, it was a small town built around the castle of the counts of Holland. That same castle, much rebuilt, now stands at the heart of a city which is home to half a million people. It is surrounded by public buildings, such as the Mauritshuis *(see pp190–91)*, and protected to the north by the remains of a moat which forms the Hofvijver (lake). To the west is the seaside town of Scheveningen *(see p193)*.

🏛 Mauritshuis
See pp190–91.

🏛 Binnenhof
Binnenhof 8a. **Tel** (070) 757 0200. **Open** for guided tours only; book via website. **Closed** Sun & public hols. 🅿 🎫 **W** prodemos.nl

By the side of the Hofvijver is the Binnenhof courtyard. In the centre of this stands the fairy-tale, double-turreted Gothic Ridderzaal (Hall of the Knights). This was the 13th-century dining hall of Floris V, Count of Holland *(see p23)*. Since 1904, the hall's function has been mostly ceremonial; it is used for the opening of the Dutch Parliament by the monarch (Prinsjesdag, the third Tuesday in September), and for other state occasions. It is open to visitors when parliament is not in session. A tour takes in one of the two former debating chambers.

🏛 Museum Bredius
Lange Vijverberg 14. **Tel** (070) 362 0729. **Open** 11am–5pm Tue–Sun. **Closed** 1 Jan & 25 Dec. 🅿 🎫 **W** museumbredius.nl

Dr Abraham Bredius was an art historian and collector as well as director of the Mauritshuis *(see pp190–91)* from 1895 to 1922. On his death in 1946, he bequeathed his vast collection of 17th-century art to the city of Den Haag. This bequest is displayed in a distinguished 18th-century merchant's house on the north side of the Hof-vijver, and features around 200 Golden Age paintings – famous works by Dutch Masters such as Rembrandt *(see pp64–5)* and Jan Steen *(see p131)*, and others by lesser-known artists.

The building itself has under-gone considerable renovation and boasts a fine collection of antique furniture, delicate por-celain and elaborate silverware.

🏛 Grote Kerk
Rond de Grote Kerk 12. **Tel** (070) 302 8630. **Open** during summer months, check website for details. 🅿 **W** grotekerkdenhaag.nl

In its present form, the Grote Kerk dates mainly from 1539, but major rebuilding between 1985 and 1987 has restored it to its former glory. Its most impressive feature is a stained-glass window which depicts Charles V, the Holy Roman Emperor *(see pp26–7)*, kneeling at the feet of the Virgin Mary. The church is at the centre of Den Haag's shopping area.

Coat of arms on façade of Rijksmuseum Gevangenpoort

🏛 Rijksmuseum Gevangenpoort
Buitenhof 33. **Tel** (070) 346 0861. **Open** 10am–5pm Tue–Fri, noon–5pm Sat & Sun. **Closed** 1 Jan, 3rd Tue in Sep, 25 Dec. 🅿 🎫 (every hour; obligatory. Last tour: 3:45pm) 📷 **W** gevangenpoort.nl

The Gevangenpoort (prison gate) was originally the main gateway to the 14th-century castle of the counts of Holland. Later, it was turned into a jail, becoming infamous during a period of violent social unrest in the late 17th century when burgomaster Cornelis de Witt *(see p29)* was confined and tortured here. Both he and his brother Jan were subsequently tried for heresy, and torn limb from limb outside the prison gate by a rioting mob.

Now a prison museum, on display is a unique collection

The Hofvijver and parliament buildings in Den Haag

Paintings in Galerij Prins Willem V

kabinet – the 18th-century Dutch word for an art gallery. The Galerij is the oldest art gallery in the Netherlands. The 18th-century fashion for covering every available inch of wall space with paintings has been retained, and so several pictures are hung high and close together. Many of Prince William's original purchases are still to be seen. Old Master paintings by Rembrandt, Jan Steen and Paulus Potter (1625–54) are included in a collection that consists principally of typically Dutch Golden Age landscapes, genre works, "conversation pieces" and recreations of historical events *(see p131)*.

of torture instruments, accompanied by a stereo soundtrack of blood-curdling screams.

Ⅲ Galerij Prins Willem V

Buitenhof 33. **Tel** (070) 302 3456.
Open noon–5pm Tue–Sun.
Closed 1 Jan, 25 Dec. 🅿 🅲 🅶
W galerijprinswillemv.nl

In his youth, Prince William V *(see p33)* was a collector of Golden Age paintings. His collection was opened to the public in 1774, inside this former inn, which the prince had converted for use as his

Ⅲ Haags Historisch Museum

Korte Vijverberg 7. **Tel** (070) 364 6940.
Open 10am–5pm Tue–Fri, noon–5pm Sat–Sun. **Closed** 1 Jan, 3rd Tue in Sep, 25 Dec. 🅿 🅶 🅲 🅿 🅿 🅰
W haagshistorischmuseum.nl

Den Haag's history museum is in the Sebastiaansdoelen, a Dutch Classical mansion built in 1636 and the former headquarters of the Civic Guard of St Sebastian. Exhibitions tell the story of Den Haag's growth since the Middle Ages. The displays are changed

periodically and are drawn from the city's collection of landscapes, portraits and genre paintings *(see p131)* as well as 17th- and 18th-century furnishings.

The 17th-century façade of the Haags Historisch Museum

Den Haag City Centre

① Grote Kerk
② Rijksmuseum Gevangenpoort
③ Galerij Prins Willem V
④ Museum Bredius
⑤ Binnenhof
⑥ Haags Historisch Museum
⑦ Mauritshuis

Key to Symbols *see back flap*

The Mauritshuis

The Count of Nassau, Johann Maurits, commissioned this graceful house while he was the governor of Brazil. It was completed in 1644 by Pieter Post and Jacob van Campen in Dutch Classical style with influences from Italian Renaissance architecture, and enjoys wonderful views across the Hofvijver *(see p188)*. The mansion was bequeathed to the state after Maurits's death in 1679, and has been the home of the Royal Picture Gallery since 1822. The collection is small, but almost every painting is a superb work by one of the Old Masters. This, combined with the exquisite presentation in elegant period rooms, makes the Mauritshuis one of the finest galleries in the Netherlands.

★ **The Anatomy Lesson of Dr Nicolaes Tulp** (1632)
One of the highlights of the Mauritshuis collection is Rembrandt's painting of surgeons examining a corpse. It reflects the burgeoning contemporary interest in anatomy and science.

Gallery Guide

The Mauritshuis is a small gallery set on three floors. The arrangement of the paintings changes frequently in order to cover all aspects of the collection, but you can check the current display on the museum's website. Information sheets and an audio tour are available in English. The Royal Dutch Shell Wing, a new exhibition wing, is connected to the historic building by an underground foyer, which also houses a brasserie and a museum shop. The main entrance is through the underground foyer.

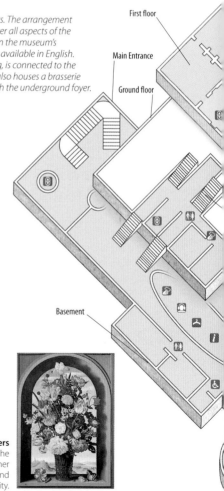

First floor

Main Entrance

Ground floor

Basement

Portrait of a Man from the Lespinette Family (c.1485–90)
Thought to be a work by Antonello da Messina until the 19th century, this tightly framed portrait has now been attributed to Hans Memling.

Vase with Flowers in a Niche (c.1618) Ambrosius Bosschaert the Elder captured the beauty of early summer flowers, but the flies buzzing around remind us of mortality.

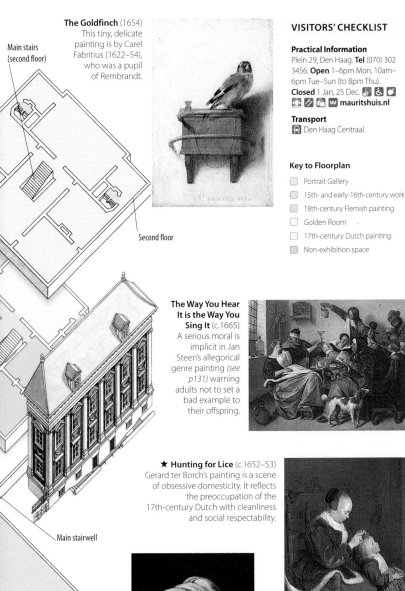

The Goldfinch (1654)
This tiny, delicate painting is by Carel Fabritius (1622–54), who was a pupil of Rembrandt.

Main stairs (second floor)

Second floor

Main stairwell

Key to Floorplan

- Portrait Gallery
- 15th- and early-16th-century work
- 18th-century Flemish painting
- Golden Room
- 17th-century Dutch painting
- Non-exhibition space

The Way You Hear It is the Way You Sing It (c.1665)
A serious moral is implicit in Jan Steen's allegorical genre painting *(see p131)* warning adults not to set a bad example to their offspring.

★ **Hunting for Lice** (c.1652–53)
Gerard ter Borch's painting is a scene of obsessive domesticity. It reflects the preoccupation of the 17th-century Dutch with cleanliness and social respectability.

★ **Girl with a Pearl Earring** (c.1665)
This haunting portrait was painted during the most successful middle period of Jan Vermeer's career. The model may have been his daughter, Maria.

🖼 Vredespaleis

Carnegieplein 2. **Tel** (070) 302 4242.
Open Tue–Sun (visitors' centre). 🖼
Sat & Sun only; compulsory (check
dates and book tickets via website).
Closed public hols and when court is
in session. 🖼 🖼 **vredespaleis.nl**

In 1899, Den Haag played host
to the first international peace
conference. This then led to the
formation of the Permanent
Court of Arbitration, which had
the aim of maintaining world
peace. To provide a suitably
august home for the court, the
Scottish-born philanthropist,
Andrew Carnegie (1835–1919)
donated $1.5 million towards
the building of the mock-Gothic
Vredespaleis (peace palace),
which was designed by French
architect Louis Cordonnier.

The enormous palace was
completed in 1913, and many of
the member nations of the
Court of Arbitration contributed
to the interior's rich decoration.
Today the Vredespaleis is the
seat of the United Nations'
International Court of Justice,
which was formed in 1946 as
successor to the Permanent
Court of Arbitration.

🖼 Gemeentemuseum Den Haag

Stadhouderslaan 41. **Tel** (070) 338
1111. **Open** 11am–5pm Tue–Sun.
Closed 1 Jan, 27 Apr, 25 Dec. 🖼 🖼
🖼 🖼 🖼 🖼 **gemeentemuseum.nl**

This is one of the town's finest
museums. The building was the
last work of HP Berlage, the father
of the architectural movement
known as the Amsterdam School
(*see p99*). The museum was
completed in 1935, a year after
his death, and is built in sandy-
coloured brick on two storeys
round a central courtyard.

Vredespaleis, home to the International Court of Justice

The exhibits are displayed in
three sections. Highlights of the
superb applied arts section
include antique delftware,
Islamic and Oriental porcelain
and the world's largest collection
of paintings by Piet Mondriaan
(*see p138*).

Costumes and musical
instruments dating from the
15th to the 19th centuries are
too fragile to be on permanent
display, though selected items
are regularly exhibited.

The labyrinthine basement is
the stage for the "Wonderkamers"
– the Wonder Rooms – which
hold quirky displays of artworks
from all the collections, aimed
especially at teenage visitors.

🖼 Panorama Mesdag

Zeestraat 65. **Tel** (070) 310 6665.
Open 10am–5pm Mon–Sat, noon–
5pm Sun. **Closed** 1 Jan, 25 Dec. 🖼
🖼 **panorama-mesdag.com**

This painted cyclorama is
important both as a work of
Dutch Impressionism and as a
rare surviving example of 19th-
century entertainment. The
vast painting is 120 m (400 ft)
around and lines the inside
wall of a circular, canopied
pavilion. The artwork shows
the old fishing village of
Scheveningen.

The astonishingly realistic
effect of the painting is
achieved through the brilliant
use of perspective, enhanced
by natural daylight from above.
It was painted in 1881 by
members of the Dutch
Impressionist School, led by
HW Mesdag (1831–1915) and
his wife, Sientje (1834–1909).
George Hendrik Breitner (1857–
1923) later added a group of
cavalry officers charging along
the beach on horseback. The
building itself has been
renovated and extended,
creating more space for
temporary exhibitions.

Gemeentemuseum Den Haag (1935), designed by HP Berlage

Omniversum

President Kennedylaan 5. **Tel** (0900) 666 4837. **Open** daily.
omniversum.nl

The Omniversum is a cross between a planetarium and a space-age cinema, and is especially appealing to children. It has a high-tech sound system and a massive dome-shaped screen, onto which films and lasers are projected. These are combined to create stunning three-dimensional images of space exploration, volcanic eruptions and life beneath the ocean's surface.

Madurodam

George Maduroplein 1. **Tel** (070) 416 2400. **Open** daily.
madurodam.nl

Madurodam is a model of a composite Dutch city, built to a scale of 1:25. It incorporates replicas of the Vredespaleis and Binnenhof in Den Haag, the canal houses of Amsterdam, Rotterdam's Europoort *(see p201)* and Schiphol airport, along with windmills, polders, bulbfields and a nudist beach. At night it is illuminated by 50,000 tiny lights.

The model city was opened by Queen Juliana in 1952. It was conceived by JML Maduro as a memorial to his son George, who died at Dachau concentration camp in 1945.

Miniature church in a miniature city, Madurodam

16 Scheveningen

45 km (28 miles) SW of Amsterdam.
52,000. Thu.
denhaag.com

This resort is a 15-minute tram-ride from the centre of Den Haag. Like many Dutch seaside towns, it had its heyday in the 19th century, and is now a mixture of faded gentility and seediness. Even so, it has retained its popularity as a holiday destination, mainly due to stretches of clean, sandy beaches as well as a pier, built in 1961, but closed since 2013. There is no shortage of places to eat, including some good seafood restaurants. The imposing French Empire-style Kurhaus, now a luxury hotel, was built in 1885 when Scheveningen was still an important spa town.

Modern amenities include the **Sea Life Scheveningen**, nearby, where visitors can walk in see-through tunnels for underwater views of stingrays, sharks and other forms of sea life. It is also a sanctuary for all kinds of wounded marine creatures.

The town has swallowed up the original fishing village of Scheveningen Haven, which has still managed to maintain some of its traditional fishing industry. The south side of the harbour is the departure point for tourists' fishing trips.

Close by is the **MuZee Scheveningen**, which combines exhibits of marine life from around the world with displays on life in the village at the turn of the 20th century.

MuZee Scheveningen

Neptunusstraat 92. **Tel** (070) 350 0830. **Open** Tue–Sun. **Closed** 1 Jan, 25 Dec. **muzee.nl**

Sea Life Scheveningen

Strandweg 13. **Tel** (070) 354 2100. **Open** daily. **Closed** 25 Dec. **visitsealife.com**

Holiday-makers on Scheveningen's popular sandy beach

⓱ Street-by-Street: Delft

The origins of Delft date from 1075 and its prosperity was based on weaving and brewing. However, a massive explosion at the national arsenal destroyed much of the medieval town in October 1645. The centre was rebuilt in the late 17th century and the sleepy old town has changed little since then – gabled Gothic and Renaissance houses still line the tree-shaded canals. Activity centres on the market square, bordered by the landmarks of the Stadhuis and Nieuwe Kerk. Visitors can dip into the scores of shops selling antiques and expensive, hand-painted delftware. Tours of local factories are available, and their shops are often reasonably priced.

★ Stedelijk Museum Het Prinsenhof
Here you can see bullet holes where William of Orange was murdered in 1584.

★ Oude Kerk
The 13th-century Oude Kerk contains tombs of eminent Delft citizens like Antonie van Leeuwenhoek, inventor of the microscope.

Oude Delft is lined with Renaissance canal houses.

SCHOOLSTRAAT

ST AGATHA PLEIN

OUDE DELFT

HIPPOLYTUSBUURT

NIEUWSTRAAT

BOTER BRUG

WIJNHAVEN

OUDE DELFT

PEPERSTRAAT

Chapel of St Hippolytus
This simple, red-brick Gothic chapel (1396) was used as an ammunition store during the Alteration (see pp26–7).

| 0 metres | 50 |
| 0 yards | 50 |

Key

 Suggested route

View of Delft (c.1660)
Jan Vermeer's painting captures the town of Delft on a gloomy summer afternoon. The original spire of the Nieuwe Kerk is clearly visible in the distance.

The Waag (1770) is now a theatre.

Vermeer Centrum Delft

Stadhuis (1618)
The Renaissance town hall was designed by Hendrick de Keyser and is adorned with stone lions' heads. It was built around a Gothic tower of the 13th century.

HOORSTRAAT

VROUWJUTTENLAND

DEVLOUW

VOLDERSGRACHT

KERKSTR

MARKT

OUDE LANGENDIJK

★ **Nieuwe Kerk**
The church was built in erratic bursts over many years *(see p196)*. Inside, this statue of Prince William of Orange reclines at the heart of his elaborate mausoleum.

Vleeshal (1650)
The façade of the old meat market is decorated with animal heads. After 1872 it was used as a corn exchange.

Exploring Delft

The charming town of Delft is known the world over for its blue-and-white pottery, but is equally famous as the resting place of William of Orange (1533–84), one of the most celebrated figures in Dutch history. He commanded the Dutch Revolt against Spanish rule from his headquarters in Delft, and his victory resulted in religious freedom and independence for the Dutch people *(see pp26–7)*. Delft was also the birthplace of artist Jan Vermeer (1632–75), whose talent was so underrated during his lifetime that he died in extreme poverty.

🔼 Oude Kerk

Heilige Geestkerkhof. **Tel** (015) 212 3015. **Open** 9am–6pm Mon–Sat (Nov–Jan: 11am–4pm Mon–Fri, 10am–5pm Sat; Feb–Mar: 10am–5pm Mon–Sat). 🚻 ♿
Ⓦ **onkd.nl**

Although a church has existed on this site since the 11th century, the original building has been added to many times. The ornate, but leaning, clock tower was built in the 14th century,

and the flamboyant Gothic north transept was added in the early 16th century. The interior is dominated by the carved wooden pulpit with overhanging canopy. The simple stone tablet at the east end of the north aisle marks the burial place of Jan Vermeer. In the north transept lies Admiral Maarten Tromp (1598–1653), who routed the English fleet in 1652. Admiral Piet Heyn (1577–1629), who captured

The imposing Renaissance pulpit (1548) of the Oude Kerk

the Spanish silver fleet in 1628, is in the chancel.

🔼 Nieuwe Kerk

Markt. **Tel** (015) 212 3025. **Open** Apr–Oct: 9am–6pm Mon–Sat; Nov–Jan: 11am–4pm Mon–Fri, 10am–5pm Sat; Feb–Mar: 10am–5pm Mon–Sat. 🚻
Ⓦ **onkd.nl**

The Nieuwe Kerk was built between 1383 and 1510, but much of the original structure was restored following a fire in 1536 and an explosion at the national arsenal in 1654. Work on the church continued for many years, and it was not until 1872 that PJH Cuypers *(see pp34–5)* added the statuesque 100-m (320-ft) tower to the Gothic façade.

The burial vaults of the Dutch royal family are in the crypt of this empty, cavernous church, but the most prominent feature is the mausoleum of William of Orange. The richly decorated tomb was designed by Hendrick de Keyser *(see p92)* in 1614 and is carved from black and white marble, with heavy gilded detailing. At its heart is a sculpture of William in his battle dress, and at each corner stand bronze figures representing the Virtues. Close to William is his dog, who died days after him, and at the foot of the tomb is a trumpeting angel – symbol of Fame. Due to the restoration work in 2016, opening times vary. Check the church's website before visiting.

The Nieuwe Kerk in Delft's market square

Delftware

The blue-and-white tin-glazed pottery, known as delftware, was developed from majolica and introduced to the Netherlands by immigrant Italian potters in the 16th century. Settling around Delft and Haarlem, the potters made wall tiles, adopting Dutch motifs such as animals and flowers as decoration. Trade with the east brought samples of delicate Chinese porcelain to the Netherlands, and the market for coarser Dutch majolica crashed. By 1650, local potters had adopted the Chinese model and designed fine plates, vases and bowls decorated with Dutch landscapes, and biblical and genre scenes. In 1653, De Porceleyne Fles was one of 32 thriving potteries in Delft. Today, it is one of two Delftware factories still in production, and is open for guided tours (www.royaldelft.com).

Hand-painted 17th-century Delft tiles

Vermeer Centrum Delft

Voldersgracht 21. **Tel** (015) 213 8588. **Open** 10am–5pm daily. **Closed** 1 Jan, 25 Dec. Fri & Sun (in Dutch only). **vermeerdelft.nl**

Little is known about the life of Delft's most famous and enigmatic artist, Johannes Vermeer (1632–75). In a series of beautifully designed displays, the Vermeer Centrum uncovers some of the mysteries surrounding this artist.

In the basement, visitors are introduced to the artist and the city where he lived all his life. Life-size copies of all his paintings are on display, including *The Girl with a Pearl Earring* (1665-67). On the upper floors, some of his painting techniques are explained, particularly his use of perspective, colour and light.

Changing exhibitions focus on the symbolic messages in his paintings.

Stedelijk Museum Het Prinsenhof

St Agathaplein 1. **Tel** (015) 260 2358. **Open** 11am–5pm Tue–Sun (daily Jun–Aug). **Closed** 1 Jan, 25 Dec. **prinsenhof-delft.nl**

This tranquil Gothic building, formerly a convent, now houses Delft's historical museum but is better known as the place where William of Orange was assassinated.

He requisitioned the convent in 1572 for his headquarters during the Dutch Revolt. In 1584, by order of Philip II of Spain *(see pp26–7)*, William was shot by Balthasar Gerards. The bullet holes in the main staircase wall can still be seen.

The museum houses a rare collection of antique Delftware, displayed alongside tapestries, silverware, medieval sculpture and a series of portraits of the Dutch royal family.

Royal Delft

Koninklijke Porceleyne Fles, Rotterdamseweg 196. **Tel** (015) 251 2030. **Open** 9am–5pm daily (Nov–Mar: noon–5pm Sun). **Closed** 1 Jan, 25 & 26 Dec. **royaldelft.com**

There were once more than 30 delftware factories in the area. De Porceleyne Fles (established in 1653) is the only factory still producing the typical white pottery with delicate blue hand-painted decorations known as delftware. A visit includes a tour of the factory and the opportunity to watch the artists at work.

There is a small museum displaying authentic pieces produced by the factory. Vermeer's dining room has been faithfully recreated, and the Royal Treasury shows the delftware especially designed for the Dutch royal family.

If you fancy trying your hand at creating your own decorative masterpiece, it is possible to sign up for a workshop of earthenware painting with Delft Blue paint. The lunchroom serves afternoon tea (advance booking required), allowing you the chance to sip tea and nibble petit fours from fine Delft Blue crockery.

Fine gabled façades along Binnenwatersloot in the centre of Delft

St Janskerk, Gouda

The original Catholic church of 1485 was rebuilt in Gothic style after it was razed by fire in 1552. Between 1555 and 1571, a series of remarkable stained-glass windows were donated to the church by wealthy Catholic benefactors such as Philip II of Spain. After the Alteration *(see pp26–7)* the church became Protestant, but even the iconoclasts could not bring themselves to destroy the windows – in fact Protestant patrons, such as the aldermen of Rotterdam, continued to donate windows until 1603. Depicting contemporary figures and events, the stained glass is rich in political symbolism, using biblical stories to make coded reference to the conflict between Catholic and Protestant, and Dutch and Spanish that led to the Dutch Revolt in 1572.

The Nave
At 123 m (403 ft), the nave is the longest in the Netherlands. Memorial slabs cover the floor.

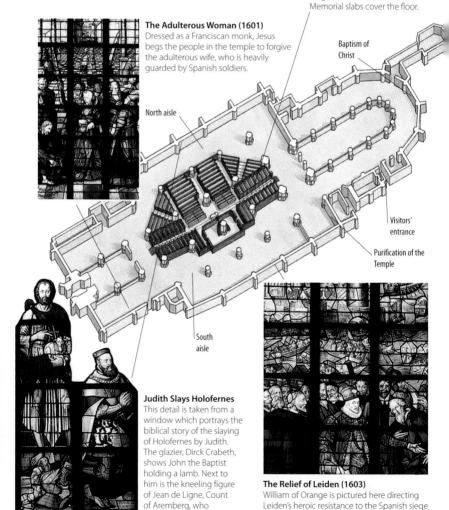

The Adulterous Woman (1601)
Dressed as a Franciscan monk, Jesus begs the people in the temple to forgive the adulterous wife, who is heavily guarded by Spanish soldiers.

North aisle

Baptism of Christ

Visitors' entrance

Purification of the Temple

South aisle

Judith Slays Holofernes
This detail is taken from a window which portrays the biblical story of the slaying of Holofernes by Judith. The glazier, Dirck Crabeth, shows John the Baptist holding a lamb. Next to him is the kneeling figure of Jean de Ligne, Count of Aremberg, who commissioned the window.

The Relief of Leiden (1603)
William of Orange is pictured here directing Leiden's heroic resistance to the Spanish siege of 1574 *(see p186)*.

View over Gouda with St Janskerk in the background

Purification of the Temple
The window was donated by
William of Orange *(see p26)* in 1567.
The detail shows dismayed traders
watching Jesus drive the
moneylenders from the temple. It
represents the Dutch desire to expel
the Spanish from their country.

Baptism of Christ (1555)
John the Baptist is shown
baptizing Christ in the river
Jordan. The window was donated
by the Bishop of Utrecht.

⑱ Gouda

50 km (31 miles) S of Amsterdam.
🚊 72,000. 🚉 🛈 Markt 35. (0182)
589 110. 🧀 cheese market: Apr–Aug:
10am–1pm Thu; general market: Thu
& Sat; antiques: Jun–Aug, Wed.
W welcometogouda.com

Gouda received its charter from
Count Floris V *(see p23)* in 1272.
Situated at the confluence of
two rivers, the town became
the centre of a successful
brewing industry in the 15th
century. The growth of the
cheese trade during the 17th
century brought more
prosperity. Today, the name of
Gouda is synonymous with its
famous full-bodied cheese.
There is a cheese market in
summer, and the twice-weekly
general market offers local
cheeses and crafts. There is also
a Candle Festival the second or
third Tuesday in December. All
these markets take place in the
huge square around the
Stadhuis which, dating from
1450, is one of the oldest town
halls in the Netherlands. The
building bristles with pinnacles
and miniature spires in Flemish
Gothic style. The main attraction
of the town is the stained-glass
windows in St Janskerk.

🏛 Museum Gouda
Achter de Kerk 14. **Tel** (0182) 331
000. **Open** 11am–5pm Tue–Sun.
Closed 1 Jan, 27 Apr, 25 Dec. 🎒
W museumgouda.nl

An arched gatehouse (1609)
leads into the leafy courtyard of
this delightful museum. The
Catharina Gasthuis was built in
the 14th century as a hospice
for travellers, later becoming an
almshouse for the elderly.
Converted into a museum in
1910, it houses Civic Guard
portraits and landscapes by
Dutch Impressionists.

🏛 Museumhaven Gouda
Between Mallegatsluis and
Guldenbrug. **Open** daily.
W museumhavengouda.nl

Gouda was once an important
inland shipping port where
goods were moved from large
sailing vessels to flat-bottomed
boats that could navigate the
shallow canals. Eighteen such
boats are moored at the
museum harbour, where
visitors can explore Gouda's
shipping history. The restored
boats are privately owned and
so cannot be boarded.

Early 17th-century gatehouse of the
Museum Gouda

⑲ Rotterdam

Rotterdam occupies a strategic position where the Rijn (Rhine), Europe's most important river, meets the North Sea. Barges from Rotterdam transport goods deep into the continent, and ocean-going ships carry European exports around the world. This made Rotterdam a prime target for aerial bombardment during World War II, and the city's ancient heart was destroyed. Much of the city has been rebuilt in experimental styles, resulting in some of Europe's most original and innovative architecture. The Europoort is now Europe's largest container port, stretching for 40 km (25 miles) along the river banks.

Modern architecure of Rotterdam, with the De Rotterdam building on the right

Exploring Rotterdam

Much of Oudehaven, the old harbour area of Rotterdam, was bombed in World War II. It has largely been rebuilt in daring and avant-garde styles. The pencil-shaped apartment block, **Blaaktoren**, and the adjacent "cube houses", **Kubuswoningen**, designed by architect Piet Blom, were built in 1982–4. The latter are extraordinary apartments, set on concrete stilts and tilted at a crazy angle. Residents have specially designed furniture to fit the sloping rooms.

The Markthal in Rotterdam, the Netherlands' first covered market

The river banks and the Kop van Zuid, the former port area on the south bank, were redeveloped in the 1990s. Eye-catching buildings here include Renzo Piano's KPN Telecom head office and Rem Koolhaas's **De Rotterdam**, a 150-m- (492-ft-) high building with three irregularly stacked, interconnected towers.

The **Markthal**, designed by Dutch architecture firm MVRDV and opened in 2014, is a huge indoor market place and housing development covered by an imposing arch. The inner roof has colourful tiles designed by artists Arno Coenen and Iris Roskam.

In the Golden Age, maritime trade brought wealth to Dutch towns with access to the sea. Delft (see pp194–7) lacked a harbour, so its citizens built a 12-km (7.5-mile) canal from the town to the Nieuwe Maas river, and constructed **Delfshaven** – a purpose-built village

complete with harbour which remains a pretty corner of the city, with 18th-century warehouses converted into restaurants and cafés.

🏛 Museum Boijmans Van Beuningen Rotterdam
See pp202–3.

🏛 Maritiem Museum Rotterdam
Leuvehaven 1. **Tel** (010) 413 2680.
Open 10am– 5pm Tue–Sat, 11am–5pm Sun & public hols (Jul & Aug: also Mon). **Closed** 1 Jan, 27 Apr, 25 Dec. 🐾 ♿ ⬛ ✓ 📷
W maritiemmuseum.nl

Prince Hendrik, brother of King William III, founded this museum in 1873. Its main highlight is an iron-clad warship called De Buffel, built in 1868. Completely renovated, it boasts opulent officers' quarters with the atmosphere of a gentleman's club, and a small fleet of barges and steamships.

🏛 Kunsthal
Westzeedijk 341. **Tel** (010) 440 0301. **Open** 10am–5pm Tue–Sat, 11am–5pm Sun & public hols. **Closed** 1 Jan, 27 Apr, 25 Dec. 🐾 📷 ⬛ W kunsthal.nl

From costume and art, to inventions and photography, the Kunsthal delivers exciting exhibitions that alternate between "high art" and pop culture. The building was designed by Rotterdam's Rem Koolhaas, whose designs include the Beijing headquarters for China Central Television.

Peaceful canal houses in a quiet corner of Delfshaven

🏛 Nederlands Fotomuseum

Gebouw Las Palmas, Wilhelminakade 332. **Tel** (010) 203 0405. **Open** 10am–5pm Tue–Fri, 11am–5pm Sat & Sun. **Closed** 1 Jan, 27 Apr, 25 Dec. 🅿 🚻 📷 🌐 nederlandsfotomuseum.nl

The restored former warehouse Las Palmas houses the Dutch Photography Museum, which has extensive archives covering Dutch photographers. Exhibitions showcase treasures from the archives alongside works by foreign photographers, comparing and contrasting the works. Prints are available at the museum shop.

🏛 Wereldmuseum Rotterdam

Willemskade 25. **Tel** (010) 270 7172. **Open** 10:30am–5:30pm (restaurant to 10pm) Tue–Sun. **Closed** 1 Jan, 27 Apr, 25 Dec. 🚻 📷 🅿 🌐 wereldmuseum.nl

During the 17th century, the city fathers amassed a superb ethnological collection. The Wereldmuseum displays 1,800 artifacts from Indonesia, the Americas and Asia, and presents audiovisual displays of theatre, film, dance and music. A café-restaurant offers river views.

Euromast against the skyline

🔭 Euromast

Parkhaven 20. **Tel** (010) 436 4811. **Open** Apr–Sep: 9:30am–11pm daily; Oct–Mar: 10am–11pm daily. Platforms close at 10pm 🚻 ♿ 📷 🅿 🌐 euromast.nl

Visitors ride a high-speed lift up the first 100 m (328 ft) of the Euromast to enjoy sweeping views of Rotterdam. This lower section, built in 1960, has a viewing platform with a restaurant and exhibition area. In 1970 the Space Tower added another

VISITORS' CHECKLIST

Practical Information
65 km (40 miles) SW of Amsterdam. 🗺 618,000. 🛈 Coolsingel 195–197. (010) 790 0185. 🎬 Rotterdam Film Festival: end Jan–begin Feb; North Sea Jazz Festival: 2nd weekend of Jul. 🌐 rotterdam.info

Transport
🚉 Stationsplein. ✈ 6 km (4 miles) NW.

85 m (272 ft) to make this the tallest construction in the Netherlands. An exterior "space cabin" ascends 58 m (190 ft) from the viewing platform.

Spido

Havenrondvaarten Willemsplein 85. Tel (010) 275 9988. Europoort: **Open** daily. Boat tours: **Open** daily **Closed** 1 Jan, 25 Dec. 🅿 🌐 spido.nl

These wharves and quays service about 32,000 container ships a year. A boat tour is an ideal way of seeing the city's port, built between 1958 and 1975. Cyclists and motorists follow the 48-km (30-mile) Haven Route (harbour route) along the Nieuwe Maas.

Rotterdam City Centre

① Kubuswoningen
② Kunsthal
③ Maritiem Museum Rotterdam
④ Museum Boijmans Van Beuningen Rotterdam
⑤ Wereldmuseum Rotterdam

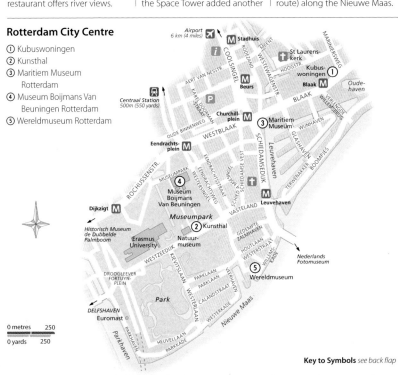

0 metres 250
0 yards 250

Key to Symbols *see back flap*

Museum Boijmans Van Beuningen Rotterdam

The museum is named after two art connoisseurs, FJO Boijmans, who bequeathed his paintings to Rotterdam in 1847, and DG van Beuningen, whose heirs donated his collection to the state in 1958. The resulting collection is one of The Netherlands' finest. First displayed in the nearby Schielandshuis, the collection was moved to the present gallery at Museumpark in 1935. Known for its supreme series of Old Master paintings, the collection also covers the whole spectrum of art, from the medieval works of Jan van Eyck to rare glassware, Surrealist paintings and contemporary art.

The museum's grounds include a sculpture garden

Three Marys at the Tomb (1425–35)
Brothers Jan and Hubert van Eyck collaborated on this colourful work, which shows the three Marys at the tomb of the resurrected Christ.

First floor

Nautilus Cup (1590)
A beautiful example of Dutch Renaissance art, this cup contains ornamental motifs relating to the sea and is crowned with Neptune sitting on a dolphin.

Key to Floorplan

- Old Masters
- Art: 18th century–1945
- Applied Arts and Design
- Free entrance exhibition space
- Temporary exhibition space
- Non-exhibition space

Thetis Receiving the Arms of Achilles from Vulcanus (1630–35)
This oil sketch by Peter Paul Rubens is one of a series inspired by Achilles' life.

★ **The Tower of Babel (c.1556)**
Pieter Bruegel took his theme from the Old Testament, and showed the elaborate ten-storey edifice teeming with frenetic activity.

Museum Guide

The museum is vast and the displays change regularly. Signposting to the museum's main sections is clear, however, and attendants are well adept at directing visitors. For Bruegel and Rembrandt follow signs to the Old Masters Collection, and for Dali and Magritte look for the Art: 18th century–1945 section.

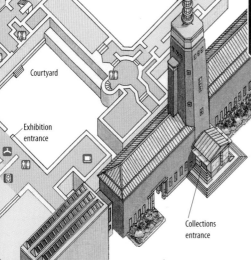

Pavilion

Basement

Ground floor

Tower

Courtyard

Collections entrance

Exhibition entrance

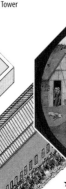

★ **The Pedlar (c.1502)**
Hieronymus Bosch's painting shows mankind trying to avoid the hazards of life, but with sin out to trap him at every turn.

★ **Titus at his Desk (1655)**
Rembrandt portrayed his sickly son in introspective mood, bathed in a tender light which heightens the ghostly pallor of his brooding features.

⑳ Utrecht

Utrecht was founded by the Romans in AD 47 to protect an important river crossing on the Rijn (Rhine). The town was among the first in the Netherlands to embrace Christianity. In 700, St Willibrord (658–739), a missionary from northern England, established a bishopric here, known as Het Sticht. Utrecht grew in importance as a religious centre throughout the Middle Ages, extending its control over much of the Netherlands until 1527, when Bishop Hendrik of Bavaria was obliged to sell all his temporal powers to Charles V *(see pp26–7)*. The city centre still retains many of its medieval churches and monasteries, but these now stand alongside modern blocks and a vast undercover shopping complex. The Oudegracht (old canal) threads its way through the city, flowing 5 m (16.5 ft) below ground level to prevent flooding. Today, it is lined with broad quays, cellar bars and cafés.

The headquarters of the Dutch railways are based in Utrecht, so it is fitting that the town has a superb railway museum in the restored 19th-century Maliebaan station. Inside there are specialist technical displays, engines and modern rail accessories. Outside, children can explore steam engines, carriages, trams and signal boxes. The museum includes five railway "worlds", each with its own theme.

Organ in the Speelklok museum

The Gothic Domtoren

🕍 Domtoren

Via VVV Utrecht, Domplein 9. **Tel** (030) 236 0010. 📷 every hour. Apr–Sep: 11am–4pm daily (from noon Mon, Sun); Oct–Mar: noon, 2pm & 4pm Sun–Fri; 11am–4pm Sat. **Closed** 1 Jan, 27 Apr, 25 & 26 Dec. 🦽 **W** domtoren.nl

The soaring Domtoren is a Gothic masterpiece and one of the tallest towers in the Netherlands at 112 m (367 ft) high. It was completed in 1382, on the site of the small, 8th-century church of St Willibrord. In 1674, the tower, which has always stood apart from the Domkerk, survived a massive hurricane that destroyed the nave of the cathedral. The Domtoren continues to dominate Utrecht's skyline.

🕍 Domkerk

Achter de Dom 1. **Tel** (030) 231 0403. **Open** daily; phone for times. 🦽 💻 🖼 **W** domkerk.nl

Construction of the cathedral began in 1254. Today, only the north and south transepts, two chapels and the choir remain, along with the 15th-century cloisters and a chapterhouse (1495), now part of the university. It was here that the Union of Utrecht *(see p27)* was signed in 1579 by John, Count of Nassau, brother of William of Orange. Outside the church is a giant boulder, dated 980 and covered with runic symbols. It was presented to Utrecht by the Danish people in 1936, to commemorate Denmark's early conversion to Christianity by missionaries from Utrecht.

🛤 Nederlands Spoorwegmuseum

Maliebaanstation. **Tel** (030) 2306 206. **Open** 10am–5pm Tue–Sun & public hols. **Closed** 1 Jan, 27 Apr. 🖼 🦽 📷 🖼 **W** spoorwegmuseum.nl

🎵 Museum Speelklok

Buurkerk on Steenweg 6. **Tel** (030) 231 2789. **Open** 10am–5pm Tue–Sun. **Closed** 1 Jan, 27 Apr, 25 Dec. 📷 🖼 🦽 💻 🖼 **W** museumspeelklok.nl

This magical place is located in the 13th-century Buurkerk, one of Utrecht's oldest churches. It has a collection of mechanical musical instruments, from the 18th century to the present day. Fairground organs compete with music boxes, clocks, carillons, pianolas and automated birds. These instruments are demonstrated on guided tours, during which visitors are encouraged to sing and dance along. The restoration of instruments can be observed in the workshop.

🏛 Centraal Museum

Nicolaaskerkhof 10. **Tel** (030) 236 2362. **Open** 11am–5pm Tue–Sun. **Closed** 1 Jan, 27 Apr, 25 Dec. 💻 🖼 **W** centraalmuseum.nl

Housed in an old convent, Centraal Museum is only a ten-minute walk from the city centre. At the heart of the

Steam engine and guard's box, Nederlands Spoorwegmuseum

Gerrit Rietveld's Schröderhuis (1924), part of the Centraal Museum

collection is a series of portraits by artist Jan van Scorel (1495–1562). On visiting Rome, van Scorel absorbed ideas from Italian Renaissance painting and he became the first Dutch artist to paint group portraits. These established the tradition leading to the superb 16th-century Civic Guard portraits (see p83).

Another of the museum's highlights is Gerrit Rietveld's Schröderhuis, Prins Hendriklaan 50. Designed in 1924 and regarded as the apogee of De Stijl architecture (see p138) (tours by appointment).

The museum also holds exhibitions of contemporary art, fashion and design.

🏛 Pieterskerk

Pieterskerkhof. **Tel** (030) 231 1485. **Open** noon–4pm Sat; Jul–mid-Sep: 11am–5pm Tue–Sat.

Built of tufa (limestone) with red sandstone columns, the church was completed in 1048. A rare Dutch example of German Romanesque architecture.

🏛 Museum Catharijneconvent

Lange Nieuwstraat 38. **Tel** (030) 231 3835. **Open** 10am–5pm Tue–Fri (from 11am Sat, Sun & public hols). **Closed** 1 Jan, 27 Apr. 🅿 ♿ 🖂 📷 **w** catharijneconvent.nl

The beautiful former convent of St Catherine (1562) is now home to this fascinating museum. It deals with the often-troubled history of religion in the Netherlands and also houses an award-winning collection of medieval art. Sculptures, gold and silver work, manuscripts, paintings, ecclesiastical clothing and jewel-encrusted miniatures are displayed in rooms round the cloister.

On the upper floors of the museum is a series of model church interiors, highlighting the variety of Dutch religious philosophies through the ages. They range from the lavish statues, paintings and elaborate altar in a Catholic church to the more austere, unadorned interiors typical of Protestant churches.

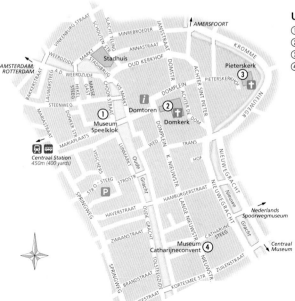

Utrecht City Centre
① Museum Speelklok
② Domtoren and Domkerk
③ Pieterskerk
④ Museum Catharijneconvent

| 0 metres | 200 |
| 0 yards | 200 |

㉑ Nationale Park De Hoge Veluwe

Made up of 5,400 ha (13,344 acres) of woodland, fen, heath and sand drifts, the Netherlands' largest nature reserve is home to thousands of rare plants, wild animals and birds. Also located in the park are the Museum Kröller-Müller, with more than 250 works by Van Gogh, and an outdoor sculpture garden, the Beeldentuin. Beneath the Visitors' Centre is the Museonder, with audiovisual displays about the earth's sub-surface, including an earthquake simulator. Cars are allowed on the main roads of the reserve, and parking areas are provided.

Jachthuis St Hubertus
This hunting lodge was built in 1920 by HP Berlage (see p81) for the park's wealthy patrons, the Kröller-Müllers.

★ Museum Kröller-Müller
Besides Van Gogh's *Café Terrace at Night* (1881), the museum has a collection of early Flemish masters and works by modern artists.

★ Beeldentuin
Jean Dubuffet's *Jardin d'Email*, shown here, is one of the striking modern sculpures on display in this 11-ha (27-acre) sculpture park. The Beeldentuin also provides an elemental setting for works by Auguste Rodin, Alberto Giacometti and Barbara Hepworth.

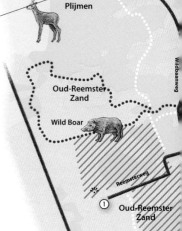

Otterlose Zand

De Wetweg

Houtkampweg

Moufflon

Kroekelweg

Plijmen

Oud-Reemster Zand

Wild Boar

Oud-Reemster Zand

Oud-Reemst

Reemsterweg

Wildbaanweg

Fran Ber

Picnicking
Tables are provided near the Visitors' Centre. Picnicking is allowed everywhere except in areas set aside for the animals.

Free White Bicycles
At the Visitors' Centre bikes are available for exploring the park.

VISITORS' CHECKLIST

Practical Information
80 km (50 miles) SE of Amsterdam.
Tel (0800) 835 3628. **Open** Apr:
8am–8pm; May, Aug: 8am–9pm;
Jun, Jul: 8am–10pm; Sep:
9am–8pm; Oct: 9am–7pm; Nov–
Mar: 9am–6pm. 🚗 ♿ 🅿️
Regulations: Do not camp, or
disturb the animals. Vehicles must
not leave the road. Do not light
fires outside designated areas.
Keep dogs on a leash.
🌐 **hogeveluwe.nl** Museum
Kröller-Müller: Houtkampweg 6,
Otterlo. **Tel** (0318) 591 241.
Open 10am–5pm Tue–Sun &
public hols. **Closed** 1 Jan. 🚗 ♿
📷 🖥 🌐 **kmm.nl**

Transport
🚌 108 from Ede-Wageningen,
change to 106 at Otterlo; 108
from Apeldoorn to Hoenderloo.
Entrances: Otterlo, Schaarsbergen,
Hoenderloo. Nationale Park
Visitors' Centre: Otterlo.

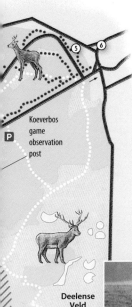

| 0 kilometres | 2 |
| 0 miles | 1 |

Koeverbos
game
observation
post

Deelense
Veld

eelense
Zand

Game Hides and Observation Points
Special viewing areas (see map) allow the
wildlife, like red deer, moufflon sheep and
wild boar, to remain undisturbed.

Key
▬▬ Main road
••• Walk route
▪▪▪ Cycle path
▢ Forest
▨ Heath
▢ Sand drifts
▨ No access

KEY
① **Bosje van Staf game
   observation post**
② **Nieuwe Plijmen game
   observation post**
③ **Visitors' Centre and Museonder**
④ **Otterlo entrance**
⑤ **Camp site**
⑥ **Hoenderloo entrance**
⑦ **Schaarsbergen entrance**

㉒ Arnhem

80 km (50 miles) SE of Amsterdam. 🏠
148,000. 🚊 🚌 ℹ️ Stationsplein 13.
0900 112 2344. 🚢 ♿ ⛪ 🏳️ 🅿️ Sat.
🌐 **vvvarnhem.nl**

Capital of Gelderland province,
Arnhem was all but destroyed
between 17 and 27 September
1944, in one of the most famous
battles of World War II. The city
still retains a number of
reminders of the conflict, such
as the John Frost Bridge, scene
of some of the heaviest fighting.
The bridge is named after the
commanding officer of the 2nd
Parachute Battalion, which
fought to hold the bridgehead
for four days.

🏛 Airborne Museum Hartenstein
Utrechtseweg 232, Oosterbeek.
Tel (026) 333 7710. **Open** daily.
Closed 25 Dec. 🚗 ♿ 🖥
📷 🌐 **airbornemuseum.com**

The museum traces the course of
the struggle to take Arnhem,
using models, slides, taped
commentaries and original film
footage. The collection is in Villa
Hartenstein near Ooster-beek,
used by the Commander of the
1st British Airborne Division,
General Urquhart.

John Frost Bridge, Arnhem

🏛 Nederlands Openluchtmuseum
Schelmseweg 89. **Tel** (026) 357 6111.
Open Apr–Oct: 10am–5pm daily;
Dec–mid-Jan: 11am–5pm Mon–Fri,
10am–6pm Sat & Sun; mid-Jan–Mar
& Nov: 11am–4:30pm Sat & Sun (park
only). **Closed** 1 Jan, 24 Dec. 🚗 ♿
🖥 🌐 **openluchtmuseum.nl**
Situated in a wooded park, this
museum recreates the traditional
architecture and folklore from
1800 to 1950. Founded in 1912,
about 100 farmhouses, barns,
windmills and workshops have
since been erected here, many of
them furnished in period style.
The museum staff dress up in
traditional costume.

㉓ Paleis Het Loo

Stadholder William III *(see p29)* built Het Loo in 1686 as a royal hunting lodge. Generations of the House of Orange used the lodge as a summer palace. Because of its magnificence, it was regarded as the "Versailles of the Netherlands". The main architect was Jacob Roman (1640–1716); the interior decoration and layout of the gardens were the responsibility of Daniel Marot (1661–1752). The building's Classical façade belies the opulence of its lavish interior; after extensive restoration work was completed on both in 1984, the palace was opened as a museum.

Monogram (c.1690) of William and Mary, king and queen of England.

★ **State Bedroom of Stadholder William III (c.1695)**
The wall coverings and draperies in this luxurious bedroom are of rich crimson damask.

KEY

① **King's Garden**

② **Stadholder William III's Closet (1690)** was William's private study with walls covered in embossed scarlet damask. His favourite paintings and delftware pieces are exhibited here.

③ **King William III's bedroom**

④ **Bedroom of Queen Mary II**

⑤ **Queen's Garden**

⑥ **Picture gallery**

⑦ **Library**

⑧ **The East Wing** houses the royal collections of clocks, dinner services and other household items.

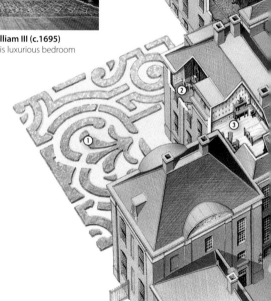

Classic Cars
This 1925 Minerva, was owned by Prince Hendrik, consort of Queen Wilhelmina. It is one of the royal family's many vintage cars, which are on display in the stable block (1910).

★ **Old Dining Room (1686)**
In 1984, six layers of paint were removed from the marbled walls, now hung with tapestries depicting scenes from Ovid's poems.

VISITORS' CHECKLIST

Practical Information
85 km (53 miles) SE of Amsterdam. Koninklijk Park 1, Apeldoorn. **Tel** (055) 577 2400. Palace & Gardens:
Open 10am–5pm Tue–Sun.
Closed 1 Jan, 27 Apr. 🅿 ♿ 🎁
🖊 w paleishetloo.nl

Transport
🚆 Apeldoorn, then bus 10, 16, 202.

Main entrance

★ **Formal Gardens**
The gardens combine plants, statuary and fountains in Classical style. The Fountain of the Celestial Sphere stands in the Lower Garden.

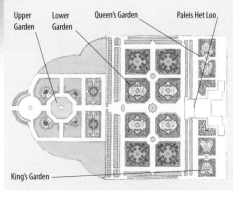

Upper Garden

Lower Garden

Queen's Garden

Paleis Het Loo

King's Garden

The Formal Gardens

Old prints, records and plans were used as the guidelines for recreating Het Loo's formal gardens, which lie in the vast acres behind the palace. Grass was planted over the original walled and knot gardens in the 18th century, and this was cleared in 1975. By 1983, the intricate floral patterns had been re-established, replanting had begun, the Classical fountains were renovated and the water supply fully restored. The garden reflects the late 17th-century belief that art and nature should operate in harmony.

Layout of the formal section of the gardens

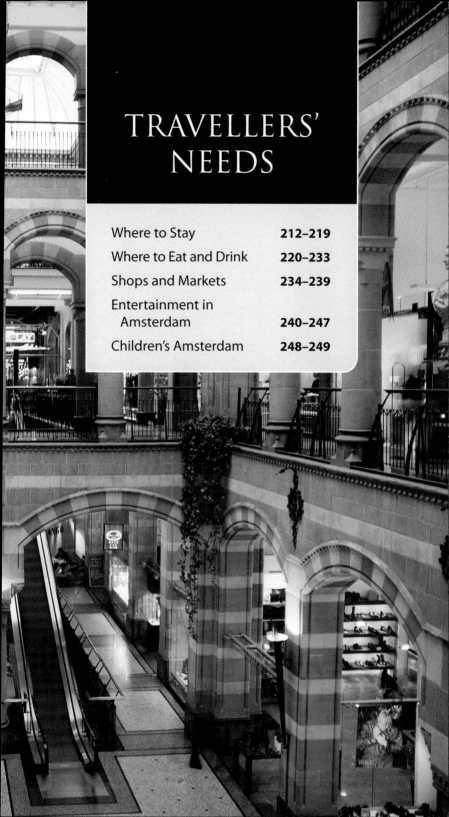

TRAVELLERS' NEEDS

WHERE TO STAY

Amsterdam offers a choice of top-quality, centrally located accommodation options to suit every budget. These range from luxurious five-star hotels to the more basic, budget-friendly options. In between, there are some bed-and-breakfasts (B&Bs) or family-run, small canalside hotels, often with good views. Accommodation can even be found on the water, in the form of canal boat rentals. During the busy summer months, most lodgings can be full, and it is wise to book well in advance. The listings on pages 216–19 include hotels that suit every taste and price range.

Lovely garden at the Canal House in Western Canal Ring (see p216)

Choosing a Hotel

Most of Amsterdam's hotels are clustered in a few areas. The most popular places to stay, unsurprisingly, are along the scenic canals. The neighbourhoods near the museums and Vondelpark are also popular. More suited to budget travellers is the area around Centraal Station and the Red Light District, where it is possible to find one or two gems in less picturesque surroundings.

Hotels in Amsterdam are generally expensive. However, the recent impacts of economic crisis on travel has seen prices drop and special offers increase. Visitors may also find the rooms to be smaller than in other European cities. The most beautiful hotels, typical of the city, are found along the main canal belt, the Grachtengordel. Many of these buildings are listed monuments and thus cannot be altered, so you will often come across very steep stairs and no lifts.

Hotels in the Museum Quarter tend to be a little more spacious and are often set in elegant villas, redesigned old schools, or other commercial buildings. This sedate area is near many of Amsterdam's cultural hotspots such as the Rijksmuseum, the Concertgebouw and the Van Gogh Museum.

Hotels which are aimed at the business traveller are mostly clustered around the RAI exhibition centre in the south, near the office blocks of the Zuidas or close to Centraal Station. The location of a hotel in Amsterdam, however, does have little effect on the price; the cost of a hotel outside the centre will differ little from a hotel of a similar standard that is situated in the heart of the town.

The **I amsterdam Visitor Centre** publishes a comprehensive list of accommodation in the city, which is available at their offices in Schiphol Airport as well as Centraal Station and

Netherlands Board of Tourism and Conventions (NBTC) offices around the world.

Room Rates

There are no hard and fast rules as to whether a hotel's advertised rates always include breakfast or the compulsory 5.5 per cent City Tourist Tax, though the price guide in the following listings does factor in any additional charges. Generally, breakfast tends to be included, except in hotels at the very top and bottom ends of the price scale. If you are staying in the Grachtengordel, note that rooms with canal or garden views generally cost more, irrespective of the hotel grading.

There are several tips that can help budget-conscious travellers. For those travelling in a group, many hotels have larger or family rooms for

Hotel de l'Europe, overlooking Muntplein (see p218)

◀ Magna Plaza shopping mall

Well-equipped room with canal views in DoubleTree hotel, Nieuwe Zijde *(see p219)*

sharing, or will add beds for a fraction of the room price. Accommodation with shared bathrooms is also quite light on the pocket. For those travelling alone, single occupation of a double room is usually a bad idea and will rarely invite a discount. The best option for single travellers is to make use of one of the many hostels in the city. Some can be particularly unique and charming; especially those located in canal boats along the picturesque waterways.

Special Offers

Many hotels, especially private ones, have lower rates between November and March, although they tend to peak around Christmas and New Year. Some even throw in a complimentary boat trip and/or free museum admissions. When booking, it is always worthwhile to ask about any special offers that might be available when you visit.

Chain hotels, of which there are many, almost always have promotion packages on, so a little research and early booking always gets discounted rates. Some chains offer cheaper weekend rates. For good deals in all classes of hotels, whether chain or private, it is worth checking a reputable reservations website such as **Hotels.nl** and **Booking.com**. The websites of agencies such as **Expedia**, **Lastminute.com** and **Kayak** usually have good offers as well. On some

of these, travellers can save money by booking flights and hotels together.

Booking and Paying

The busiest times of year for Amsterdam hotels are April (tulip season and King's Day), August and the Christmas and New Year period. If you want to visit during these times, it is advisable to book a room months ahead to get a good deal. Watch out for holidays such as King's Day, when rooms may be booked up to a year in advance.

Amsterdam is such a popular city that it is often difficult to book a last-minute room at any time of the year, so planning ahead – especially if you intend to stay in a Grachtengordel hotel – is recommended.

Booking a room via telephone, website or email is invariably straightforward as most hotel staff are familiar with English. All the chains and finer hotels take credit card payments as do an increasing number of privately-owned hotels.

Many establishments will ask for a deposit to hold a reservation. This could be anything from 10 per cent up to the cost of a first night's stay. For hotels that don't accept credit cards, the final bill settlement will need to be in cash. Costs for cancellations vary; the later you cancel, the more you pay. Many hotels will charge up to 100 per cent of the cost for last minute cancellations.

If you arrive in Amsterdam

without a room reservation, then the I amsterdam Visitor Centre at Schiphol Airport, Centraal Station or Leidseplein can book one for you, but this service will incur a small fee. Hotels can also be found and booked through the I amsterdam website.

Hotel Gradings

The star system used by Benelux Hotel Classification ranges from one-star (may have shared bathrooms) to five stars (rooms must be of a minimum size and the hotel must have plenty of amenities). These stars relate entirely to facilities and not to location or attractiveness, you therefore may find that a small, cheap hotel on a canal is more charming than a bland, corporate one, but that the more appealing of the two will have fewer stars.

The elegant foyer of the InterContinental Amstel Amsterdam *(see p219)*

A spacious executive double guest room in the Marriott in the Museum Quarter *(see p219)*

What to Expect

The only establishments that have on-site restaurants are the larger chains or very expensive hotels. On the other hand, quite a sizeable number of hotels, including the smallest ones, have bars that provide at least some snacks. The rest of the lodgings usually provide just bed and breakfast, although bigger places may also have communal lounge areas.

Breakfast usually comprises a continental buffet, which largely includes coffee, bread rolls and conserves, cheese, meats and boiled eggs. While in the past only the most expensive hotels provided a hot buffet, these days the trend is for most hotels to feature a good breakfast spread.

Make sure to get a description of the room before booking, or you may not find the splendid canal vistas you had hoped for. Most rooms are on the small side and come with a TV and telephone. An increasing numbers of hotels – even budget ones – now provide Wi-Fi, though this is not always free of charge. Bathrooms can be tiny and, as with Amsterdam apartments, bathtubs are a luxury rather than standard.

Travelling with Children

Amsterdam is generally a child-friendly place, and although some of the more exclusive places discourage younger travellers, most places welcome them. Many of the chains and bigger hotels allow children (usually up to two) to stay free in their parents' rooms and some provide free breakfasts. Others may offer reduced rates or charge a small fee to rent babies' cots. In many hotels, babysitting services are available for a fee.

Gay Hotels

Amsterdam is a gay-friendly city, so there are no problems staying anywhere. If, however, you do want to sample the city's gay hotels, the most popular and well known is the Golden Bear *(see p217)*, at the heart of the Kerkstraat gay scene. **ITC**, near Rembrandtplein, is also popular with both gay and lesbian travellers. The city lacks lesbian-only accommodation, but the **Quentin**, near Leidseplein is a popular choice.

The monthly magazine *Gay&Night* gives a full overview of all things gay and lesbian and is available at **Pink Point** and the **Vrolijk** bookshop. It is also included in the information kit on gay Amsterdam and can be ordered from **GAYtic** *(see p255)*.

Disabled Travellers

While charming, the cobbled streets, tall or narrow houses and steep stairs can cause problems for disabled tourists. Since so many hotels on the canal belt have a protected status and cannot be renovated, there are few lifts. Wheelchair access is therefore often only viable in chain hotels or top-price establishments.

Hostels

Hostels are very popular in Amsterdam, and generally cater to a, young back-packing crowd. Most hostels, with the exception of **Stayokay**, are privately owned and have dorm accommodation, though some have private rooms as well. Many places also have cheap, cheerful bars on site. A relatively new hostel in the Amsterdam-Zuidoost, **Hostelle** offers women-only accommodation. Note that some hostels have curfews as well. Those near Centraal Station can be less pleasant than elsewhere, so do exercise caution when booking.

Camping

Amsterdam is well served by camp sites. While none of these are in the city centre, they are easily accessible via good public transport links. Open between March and October, **Gaasper Camping** is good for families, with watersporting opportunities nearby. The **Amsterdamse Bos** site is set in acres of recreational woodland, perfect for children. To the north, **Vliegenbos** is great for exploring pretty Waterland villages *(Apr– Sep)*. Open year-round, **Zeeburg** is the nearest to the city centre. Rental huts are available, and a tram stop is located within walking distance.

Self-catering

There are few self-catering options in Amsterdam as apartment space is at a premium. The I amsterdam Visitor Centre's hotel brochure lists letting agents, who sometimes stipulate a minimum stay of a week. The website **City Mundo** is also a good place to research possibilities. Of the hotels recommended in this guide, Bridge Hotel *(see p216)*, Residence Le Coin *(see p217)* and Amsterdam House *(see p218)* offer the best self-catering options.

Staying in Private Homes

Since real estate is at a premium and Amsterdam flats tend to be tiny, guesthouse stays in people's homes are severely limited. Nevertheless, **Bed and Breakfast Nederland** is an excellent resource for finding places that are available.

Beyond Amsterdam

The NBTC's website lists more than 2,000 hotels throughout the Netherlands, with comprehensive information about each of them. Although this guide does not cover hotels outside Amsterdam, the information about booking and paying, hotel gradings, hostels and camping applies across the entire country.

Recommended Hotels

The places to stay recommended on pages 216–19 feature a wide selection in Amsterdam to suit every budget and requirement. These include the best canalside, retreats, luxurious hotels, superb getaways with character and lodgings catering to families and to business travellers.

The DK Choice label identifies accommodation that has been chosen for one or more exceptional qualities. A hotel may feature state-of-the-art luxury and top-class amenities, be situated in a historic building or it may be particularly comfortable and offer excellent value for money. Whatever the reason, these guarantee a memorable stay.

Modern exterior of the Amsterdam Hilton *(see 219)*

DIRECTORY

Choosing a Hotel

I amsterdam Visitor Centre
Centraal Station:
Stationsplein 10, 1012 AB.
Schiphol Airport:
Arrivals Hall 2 at
Schiphol Plaza.
Tel 702 6000.
W **iamsterdam.com**

NBTC
PO Box 63740, 2502 JL
Den Haag.
Tel 070 370 5705.
W **holland.com**

Special Offers

Booking.com
W **booking.com**

Expedia
W **expedia.com**

Hotels.nl
W **hotels.nl**

Kayak
W **kayak.com**

Lastminute.com
W **lastminute.com**

Gay Hotels

ITC
Prinsengracht 1051,
1017 JE. **Map** 5 A3.
Tel 623 0230.
W **itc-hotel.com**

Pink Point
Westermarkt, 1016 DH.
Map 1 B4. **Tel** 428 1070.
W **pinkpoint.org**

Quentin
Leidsekade 89, 1017 PN.
Map 4 D1.
Tel 894 3004.
W **quentinhotels.com**

Vrolijk
Paleisstraat 135, 1012 ZL.
Map 7 B3. **Tel** 623 5142.
W **vrolijk.nu**

Hostels

Hostelle
Frankemaheerd 2, 1102
AN. Amsterdam Zuidoost.
Tel 770 3504.
W **hostelle.com**

Stayokay
Stadsdoelen (city centre).
Map 7 C4. **Tel** 624 6832.
W **stayokay.com**

Camping

Amsterdamse Bos
Kleine Noorddijk 1,
1187 NZ, Amstelveen.
Tel 641 6868.
W **camping amsterdamsebos.nl**

Gaasper Camping
Loosdrechtdreef 7,
1108 AZ. **Tel** 696 7326.
W **gaaspercamping.nl**

Vliegenbos
Meeuwenlaan 138,
1022 AM. **Tel** 636 8855.
W **vliegenbos.com**

Zeeburg
Zuider IJdijk 20, 1095 KN .
Tel 694 4430.
W **campingzeeburg.nl**

Self-Catering

City Mundo
W **citymundo.nl**

Staying in Private Homes

Bed and Breakfast Nederland
W **bedandbreakfast nederland.nl**

Where to Stay

Canalside/Waterside

Oude Zijde

MISC €€
Kloveniersburgwal 20, 1012 CV
Tel *330 6241* **Map** 8 D3
W misceatdrinksleep.com
Themed rooms include the
Rembrandt Room and Baroque
Room. Serves breakfast till noon.

Nieuwe Zijde

Estheréa €€
Singel 303–309, 1012 WJ
Tel *624 5146* **Map** 7 A3
W estherea.nl
Elegant, family-run hotel with a
library, a canal-view lounge and
a 24-hour bar. Attentive staff.

Western Canal Ring

Chic & Basic €
Herengracht 13–19, 1015 BA
Tel *522 2345* **Map** 2 D3
W chicandbasic.com
Several 300-year-old canal
houses contain white,
minimalist rooms.

Hotel Brouwer €
Singel 83, 1012 VE
Tel *624 6358* **Map** 7 B1
W hotelbrouwer.nl
Simple rooms are named after
Dutch artists. Great canal views.

't Hotel €€
Leliegracht 18, 1015 DE
Tel *422 2741* **Map** 7 A2
W thotel.nl
Featuring 1920s-influenced
furniture, this lovely hotel has
light, airy rooms.

Sunhead of 1617 €€
Herengracht 152, 1016 BN
Tel *626 1809* **Map** 7 A2
W sunhead.com
This cosy and romantic B&B offers
magnificent views. There's an
impressive breakfast spread.

The Times Hotel €€
Herengracht 135–137, 1015 BG
Tel *330 6030* **Map** 7 A2
W thetimeshotel.nl
Set in canal houses dating from
1650, this hotel offers a mix of
tradition and modern comfort.

Canal House €€€
Keizersgracht 148, 1015 CX
Tel *622 5182* **Map** 7 A1
W canalhouse.nl
Boutique hotel with 17th-century
façade and period features. Pretty
garden and excellent breakfast.

Central Canal Ring

De Leydsche Hof €
Leidsegracht 14, 1016 CK
Tel *638 2327* **Map** 7 A5
W hoteldeleydschehof.com
This cosy family-run hotel with a
genteel feel has en suite rooms
with fridge and tea/coffee facilities.

Amsterdam Wiechmann €€
Prinsengracht 332, 1016 HX
Tel *626 3321* **Map** 1 B5
W hotelwiechmann.nl
Cosy rooms have chintzy decor
and eccentric knick-knacks. The
breakfast room has canal views.

Eastern Canal Ring

Seven Bridges Hotel €€
Reguliersgracht 31, 1017 LK
Tel *623 1329* **Map** 5 A3
W sevenbridgeshotel.nl
Housed in a former 17th-century
merchant house, rooms feature
antique furnishings.

DK Choice

Banks Mansion €€€
Herengracht 519–525, 1017 BV
Tel *420 0055* **Map** 7 B5
W carlton.nl/banksmansion
Set in an iconic former bank
building, this hotel has a "full
service concept" – everything
from breakfast to the bedroom
mini bar is included in the price.
The rooms feature Frank Lloyd
Wright-inspired decor, pristine
bathrooms and a pillow menu.
The hotel won the Tripadvisor
Travellers' Choice award in 2013.

Plantage

Hotel Adolesce €
Nieuwe Keizersgracht 26, 1018 DS
Tel *626 3959* **Map** 8 F5
W adolesce.nl
Clean, unfussy budget option
with en suite rooms. No breakfast,

Price Guide

Prices are based on one night's stay in
high season for a standard double room,
inclusive of service charges and taxes.

€	up to €150
€€	€150–€250
€€€	over €250

but there is 24-hour free
access to food and drinks in
the lounge.

The Bridge Hotel €€
Amstel 107-111
Tel *623 7068* **Map** 5 B3
W thebridgehotel.nl
This decent budget hotel with
simple but bright rooms is in a
former stonemason's workshop.

Hermitage €€
Nieuwe Keizersgracht 16, 1018 DR
Tel *623 8259* **Map** 5 B3
W hotelhermitageamsterdam.com
Centrally located hotel set in a
1733 canal house, with en suite
rooms simply decorated in
shades of grey and silver.

Hotels with Character

Oude Zijde

DK Choice

Hôtel Droog €€€
Staalstraat 7B, 1011 JJ
Tel *217 0100* **Map** 7 C4
W hoteldroog.com
The eponymous creation of the
famous Dutch design group,
Hôtel Droog offers excellent
hospitality with the ambience
of an art gallery. It has just one
apartment for guests but
boasts many unique features,
including a courtyard fairy-
tale garden, a café, a beauty
salon, a fashion boutique, an
art gallery and a design store.

Cosy room with wooden furniture at Canal House in Western Canal Ring

Nieuwe Zijde

Die Port van Cleve €€
Nieuwezijds Voorburgwal 176, 1012 SJ
Tel *714 2000* **Map** 7 B2
W dieportvancleve.com
On the site of the original 1864
Heineken brewery, this hotel has
luxurious rooms with a Delfts
Blauw theme. Excellent restaurant.

Hotel Sint Nicolaas €€
Spuistraat 1A, 1012 SP
Tel *626 1384* **Map** 7 C1
W hotelnicolaas.nl
Set in a former harbour office and
mattress factory, this hotel offers
uniquely shaped en suite rooms
with plush furnishings.

Kamer 01 €€€
Singel 416, 1016 AK
Tel *06 5477 6151* **Map** 7 A4
W kamer01.nl
Situated in a listed 1585 building
with authentic original features,
this cosy B&B has just three rooms.

Western Canal Ring

The Toren €€€
Keizersgracht 164, 1015 CZ
Tel *622 6352* **Map** 7 A1
W thetoren.nl
Award-winning hotel located in
a former merchant's house and
World War II hiding place.

Central Canal Ring

Back Stage Hotel €
Leidsegracht 114, 1016 CT
Tel *624 4044* **Map** 4 D1
W backstagehotel.com
Hotel for music lovers; black-and-
white, rock'n'roll themed decor
and iPod docks in all rooms.

The Golden Bear €
Kerkstraat 37, 1017 GB
Tel *624 4785* **Map** 4 E1
W quentingoldenbear.com
Located in two 1731 buildings,
this popular gay hotel has bright
and cheerful rooms.

Dikker & Thijs Fenice Hotel €€
Prinsengracht 444, 1017 KE
Tel *620 1212* **Map** 4 E1
W dtfh.nl
Luxury hotel in an 18th-century
warehouse. Traditional ambience
and an in-house art gallery.

Eastern Canal Ring

Between Art and Kitsch €
Ruysdaelkade 75, 1072 AL
Tel *679 0485* **Map** 4 E4
W between-art-and-kitsch.com
Cosy B&B with basic amenities.
Rooms are furnished with
pastiche Baroque decoration
and Art Deco touches.

Exterior of the stylish Hôtel Droog, housed
in a 17th-century building in Oude Zijde

Cake Under My Pillow €
Jacob van Campenstraat 66, 1072 BH
Tel *751 0936* **Map** 4 F3
W cakeundermypillow.nl
Charming B&B with individually
themed rooms and a communal
kitchen. Free baked treats.

Museum Quarter

Atlas Hotel €
van Eeghenstraat 64, 1071 GK
Tel *676 6336* **Map** 3 C3
W hotelatlas.nl
Peaceful Art Nouveau villa with
ornate gables and stained glass.
The rooms are decorated with
original artworks.

**Conscious Hotel Museum
Square** €
de Lairessestraat 7, 1071 NR
Tel *671 9596* **Map** 4 D4
W conscioushotels.com
Eco-friendly hotel filled with
plants. Serves organic breakfasts.

Sandton Hotel De Filosoof €
Anna van den Vondelstraat 6, 1054 GZ
Tel *683 3013* **Map** 3 C2
W sandton.eu/amsterdam
Best suited to budding
intellectuals, the rooms here
are based on a philosophy or
philosopher. Extensive library.

Further Afield

Bicycle Hotel €
van Ostadestraat 123, 1072 SV
Tel *679 3452*
W bicyclehotel.com
Solar-powered panels and bicycle
rentals at this eco-friendly hotel.

Lloyd Hotel €
Oostelijke Handelskade 34, 1019 BN
Tel *561 3636*
W lloydhotel.com
Lloyd hotel offers a choice of one-
to-five star rooms. It hosts events
focusing on art and culture.

Family-Friendly

Oude Zijde

Résidence Le Coin €€
Nieuwe Doelenstraat 5, 1012 CP
Tel *524 6800* **Map** 7 C4
W lecoin.nl
Spacious, apartment-style rooms
have bright, modern decor, big
windows and kitchenettes.

Nieuwe Zijde

Avenue €€
Nieuwezijds Voorburgwal 33, 1012 RD
Tel *530 9530* **Map** 7 C1
W avenue-hotel.nl
Set in nine canal houses, this hotel
has various family rooms. Packed
lunches are available on request.

Citadel €€
*Nieuwezijds Voorburgwal 98–100,
1012 SG*
Tel *627 3882* **Map** 7 B2
W hotelcitadel.nl
Basic, modern rooms have great
cityscapes of Amsterdam.

Hotel Des Arts €€
Rokin 154–156, 1012 LE
Tel *620 1558* **Map** 7 B4
W hoteldesarts.nl
Cosy place with colourful, split-
level family rooms.

Rho Hotel €€
Nes 5–23, 1012 KC
Tel *620 7371* **Map** 7 C3
W rhohotel.com
An elegant hotel with a delicious
buffet breakfast and private
parking. Pets welcome.

Western Canal Ring

Linden Hotel €€
Lindengracht 251, 1015 KH
Tel *622 1460* **Map** 1 B3
W lindenhotel.nl
The modern and cleverly
designed rooms at this unique
triangular-shaped hotel include
family triple and quadruple rooms.

Central Canal Ring

Hotel Nadia €
Raadhuisstraat 51, 1016 DD
Tel *620 1550* **Map** 7 A2
W nadia.nl
In a central location, Hotel Nadia
has small and basic rooms. Baby
cots and babysitting are available
on request.

La Bohème €€
Marnixstraat 415, 1017 PK
Tel *624 2828* **Map** 4 E2
W la-boheme-amsterdam.com
This simple and cosy hotel offers
a free babysitting service.

For more information on types of hotels *see pages 212–15*

Handsome exterior of Ambassade Hotel in Central Canal Ring

Eastern Canal Ring

Hotel de Munck €
Achtergracht 3, 1017 WL
Tel *623 6283* **Map** 5 B3
W hoteldemunck.nl
Bright, cheerful hotel situated in a former sea captain's house, with group and family rooms.

Museum Quarter

Hotel Hestia €
Roemer Visscherstraat 7, 1054 EV
Tel *618 0801* **Map** 4 D2
W hotel-hestia.nl
Small, private hotel aimed at families and groups. Rooms for up to five. Pets welcome.

Hotel Jupiter €
2e Helmersstraat 14, 1054 CJ
Tel *618 7132* **Map** 4 D2
W jupiterhotel.nl
Family-run, cash-only hotel with shared facilities. Good continental breakfasts.

Hotel Museumzicht €
Jan Luijkenstraat 22, 1071 CN
Tel *671 2954* **Map** 4 E3
W hotelmuseumzicht.com
Basic hotel with 1950s and 60s-style vintage decor. Serves great organic breakfasts.

Stayokay City Hostel Vondelpark €
Zandpad 5, 1054 GA
Tel *589 8996* **Map** 4 D2
W stayokay.com/vondelpark
Great value hostel with accommodation ranging from double rooms to 20-bed dorms.

Best Western Apollo Museum Hotel €€
PC Hooftstraat 2, 1071 BX
Tel *662 1402* **Map** 4 E2
W apollohotelresorts.com/museum
Well-equipped chain hotel with amenities such as buffet breakfast, cots and airport shuttle service.

The Neighbour's Magnolia €€
Willemsparkweg 205, 1071 HB
Tel *676 9321* **Map** 3 C4
W magnoliahotelamsterdam.com
This B&B has bright rooms and a view of the splendid magnolia tree next door. Spacious family room.

Plantage

DK Choice

Amsterdam House €
's-Gravelandseveer 3–4, 1011 KM
Tel *626 2577* **Map** 7 C4
W amsterdamhouse.com
Amsterdam House has well-furnished bedrooms and apartments in colourful accents. For a memorable on-the-water experience, rent a houseboat with fully equipped kitchens and bathrooms, TV and stereo. Also serves organic breakfasts. Pets welcome. Great for groups.

Rembrandt €
Plantage Middenlaan 17, 1018 DA
Tel *627 2714* **Map** 6 D2
W hotelrembrandt.nl
Housed in a listed building with period features and murals, this hotel also has a library and garden.

Luxury
Oude Zijde

Grand Hotel Amrâth Amsterdam €€
Prins Hendrikkade 108, 1011 AK
Tel *552 0000* **Map** 8 E2
W amrathamsterdam.com
This impressive early 20th-century building is decorated with stained-glass and wood panelling.

The Grand €€€
Oudezijds Voorburgwal 197, 1012 EX
Tel *555 3111* **Map** 7 C3
W sofitel-legend-thegrand.com
A deluxe hotel with modern decor and a stunning marble foyer.

Hotel de l'Europe €€€
Nieuwe Doelenstraat 2–14, 1012 CP
Tel *531 1777* **Map** 7 C4
W leurope.nl
Choose from simple rooms or opulent suites. Superb restaurant.

Nieuwe Zijde

INK Hotel Amsterdam €€
Nieuwezijds Voorburgwal 67, 1012 RE
Tel *721 9178* **Map** 7 B2
W accorhotels.com
Formerly a newspaper office, this hotel offers first-class luxuries such as a well-equipped fitness room.

Swissôtel Amsterdam €€
Damrak 96, 1012 LP
Tel *522 3000* **Map** 7 B2
W swissotel.com
Contemporary interiors hide behind a 19th-century façade at this hotel just off Dam Square.

NH Grand Hotel Krasnapolsky €€€
Dam Square 9, 1012 JS
Tel *554 9111* **Map** 7 C3
W nh-hotels.nl
Fabulous space with opulent decor. Luxury suites plus compact rooms. Winter Garden glasshouse is a must-visit for brunch.

Western Canal Ring

The Dylan €€€
Keizersgracht 384, 1016 GB
Tel *530 2010* **Map** 1 B5
W dylanamsterdam.com
This refined and tasteful hotel has a Michelin-starred restaurant.

Central Canal Ring

Amsterdam American Hotel €€
Leidsekade 97, 1017 PN
Tel *556 3000* **Map** 4 E2
W edenamsterdamamericanhotel.nl
Stunning Art Deco hotel with sleek, modern design. Lovely fountained terrace.

Ambassade Hotel €€€
Herengracht 341, 1016 AZ
Tel *555 0222* **Map** 7 A4
W ambassade-hotel.nl
Spread across 10 canal houses, Ambassade offers spacious rooms and has an interesting library.

Hotel Pulitzer €€€
Prinsengracht 315, 1016 GZ
Tel *523 5235* **Map** 1 B5
W pulitzeramsterdam.com
Set across 25 adjoining 17th- and 18th-century canal houses. Timber ceilings run throughout.

Eastern Canal Ring

Hotel Seven One Seven €€€
Prinsengracht 717, 1017 JW
Tel *427 0717* **Map** 4 E2
W 717hotel.nl
Small and exclusive hotel with suites named after famous writers and musicians, and decorated with fresh flowers.

Museum Quarter

The College Hotel €€
Roelof Hartstraat 1, 1071 VE
Tel *571 1511* **Map** 4 E5
W thecollegehotel.com
This is a stylish boutique hotel with chic decor. Staff are students training in the craft of hospitality.

DK Choice

Conservatorium   €€€
Van Baerlestraat 27, 1071 AN
Tel *570 0000*   **Map** 4 D3
Ⓦ conservatoriumhotel.com
This former 19th-century bank
is now the sleek hotel
Conservatorium, designed by
architect Piero Lissoni. The
hotel boasts high ceilings
and a beautiful atrium. Many
of the rooms are duplexes
furnished with luxury linen,
state-of-the-art technology,
and offer amazing views. There
are excellent spa facilities and a
fitness centre as well.

Fusion Suites   €€€
Roemer Visscherstraat 40, 1054 EZ
Tel *618 4642*   **Map** 4 D2
Ⓦ fusionsuites.com
This hideaway provides large
luxury suites with rich antique
furnishings and an emphasis on
personal service. Some rooms
include whirlpools.

Plantage

**InterContinental Amstel
Amsterdam**   €€€
Professor Tulpplein 1, 1018 GX
Tel *622 6060*   **Map** 5 B4
Ⓦ amsterdam.intercontinental.com
A favourite with royalty and rock
stars, this sumptuously decorated
hotel offers first-class service and
a Michelin-starred restaurant.

Further Afield

Okura   €€
Ferdinand Bolstraat 333, 1072 LH
Tel *678 7111*
Ⓦ okura.nl
A superior hotel with elegantly
decorated rooms, Okura has
Michelin-starred Japanese and
French restaurants, a panoramic
champagne bar and a luxury spa.

Business

Oude Zijde

Radisson Blu Hotel   €€
Rusland 17, 1012 CK
Tel *623 1231*   **Map** 7 C4
Ⓦ radissonblu.com
This hotel has spacious rooms
with timber ceilings and modern
decor. It offers conference facilities.

Nieuwe Zijde

DK Choice

DoubleTree   €€
Oosterdoksstraat 4, 1011 DK
Tel *530 0800*   **Map** 8 E1
Ⓦ doubletree3.hilton.com
A large hotel with stunning
harbour views, DoubleTree offers
four-star amenities including a
fitness room and a DVD library.
Every room is equipped with an
iMac computer, which also
functions as a TV. Sixteen
conference halls are available,
plus remote printing facilities.

NH Barbizon Palace   €€
Prins Hendrikkade 59–72, 1012 AD
Tel *556 4564*   **Map** 8 D1
Ⓦ nh-hotels.com
A hotel with classic decor and a
Michelin-starred restaurant.

Park Plaza Victoria Hotel   €€
Damrak 1–5, 1012 LG
Tel *623 4255*   **Map** 7 C1
Ⓦ parkplaza.com/amsterdam
Built in 1890, this hotel offers
beautiful surroundings plus a spa
and video conference facilities.

Renaissance Amsterdam   €€€
Kattengat 1, 1012 SZ
Tel *621 2223*   **Map** 7 C1
Ⓦ renaissanceamsterdam.com
Excellent hotel with an impressive
17th-century Koepelkerk dome.

Eastern Canal Ring

NH Schiller   €€
Rembrandtplein 26, 1017 CV
Tel *554 0700*   **Map** 7 C5
Ⓦ nh-hotels.com
Charming hotel in a historic
building with Art Deco
furnishings and beautiful stained-
glass windows.

Museum Quarter

Marriott   €€
Stadhouderskade 12,1054 ES
Tel *607 5555*   **Map** 4 D2
Ⓦ marriott.com
Large chain hotel with rooms in
warm hues. Facilities include a
business centre, 24-hour gym
and sauna. Pets welcome.

Memphis   €€
De Lairessestraat 87, 1071 NX
Tel *673 3141*   **Map** 3 C4
Ⓦ embhotels.nl
Smart and stylish hotel with mod
cons such as flatscreen TVs, iPod
docks and tea/coffee facilities.

Further Afield

citizenM   €
Prinses Irenestraat 30, 1077 WX
Tel *811 7090*
Ⓦ citizenm.com
A thoroughly modern and stylish
hotel with touch-screen check-in.
Online reservations only.

Savoy Hotel Amsterdam   €
Ferdinand Bolstraat 194, 1072 LW
Tel *644 7445*   **Map** 4 F5
Ⓦ savoyhotel.nl
This conveniently located hotel
has large, bright rooms, and
facilities for small conferences.

Amsterdam Hilton   €€
Apollolaan 138, 1077 BG
Tel *710 6000*   **Map** 3 C5
Ⓦ amsterdam.hilton.com
Famous for John Lennon and
Yoko Ono's "bed-in for peace".
This luxurious hotel offers
excellent business facilities.

Bilderberg Garden Hotel   €€
Dijsselhofplantsoen 7, 1077 BJ
Tel *570 5600*   **Map** 3 C5
Ⓦ bilderberg.nl
Located in a quiet, upmarket
area, this hotel has extensive
conference facilities. There is a
comfortable lounge area for
post-dinner drinks.

Mövenpick   €€
Piet Heinkade 11, 1019 BR
Tel *519 1200*   **Map** off map
Ⓦ moevenpick-amsterdam.com
This waterfront hotel has
wonderful views over IJ river. Free
shuttle service to Centraal Station.

Nineteenth-century façade of Swissôtel Amsterdam, Nieuwe Zijde

For more information on types of hotels *see pages 212–15*

WHERE TO EAT AND DRINK

Though the Netherlands may not enjoy the gastronomic reputation of France or Italy, there are plenty of opportunities to enjoy good food at reasonable prices, especially in Amsterdam. Many cafés and bars serve tempting snacks, or *lekkertjes*, and some *eetcafés* provide full three-course menus at reasonable prices *(see pp232–3)*. In addition to the many Dutch restaurants, renowned for their generous portions, there are myriad eateries offering a range of international culinary delights, especially Thai, Italian and Indonesian. Most restaurants have a good selection of local and international wines, and there are cosy bars and a plethora of brown cafés *(see p50)* as well. The restaurant listings in this guide *(see pp224–31)* have been selected for their quality, atmosphere and good value.

Where to Eat

Amsterdam is a small city, and most of the restaurants listed in this guide are fairly centrally located. The highest concentrations of restaurants are along the Zeedijk and the Red Light District in Oude Zijde; along Spuistraat in the Nieuwe Zijde; and around the Jordaan in Western Canal Ring. A wide range of restaurants can also be found along the Leidseplein in Central Canal Ring, on Reguliersdwarsstraat and Utrechtsetraat in the Eastern Canal Ring and along the Van Baerlestraat in the Museum Quarter. Cheap meals are particularly easy to find and enjoy in many of the city's *eetcafés*. For lunch, there are numerous bakeries, coffee or bagel bars and cafés.

What to Eat

The wide range of international dishes available in Amsterdam reflects the multicultural nature of the city. Many fine-dining restaurants fuse French culinary techniques with Mediterranean, Asian or seasonal Dutch ingredients. There is also an increasing emphasis on organic produce and use of sustainably sourced fish.

Since Indonesia was once a Dutch colony, Amsterdam is one of the best places in Europe to sample its diverse flavours. Much of the cooking may lean more towards Chinese, but it is possible to sample some genuine Indonesian food. Suriname was another former colony, and the cuisine is a wonderful mix of Indian, African, Indonesian, Dutch, Chinese and Portuguese flavours. Most Surinamese restaurants lie outside the city centre, but the Kam Yin *(see p225)*, close to Centraal Station, is a good place to enjoy this amazing cuisine. Japanese and Thai restaurants are very popular and offer affordable meals. Italian, Spanish and Mediterranean cuisines are other favourites, with a number of authentic, regional or family-run restaurants around the city.

Elegantly laid-out table at Srikandi in the Museum Quarter *(see p230)*

Indian, Mexican and African food can also be easily found, and vegetarians are well catered for. Some of the best-loved vegan and vegetarian eateries can be found by the canalside in the Jordaan area.

What to Drink

Beer is the preferred drink in most Dutch cafés and bars *(see pp50–51)*, and all have a wide selection of local and imported brews. Wine is widely available, and nearly all restaurants in the city offer a good choice. Fine-dining places serve excellent French, international and organic wines, while many Spanish and Italian restaurants also feature local wines. The listings on the following pages include several restaurants that boast an exceptional wine list. Cocktail fever has also swept through the city, with many establishments offering a good range.

Restaurants specializing in traditional cuisine tend to have the best selection of *jenevers* (Dutch gin). For an authentic

Bottles on display in the bar at Nomads in Central Canal Ring *(see p228)*

jenever experience, visit a good *proeflokalen* (tasting house) and sample the huge range of delicious flavours available.

How Much to Pay

As across Europe, almost all of the restaurants in Amsterdam display a menu in the window. This gives the prices, which include VAT (BTW), and sometimes service charges. Prices vary markedly in the city and a meal at a luxurious restaurant can cost more than €50 per head. However, Amsterdam also has a wide choice of places serving meals at under €30 per person. The cost of drinks is invariably extra and the mark-up levied by a restaurant, especially on wine, can be high.

Opening Times

Although the Dutch do not view lunch as the main meal, many of the better restaurants in town are now beginning to open during the day. Many designer bars and brown cafés also serve lunch from around noon to 2 or 3pm. Dinner is served from 6pm onwards, and last orders are often taken as early as 10pm in most restaurants. However, some restaurants, particularly those in the central areas, have started to remain open until considerably later, especially on the weekends. Many places do not open at all on Mondays, although this is also changing, especially during peak tourist periods.

The picturesque terrace of Café de Jaren in Oude Zijde *(see p224)*

Charming glass dining room of De Kas restaurant *(see p231)*

Making a Reservation

When visiting one of the city's more celebrated restaurants, it is always wise to reserve ahead. However, some of the most popular and affordable restaurants do not take bookings. The listings indicate places where booking is advisable. Popular brown cafés and designer bars can also become crowded in the evening, but few of them take reservations.

Reading the Menu

The menus at many restaurants are written in Dutch, English and French or German. Most waiters and waitresses in the city speak good English, and often another European language, so it is rarely a problem ordering a meal anywhere in Amsterdam.

Etiquette

Most restaurants in Amsterdam are relaxed, so smart-casual dress is suitable almost everywhere. Although there is nothing to stop you from dressing up for special occasions, few places insist on a tie. For eating out with children, see page 249.

Smoking

Since July 2008, smoking has been banned in all Dutch cafés, restaurants, hotels and other public areas. The ban also includes "smoking" coffeeshops *(see p51)* where, in theory, owners must provide special rooms for their smoking clientele.

Disabilities

Disabled visitors will be able to get into the majority of ground-floor restaurants in the city. However, toilets can be difficult to get to as access is often via steep stairs.

Tipping

A service charge of 15 per cent is sometimes automatically included in the bill in restaurants, cafés and bars. This rarely goes to the server, however, so most locals leave a gratuity of about 10 per cent on the table.

Recommended Restaurants

The restaurants and cafés recommended in this guide have been chosen over a wide range of cuisines to suit every budget and taste. These include the best places in town to get *pannenkoeken* (pancakes), relaxed cafés that can be visited for a simple sandwich or salad, as well as sophisticated Michelin-starred restaurants that offer an unforgettable fine-dining experience.

The DK Choice designation identifies restaurants that are especially good for a particular reason. These may include an exceptionally romantic place to dine, a restaurant with splendid views or fabulous outdoor seating or a café offering amazing cuisine or a signature dish at excellent value.

The Flavours of Amsterdam

From its street-corner fish stalls to its cafés and top-flight gourmet restaurants, eating out in Amsterdam can be full of surprises. Traditional Dutch cuisine may be simple, wholesome and hearty, but the variety of food on offer in the city is huge and influenced by culinary styles from across the globe. Holland was once a major colonial power and its trading ships brought back exotic ingredients, ideas and people from former colonies to settle. Dutch chefs branched out and tried new flavours, and as such, "fusion" food has long been a feature of Amsterdam's menus.

Edam cheese

Sampling pickled herring at one of Amsterdam's many fish stalls

Home-Grown Staples

The typical Dutch menu offers good, solid fare. Plainly prepared fish or meat is served with well-cooked vegetables. Pork, hams and all kinds of sausages are popular. The North Sea provides plenty of fresh fish, especially cod, herring and mackerel, as well as its own variety of tiny brown shrimps. Leafy green vegetables, such as cabbage, endive (chicory) and curly kale make regular appearances, frequently mashed with the ubiquitous potato. Sauerkraut arrived from Germany long ago and is now considered a native dish, as are French fries dowsed in mayonnaise, which are a Belgian import. The world famous Gouda and Edam cheeses are sold at various stages of maturity, and with flavourings such as cloves, cumin or herbs.

The Melting Pot

Amsterdam has long had a reputation for religious and political tolerance. Refugees who found a safe haven there brought along their own styles

Fried tofu with *sambal oelek* (chilli sauce)

Bami goreng (fried noodles with chicken and shrimp)

Steamed rice

Prawn crackers

Gado-gado (vegetable salad with peanut sauce)

Satay ayam (chicken satay)

Selection of typical *rijsttafel* dishes

Local Dishes and Specialities

Brown shrimp

Dining out in Amsterdam is almost guaranteed to come up with some curious quirks. Cheese, ham and bread are standards at breakfast, but you may also find *ontbijtkoek* (gingerbread) and *hagelslag* (grains of chocolate) to sprinkle over bread. Ham and cheese are also lunchtime staples, often served in a bread roll with a glass of milk, though more adventurous sandwiches and salads are creeping in. Numerous pancake houses provide both sweet and savoury snacks throughout the day. The evening is the time when Amsterdam's eateries have the most to offer. The soups and mashed vegetables of Dutch farmhouse cooking sit alongside spicy Indonesian delights, as well as innovative cuisine from some of Amsterdam's fine chefs.

Erwtensoep is a thick pea and smoked sausage soup, which is often served with rye bread and slices of ham.

Baskets of wild mushrooms at an organic market

of cooking. In the 16th century, Jews fleeing persecution in Portugal and Antwerp were some of the first foreigners to make their home in the city. Today, Amsterdammers count as their own such Jewish specialities as *pekelvlees* (salt beef), pickled vegetables (often served as salad) and a variety of sticky cakes, now found mostly in the more old-fashioned tea rooms.

The 20th century saw an influx of immigrants from Turkey and several North African countries. Large Arab and Turkish communities have become established in Amsterdam. As a result, restaurants with menus that feature Middle-Eastern style stuffed vegetables, succulent stews and couscous, are almost everywhere. Falafel (fried chickpea balls) are readily available from roadside take-aways and are now one of the city's favourite late-night snacks. Ethiopians, Greeks, Thais, Italians and Japanese are among other waves of immigrants to make their culinary mark, and most recently traditional British fare has become popular.

Gouda on offer in an Amsterdam cheese shop

Indonesian Legacy

The Dutch began colonizing Indonesia in the 17th century and ruled the southeast Asian archipelago right up until 1949. Indonesian cuisine has had a marked influence on eating habits in Holland. Ingredients once regarded as exotic have crept into Dutch dishes. It is now commonplace to spice up apple pies and biscuits with cinnamon, which is sometimes even used to flavour vegetables. Coconut and chillis are very popular flavourings, too, and sampling a *rijsttafel* (see below) is considered one of the highlights of any trip to Amsterdam.

The Rijsttafel

Dutch colonialists in Indonesia often found that the modest local portions failed to satisfy their hunger. To match their larger appetites, they created the *rijsttafel* (literally "rice-table"). It consists of around 20 small spicy dishes, served up with a shared bowl of rice or noodles. Pork or chicken satay (mini kebabs with peanut sauce) and *kroepoek* (prawn crackers) usually arrive first. A selection of curried meat and vegetable dishes follows, with perhaps a plate of fried tofu and various salads, all more or less served together. A sweet treat, such as bananas fried in batter, rounds it all off.

Shrimp croquettes are shrimps in a creamy sauce, coated in breadcrumbs and deep-fried until golden.

Stamppot is a hearty dish of curly kale, endive (chicory) and crispy bacon mixed with mashed potato.

Nasi goreng, an Indonesian-style dish of egg-fried rice with pork and mushrooms, is also popular for a *rijsttafel*.

Where to Eat and Drink

Oude Zijde

A-Fusion €
Asian **Map** 8 D2
Zeedijk 130, 1012 BC
Tel *330 4068*
Trendy fusion restaurant serving
small, tapas-sized portions. Try
the beef with black peppers,
crispy chicken steak or sushi.

De Bakkerswinkel €
Bakery **Map** 7 C2
Warmoesstraat 69, 1012 HX
Tel *489 8000*
Everything in this café is home-
made, down to the jam. Sample
traditional English scones here.

Ganesha Indian Restaurant €
Indian **Map** 8 E1
Geldersekade 5 HS, 1011 EH
Tel *320 7302* **Closed** *lunch*
Good-value authentic Indian
restaurant. Popular choices include
tandoori grills (marinated meat
or seafood, cooked in a clay oven).

Golden Chopsticks €
Chinese **Map** 7 C3
Oude Doelenstraat 1, 1012 ED
Tel *620 7040*
This Hong Kong-style eatery has
a diverse menu. Try the steamed
oysters and sautéed lobster.

Bird €€
Thai **Map** 8 D2
Zeedijk 72–74, 1011 HB
Tel *620 1442* **Closed** *lunch daily*
Decorated with artworks, Bird is
renowned for its Thai curries. The
à la carte and set menus are
great value.

Café Bern €€
European **Map** 8 D3
Nieuwmarkt 9, 1011 JR
Tel *622 0034*
Café popular with locals. Signature
dishes include cheese fondue and
entrecôte (steak). A range of spirits
and house wines is on offer.

Café de Engelbewaarder €€
Brown Café **Map** 8 D4
Kloveniersburgwal 59, 1011 JZ
Tel *625 3772*
Traditional brown café. The weekly
changing menu has European
and seasonal dishes. Pinball
machines. Live jazz on Sundays.

Café de Jaren €€
European **Map** 7 C4
Nieuwe Doelenstraat 20–22, 1012 CP
Tel *625 5771*
Multistorey grand café with
a waterside terrace. The menu

includes soups, sandwiches and
more hearty meals. Good wine list.

Éénvistwéévis €€
Seafood **Map** 5 C1
Schippersgracht 6, 1011 TR
Tel *623 2894* **Closed** *Sun & Mon*
The chef at this intimate
restaurant combines the catch
of the day with organic, seasonal
ingredients to create fresh and
flavoursome dishes.

Geisha €€
Asian **Map** 8 E2
Prins Hendrikkade 106a, 1011 AJ
Tel *626 2410* **Closed** *Sat lunch; Sun*
Geisha serves modern and varied
Asian cuisine in stylish interiors.
Favourites include Kobe steak,
Szechuan lobster and lychee
sorbet. Sample cocktails or sake
with Asian titbits at the bar.

Hemelse Modder €€
International **Map** 8 E2
Oude Waal 11, 1011 BZ
Tel *624 3203* **Closed** *lunch*
This restaurant fuses international
cuisine with strong Mediterranean
influences. Do not miss the
signature namesake "Heavenly
Mud" chocolate mousse.

Kilimanjaro €€
African **Map** 8 F4
Rapenburgerplein 6, 1011 VB
Tel *622 3485* **Closed** *lunch; Mon*
Friendly, pan-African restaurant.
Specialities from across the vast
continent include West African
antelope stew. Charming terrace.

Latei €€
International **Map** 8 D2
Zeedijk 143, 1012 AW
Tel *625 7485* **Closed** *Sun–*
Wed dinner
This split-level café, which
doubles as a bric-a-brac shop,
has a regularly changing fusion
menu of home-made organic
vegetarian, vegan, meat and
seafood dishes.

Me Naam Naan €€
Thai **Map** 8 D3
Koningsstraat 29, 1011 ET
Tel *423 33 44* **Closed** *lunch; Mon*
Authentic Thai restaurant serving
classic cuisine. Do not miss the
koeng choechie (shrimps and Thai
aubergine in spicy red curry).

Olijfje €€
Mediterranean **Map** 8 E4
Valkenburgerstraat 223 D, 1011 MJ
Tel *330 4444* **Closed** *lunch; Mon*
Everything at Olijfje is freshly
made with quality olive oil. The

menu consists of good-value
Mediterranean cuisine, including
tapas, grilled dishes and organic
chicken. No pork served.

Oriental City €€
Chinese **Map** 7 C3
Oudezijds Voorburgwal 177–179,
1012 EV
Tel *626 8352*
Multistorey Chinese restaurant
specializing in Cantonese and
Szechuan dishes. The diverse
menu features crispy duck
and oysters. Sunday brunch
dim sum are a must-try.

Blauw aan de Wal €€€
Mediterranean **Map** 8 D3
Oudezijds Achterburgwal 99,
1012 DD
Tel *330 2257* **Closed** *Mon & Sun*
Hidden in a narrow alleyway,
this is a stylish restaurant with
rustic brick walls and wooden
beams. It serves delicious
Mediterranean fusion food.
Outstanding wine list.

Bridges €€€
Seafood **Map** 7 C3
Oudezijds Voorburgwal 197, 1012 EX
Tel *555 3560* **Closed** *Sat &*
Sun lunch
Refined seafood restaurant in
the Grand hotel. The modern
interior has a wall mural by artist
Karel Appel. It offers exquisitely
prepared crab, lobster and
delicate, divine fish *tartaar*.
Fantastic wines.

Guests enjoying a meal at the popular Café
de Jaren, Oude Zijde

Relaxed interior of Olijfje in Oude Zijde

DK Choice

Greetje €€€
Dutch **Map** 8 F3
Peperstraat 23, 1011 TJ
Tel *779 7450* **Closed** *lunch*
This traditional restaurant is very popular with locals. The menu changes every two months and features authentic Dutch cuisine. Specialities include grilled sugarbread with duck liver, *bloedworst* (blood sausage) with apple compote and *trekdrop* (liquorice) ice cream. Reservations recommended.

In de Waag €€€
European **Map** 8 D3
Nieuwmarkt 4, 1012 CR
Tel *422 7772*
This fusion kitchen is set in a former 15th-century city gate and is atmospherically lit by 300 candles. The eclectic menu includes delectable desserts. Above the restaurant is the room where Rembrandt sketched *Anatomy Lesson of Dr Tulp.*

Looks €€€
French **Map** 8 D2
Binnen Bantammerstraat 7, 1011 CH
Tel *320 0949* **Closed** *lunch; Sun*
This characterful restaurant sports a decor to match the menu: a fusion of classic and modern. Try the signature Surf and Turf (entrecôte and Canadian lobster). Excellent wine list.

Nieuwe Zijde

Català €
Spanish **Map** 7 A4
Spuistraat 299, 1012 VS
Tel *623 1141*
Small tapas bar with rustic interiors and a pavement terrace good for people-watching. It serves popular fish dishes such as rice

with shellfish, grilled swordfish and monkfish. Try the famous *pata negra jamon* (Iberian ham).

Getto Food & Drink €
International **Map** 8 D2
Warmoesstraat 51, 1012 HW
Tel *421 5151* **Closed** *Mon*
This gay-friendly restaurant serves home-style cooking. Burgers are named after famous Amsterdam drag queens: Jennifer Hopeless has bacon, guacamole and melted cheese filling.

Greenwoods €
English **Map** 7 B1
Singel 103, 1012 VG
Tel *623 7071*
Welcoming English-style tearoom. Choose between the breakfast, lunch or tea menus. Highlights include the full English breakfast with sausages and baked beans, and the Classic High Tea with real clotted cream.

DK Choice

Kam Yin €
Surinamese, Chinese **Map** 8 D1
Warmoesstraat 6, 1012 JD
Tel *625 3115*
An Amsterdam institution, Kam Yin is a great place for quick, delicious food. The extensive menu includes traditional Surinamese *roti* (pancake with vegetables or meat), *broodje pom* (chicken casserole sandwich) and Chinese *rijsttafel*. This simple restaurant is well worth a visit.

Moti Mahal €
Indian **Map** 7 C1
Nieuwezijds Voorburgwal 34, 1012 SB
Tel *625 0330* **Closed** *lunch*
Long-standing authentic Indian restaurant. Locals enjoy dishes such as butter chicken, *tikka masala* and *vindaloo*. Relish the delicious *kheer badami* (rice pudding with nuts and raisins).

Sushi €
Japanese **Map** 7 B4
Taksteeg 3 BG, 1012 PB
Tel *422 8978* **Closed** *Wed*
No-frills restaurant serving delicious sushi rolls and lamb chops. A range of fixed menus is available – try *Unadon*, which includes miso soup, Japanese salad and marinated eel.

Tibet €
Chinese **Map** 8 D2
Lange Niezel 24, 1012 GT
Tel *624 1137*
Relaxed eatery with eclectic decor. There is a choice of Chinese Szechuan dishes alongside staple Tibetan fare such as *momo* (dumplings). Asian lunch (rice or noodle dishes) is also served.

1e Klas €€
International **Map** 8 D1
Stationsplein 15, 1012 AB
Tel *625 0131*
Grand café-restaurant in a former first-class waiting room on platform 2B in Centraal Station. The extensive menu consists of bar snacks, meal-sized salads and Argentinian steak.

Barco €€
European **Map** 8 F2
Oosterdokskade10, 1011 AE
Tel *626 9383* **Closed** *lunch*
Laid-back café with a lovely deck terrace, set on an old canal barge. Typical European fare includes simply prepared meat and fish and a few vegetarian options. Live music Thursday to Saturday evenings.

Brasserie Harkema €€
French **Map** 7 B4
Nes 67, 1012 KD
Tel *482 2222*
Immensely popular Parisian-style brasserie. Feast on delights such as guinea fowl marinated in sage and olive oil. Book ahead.

Unique boat setting of Barco, Nieuwe Zijde

Côte Ouest €€
French **Map** 7 B2
Gravenstraat 20, 1012 NM
Tel *320 8998* **Closed** *Tue & Wed lunch; Mon*
Specializing in Breton dishes, the menu at Côte Ouest includes traditional savoury buckwheat galettes with toppings such as warm goat's cheese or smoked salmon, and mussels cooked in cider, with apple and bacon.

Kapitein Zeppos €€
Mediterranean **Map** 7 B4
Gebed Zonder End 5, 1012 HS
Tel *624 2057*
Tucked down a tiny alley, lit by fairy lights, this café-restaurant has an eclectic decor with an open roof. The seasonal menu includes cheese fondue served in a bread bowl. Occasional live music.

Trattoria Caprese €€
Italian **Map** 7 A4
Spuistraat 259, 1012 VR
Tel *620 0059* **Closed** *Mon lunch*
Delicious slow-cooked dishes are made with locally sourced organic ingredients. Try the risotto with octopus, parsley and lemon zest and the panna cotta with orange compote.

Van Kerkwijk €€
International **Map** 7 B3
Nes 41, 1012 KC
Tel *620 3316*
Café-like atmosphere with small wooden tables. A daily changing menu offers an eclectic mix of cuisines from French and Italian to Moroccan and Indonesian.

De Compagnon €€€
French **Map** 8 D1
Guldehandsteeg 17, 1012 RA
Tel *620 4225* **Closed** *Sun*
Intimate fine-dining restaurant with an organic seasonal menu. Perennial favourites include goose liver and *côte de boeuf* (prime rib). Exceptional wine list.

Supperclub €€€
International **Map** 7 B3
Jonge Roelensteeg 21, 1012 PL
Tel *344 6400* **Closed** *lunch*
Dine on a five-course menu comprising world cuisine while reclining on large, comfortable, white beds. DJs, video art and offbeat performers add to the incredible experience.

Vermeer €€€
European **Map** 8 D1
Prins Hendrikkade 59–72, 1012 AD
Tel *556 4885* **Closed** *lunch; Sun*
This Michelin-starred restaurant in NH Barbizon Palace hotel offers French-inspired, seasonal delights

made with locally sourced organic ingredients. Try the nine-course tasting menu. Inspired wine list.

D'Vijff Vlieghen €€€
Dutch **Map** 7 A4
Spuistraat 294–302, 1012 VX
Tel *530 4060* **Closed** *lunch*
Sample fine, traditional cuisine amidst original Rembrandt etchings and 17th-century furnishings. Enjoy the lightly smoked duck breast or choose the chef's "surprising" menu, which has a choice of four, five or six courses.

DK Choice

Visrestaurant Lucius €€€
Seafood **Map** 7 A3
Spuistraat 247, 1012 VP
Tel *624 1831* **Closed** *lunch*
Named after the freshwater fish *esox lucius* (pike), this French bistro-style restaurant specializes in delicious seafood. Popular with locals, it serves simply cooked dishes with an emphasis on fresh ingredients. The excellent *plateau fruits de mer* features a selection of shellfish such as lobster, crab, oysters and langoustines.

Western Canal Ring

DK Choice

Pancake Bakery €
International **Map** 7 A1
Prinsengracht 191, 1015 DS
Tel *625 1333* **Closed** *Breakfast*
A variety of pancakes are served at this family-run bakery. Choose from international favourites such as Egyptian with lamb, paprika and garlic sauce, and Italian Caprese with tomatoes, onion, mozzarella, pesto and fresh basil. Alternatively, try the classic Dutch with bacon and cheese or syrup and powdered sugar. Wash them down with house wine.

Piqniq €
Café **Map** 1 C3
Lindengracht 59, 1015 KC
Tel *320 3669* **Closed** *dinner*
Choose from home-made mini-sandwiches, bite-size quiches and cakes. Gluten-free options.

Semhar €
Ethiopian **Map** 1 A4
Marnixstraat 259–261, 1015 WH
Tel *638 1634* **Closed** *lunch; Mon*
The friendly and spacious Semhar serves traditional Ethiopian and Eritrean food.

Entrance to the delightful café-restaurant Kapitein Zeppos in Nieuwe Zijde

Speciality pancakes are served with every meal. Be sure to try the exotic beers (palmnut, banana, coconut and quinoa) or the Ethiopian coffee.

Black and Blue €€
Steakhouse **Map** 1 B4
Leliegracht 46, 1015 DH
Tel *625 0807*
Excellent organic Angus steaks are cooked on a charcoal grill and served with home-made sauces at this laid-back eatery. As an accompaniment, choose a salad with a range of dressings.

De Bolhoed €€
Vegetarian **Map** 1 B3
Prinsengracht 60–62, 1015 DX
Tel *626 1803*
Imaginative international dishes with a daily vegan choice are served at this vegetarian restaurant. Delectable desserts include banana cream pie. Delightful canalside terrace. Reserve ahead.

Daalder €€
French **Map** 1 C3
Lindengracht 90–92, 1015 KK
Tel *624 8864*
Fine French dining with a twist. The weekly three- or four-course chef's menu features delicacies such as sea bass on bread crust, black Angus beef and glazed pork cheek. Suggested wines with each dish.

Mantoe €€
Afghani **Map** 1 B4
Tweede Leliedwarsstraat 13
Tel *421 6374* **Closed** *Tue*
Amsterdam's first Afghani restaurant, Mantoe offers a daily "surprise" four- or five-course menu comprising specialities that are spicy and rich in flavour.

Stout!
International €€   **Map** 1 C3
Haarlemmerstraat 73, 1013 EL
Tel *616 3664*
This hip restaurant offers creative international fare. Try the Stout Plateau of ten small treats or the catch of the day. Live DJ on Saturday nights.

Bordewijk
Mediterranean €€€   **Map** 1 C3
Noordermarkt 7, 1015 MV
Tel *624 3899*   **Closed** *Mon & Sun*
Renowned designer restaurant offering superb food made with seasonal ingredients. The menu comprises fresh pasta, wild game, and signature offal dishes. Excellent wine list. Book ahead.

Chez Georges
French €€€   **Map** 7 A1
Herenstraat 3, 1015 BX
Tel *626 3332*   **Closed** *Sun*
A must for gourmands, this small restaurant offers a seasonal Burgundian menu. The five-course set meal consists of salad, fish, Scottish beef with morel sauce and dessert. Fine wine selection.

Lof
International €€€   **Map** 1 C3
Haarlemmerstraat 62, 1013 ES
Tel *620 2997*   **Closed** *lunch; Sun & Mon*
The hugely popular Lof relies on seasonal food. The delicious offerings vary daily and range from French to Asian cuisines.

Central Canal Ring

Bagels and Beans
Café €   **Map** 7 A5
Keizersgracht 504, 1017 EJ
Tel *330 5508*   **Closed** *dinner*
Casual chain café with high ceilings, newspapers and free Wi-Fi. It offers a variety of breakfast, brunch and lunch menus.

Fou Fow Ramen
Japanese €   **Map** 1 B5
Elandsgracht 2A, 1016 TV
Tel *845 0544*   **Closed** *Mon; Tue–Thu lunch*
This trendy eatery serves authentic ramen noodles in meat or vegetarian broth. Try the classic *tonkotsu* (pork) ramen. Side dishes include steamed dumplings.

Goodies
Mediterranean €   **Map** 7 A4
Huidenstraat 9, 1016 ER
Tel *625 6122*
Freshly prepared food using organic ingredients is served at this informal diner. The menu

Interior of Los Pilones, bringing a taste of Mexico to Amsterdam's Central Canal Ring

comprises meal-sized salads, tapas-style dishes, excellent ravioli and home-made cakes.

Pancakes! Amsterdam
Dutch €   **Map** 1 B5
Berenstraat 38, 1016 GH
Tel *528 9797*
Choose from a variety of Dutch and international pancakes. All the ingredients are sustainably sourced, and the flour comes from a Dutch grain mill in Hoofddorp, just outside of Amsterdam. Good kids' menu.

Pancake Corner
Dutch €   **Map** 4 E2
Kleine Gartmanplantsoen 51, 1017 RP
Tel *627 6303*
Basic creperie with a varied menu. Popular picks include pancakes with spinach and goat's cheese and pizza-style options. Try the chunky banana pancake with chocolate sauce, whipped cream and walnuts.

Akitsu
Japanese €€   **Map** 1 A5
Rozengracht 230, 1016 SZ
Tel *625 3254*   **Closed** *lunch; Mon*
Authentic Japanese restaurant with an open kitchen. Guests can choose to sit on tatami mats to eat their meal. Try the locals' favourite, bluefin tuna.

Outside seating at the popular Pancakes! Amsterdam

Aphrodite
Greek €€   **Map** 4 E2
Lange Leidsedwarsstraat 91, 1017 NH
Tel *622 7382*   **Closed** *lunch; Mon*
Cosy little Greek restaurant with modern interiors and a pleasant ambience. The extensive menu features grilled and baked meat and seafood dishes.

DK Choice

Balthazar's Keuken
International €€   **Map** 1 B5
Elandsgracht 108, 1016 VA
Tel *420 2114*   **Closed** *Sun–Tue*
The shabby-chic Balthazar's Keuken is owned by chefs Karin and Alain. With an open kitchen and a clutter of hanging pots and pans, it gives the feeling of dining at someone's home. Guests are offered a weekly changing three-course menu with up to five appetizers and pre-chosen wine.

Brix
Fusion €€   **Map** 1 C5
Wolvenstraat 16, 1016 EP
Tel *639 0351*
Hip restaurant with a dynamic fusion kitchen. There is a choice of small dishes such as polenta, plus hearty fish and chips, full pasta meals, snacks and desserts.

Los Pilones
Mexican €€   **Map** 7 A5
Kerkstraat 63, 1017 GC
Tel *320 4651*   **Closed** *lunch*
This cantina serves the best Mexican food in the city. Favourites include nachos, tacos and quesadillas. Do not miss the enchiladas with chocolate sauce. Many different brands of tequila.

Proeverij 274
Dutch €€   **Map** 1 B5
Prinsengracht 274, 1016 HH
Tel *421 1848*   **Closed** *lunch*
Warm and romantic restaurant in a beautiful canal house. The small, creative menu features organic and fresh regional produce. Good wine choices. Book ahead.

Middle Eastern-style decor with floor mats and cushions at Nomads, Central Canal Ring

Puri Mas €€
Indonesian   Map 4 E2
Lange Leidsedwarsstraat 37–41,
1017 NG
Tel *627 7627*   Closed *lunch*
This popular Indonesian
restaurant offers good-value
set menus. The *rijsttafel* is served
with four types of rice dishes.
Vegetarian, gluten-free and
halal meals on request.

Restaurant Portugalia €€
Portuguese   Map 4 E1
Kerkstraat 35, 1017 GB
Tel *625 6490*   Closed *lunch*
Family-run restaurant serving
simple cuisine. Try the *cataplana*
(single-pan) dishes such as clams,
smoked pork and potatoes in a
cream sauce. There are vegetarian
options and a children's menu.

Stoop en Stoop €€
Dutch   Map 4 E2
Lange Leidsedwarsstraat 82, 1017 NM
Tel *620 0982*   Closed *Sun lunch*
This cosy Dutch eatery offers
generous, hearty meals with an
emphasis on fish and meat dishes.
Excellent spare ribs, mussels and
chicken satay. Good beers.

Struisvogel €€
French/International   Map 1 B5
Keizersgracht 312, 1016 EX
Tel *423 3817*   Closed *lunch*
Set in the cellar of a canal house,
this cosy restaurant specializes in
unusual meats such as springbok
(antelope) and wild Scottish deer.
Try the apple raisin crumble with
vanilla ice cream.

Blue Pepper €€€
Indonesian   Map 4 D1
Nassaukade 366, 1054 AB
Tel *489 7039*   Closed *lunch*
Traditional Indonesian fare with a
modern twist. The 14-course
rijsttafel is a fantastic gourmet
experience. There are also smaller
four- or five-course rice tables.

Hosokawa €€€
Japanese   Map 4 E2
Max Euweplein 22, 1017 MB
Tel *638 8086*   Closed *lunch; Tue*
Authentic, upmarket Japanese
restaurant. Guests can watch the
meals being prepared in the
open kitchen. Signature dishes
include sushi and teppan-yaki.

Nomads €€€
Middle Eastern   Map 1 A5
Rozengracht 133
Tel *344 6401*   Closed *lunch*
Inspired by nomadic culture, the
decor has warm lighting and soft
cushions. There is a three-course
menu and smaller dishes. DJs,
live music, belly dancers or
storytellers feature most evenings.

Restaurant Vinkeles €€€
French   Map 1 B5
Keizersgracht 384, 1016 GB
Tel *530 2010*   Closed *lunch; Sun*
Famous Michelin-starred restaurant serving French cuisine. Sit
among 18th-century bakery ovens
or on the 19th-century salon
boat. Try the Anjou *duif* (pigeon).

Eastern Canal Ring

Azmarino €
African   Map 5 A5
Tweede Sweelinckstraat 6, 1073 EH
Tel *671 7587*   Closed *lunch; Mon*
Decorated with traditional
African furnishings, Azmarino
offers a classic menu of mild and
spicy meats, eggs in red sauce,
and *enjera* (pancakes) with
meat or vegetable sauces.

Bazar €
International   Map 5 A5
Albert Cuypstraat 182, 1073 BL
Tel *675 0544*
This colourful restaurant serves a
mouthwatering range of North
African, Morrocan and Turkish

cuisines. The signature dish,
Bizarre Bazar, is a fantastic mixed
grill featuring a selection of
meats, fish and vegetables.

Golden Temple €
Vegetarian   Map 5 A3
Utrechtsestraat 126
Tel *626 8560*   Closed *lunch*
A varied menu of vegetarian and
vegan dishes. Try an Indian or
Nepali *thali* (selection of small
dishes), a Mediterranean or
Middle Eastern *mezze* platter.

Hans en Grietje €
Dutch   Map 4 F2
Spiegelgracht 27, 1017 JP
Tel *624 6782*
On a busy corner near the
Rijksmuseum, Hans en Grietje
is a great spot for pancakes,
sandwiches and salads.

Kingfisher €
Café   Map 4 F4
Ferdinand Bolstraat 24, 1072 LK
Tel *671 2395*
Good-value food including goat's
cheese croquettes, club sand-
wiches and spicy lamb burgers.
The day menu has meat, fish and
vegetarian dishes. Free Wi-Fi.

Village Bagels €
Café   Map 4 F2
Vijzelstraat 137, 1017 HJ
Tel *427 2213*
Housed in a listed building, this
café offers real New York-style
bagels, fresh juices and espresso.

Zushi €
Japanese   Map 7 C5
Amstel 20, 1017 AA
Tel *330 6882*
A large, bright restaurant with a
conveyor belt of delicacies. Plates
are colour-coded according to
price. Soups, tempura and grill
dishes can be ordered separately.
Try the green-tea ice cream.

Bouchon du Centre €€
French   Map 5 A4
Falckstraat 3, 1017 VV
Tel *330 1128*   Closed *Sun–Tue*
French bistro with red-and white-
checked tablecloths and black-
and-white-floor tiles. Traditional
fare includes blood sausages and
a range of cheese from Lyon. By
reservation only.

Buffet van Odette €€
Brasserie   Map 4 F2
Prinsengracht 598, 1017 KS
Tel *423 6034*   Closed *Tue*
Light and sunny eatery with a
great terrace. Popular dishes
include truffle cheese omelette,
steak sandwich and sticky toffee
cake. Reservations recommended.

For key to prices see page 224

Coffee & Jazz €€
Indonesian **Map** 5 A3
Utrechtsestraat 113, 1017 VL
Tel *624 5851* **Closed** *Sat lunch; Sun & Mon*
This relaxed restaurant has a top-notch Indonesian chef. Sample the world-famous chicken satay, or give the chef free rein to surprise. Occasional live jazz.

Rose's Cantina €€
South American **Map** 7 B5
Reguliersdwarsstraat 38–40, 1017 BM
Tel *625 9797* **Closed** *lunch*
Established restaurant with an emphasis on Mexican dishes like tacos and quesadillas. The speciality, Rose's house burger served with pickled jalapeños, cheese and bacon, is a must.

Take Thai €€
Thai **Map** 5 A3
Utrechtsestraat 87, 1017 VK
Tel *624 0577* **Closed** *lunch*
Authentic Thai cuisine served in minimalist interiors. Enjoy classics such as fishcakes and red and green curries. The à la carte menu offers beef, seafood, chicken and vegetarian dishes.

Vamos A Ver €€
Spanish/Catalonian **Map** 5 A5
Govert Flinckstraat 308, 1073 CJ
Tel *673 6992* **Closed** *lunch; Tue*
This no-frills restaurant offers excellent Catalonian fare. Wide selection of tapas. Specialities include *paella* (Spanish rice dish) and *zarzuela* (seafood stew).

De Waaghals €€
Vegetarian **Map** 4 F3
Frans Halsstraat 29, 1072 BK
Tel *679 9609* **Closed** *lunch*
International cuisine made with organic produce. The menu focuses on a different country every month. The Brazilian menu, for example, may offer roasted pumpkin, bean stew, cheese balls and avocado dip.

Le Zinc... et les Autres €€
French **Map** 5 A3
Prinsengracht 999, 1017 KM
Tel *622 9044* **Closed** *lunch; Sun & Mon*
In a beautifully restored ware-house, this stylish restaurant serves hearty, rustic cuisine, such as fish soup with seasonal seafood and saffron potatoes. Good wine list.

Dik & Cunningham €€€
French/Mediterranean **Map** 5 A3
Kerkstraat 377, 1017 HW
Tel *422 2766* **Closed** *Sat lunch; Sun*
A smart, split-level restaurant serving eclectic dishes such as tuna with langoustine, avocado

with preserved lemon and wild duck with dried mulberries.

Sluizer €€€
International **Map** 5 A3
Utrechtsestraat 41-45, 1017 VH
Tel *622 6376* **Closed** *lunch*
Two great restaurants under one roof – Specialties and Fish – offer extensive à la carte and changing choice menus, with international meat, fish and vegetarian options.

DK Choice

Utrechtsedwarstafel €€€
European **Map** 5 B3
Utrechtsedwarsstraat 107, 1017 WD
Tel *625 4189* **Closed** *lunch; Sun–Tue*
Fine dining in an intimate and informal setting. There is no menu – guests choose the number of courses (three to five) and the details are left to the owners. Expect exceptional culinary delights such as melted *bleu d'auvergne* (French blue cheese) with caramelized pears. The chef explains the dishes he has prepared and the food is paired with the perfect wine.

Museum Quarter

De Bakkerswinkel €
Bakery **Map** 4 E5
Roelof Hartstraat 68, 1071 VM
Tel *662 3594* **Closed** *dinner; Mon*
Part of a home-grown chain, this bakery has delicious scones with

clotted cream, home-made cakes, quiches, sandwiches, savoury pastries and wonderful cheesecake.

Het Blauwe Theehuis €
European **Map** 3 C3
Vondelpark 5, 1071 AA
Tel *662 0254* **Closed** *winter; dinner Mon–Wed*
Housed in a 1937 octagonal concrete, steel and glass structure with a huge terrace overlooking the Vondelpark, the "Blue Teahouse" has a European menu of both dinner and finger foods.

Cobra Café €
International **Map** 4 E3
Hobbemastraat 18, 1071 ZB
Tel *470 0111* **Closed** *dinner*
This trendy, modern brasserie in the museum square has a varied menu. It has a large, sunny terrace for summer dining.

Café Toussaint €€
International **Map** 4 D1
Bosboom Toussaintstraat 26, 1054 AS
Tel *685 0737*
The emphasis is on healthy fare such as soups, sandwiches and tapas at this charming café with an open kitchen and a romantic terrace. There are good vegetarian options.

Due Napoletani €€
Italian **Map** 4 E4
Hobbemakade 61–63, 1071 XL
Tel *671 1263* **Closed** *Tue*
Chic Italian cuisine is served in a cosy and informal setting. Savour the popular *pasta al parmigiano*. Warm and friendly staff.

Tables laid out at the cheerful De Waaghals restaurant in Eastern Canal Ring

For more information on types of restaurants *see pages 220–21*

Brasserie van Baerle, a fine-dining French restaurant in Museum Quarter

De Griekse Taverna €€
Greek   **Map** 4 E4
Hobbemakade 64–65, 1071 XM
Tel *671 7923*   **Closed** *lunch*
Typical dishes include *moussaka*
(baked aubergine dish) and
18 different sorts of *mezze*.
Traditional live music and dancing
in the evenings. Book ahead.

Pheun Thai €€
Thai   **Map** 4 E4
Hobbemakade 71, 1071 XM
Tel *427 4537*   **Closed** *lunch*
Authentic specialities include
shrimp soup with lemon and fish
with *sambal* (spicy South Asian
condiment). Great-value three- or
four-course set menus.

Pompa €€
Mediterranean   **Map** 4 D3
Willemsparkweg 6, 1071 HD
Tel *662 6206*
A friendly eatery offering a three-
course daily menu. There are also
tapas and platters such as the
Vegetariano with peppers, tzatziki,
hummus and grilled aubergine.

Sama Sebo €€
Indonesian   **Map** 4 E3
P C Hooftstraat 27, 1071 BL
Tel *662 8146*   **Closed** *Sun*
The oldest and most famous
Indonesian restaurant in town
with authentic food. Order the
rijsttafel, comprising 17 dishes,
or assemble one from the à la
carte menu. Reserve ahead.

The Seafood Bar €€
Seafood   **Map** 4 D3
van Baerlestraat 5, 1071 AL
Tel *670 8355*
Trendy seafood bar with a relaxed
ambience. The menu changes
every three months, though
some favourites, including fish
and chips and *fruits de mer*
(seafood platter), remain.

Solo €€
European   **Map** 4 D4
van Baerlestraat 35–37, 1071 AP
Tel *662 2655*   **Closed** *Mon*
Deluxe grand café situated
in a former fire station. It serves

an inspired mix of Italian
and French cuisine. The
Scroppino cocktail features
Venetian lemon ice, vodka
and prosecco.

Srikandi €€
Indonesian   **Map** 4 E2
Stadhouderskade 31, 1071 ZD
Tel *664 0408*
Art and music create an
authentic atmosphere to
savour traditional Indonesian
fare. Srikandi is known for the
rijsttafel, featuring 18 dishes.
There are very good vegetarian
options. Reservations required.

Valerius €€
International   **Map** 3 C4
Banstraat 14, 1071 JZ
Tel *471 3976*   **Closed** *Sun,
Mon & Tue dinner*
This modern café has a
deliciously varied international
menu. Starters range from
Moroccan savoury pastries to
Italian aubergine-stuffed ravioli.
Mains include excellent
risotto and lamb marinated
in honey and coriander.

Brasserie van Baerle €€€
French   **Map** 4 E4
van Baerlestraat 158, 1071 BG
Tel *679 1532*   **Closed** *Sat &
Mon lunch*
A French-style brasserie popular
with Dutch celebrities, van
Baerle serves classic, mouth-
watering dishes such as roast
poussin, steak tartare, eggs
Benedict and Caesar salad. Excep-
tional wine list. Reserve ahead.

The College Hotel €€€
Dutch   **Map** 4 E5
Roelof Hartstraat 1, 1071 VE
Tel *571 1511*
The renovated gymnasium
of an 1895 school building is
home to a renowned gourmet
restaurant. It offers classic Dutch
cuisine with a modern twist.

Le Garage €€€
French   **Map** 4 E4
Ruysdaelstraat 54–56, 1071 XE
Tel *679 7176*   **Closed** *Sat & Sun lunch*
In a renovated garage, this chic
bistro with plush red seating is a
celebrity haunt. The French-
inspired fare has an emphasis on
organic produce. Superb wines.

DK Choice

Momo €€€
Asian   **Map** 4 E4
Hobbemastraat 1, 1071 XZ
Tel *671 7474*   **Closed** *Sun lunch*
An uber-trendy bar-restaurant,
Momo offers quality Asian fusion
cuisine packed with flavour.
Choose from a selection of
tapas-sized dishes or opt for a
fixed set menu of 10 dishes.
Regulars enjoy delicacies such
as Wagyu beef, sushi with soft
shell crab and duck with foie
gras. Live DJs at weekends.

Willems €€€
French   **Map** 3 C4
Willemsparkweg 177, 1071 GZ
Tel *752 1973*   **Closed** *Mon lunch*
French-inspired cuisine. Popular
dishes include oysters, salmon,
risotto and steak tartare. The
signature six-course Willems
Keuze menu includes a fish
course and cheese plate.

Plantage

Aguada €
International   **Map** 5 C3
Roetersstraat 10, 1018 WC
Tel *620 3782*   **Closed** *lunch*
Tiny, family-run café-restaurant
with an informal atmosphere.
The changing menu includes
a range of international cuisine
such as Indian, Italian and Dutch,
to name a few. Try the speciality,
cheese fondue.

The atmospheric dining room at The College Hotel in the Museum Quarter

Elegant table setting at Ciel Bleu, on the 23rd floor of the Okura hotel

Café Kadijk €
Indonesian **Map** 6 D1
Kadijksplein 5, 1018 AB
Tel *617 744 411* **Closed** *lunch*
A popular choice with students, Café Kadijk offers good-value, delicious fare. Try the spicy *rendang*, beef stewed in coconut sauce, or enjoy a complete *rijsttafel* served on a big plate.

Palorma €
Italian **Map** 5 C2
Plantage Kerklaan 28, 1018 TC
Tel *625 3434*
This takeaway restaurant serves fantastic Italian food made with the freshest ingredients. Large portions and reasonable prices. Great vegetarian lasagne.

DK Choice

De Pizzabakkers €
Italian **Map** 5 C2
Plantage Kerklaan 2, 1018 TA
Tel *625 0740*
De Pizzabakkers is the place for excellent, authentic Italian pizzas. The crispy, thin pizzas are baked in a traditional wood oven and toppings are made using fresh, locally sourced ingredients. The menu also includes a range of *antipasti*, salads, tasty desserts and vegetarian choices. Guests can enjoy a good prosecco while waiting and kids get some dough to play with. Payment is by credit or debit card only.

Amstelhaven €€
European **Map** 5 C4
Mauritskade 1, 1091 EW
Tel *665 2672*
Unique bar-restaurant with a huge waterside terrace; many patrons arrive by boat. More of an event venue than a restaurant, it regularly hosts live DJs, music, concerts and performances.

Bloem €€
European **Map** 6 D2
Entrepotdok 36, 1018 AD
Tel *330 0929*
The place to go for a delicious and healthy breakfast, lunch or dinner. The bread, fruit, vegetables and meat are all organic, and the fish is sustainably sourced.

Elkaar €€
Mediterranean **Map** 6 E3
Alexanderplein 6, 1018 CG
Tel *330 7559* **Closed** *Sat lunch*
Intimate restaurant with a Mediterranean kitchen. There is a choice of à la carte or changing three-, four- and five-course menus. Try the deer ham with nuts and red port dressing. Extensive wine list.

Neva €€
French **Map** 8 D5
Amstel 51, 1018 EJ
Tel *530 7483* **Closed** *dinner*
Sleek, understated museum café in the Hermitage Amsterdam. The fixed and à la carte menus have fish, meat and vegetarian dishes. Excellent wines.

Paerz €€
French **Map** 6 D2
Entrepotdok 64, 1018 AD
Tel *623 2206* **Closed** *Mon & Tue*
Enjoy seasonal, French-inspired cuisine in warm and cosy interiors. In summer, dine on the sunny terrace with fine canal views. Good-value chef's menu.

Tempura €€
Japanese **Map** 5 C2
Plantage Kerklaan 26, 1018 TC
Tel *428 7132* **Closed** *lunch; Mon*
Japanese-style brasserie with an extensive menu of sushi, yakitori and tempura as well as grilled and vegetarian dishes. Specialities include squid and St Jacques sashimi. Good set menus.

La Rive €€€
French/Mediterranean **Map** 5 B4
Professor Tulpplein 1, 1018 GX
Tel *520 3264* **Closed** *lunch; Mon*
Michelin-starred restaurant in the deluxe Intercontinental Amstel hotel. The flavourful French and Mediterranean cuisine is made using the highest quality seasonal produce. Outstanding wines.

Further Afield

Blauw €€
Indonesian **Map** 3 A4
Amstelveenseweg 158–160, 1075 XN
Tel *675 5000* **Closed** *lunch*
One of the better-known Indonesian restaurants in town. The decor is stylish and intimate. Order one of the huge *rijsttafel*.

Ciel Bleu €€€
French **Map** 4 F5
Ferdinand Bolstraat 333, 1072 LH
Tel *678 7450* **Closed** *Sun*
A Michelin-starred fine-dining restaurant situated in the luxurious Okura hotel, Ciel Bleu is known for its innovative dishes and terrific views of Amsterdam.

DK Choice

De Kas €€€
Mediterranean
Kamerlingh Onneslaan 3, 1097 DE
Tel *462 4562* **Closed** *Sat lunch, Sun; Christmas*
Dine among lush plants in this upmarket, organic restaurant set within a 1920s greenhouse. The Michelin-starred chef, owner and grower Gert Jan Hageman uses herbs and seasonal vegetables cultivated in the adjacent nursery. De Kas offers two- and three-course fixed menus, and good vegetarian options are available as well. Reserve the Chef's Table in the kitchen or the romantic terrace in summer.

Beautiful glass façade of the waterfront De Kas restaurant

For more information on types of restaurants *see pages 220–21*

Light Meals and Snacks

In addition to the normal assortment of burger joints, pizzerias and the like, most Dutch cafés and bars serve food ranging from simple bar snacks to a three-course meal. Those that offer lunchtime snacks and an evening meal are generally known as *eetcafés*. While the choice of dishes tends to be limited, the quality is generally high and prices are often very reasonable. Some *eetcafés* have started serving more adventurous dishes and generally offer a good vegetarian selection. However, café and bar kitchens close early and it is difficult to get a meal after 9pm. For more information on cafés and bars, including a selection of the top ten in Amsterdam, see pages 48–9.

Bars and Street Stalls

Almost all bars serve a range of snacks. The standard selection of nibbles includes olives, chunks of Dutch cheese served with mustard and *borrelnoten* (nuts with a savoury coating). More substantial tapas-like snacks include *bitterballen* (deep-fried meatballs), *vlammetjes* (deep-fried batter envelopes similar to meat and vegetable spring rolls) and *osseworst* (a spicy mince-beef sausage).

Given the maritime tradition of the Netherlands, it is worth trying the fish dishes available in bars and from stalls on the street, such as herring served with onion or gherkins. Pizza, sandwiches and hamburgers are also commonly available from stalls. However, the most popular snack from street stalls is French fries or *patat frites*, which are served with mayonnaise in a plastic tray or a paper cone (see p222).

Pancake Houses

Pancakes (*pannenkoeken*) are a popular, value-for-money light meal in Amsterdam. The French-style *crêpe* is believed to have been adopted in the Netherlands during the Napoleonic occupation (see pp32–3) as a way of using up leftovers.

These days there is nothing penny-pinching about the wide range of sweet and savoury toppings available at most pancake houses in Amsterdam. It is not uncommon to find up to 70 varieties on offer and you can usually combine any of these to create the pancake of your choice. The best places include **De Carrousel**, **Boerderij Meerzicht**, **The Pancake Bakery** and **Upstairs**. Portions may seem small, but they are deceptively filling. Pancakes and waffles served with syrup are also available as the staple snack at smoking coffeeshops (see p51).

Brown Cafés and Bars

The term *eetcafés* is usually applied to traditional brown cafés (see also p48) that also serve food. These often offer much better value and a more relaxed ambience than many small restaurants. Outstanding brown cafés include **De Prins**, **Het Molenpad**, **Café du Lac**, **Ruis onder de Bomen**, **De Reiger**, and **De Engelbewaarder**, which have extensive and appealing menus. Not surprisingly, they often get crowded and it can be hard to find a free table.

The majority of basic *eetcafés* just offer filling home-made fare, such as sandwiches, soups, salads, omelettes and chips. The only unfamiliar dishes you are likely to come across are *uitsmijter* (a large open sandwich with roast beef or ham, topped with fried eggs) and *erwtensoep* (a thick pea soup with pork). Of the cheaper, more down-to-earth varieties of *eetcafés*, **De Doffer** serves filling food that is excellent value and it has the attraction of a billiard room. Another old favourite is **Café Gambrinus** in the Pijp area. Both places attract a young, lively crowd and are popular with students. **Van Puffelen** offers more formal French-style dishes. All meals are served in the back extension and adjacent building of this intimate brown café, which has an impressive 19th-century interior. For the best French fries in the city, head to **Vleminckx Vlaamse Friteshuis**.

Designer Bars

An extensive range of food is offered in some of the more up-market designer bars (see p51). This type of bar is invariably more expensive than other types of cafés and bars in the city and in most cases the quality of the fare does not justify such inflated prices. **Café Schiller**, housed in a beautiful Art Deco building on Rembrandtplein, is an honourable exception. Amid portraits of 1930s cabaret stars painted by Frits Schiller, you can enjoy a value-for-money selection of snacks and meals in an evocative period bar. Both **Walem** and **De Balie** also serve tasty food in a stylish setting. **Morlang**, next door to Walem, is less chic, but the food definitely is better value, and the trendy **Caffé Esprit** is very popular with Kalverstraat shoppers.

Specialist Cafés

If you feel like trying something different, sample the delicious food at the Flemish cultural centre **De Brakke Grond**, where international dishes with a Belgian twist are served in both the café and the restaurant. **De Zotte** also serves down-to-earth Flemish food and stocks a huge variety of Belgian beers. While the quality of the food may not be that exceptional, the portions certainly are large enough to soak up the strongest of beers. Café-restaurant **Stanislavski** occupies almost the entire ground floor of the Stadsschouwburg (see p113). Named after the famous Russian theatre director, it has an atmosphere reminiscent of Paris or Berlin. Here, you can while away your day from breakfast until the small hours, enjoying the food and mingling with the eclectic theatre crowd.

DIRECTORY

Pancake Houses

Boerderij Meerzicht
Koenenkade 56.
Amsterdamse Bos.
Tel 679 2744.

De Carrousel
Tweede
Weteringplantsoen 1.
Map 4 F3.
Tel 625 8002.

The Pancake Bakery
Prinsengracht 191.
Map 1 B4.
Tel 625 1333.

Upstairs
Grimburgwal 2.
Map 7 B4.
Tel 626 5603.

Brown Cafés and Bars

Café Gambrinus
Ferdinand Bolstraat 180.
Map 4 F5.
Tel 671 7389.

Café du Lac
Haarlemmerstraat 118.
Map 1 C3.
Tel 624 4265.

De Doffer
Runstraat 12–14.
Map 4 E1.
Tel 622 6686.

't Doktertje
Rozenboomsteeg 4.
Map 7 B4.
Tel 626 4427.

De Engelbewaarder
Kloveniersvoorburgwal 59.
Map 8 D3.
Tel 625 3772.

Het Molenpad
Prinsengracht 653.
Map 4 E1.
Tel 625 9680.

Pieper
Prinsengracht 424.
Map 4 E1.
Tel 626 4775.

De Prins
Prinsengracht 124.
Map 1 B4.
Tel 624 9382.

Van Puffelen
Prinsengracht 375–377.
Map 1 B4.
Tel 624 6270.

De Reiger
Nieuwe Leliestraat 34.
Map 1 B4.
Tel 624 7426.

Ruis onder de Bomen
Van der Helstplein 9.
Tel 364 0354.

De Tuin
2e Tuindwarsstraat 13
(near Westerstraat).
Map 1 B3.
Tel 624 4559.

Vleminckx Vlaamse Friteshuis
Voetboogstraat 33.
Map 7 B4.
Tel 624 6075.

Proeflokalen and Modern Tasting Bars

De Drie Fleschjes
Gravenstraat 18.
Map 7 B2.
Tel 624 8443.

In De Wildeman
Kolksteeg 3.
Map 7 C1.
Tel 638 2348.

Mulliner's Wijnlokaal
Lijnbaansgracht 266–267.
Map 4 E2.
Tel 627 9782.

Whisky Café L&B Limited
Korte Leidsedwarsstraat 82–84.
Map 4 E2.
Tel 553 5151.

Grand Cafés and Designer Bars

De Balie
Kleine Gartman-plantsoen 10.
Map 4 E2.
Tel 553 5130.

Het Blauwe Theehuis
Vondelpark 5.
Map 3 C3.
Tel 662 0254.

Café Americain
American Hotel,
Leidsekade 97.
Map 4 E2.
Tel 556 3000.

Café Luxembourg
Spui 22–24.
Map 7 B4.
Tel 620 6264.

Café Schiller
Rembrandtplein 26.
Map 7 C5.
Tel 624 9846.

Caffè Esprit
Spui 10. Map 7 B4.
Tel 639 2589.

De Jaren
Nieuwe Doelenstraat 20–22.
Map 7 C4.
Tel 625 5771.

De Kroon
Rembrandtplein 17.
Map 7 C5.
Tel 625 2011.

Morlang
Keizersgracht 451.
Map 7 A5.
Tel 625 2681.

Walem
Keizersgracht 449.
Map 7 A5.
Tel 625 3544.

Smoking Coffeeshops

Abraxas
Jonge Roelensteeg 12.
Map 7 B3.
Tel 625 5763.

The Bulldog
Leidseplein 15.
Map 4 E2.
Tel 627 1908.

The Grasshopper
Nieuwezijds Voorburgwal 59. Map 7 A4.
Tel 624 6753.

Happy Feelings
Kerkstraat 51.
Map 4 E1.
Tel 423 1936.

Rusland
Rusland 16.
Map 7 C4.
Tel 627 9468.

Siberië
Brouwersgracht 11.
Map 1 C3.
Tel 623 5909.

Coffeeshops and Salons de Thé

Arnold Cornelis
Elandsgracht 78.
Map 1 B5.
Tel 625 8585.

Bagels & Beans
Ferdinand Bolstraat 70.
Map 4 F4.
Tel 672 1610.

Coffee Company
Haarlemmerdijk 62.
Map 1 C2.
Tel 624 4278.

Konditorei Taart van m'n Tante
Ferdinand Bolstraat 10.
Map 4 F3.
Tel 776 4600.

De Laatste Kruimel
Langebrugsteeg 4.
Map 7 B4.
Tel 423 0499.

Pompadour
Huidenstraat 12.
Map 7 A4.
Tel 623 9554.

Tazzina
Brouwersgracht 139.
Map 1 B2.
Tel 330 4649.

Specialist Cafés

De Brakke Grond
Nes 43.
Map 7 B3.
Tel 422 2666.

Stanislavski
Leidseplein 25.
Map 4 E2.
Tel 795 9995.

De Zotte
Raamstraat 29.
Map 4 E1.
Tel 626 8694.

SHOPS AND MARKETS

Amsterdam has a huge range of shops and markets, so if you are present-hunting, you will find no shortage of ideas. Most of the large clothing and department stores are to be found in the Nieuwe Zijde, especially along Kalverstraat *(see p74)*, but there are many other shopping areas to discover. The narrow streets which cross the Canal Ring, such as Herenstraat and Hartenstraat, contain a diverse array of specialist

shops selling everything from ethnic fabrics and beads to unusual games and handmade dolls. The best luxury fashion is to be found on the classy PC Hooftstraat and Van Baerlestraat. However, if you are looking for a bargain, take time to explore the street markets and numerous second-hand shops. Here you can pick up recent fashion items and worn leather jackets cheaply.

Atrium of the Magna Plaza in the former Postkantoor

Opening Hours

Shops are usually open from 9am or 10am to 6pm Tuesday to Saturday and from 1pm to 6pm on Monday *(see p253)*. Many shops are now also open on Sundays. In the city centre, shops stay open until 9pm on Thursdays. However, legislation does allow shopkeepers in the city centre to remain open between 7am and 10pm seven days a week. Retailers are most likely to take advantage of this law in the run-up to Sinterklaas *(see p55)* and during Christmas.

How to Pay

Cash in euros is the most popular method of payment, followed by debit card. If you intend to use a credit card, ask if they are accepted before buying. Although cards are becoming more widely used, some small shops may only accept them for non-sale items and goods costing more than €45, or if they are accepted, an

extra charge may be incurred. It is not possible to pay with traveller's cheques in shops. These can be cashed at GWK bureaux de change offices *(see p258)*. Many shops do not accept €100 or higher bills. Also, it is common practice to round off the prices to the nearest 5 cents.

VAT Exemption

Most Dutch goods are subject to value-added tax (BTW) of either 19 per cent for clothes and other goods, or 6 per cent for books. Non-EU residents are entitled to a refund, subject to certain conditions. Shops which stock the relevant forms will have a sign saying "Tax free for tourists". On leaving the country, present your goods, receipt and the form at customs who will refund you 10 per cent of the purchase price of your goods. Refunds are only made on purchases that are above €50.

Sales

Sales take place mainly in January and July but smaller shops and boutiques may offer discount items at any time. *Uitverkoop* describes anything from a closing-down sale to a stock-clearance sale, while *korting* merely indicates that discounts are being offered.

Towards the end of a sale, further discounts, which will be calculated at the till, are often subtracted from the marked-down price. Beware of clothes rails marked, for example, *VA 40* or *Vanaf 40* as

this sign means "From 40" – the items cost €40 or more, rather than exactly €40.

Department Stores and Malls

Perhaps Amsterdam's best-known department store is **De Bijenkorf** on Dam square, often described as the Dutch Harrods. It has a huge perfumery, and stocks a wide range of men's and women's clothing, plus toys, soft furnishings and household goods. At Christmas it devotes a whole floor to decorations. Among the less expensive stores, **Hema** is very popular for household goods, children's clothes and underwear. Also popular for basic items is **Vroom & Dreesmann**. The only shopping malls in central Amsterdam are the Kalvertoren (Kalverstraat, near Singel) and Magna Plaza, which is housed in the old Postkantoor building *(see p80)*. The impressive, vaulted interior of this former head post office now contains a huge assortment of upmarket boutiques and shops.

Markets

Amsterdammers' love of street trading is most graphically illustrated on 27 April during King's Day *(see p52)*, when Amsterdam turns into the biggest flea market in the world, as local people crowd the city to sell off all their unwanted junk. Such is the crush of eager bargain hunters that the entire city centre is closed to traffic during the festivities.

As Amsterdam still resembles a collection of small villages, every district has its own local market. The best-known of these, because of its size, is the Albert Cuypmarkt (see p124) in the Pijp district, which sells a wide assortment of food, both Dutch and ethnic. This market is also good for cheap clothes and reasonably priced flowers.

Apart from the local markets, Amsterdam has a wide range of specialist markets. Seasonal flowers are on sale at the Bloemenmarkt (see p125). Another market popular with tourists is Waterlooplein flea market (see p65). Despite the crowds, vigilant collectors can still seek out the odd bargain among the bric-a-brac; there is also a selection of new and second-hand clothes for sale.

Browsers will be fascinated by the hundreds of stalls at the Antiekcentrum Amsterdam (see p115), which sell anything from antique dolls to egg cups. Every Wednesday and Saturday on the Nieuwezijds Voorburgwal there is a specialist market for stamp and coin collectors. On Fridays there is a second-hand bookmarket on Spui. Gourmets should head for the Noordermarkt (see p94), which holds an organic food market on Saturdays. The best prices, however, are to be found about 25 km (16 miles) north-west of Amsterdam in the port town of Beverwijk, where the **Beverwijkse Bazaar**, open weekends from 8:30am until 6pm, is one of Europe's largest indoor flea markets selling

Azzurro, a smart boutique on PC Hooftstraat (see p238)

clothing and accessories, toys, jewelry, beauty products, furniture and electrical goods. Next door, the market continues with a cross-section of Asian merchandise, including rugs, carpets, pottery, crafts and food.

Smoked fish on display at the Albert Cuypmarkt

Specialist Shops

Dotted throughout Amsterdam are dozens of small specialist shops. One of the more unusual is **Condomerie Het Gulden Vlies**, located in a former squat, which sells condoms from all over the world. Equally unusual is **Christmas Palace**, which sells festive adornments all year

round, and **Party House**, which has a vast collection of paper decorations. **Capsicum Natuurstoffen** has a huge selection of exotic silks and linens, while **Coppenhagen Kralen** has more than 1,000 different types of beads. It is also worth making time to explore **Joe's Vliegerwinkel** for its wide range of kites, **Simon Levelt** for tea and coffee, or **Hooy & Co.** for an array of wonderful-smelling herbs. The **Nine Streets** area (cross-streets in the Western Canal Ring section) is a treasure trove of boutiques and specialist shops.

Books, Newspapers and Magazines

As books are subject to Value-Added tax in the Netherlands, you may find them slightly more expensive than at home. English-language books are generally available, particularly at **The American Book Center**, **Waterstone's** and **The English Bookshop**. Holiday reading can be picked up very cheaply at second-hand book-shops, such as **The Book Exchange**. Collectors of comics should not miss a visit to **Lambiek**. Most city-centre newsagents stock foreign papers. *Het Financieel Dagblad* has a daily business update in English and publishes a weekly English-language edition. *A-Mag (see p240)* is a useful listings magazine, as is the monthly *Time Out* magazine.

A selection of seasonal flowers, including sunflowers, roses and lilies at a market stall

What to Buy in Amsterdam

Amsterdam has hundreds of tourist shops selling souvenirs, but those looking for something different will find a better selection of genuine Dutch items in one of the city's specialist shops or even at an ordinary supermarket. Authentic delftware is only found at a handful of licensed dealers, but there are still many jewellers selling anything from uncut stones to second-hand diamond rings. Dutch cheese, chocolate and locally produced beers and *jenevers* offer a flavour of the city, while a bunch of flowers is always appreciated.

Ceramics
Finely detailed model canal houses can be be bought singly or by the row.

Droste chocolate pastilles

Sweet and salty varieties of drop liquorice

Dutch Sweets
Handmade Belgian chocolates and Droste pastilles are both delicious, but salty liquorice is an acquired taste.

Hand-made Belgian chocolates

Flowers
Bulbs and cut flowers are a colourful reminder of the city and, due to greenhouse production, many blooms are available all year round.

Tulip bulbs

A bunch of fresh tulips

Two popular brands of beer

Gouda Cheese
There are many types of Gouda of different maturity *(see p238)*. Any shop will be happy to let you try a slice before making a purchase.

Beer in Amsterdam
A huge variety of imported, bottled beers are sold in Amsterdam as well as many local brews *(see p238)*.

Sturdy stone flagons of *jonge* and *oude jenever (see pp50–51)* – also available in flavoured varieties

Dutch windmill prints

Old Maps and Prints
Historically famous for cartography, Amsterdam has a good selection of new and old maps, and many second-hand bookshops stock etchings.

Reproductions of old maps of Amsterdam and Russia

Diamond brooch

Chain-link, diamond-encrusted bracelet

Diamonds
Diamond-cutting was first established in Amsterdam during the 16th century. The city is still one of the major diamond centres.

Different coloured brilliant-cut diamonds

Royal Delft
In response to the demand for Chinese design, more than 30 factories sprang up in Delft in the 17th century, producing distinctive blue-and-white ceramics (see p197). Today, only De Porceleyne Fles still makes real delftware. Items from this factory are sold with a certificate of authenticity.

Polychrome jug painted in colours used on 17th-century majolica

Pynaker tobacco jar influenced by Japanese Imari ware

Plate painted in traditional Delft blue

Painter's initials

Year code – DB means 1982

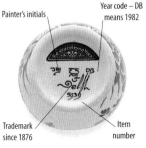

Trademark since 1876

Item number

Genuine De Porceleyne Fles marks

Delft-blue vase

17th-century plate made for rich family

Decorative 17th-century fireplace tile

Antique Delft
Old delftware is highly sought after and expensive, but Delft fireplace tiles can be picked up more cheaply.

Where to Shop in Amsterdam

The Netherlands is justly famous for its flowers, beer and cheese. A wide choice of these indigenous products is available in Amsterdam, which has also long been regarded as the world centre for diamonds. Owing to the large numbers of overseas settlers living in Amsterdam and the cosmopolitan outlook of its residents, it is easy to find a selection of foreign goods in the city. These range from Indonesian beads to French designer wear.

Fashion and Clothes

Van Baerlestraat and PC Hooftstraat contain numerous designer boutiques such as **Azzurro**, offering top names like Alexander McQueen and the leading French and Italian designer labels. The smart set from the Canal Ring haunt the stylish **The People of the Labyrinths** and **Pauw** for their timeless clothes and accessories.

Boutiques in the Nieuwe Zijde offer less pricey items. The French designer **Agnès B** has her own shop along Rokin selling classic designer wear. **Robin & Rik** on Runstraat sells handmade leather clothes and accessories. In Magna Plaza shopping mall, **Sissy Boy** specializes in refined classic suits as well as eye-catching designs. The ultra-hip **Abercrombie & Fitch** sells sporty leisurewear.

Well-priced and stylish second-hand clothes can be found at shops such as **Zipper**. For the widest choice of fashionable boots and shoes, **Dr Adams** is almost a Dutch institution.

Antiques and Furnishings

While you can pick up the odd bargain on Waterlooplein (see p65) and at the Noordermarkt (see p94), the best place for antiques is around Spiegelgracht. A wide selection of shops sell everything from 17th-century tiles to icons. **Peter Pappot** specializes in paintings by Dutch and French expressionists. It is also interesting to visit an auction house. Both **Sotheby's** and **Christie's** have branches in Amsterdam. **Antiekcentrum Amsterdam** (see p115), the largest antiques centre in the Netherlands, has a potpourri of odds and ends, while **Fanous**

Ramadan has a colourful collection of Arabic lampshades, pottery and furniture.

Flowers and Bulbs

No Dutch person would dream of visiting a friend without a bunch of flowers, so Amsterdam is crowded with flower shops. Worth visiting are **Madelief**, for a vast assortment of colourful domestic blooms, and **Gerda's Bloemen en Planten**, for its stock of tropical flowers.

Cut flowers are cheapest at Albert Cuypmarkt (see p124), but Bloemenmarkt (see p125) has a better selection, as well as hundreds of bulbs and tubers. It also sells potted plants, but due to customs regulations, these usually can't be exported.

Diamonds

Amsterdam has a long tradition of cutting and polishing diamonds (see p34). It is still possible to purchase loose stones and diamonds in a new setting at one of the city's many diamond-cutting centres, such as **Gassan Diamonds** or Coster Diamonds (see p134). The city is also well stocked with jewellers, several specializing in diamonds. The best second-hand jewellery can be found in the fascinating antique shops around Spiegelgracht.

Cheese

You can buy a good selection of cheese at street markets and specialist shops such as **Wout Arxhoek** or **De Kaaskamer**. Instead of buying the red-wax-covered Edam, try one of the many varieties of Gouda. Mature Gouda (overjarige kaas) has a rich, salty taste and crumbly texture,

while young Gouda is softer and more buttery. This cheese is also sold with cumin (leidsekaas) or cloves (nagelkaas) (see p222).

Chocolates

Verkade and Droste are the best-known makes of chocolate in the Netherlands. For a treat, visit **Pompadour**, for its delicious hand-made chocolates, or another Amsterdam favourite, **Puccini Bomboni**.

Beers and Spirits

The Dutch are knowledgeable beer drinkers. Along with brand-name lagers like Heineken, Grolsch and Amstel, there is also a huge range of bottled beers on offer. Local specialities include Zatte, a rare, bottle-fermented beer and Wieckse Witte, a white beer. Specialist shops like **De Bierkoning** offer the widest choice and best advice.

The Dutch spirit jenever, the "father" of gin, is often sold in stone bottles and flavoured with herbs or fruit (see p50).

Pottery and Glassware

Blue-and-white pottery is stocked by most shops, but only items with a certificate are real delftware. **Rinascimento** sells the real thing from De Porceleyne Fles, one of the original Delft potteries.

The Jordaan is the best place to hunt for modern pottery, while **Glasgalerie Kuhler** has a stunning range of modern glass, and **Het Kleikollektief** offers an ever-changing choice of bright ceramics.

Posters and Prints

The best places to find good reproductions of paintings are in museum shops. **Art Unlimited** offers an excellent selection of the less famous Dutch scenes.

A range of old etchings can be found at **Hoogkamp Old Prints** and among the stalls at the Oudemanhuispoort in the Oude Zijde (see p63).

DIRECTORY

Department Stores

De Bijenkorf
Dam 1.
Map 7 B2.
Tel 0800 0818.

Hema
Kalvertoren,
Kalverstraat 212.
Map 7 B4.
Tel 311 4800.
Nieuwendijk 174–176.
Map 7 B2.
Tel 311 4800.

Vroom & Dreesmann
Kalverstraat 203.
Map 7 B5.
Tel 0900 235 8363.

Markets Outside the City

De Beverwijkse Bazaar
Montageweg 35,
1948 PH Beverwijk.
Tel 0251 262 626.
W debazaar.nl

Specialist Shops

Capsicum Natuurstoffen
Oude Hoogstraat 1.
Map 7 C3.
Tel 623 1016.

Christmas Palace
Singel 508.
Map 7 B5.
Tel 421 0155.

Condomerie Het Gulden Vlies
Warmoesstraat 141.
Map 7 C2.
Tel 627 4174.

Coppenhagen Kralen
Rozengracht 54.
Map 1 B4.
Tel 624 3681.

Jacob Hooy & Co
Kloveniersburgwal 12.
Map 8 D3.
Tel 624 3041.

Joe's Vliegerwinkel
Nieuwe Hoogstraat 19.
Map 8 D3.
Tel 625 0139.

Nine Streets
W de9straatjes.
amsterdam

Party House
Rozengracht 92b.
Map 1 B4. **Tel** 624 7851.

Simon Levelt
Prinsengracht 180.
Map 1 B4.
Tel 624 0823.

Books, Newspapers and Magazines

The American Book Center
Spui 12.
Map 7 A4.
Tel 625 5537.

The Book Exchange
Kloveniersburgwal 58.
Map 7 C4.
Tel 626 6266.

The English Bookshop
Lauriergracht 71.
Map 1 B5.
Tel 626 4230.

Lambiek
Kerkstraat 132.
Map 4 F2.
Tel 626 7543.

Waterstone's Bookseller
Kalverstraat 152.
Map 7 B4.
Tel 638 3821.

Fashion and Clothes

Abercrombie & Fitch
Leidsestraat 34-36.
Map 7 A5.
Tel 520 3910.

Agnès B
Rokin 126.
Map 7 B4.
Tel 627 1465.

Azzurro
PC Hooftstraat 142a.
Map 4 D3.
Tel 671 6804.

Dr Adams
Oude Doelenstraat 5–7.
Map 7 C3.
Tel 622 3734.

Pauw
Van Baerlestraat 48.
Map 4 D3.
Tel 673 2665.

The People of the Labyrinths
Van Baerlestraat 44.
Map 4 D3.
Tel 664 0779.

Robin & Rik
Runstraat 30. **Map** 7 B4.
Tel 627 8924.

Sissy Boy
Magna Plaza, Nieuwezijds
Voorburgwal 182.
Map 7 B2. **Tel** 740 1230.

Zipper
Huidenstraat 7. **Map** 7 A4.
Tel 623 7302.

Antiques and Furnishings

Antiekcentrum Amsterdam
Elandsgracht 109.
Map 1 A5.
Tel 624 9038.

Christie's
Cornelis Schuytstraat 57.
Map 3 C4. **Tel** 575 5255.

Fanous Ramadan
Runstraat 33. **Map** 4 E1.
Tel 423 2350.

Kitsch Kitchen
Rozengracht 8–12.
Map 1 B4. **Tel** 462 0051.

Peter Pappot
Nieuwe Spiegelstraat
30–34. **Map** 4 F2.
Tel 624 2637.

Sotheby's
Emmalaan 23.
Map 3 B4.
Tel 550 2200.

Flowers and Bulbs

Gerda's Bloemen en Planten
Runstraat 16.
Map 4 E1.
Tel 624 2912.

Madelief
Haarlemmerdijk 93.
Map 1 C2.
Tel 625 3239.

Diamonds

Gassan Diamonds
Nieuwe Uilenburgerstraat
173–175. **Map** 8 E4.
Tel 622 5333.

Cheese

De Kaaskamer
Runstraat 7. **Map** 4 E1.
Tel 623 3483.

Wout Arxhoek
Damstraat 19. **Map** 7 C3.
Tel 622 9118.

Chocolates

Pompadour
Huidenstraat 12.
Map 7 A4.
Tel 623 9554.

Puccini Bomboni
Staalstraat 17.
Map 8 D4.
Tel 626 5474.

Beers and Spirits

De Bierkoning
Paleisstraat 125.
Map 7 B3.
Tel 625 2336.

Pottery and Glassware

Fleur de Lys
Beethovenstraat 41.
Map 4 D5.
Tel 662 1737.

Galleria d'Arte Rinascimento
Prinsengracht 170.
Map 1 B4.
Tel 622 7509.

Glasgalerie Kuhler
Prinsengracht 134.
Map 1 B4. **Tel** 638 0230.

Het Kleikollektief
Hartenstraat 19.
Map 7 A3.
Tel 622 5727.

Rinascimento
Prinsengracht 170.
Map 1 B4.
Tel 622 7509.

Posters and Prints

Art Unlimited
Keizersgracht 510.
Map 7 A5.
Tel 624 8419.

Hoogkamp Old Prints
Spiegelgracht 27.
Map 4 F2. **Tel** 625 8852.

ENTERTAINMENT IN AMSTERDAM

Amsterdam offers a diverse array of world-class entertainment. A variety of performances are staged in hundreds of venues throughout the city, ranging from the century-old Concertgebouw (see p134) to the innovative Musiekgebouw aan het IJ (see p244). The Dutch passion for American jazz draws many international greats such as Pharaoh Sanders to annual events such as the North Sea Jazz Festival (see p53). The city's most popular events take place in the summer, and include the Holland Festival (see p53) and the Amsterdam Roots Festival (see p53). There is a huge choice of multilingual plays and films throughout the year. There is also plenty of free entertainment to be enjoyed from the multitude of street performers and live bands in late-night bars and cafés.

Entertainment Information

One of the most useful sources of entertainment information is *Uitkrant*, a free listings magazine (see p261). It is printed monthly and available, as are a variety of other Dutch-language listings, from theatres, cafés and bars, libraries and tourist offices. Although written in Dutch, it is easy to follow and offers the most comprehensive daily listings of what's going on.

The **I amsterdam Visitor Centre** publishes an English-language listings magazine every two months called *A-mag*. It can be picked up for a nominal price at Visitor Centres and some newsagents, or free issues can be found in selected hotels and restaurants.

Late-night bar in the Red Light District

Daily newspapers including *De Volkskrant, NRC Handelsblad* and *De Telegraaf* publish a selection of listings on Wednesdays. *Het Parool* has a Saturday supplement with a complete listing of the following week's events, including those at museums and galleries.

Booking Tickets

Amsterdam's major classical music, opera and dance performances, such as those by the Dutch National Ballet, are likely to be sold out weeks ahead of time. It is advisable to book tickets in advance to ensure the day, time and seats of your choice. For most other events, it is possible to buy tickets on the day. The **AUB** has a last-minute window (noon–7:30pm daily) selling tickets for same-day shows.

The main reservations office for entertainment and all cultural activities is the AUB, which is located in the Stadsschouwburg (see p113), accessible via the corner entrance, in Leidseplein. You can make reservations, pick up tickets in advance (a booking fee is charged) and obtain information in person or over the telephone. You can also make bookings at the venue itself, or through I amsterdam Visitor Centres. Tickets to major rock concerts can be obtained at the Tourist Board, AUB and at some of the large record shops in the city centre. Although some of the most popular club dates need to be booked in advance, entrance to clubs like the Paradiso and De Melkweg

The Stopera complex, home to the Dutch national opera and ballet companies

The Neo-Classical-style pediment of the Concertgebouw *(see p134)*

(see pp112–13) can usually be bought at the door. Going to the cinema is very popular with Amsterdammers, so it is advisable to book tickets in the afternoon for evening performances during a film's opening week. Most multiscreen cinemas provide a Dutch-speaking automated booking service. All booking offices are usually open from Monday to Saturday, between 9am and 6pm, or later. Credit cards are usually not accepted and it is important to collect reserved tickets at least an hour before the show starts, or the tickets may be resold.

Theatre sign on Nes *(see p75)*

Reduced-Price Tickets

Entry to some performances can be obtained at bargain prices for holders of the Cultureel Jongeren Passport (CJP). Valid for one year, it is available to anyone under the age of 30 for €15. Some hotels include reduced-price entry to certain events as part of their package deals – check details with your travel agent. Half-price last-minute tickets can be bought at the AUB last-minute ticket office. Several venues, such as the Concertgebouw *(see p134)*, have free lunchtime concerts throughout the year. On Fridays (Apr–Oct), the Westerkerk *(see p92)* puts on free organ recitals.

Facilities for the Disabled

Most major theatres, cinemas and concert halls in Amsterdam have unrestricted wheelchair access, and assistance is always available. A number of the city's smaller venues, however, are housed in old buildings not designed with the disabled in mind. Venues like De Kleine Komedie *(see p242)* will make special arrangements if they are notified beforehand. Cinemas also provide facilities for the hard of hearing and visually impaired. Always telephone the box office a couple of days before your visit and specify what you require.

Open-Air Entertainment

Since Amsterdammers are avid supporters of theatre and of all sorts of music, there are plenty of open-air venues operating throughout the summer. In the heart of the city, the Vondelpark open-air theatre *(see pp134–5)* stages a variety of free concerts and theatre performances. Acoustic concerts, often featuring African and Middle-Eastern musicians, are held in summer in the gardens of the Tolhuistuin *(see p247)*, reachable by the Buiksloterveer ferry behind the Centraal Station).

The Prinsengracht classical music concert *(see p53)* is performed in August on a group of canal barges. On the outskirts of the city, the scenic Amsterdamse Bos, *(see p157)* is the setting for productions of Shakespeare, Chekhov and other classical dramatists, staged in the 1,800-seat open-air amphi-theatre. In the south, Amstelpark *(see p156)* is the venue for the De Parade, where dance, theatre and circus acts perform inside a large tent, taking place at the end of July *(see p242)*. Many Amsterdammers also enjoy rowing on the Amstel; you'll find several rowing clubs dotted southwards along the river.

Useful Addresses

AUB/Last-Minute Ticket Office
Leidseplein 26.
Map 4 E2.
Ⓦ amsterdamsuitburo.nl

I amsterdam Visitor Centre
Stationsplein 10.
Map 8 D1.
Tel 702 6000.
Ⓦ iamsterdam.com

Customers enjoying café life in the popular Thorbeckeplein

Theatre, Dance and Film

Theatre and dance are important aspects of cultural life in Amsterdam, and performances take place throughout the year in dozens of venues all over the city. Experimental theatre can be found in one of the oldest streets in the city, along the Nes (see p75). Theatres on the Nes, such as De Brakke Grond, are also popular venues for radical theatre productions. The city's main locations for dance include the Meervaart, Nationale Opera & Ballet, Stadsschouwburg and the Dutch Dance Laboratory, for experimental productions. The Dutch love cinema and, though Amsterdam has only a few large cinema complexes, there is a surprising number of venues that show a variety of films, from first-run, mainstream and art, to foreign-language, revival and gay.

Theatre and Cabaret

Amsterdam has more than 50 theatre venues and boasts a number of English-speaking companies. The Toneelgroep Amsterdam is the resident theatre company at the **Stadsschouwburg**; **De La Mar**, **Westergasfabriek** and **Bellevue** are important venues for touring theatre companies.

Experimental theatre can be found at a range of locations throughout Amsterdam, including the **Westergasfabriek**. **Compagnietheater** is a small company that specializes in translating and staging the classics, as well as promoting works by young playwrights. The Orkater musical theatre company often holds performances at Stadsschouwburg and the Theater Bellevue. **Theater Amsterdam** stages long-running productions.

The annual Holland Festival (see p53) in June offers a prestigious series of opera, theatre and dance performances. It features international talent such as Peter Brook, Peter Zadek and John Jesurum. The International Theatre School Festival presents innovative performances at the **Compagnietheater**. Nearby, on the Nes (see p75), **Frascati** and **De Brakke Grond** feature productions by young directors and performers, the latter focusing on Flemish companies.

Down-river from the Nationale Opera & Ballet, near the smart Inter-Continental Amstel (see p219), the **Koninklijk Theater Carré** plays host to long-running international musicals such as Les Misérables and Cyrano. The **Koninklijk Theater Carré** is often the setting for elegant premieres attended by members of the Dutch royal family. Closer to the Nationale Opera & Ballet and also facing the Amstel is the charming 17th-century **De Kleine Komedie**. It can seat an audience of up to 500 and offers a perfect setting for cabaret. It also features stand-up comedy and occasionally has English-language theatre productions. Although De Kleine Komedie is closed throughout the summer, such is its reputation throughout Europe, that bookings must be made at least three months in advance. Stand-up comedy and improv nights (in English) also can be found at the **Rozentheater**.

Summer outdoor theatre can be seen at the Vondelpark open-air theatre (see pp134–5) and at the Amsterdamse Bos (see p157), a woodland park on the edge of town. Here, a pathway lined with Classical Greek statuary leads to a 1,800-seat amphitheatre, the venue for performances of works by classic playwrights like Shakespeare, Chekhov, Ibsen and Miller. In the south of Amsterdam, the Amstelpark (see p156) is the venue for De Parade, a tent city erected each summer in late July and early August where international dance, theatre and circus acts perform before a rapturous audience. Merrymaking often carries on into early morning .

Dance

The Netherlands possesses two world-class ballet companies, the Dutch National Ballet and the Nederlands Dans Theater (NDT). The Dutch National Ballet is housed in the 1,600- seat **Nationale Opera & Ballet** (see p65), which provides magnificent views along the Amstel river, and is renowned for its classical and modern repertoire.

The Nederlands Dans Theater (NDT) regularly performs in venues throughout the city. Ballets from its former artistic director, Jiri Kylian, are often performed, together with works by the groups' current choreographer, Paul Lightfoot. In addition to the core company, the NDT also has one other group, the Nederlands Dans Theater II, a younger company made up of dancers aged 18–21 who perform the work of established choreographers such as Hans van Manen. The company also performs the works of choreographer Lionel Hoche.

Dance is often performed at Stadsschouwburg and at Bellevue and Frascati. Westergasfabriek, the former gasworks, also holds dance performances.

Amsterdam is a laboratory for experimental dance, and many innovative performances can be seen throughout the city. They are not confined to any one venue though, so it is best to check the entertainment listings, such as Uitkrant (see p261), for full details. Experimental dance can be enjoyed regularly at top venues like the Stadsschouwburg and the **De Meervaart**. Companies to look out for include Introdans, who combine jazz with flamenco alongside other varieties of ethnic dance, and Opus One, who mix jazz, classical ballet and tap. Needless to say, the Nederlands Dans Theater's repertoire also includes experimental dance routines.

During the first two weeks of July the Stadsschouwburg and surrounding theatres host The Julidans International Festival for Contemporary Dance. Young and established choreographers and dance groups give daring and often ground-breaking performances, to great acclaim. The programme can be found on www.julidans.nl. The Holland Festival in June *(see p53)* is used as the principal platform for premieres of shows by top choreographers from both the Nederlands Dans Theater and the Dutch National Ballet. The International Theatre School Festival, also in June, focuses increasingly on dance, with performances taking place in the historic street of Nes *(see p75)*, which is one of the very oldest parts of the city.

Film

Amsterdammers love the cinema, and there are more than 45 venues in the city. All films are screened in the original language with subtitles. Movie lovers should not miss the plush Art Deco Tuschinski Theater *(see p125)*. Built between 1918 and 1921, this cinema features a luxurious foyer, stained-glass windows, tables, sofas and lamps. First-run films frequently open at the Tuschinski, and this is often the place to catch public appearances by film stars.

It is easy to find out which films are showing where, as each cinema has a listing at its entrance, and details are also posted in bars and cafés.

Programmes change on a Thursday, and most new film listings, carried in the daily newspapers, are printed on the Wednesday. *De Filmkrant* is a free monthly film magazine that carries complete listings; these are written in Dutch but very easy to understand. It is also possible to check online at www.amsterdam.filmladder.nl.

Ticket prices vary from around €7 to €12, depending on whether it is a matinée or an evening screening, although some longer films can command a slightly higher admission price.

Some of the larger cinema complexes carry afternoon matinées during the week and these usually begin at 2pm. At the weekend the schedule varies. Some of the cinemas, such as the mainstream **Pathé City** and the arthouse **Kriterion**, often schedule several showings of children's films at the weekend. For adults, the Kriterion offers a great selection of arthouse and mainstream films, with late-night screenings of cult and erotic movies.

Evening shows usually begin at either 6:30pm or 7pm, and there is a second showing at 9pm or 9:30pm, although a few cinemas

also have an 8pm screening. Some cinemas have an intermission, known as the "pauze". This is a 15-minute obligatory break that is usually scheduled to coincide exactly with the most exciting scene of the film.

If you suddenly get the urge to see a film and don't particularly mind what it is, check out Leidseplein *(see p112)*, one of the biggest gathering areas in the city, where cinemas, cafés, restaurants and bars abound.

One first-run and arthouse cinema that can be found within a 2-minute walk of Leidseplein is the eight-screen Pathé City theatre.

For arthouse films there is also the **Cinecenter**, situated on a side street just off the main square across from De Melkweg *(see p112)*; and for a real treat, **Film-theater de Uitkijk**, which is a short walk along Leidsestraat to Prinsengracht. This small, venerable 158-seat venue specializes in movie classics and, best of all, refuses to indulge in the dreaded "pauze". Dating from 1913, De Uitkijk is Amsterdam's oldest operational cinema. **The Movies** near Haarlemmerpoort *(see p95)* is a movie house specializing in films with a psychological connection. The theatre also houses a pleasant pub and restaurant.

DIRECTORY

Theatre/Cabaret

De Brakke Grond
Vlaams Cultureel Centrum,
Nes 45.
Map 7 C3.
Tel 626 6866.
w brakkegrond.nl

Compagnietheater
Kloveniersburgwal 50.
Map 7 C3.
Tel 520 5320.
w compagnietheater.nl

Frascati
Nes 63. **Map** 7 B4.
Tel 626 6866.
w theaterfrascati.nl

De Kleine Komedie
Amstel 56–58.
Map 5 B3.
Tel 624 0534.
w dekleinekomedie.nl

Koninklijk Theater Carré
Amstel 115–125. **Map** 5 B3. **Tel** 0900 252 5255.
w theatercarre.nl

De La Mar Theater
Marnixstraat 402. **Map** 4 E2. **Tel** 0900 335 2627.
w delamar.nl

Rozentheater
Rozengracht 117.
Map 1 A5. **Tel** 0900 BOOM CHICAGO.
w boomchicago.nl

Stadsschouwburg
Leidseplein 26. **Map** 4 E2.
Tel 624 2311. w ssba.nl

Theater Amsterdam
Danzigerkade 5.
Tel 900 0322.
w theateramsterdam.nl

Theater Bellevue
Leidsekade 90. **Map** 4 D1.
Tel 530 5301.
w theaterbellevue.nl

Westergasfabriek
Haarlemmerweg 8–10.
Map 1 A1. **Tel** 586 0710.
w westergasfabriek.nl

Dance

De Meervaart
Meer en Vaart 300.
Tel 410 7777.
w meervaart.nl

Nationale Opera & Ballet
Amstel 3. **Map** 7 C5.
Tel 625 5455.
w operaballet.nl
See also venues under Theatre/Cabaret

Film

Cinecenter
Lijnbaansgracht 236.
Map 4 E2.
Tel 623 6615.

Filmtheater de Uitkijk
Prinsengracht 452.
Map 4 E2.
Tel 623 7460.

Kriterion
Roetersstraat 170.
Map 5 C3.
Tel 623 1708.

The Movies
Haarlemmerdijk 161.
Map 1 B2. **Tel** 638 6016.

Pathé City
Kleine Gartmanplantsoen 15–19. **Map** 4 E2.
Tel 0900 1458.

Classical Music and Opera

Amsterdam is a city with a long and rich tradition in classical music and opera. The principal orchestral venues house some of the world's finest musical events. The city has also acquired a reputation as a centre for early music and organ recitals, with performances in traditional settings such as the English Reformed Church or the Oude Kerk. In summer, concerts can be enjoyed as you relax in one of the city's beautiful parks.

Orchestral, Chamber and Choral Music

Amsterdam's music centrepiece is the **Concertgebouw**, renowned for its acoustics and home to the celebrated Royal Concertgebouw Orchestra. International orchestras and soloists come here regularly, and each summer it hosts Robeco SummerNights concerts, which are famous for showcasing young talent. Early music is also performed here, often by the world-famous Amsterdam Baroque Orchestra and the Orchestra of the Eighteenth Century.

The **RAI** is principally a convention centre, but is often the setting for classical music and opera events. **Museum Geelvinck**, a pretty 18th-century canal house, hosts intimate chamber music concerts featuring fortepianos from its collection. Modern classical music, opera and choirs can be heard at De Melkweg (see pp112–13) and the Paradiso (see p247).

The **Bethaniënklooster**, near the Nieuwmarkt, is host to varied and interesting concerts. Leading international chamber groups

and soloists perform in the intimate setting of the old refectory of this former convent, where the oak-wood ceiling contributes to the extraordinary acoustics.

The **Muziekgebouw aan het IJ**, a 15-minute walk from Centraal Station, is Amsterdam's new grand location for innovative modern music concerts, festivals and multimedia events.

Music in Churches

Churches in Amsterdam offer concerts throughout the year. The historic church organs in the **Oude Kerk** (see pp70–71), **Nieuwe Kerk** (see pp76–7) and **Waalse Kerk** are magnificent. On the edge of Vondelpark and housed in a renovated church, Orgelpark has several organs from various historical periods, including the Renaissance. It hosts concerts and workshops for artists.

Carillon concerts are often held in the Oude Kerk and at lunchtime on Tuesdays in the **Westerkerk** (see p92). This church also hosts free organ concerts on Fridays at 1pm, April to October. The 17th-century **English**

Reformed Church holds concerts that range from Baroque to modern. Free lunch-time summer concerts are given by new ensembles and young musicians. The **Thomaskerk**, built in the 1960s, holds a free lunchtime concert every other Tuesday (except in July and August). Concerts are also held in the **Waalse Kerk** and Noorderkerk (see p94).

Opera

Built in 1988, the **Nationale Opera & Ballet** houses the Stadhuis (town hall) and the Dutch National Opera. Its nickname, the Stopera, is a combination of both names (see p65). It is one of Europe's most up-to-date theatres and features an internationally famous repertoire, as well as lesser-known and some experimental works. Opera can also be seen at the Stadsschouwburg (see p113) on Leidseplein. More experimental opera is performed at nightclubs such as the Paradiso and De Melkweg (see p247). Also, check the Holland Festival listings for world premieres (see p53).

Open-Air Concerts

The Prinsengracht concert (see p53) takes place in late August. Musicians perform on barges on the canal in front of the Hotel Pulitzer (see p218). In summer, concerts also take place in the Vondelpark open-air theatre and the Amsterdamse Bos (see p157).

DIRECTORY

Orchestral, Chamber and Choral Music

Bethaniënklooster
Barndesteeg 6.
Map 8 D3. **Tel** 625 0078.
🖳 bethanienklooster.nl

Concertgebouw
Concertgebouwplein 2–6.
Map 4 D4.
Tel 0900 671 8345.
🖳 concertgebouw.nl

Museum Geelvinck
Keizersgracht 633.

Map 5 A3. **Tel** 715 5900.
🖳 geelvinck.nl

Muziekgebouw aan het IJ
Piet Heinkade 1. **Tel** 788 20 00. 🖳 muziekgebouw.nl

RAI
Europaplein 8.
Tel 549 1212. 🖳 rai.nl

Music in Churches

English Reformed Church
Begijnhof 48.

Map 7 B4.
Tel 624 9665.

Nieuwe Kerk
Dam. **Map** 7 B2.
Tel 638 6909.

Orgelpark
Gerard Brandtstraat 26.
Map 3 C3. **Tel** 515 8119.

Oude Kerk
Oudekerksplein 23.
Map 7 C2. **Tel** 625 8284.

Thomaskerk
Prinses Irenestraat 36.
Tel 622 5170.

Waalse Kerk
Oudezijds Achterburgwal 159. **Map** 7 C3.
Tel 623 2074.

Westerkerk
Prinsengracht 281.
Map 1 B4. **Tel** 624 7766.
🖳 westerkerk.nl

Opera

Nationale Opera & Ballet
Amstel 3. **Map** 7 C5.
Tel 625 5455.
🖳 operaballet.nl

Pop, Rock and Nightclubs

Amsterdam is bursting with live music. From the omnipresent street entertainers to a whole variety of music venues and nightclubs, as well as countless music cafés, it is hard to avoid the city's rock and pop and club scene. Concerts and clubs tend to be cheap and relaxed, with few venues having a strict door policy or dress code. Local bands and musicians are encouraged, and many venues receive subsidies from the local council, so tickets, with the exception of the big-name concerts, rarely cost more than €8. Some of the best bands can be enjoyed for the price of a drink. Fierce competition means that venues and clubs come and go. For the latest information and gig guides, consult the free *Pop & Jazz Uitlijst*, available from cafés and libraries as well as the AUB ticket service and Tourist Board offices *(see p241)*. Both AUB and tourist offices sell advance tickets for major concerts. The free magazine *Uitkrant* and English-language *A-mag* also carry concert listings *(see p240)*.

Pop and Rock

Many big names tend to by-pass Amsterdam and head for Rotterdam's Ahoy and Utrecht's Vredenburg stadiums instead. However, mainstream pop and rock concerts are held at the RAI, Amsterdam Arena (home to Ajax football club), the **Heineken Music Hall** and **Ziggo Dome**. The Ziggo Dome is housed in what appears to be a sleek black box, located behind the Amsterdam Arena, seats almost 16,000 for acts such as Lady Gaga and Radiohead. Middle-of-the-road artists tend to put on shows in large theatres, such as the Theater Carré *(see p147)* and the Theater Bellevue *(see p243)*. **Club Air** and **Escape** nightclubs *(see p247)* host a variety of dance and soul acts.

For most Amsterdammers, rock and pop are synonymous with two venues – **Paradiso** and **De Melkweg**. Paradiso, housed in a converted church just off Leidseplein, is more prestigious. De Melkweg is housed in a former dairy, hence the name, the "Milky Way" *(see pp112–13)*.

Both the Paradiso and De Melkweg offer an extremely varied and entertaining programme: rock, pop, dance, rap and world music. The standards range from chart-toppers and cult heroes to local hopefuls trying their luck at one of the regular talent nights. Big-name bands which come to play in Amsterdam invariably turn up at one of these two places. Followers of rock'n'roll should visit the **Cruise-Inn**. The **Arena** is part of the well-known hotel where tourists and locals cram in to dance to the latest music played by live DJs. **The Waterhole**, located near Leidseplein, features live rock nightly.

Blues music alternates with rock at the loud and crowded **Maloe Melo**. Sweaty and beer-soaked, this place may not seem particularly inviting, but the atmosphere is convivial. From May to September, free concerts are held every Sunday afternoon in the Vondelpark open-air theatre *(see pp134–5)*, often featuring some of the country's top pop and rock acts.

Jazz

There may well be more jazz venues in Amsterdam than anywhere else in the world. The relaxing rhythms of jazz music are perfectly suited to the mood of the brown cafés and bars *(see pp48–51)*.

The city's jazz flagship is the **Bimhuis**, a venue that takes its music seriously. Commonly known as the "Bim", it is the best venue in Amsterdam for contemporary jazz and has an international reputation. In late 2005, Bimhuis moved next to the Muziekgebouw, Piet Heinkade 1.

Café-restaurant **Casablanca**, in the Red Light District on the Zeedijk, offers live jazz three or four times a week (always on Friday, Saturday and Sunday). More traditional than the Bimhuis, the music here is played by both veterans and newcomers alike.

The many jazz cafés dotted around the city are very popular. Most of them are small brown cafés where local bands perform. Late opening and free entry boost their appeal, although drinks cost a little above average. Most cafés hold weekly jam sessions, when anyone can take the stage.

Around Leidseplein are the **Alto Jazz Café** and the **Bourbon Street**. Alto is best on Wednesday evenings when Hans Dulfer, the so-called "father" of the Amsterdam jazz scene, is in residence. His daughter Candy is a regular attraction at the **De Heeren van Aemstel**. **De Engelbewaarder** has popular jam sessions on Sunday afternoons. The Vondelpark *(see pp130–31)* is also a popular jazz venue in the summer, when free open-air concerts are held here.

The Dutch passion for jazz turns to frenzy in the summer, when there is a festival held in almost every town. In July, the North Sea Jazz Festival *(see p53)* in Rotterdam, attracts some of the biggest names in jazz.

World Music and Folk

In the Netherlands the world music scene has been heavily influenced by its many immigrant communities. The West Indian, Indonesian, Maghreb, West African, Surinamese and Turkish traditions are thriving, and are actively encouraged by the city's authorities.

Occupying a disused church in the western part of the city, **Podium Mozaïek** is a multi-cultural arts centre, staging plays, music and dance performances. It attracts young artists from around the globe, but particularly those from Turkey and North Africa.

Several venues regularly schedule world music events, including De Melkweg and Paradiso. De Melkweg hosts a colourful Amsterdam Roots Festival (see p53) in June. The **Tolhuistuin**, next to the EYE Film Institute, is housed in the former Shell head office café. It offers an eclectic mix of jazz, world music, lindy hop and much more. The terrace of its café-restaurant has great views of the Amsterdam skyline across the IJ. In summer, acoustic concerts are held in the garden. **De Badcuyp**, in the lively Pijp neighbourhood, swings with salsa, tango, African music and dance options. The venue often holds free workshops highlighting Cuban dance and salsa traditions.

The indigenous folk music of the Netherlands is an acquired taste. It sounds like a mix of traditional German folk music, French chanson and old sea shanties. Large cafés around Rembrandtplein, including **Jantjes Verjaardag** and **Café Tante Roosje**, provide folk music for tourist consumption. For a more authentic experience, head for the Jordaan. In bars like **De Twee Zwaantjes** and **Café Nol** regulars sometimes burst into joyous song.

Many of Amsterdam's Irish pubs feature live music. Some of the best include **Mulligan's**, and the huge and extremely popular **O'Donnells**, where you can hear authentic fiddle playing almost every weekend. **The Old Nickel** holds regular folk and jazz nights.

Clubs and Discos

Amsterdam is well-known for its lively nightclub scene. There is little pretension here, and the mood is relaxed and carefree. Most clubs open at 11pm but don't really get going before 1am. They usually close at 4am during the week, and 5am on Friday and Saturday nights. Entrance prices are relatively low and drinks are reasonably priced. Few clubs enforce a strict dress code, but they do reserve the right to refuse admission. It is an established custom to tip the doormen on the way out.

Amsterdam was one of the very first cities to embrace house music during the late 1980s. It still dominates most clubs, but there is now more variety on offer, from disco to techno. DJs and music vary from one night to the next, so check listings for details. Most venues are situated around Rembrandtplein and Leidseplein, but you can come across some interesting places if you venture beyond the centre. Some of the disused docks across the IJ often host festivals.

Jimmy Woo dance club is famous for its tough door policy and it is hard to get into it, but once past the door, it has a great party atmosphere. It's Hong Kong hip, with plenty of black leather and a great sound system. The Westergasfabriek (see p243), located to the north of the Jordaan, is a huge former gasworks. Its buildings now house a collection of music and dance spaces such as **WesterUnie**.

Club 8, situated west of the old centre, has a pool and snooker hall. There's dancing every Saturday night when the club transforms into the Cacao Lounge, featuring R & B, Balkan beats and house muic.

A complete contrast is **Disco Dolly**, a favourite among students. The entrance charge is low (or even free) and it attracts a mixed crowd. Dance the night away on a happy mix of funk, house, disco or hip-hop played by the club's DJs.

The leading non-house club in Amsterdam is the **Sugarfactory**, with its varied and enjoyable menu of soul, funk and jazz dance.

The city's biggest dance hall is **Escape**, attracting a predominantly young crowd who usually come from out of town each weekend. The discos around Leidseplein are basically just extended bars with only small dance floors, catering for tourists and attracting a much wider age range of people. On the whole, mainstream and chart music tend to be played. **Bitterzoet** attracts a more alternative crowd and often stages live music from a wider variety of music genres. The seventh floor of a former newspaper office, which is now the Volkshotel, is home to **Canvas**, a club that is open every Friday and Saturday night from 10pm. It has a mix of musical styles played by local DJs. The outdoor terrace offers sweeping views of the city.

Gay and Lesbian Clubs

Clubbing is at the heart of Amsterdam's gay scene. The techno sounds and camp floor shows at many venues attract a trendy clientele. Crowds are often mixed and most gay clubs will rarely turn away women or straight men.

Gay nightlife used to centre around Reguliersdwarsstraat. **Club NYX** is housed in a former coach house and is spread over three floors with DJs playing on each. It attracts a young, mixed crowd. Café **Reality** attracts a Surinamese crowd and offers a mix of disco and salsa. Nowadays, the focus has moved to Zeedijk, where bars like **De Engel van Amsterdam** and **The Queen's Head** are popular.

Prik, near the Dam, is a straight-friendly gay bar, and becomes pretty busy almost every night. **De Trut** is housed in the basement of a famous former squat and packs in a mixed crowd on Sunday nights. The decor is seedy, but the dance floor is big and the drinks are cheap.

If you're interested in a mixed lesbian/gay disco head to **Club Roque**, with music from the Top 40. Details of other events are listed in the monthly Gay&Night magazine, available at many gay bars, the **Pink Point** kiosk and online at www.amsterdam4gays.com. **Gayforcing** organizes gay and lesbian bridge afternoons. The decor is imaginative and the atmosphere friendly. **Saarein II** is frequented by lesbians and gays and offers a friendly, relaxed atmosphere.

DIRECTORY

Pop and Rock

Arena
's-Gravesandestraat 51.
Map 6 D4.
Tel 850 2400.
W hotelarena.nl

Cruise-Inn
Zuiderzeeweg 29
(Amsterdam-Noord).
Tel 692 7188.
W cruise-inn.com

Heineken Music Hall
Arena Boulevard 590.
Tel 0900 687 4242.
W heineken-music-hall.nl

Maloe Melo
Lijnbaansgracht 163.
Map 4 D1.
Tel 420 4592.
W maloemelo.nl

De Melkweg
Lijnbaansgracht 234a.
Map 4 E2.
Tel 531 8181.
W melkweg.nl

Paradiso
Weteringschans 6–8.
Map 4 E2.
Tel 626 4521.
W paradiso.nl

The Waterhole
Korte Leidsedwarsstraaat
49. **Map** 4 E2.
Tel 620 8904.
W waterhole.nl

Winston International
Warmoesstraat 123–9.
Map 7 C2.
Tel 623 1380.
W winston.nl

Ziggo Dome
Arena Boulevard 6175.
Tel 0900 235 3663.
W ziggodome.nl

Jazz

Alto Jazz Café
Korte Leidsedwarsstraat
115.
Map 4 E2.
Tel 626 3249.
W jazz-cafe-alto.nl

Bimhuis
Piet Heinkade 3.
Tel 788 2188.
W bimhuis.nl

Bourbon Street
Leidsekruisstraat 6–8.
Map 4 E2.
Tel 623 3440.
W bourbonstreet.nl

Brix
Wolvenstraat 16.
Map 7 A3.
Tel 639 0351.
W cafebrix.nl

Casablanca
Zeedijk 26E.
Map 8 D2.
Tel 776 7407.
W cafecasablanca.nl

De Engelbewaarder
Kloveniersburgwal 59.
Map 8 D3.
Tel 625 3772.
W cafe-de-engelbewaarder.nl/jazz

De Heeren van Aemstel
Thorbeckeplein 5.
Map 7 C5.
Tel 620 2173.
W deheeren vanaemstel.nl

World Music and Folk

De Badcuyp
Sweelinckstraat 10.
Map 5 A5.
Tel 675 9669.
W badcuyp.nl

Café Nol
Westerstraat 109.
Map 1 B3.
Tel 624 5380.
W cafenol-amsterdam.nl

Café Tante Roosje
Rembrandtplein 5.
Map 7 C5.
Tel 820 8257.
W tanteroosje.nl

Jantjes Verjaardag
Reguliersdwarsstraat
108–114.
Map 7 D5.
Tel 778 4093.
W jantjesverjaardag.nl

MC Theater
Polonceaukade 5.
Map 1 A1.
Tel 606 5040.
W mconline.nl

Mulligan's
Amstel 100.
Map 7 C5.
Tel 622 1330.
W mulligans.nl

O' Donnell's
Ferdinand Bolstraat 5.
Map 4 F5. **Tel** 676 7786.
W odonnellsirishpub.com

The Old Nickel
Nieuwebrugsteeg 11.
Map 8 D1.
Tel 624 1912.

Podium Mozaïek
Bosen Lommerweg 191.
Tel 580 0380.
W podiummozaiek.nl

Tolhuistuin
Tolhuisweg 5.
Map 2 E2.
Tel 624 1912.
W tolhuistuin.nl

De Twee Zwaantjes
Prinsengracht 114.
Map 1 C3.
Tel 625 2729.
W detweezwaantjes.nl

Clubs and Discos

Bitterzoet
Spuistraat 2.
Map 7 C1.
Tel 421 2318.
W bitterzoet.com

Canvas
Wibautstraat 150
(7th floor).
Map 5 C5.
Tel 261 2110.
W canvas7.nl

Club 8
Admiraal de Ruijterweg
56 B. **Tel** 685 1703.
W club-8.nl

Club Air
Amstelstraat 16.
Tel 820 0670.
Map 8 D5.
W air.nl

Disco Dolly
Handboogstraat 11.
Map 7 B4.
W discodolly.nl

Escape
Rembrandtplein 11–15.
Map 7 C5. **Tel** 622 1111.
W escape.nl

Jimmy Woo
Korte Leidsedwarsstraat 18.
Map 4 E2. **Tel** 626 3150.
W jimmywoo.com

Sugarfactory
Lijnbaansgracht 238.
Map 4 E2. **Tel** 627 0008.
W sugarfactory.nl

WesterUnie
Klönneplein 4–6.
Map 1 A1.
Tel 686 9304.

Gay and Lesbian Clubs

Club NYX
Reguliersdwarsstraat 42.
Map 7 B5. W clubnyx.nl

Club Roque
Amstel 178. **Map** 7 C5.
W clubroque.nl

De Engel van Amsterdam
Zeedijk 21.
Map 8 D2.

Gayforcing
Gay & lesbian bridge club.
W gayforcing.nl

Pink Point
Westermarkt.
Map 1 B4.
Tel 428 1070.
W pinkpoint.org

Prik
Spuistraat 109.
Map 7 B2. **Tel** 320 0002.
W prikamsterdam.nl

The Queen's Head
Zeedijk 20.
Map 8 D2.
Tel 420 2475.

Reality
Reguliersdwarsstraat 129.
Map 7 C5.
Tel 639 3012.

Saarein II
Elandsstraat 119.
Map 1 B5.
Tel 623 4901.

De Trut
Bilderdijkstraat 165.
Map 3 C1.
W trutfonds.nl

CHILDREN'S AMSTERDAM

As a lively, cultural city, Amsterdam can be a fascinating place to visit with children. Its network of canals is fun to explore and many of the squares are alive with street musicians and performers. The city's many parks offer a wide range of outdoor activities and the streets are lined with tempting shops, restaurants, cafés and food stalls. Even in summer, there is no guarantee of good weather, but you can always find something to do on wet days. Some theatres and museums are geared for children and there is nearly always an English-language film showing that is suitable for children.

Practical Advice

If you are visiting Amsterdam with a very young child, a baby sling or pouch is essential. While the city centre is small enough to be covered on foot, man-oeuvring a heavy pushchair around the cobbled streets can be tough going. Negotiating one of the city's notoriously steep flights of stairs or getting on a crowded tram or canal boat with a pushchair is virtually impossible, and they are actually banned in some of the museums.

For sightseeing, it is worth taking a boat trip. Details of the options available are given on pages 272–3. Most of the operators offer discounts to children under 12 and allow toddlers to travel free. Trams are another entertaining and efficient way to get around (see p268), although they tend to be crowded at peak periods. Like all other forms of public transport in the city, children under four go for free and under-12s travel at half-price.

Children are welcome at the majority of hotels in Amsterdam (see p214). Some of the bigger ones even provide babysitting facilities. If your hotel does not offer this, **Babysit Centrale**

Kriterion provides reliable, cheap childcare. The service is 24-hour, but bookings must be made daily from 4:30 to 8pm.

Theatres and Museums

Many theatres, such as the **Circus Elleboog** and **De Krakeling**, hold children's shows on Wednesdays or Sundays and the Vondelpark (see pp134–5) stages weekly open-air shows in summer.

Seasonal attractions include the Christmas circus at the Koninklijk Theater Carré (see p147). The Amsterdam Tourist Board's monthly publication, *Uitkrant*, contains a complete listing, which is easy to understand, despite being written in Dutch (see p261). Many of Amsterdam's museums have sections which are geared for children. NEMO Science Center (see p152) is one of the best for older children, with its wide range of hands-on exhibits and buttons to press. Adventurous 6- to

Rangda witch from Bali at the Tropenmuseum

12-year-olds will like the exhibitions at Tropenmuseum Junior (see pp154–5), which brings to life the cultures and traditions of the developing world. Would-be pirates love climbing aboard the *Amsterdam*, a full-size replica of an 18th-century East Indiaman moored outside Het Scheepvaart-museum (see pp148–9). The waxworks at Madame Tussauds Scenerama (see p78) are also worth a visit, although small children may be upset by a few of the more gruesome exhibits. The **EYE Film Institute** (see p153) shows children's films on Wednesday, Saturday and Sunday afternoons. Most of Amsterdam's museums offer substantial discounts to children, and toddlers under four normally get in free.

Zoos and City Farms

Artis zoo (see pp144–5) incor-porates both covered and open-air animal pens, along with a Planetarium and the Aquarium. Cheaper, but less extensive, animal-viewing options in and around the city include the animal enclosure in the Amsterdamse Bos (see p157), donkeys and llamas in the Vondelpark (see pp134–5) and free-roaming Highland cattle in the Amstelpark (see p156).

Sports and Recreation

Amsterdam's parks provide a whole range of activities for children. The Vondelpark (see pp134–5) has well-maintained

Crocodiles basking in the Reptile House of Artis zoo (see pp144–5)

The full-size replica of the *Amsterdam*, outside Het Scheepvaartmuseum

playgrounds, free puppet shows and face-painting sessions at the Milk Bar in summer. The Amstelpark *(see p156)* and Amsterdamse Bos *(see p157)* also have a range of activities. The Electrische Museumtramlijn *(see p157)* runs regular round trips to and from the Amsterdamse Bos in vintage trams. You can also camp in designated sites in this park *(see p215)*. On a rainy day, head to **TunFun**, an indoor recreation centre for children aged up to 12.

There are a number of indoor swimming pools around Amsterdam. The best is **Miranda Bad**, a tropical paradise with water chutes, a beach and a wave machine. Indoor pools tend to close in the summer and are replaced by open-air pools, like the municipal one in Twiske, a rural park north of the IJ. The seaside, which is only a short train ride away, has miles of clean, sandy coastline.

Perhaps the most fun can be had simply exploring Amsterdam's network of canals by hiring canal bikes *(see p273)*. When the canals are frozen during a hard winter, your children will enjoy the thrill of skating around the city.

Eating Out

Children may not be welcome in some of the more expensive restaurants, but most places are tolerant, and many cafés and cheaper places have a children's menu such as chicken, chips and *appelmoes* (apple purée). At the **Kinderkookkafé** the food is cooked and served by children. Advance dinner reservations (at least a month) are essential, both for eating and for kids who want to cook.

Amsterdam also has a good selection of pancake houses *(see p232)*. Other treats include *poffertjes*, which are tiny pancakes loaded with butter and icing sugar.

Shopping

Alongside an assortment of large toyshops, there are also a few small shops that sell traditional wooden and handcrafted toys. Look out for the exquisite dolls'-house furniture at **De Kleine Eland**.

For something out of the ordinary in the way of children's clothes, go to **'t Schooltje**.

Children resting weary legs after a hard day's play

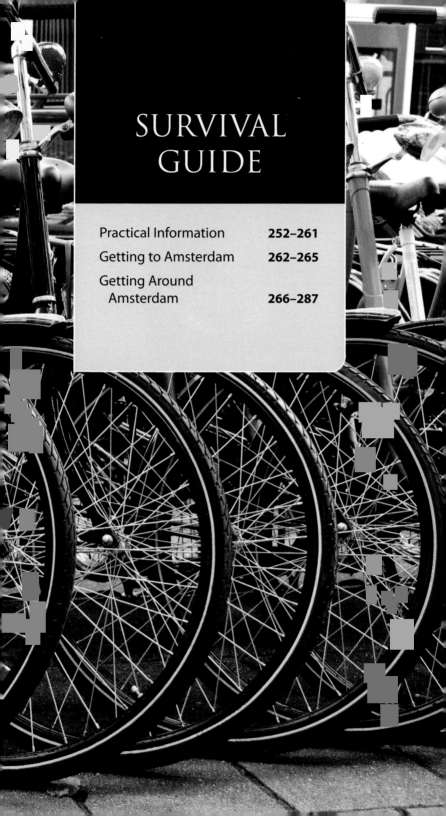

SURVIVAL GUIDE

PRACTICAL INFORMATION

Amsterdam is a cosmopolitan city, and visitors should find its citizens helpful, friendly and often multilingual. The official networks for helping tourists are efficient and straightforward. Telephones, parking meters and cash dispensers may seem familiar to European visitors, but other tourists will need to follow instructions closely. One of the particular pleasures of visiting the city is to enjoy the relatively car-free environment, which leaves more room for alternative forms of travel. Trams, water transport, bicycles and pedestrians are all given a much higher priority in the centre than motor vehicles. Indeed, the ideal way to explore the city is on foot *(see p266)* or by bicycle *(see pp270–71)*.

I amsterdam sign in the Museumplein

When to Go

High season for tourists runs from April to September, with another peak around New Year. During school summer holidays (June to August), it can be hot and humid; hotels and travel prices are also more expensive, and many tourist sights are overcrowded. For the annual national holiday, King's Day (April 27), it is often difficult to find hotel rooms unless you book well in advance. In winter there can be heavy snow or ice. Early spring and late autumn are the quietest times, but the weather can be rather cool.

Visas and Passports

For a stay lasting up to three months for the purpose of tourism, EU, US, Canadian, Australian and New Zealand nationals need only a valid passport. Other nationalities should check with the Netherlands embassy in their home country. Under the Schengen visa open-borders agreement, a visitor from a Schengen country can travel freely throughout the Schengen zone with only a valid form of ID and no passport. Immigration procedures have tightened and you may have to prove that you have sufficient funds for your stay and a return ticket. In the Netherlands, everyone over the age of 14 is required to carry ID, and this includes tourists. You can be fined for not having the correct ID. As a visitor, you will be asked to show a stamped passport.

Customs Information

EU nationals over the age of 17 are entitled to import unlimited goods for personal use, except for tobacco and alcohol on which duty has already been paid. The limits are: 800 cigarettes, 400 cigars, 1 kg of tobacco, 10 litres of spirits, 20 litres of fortified wine, 90 litres of wine and 110 litres of beer. Duty-free tobacco and alcohol are no longer available to EU citizens. However, some other duty-free goods are available at Schiphol airport after passport control. Citizens of non-EU countries must abide by the following restrictions: 200 cigarettes or 50 cigars or 250g of tobacco; 1 litre of spirits or 2 litres of sparkling or fortified wine, 16 litres of beer or a reasonable assortment of these products; other goods or gifts up to the value of €430 per adult.

Bulbs bought in Amsterdam must have a certificate of inspection from the Plant Protection Service if being taken to the USA or Canada.

Non-EU members can reclaim VAT on returning home, or at the Departure Lounge at the airport. Phone the **Customs Information** line, or see www.vatfree.nl.

If you are leaving the EU with more than €10,000, this must be declared.

Tourist Information

The Dutch Tourist Board, the VVV, which is pronounced, "fay-fay-fay", has many branches all over the Netherlands. In Amsterdam, the Amsterdam Tourism and Convention Board (ATCB), the VVV and other tourist services and businesses have merged to become I amsterdam. Amsterdam prides itself on its accessibility

The Neo-Renaissance façade of the Rijksmuseum *(see pp130–3)*

◀ Row of parked bicycles in Amsterdam

to visitors, and I amsterdam has a comprehensive network of tourist information centres. The main **I amsterdam Visitor Centre** is located in front of Centraal Station. The visitor centres offer multilingual information on sights, events, entertainment, transport and tours. They will also book hotels, plays, shows, excursions and concerts (for a small fee). I amsterdam leaflets and maps are also available from museums. The **AUB Uitburo** can provide information and tickets to cultural events.

For information before you travel, the **NBTC** (Netherlands Board of Tourism and Conventions) produces their own brochures and maps.

Be wary of using agencies unrelated to the Tourist Board or I amsterdam: the accommodation they offer can often can be uneccessarily expensive or of poor quality.

Language and Smoking Etiquette

The Dutch have been linguists for centuries, and most students learn English, some German and French. However, it's appreciated if you can handle a few niceties, such as saying *Dag* (Good day) before asking a Dutch person whether they speak English. The Dutch are quite liberal in many ways, but they retain a few conventions. Expect to shake hands often, and if you are out with a crowd it's polite to introduce yourself. When eating out in a group, the Dutch tend to pay for their share of the bill, unless it has been made clear that you are being treated.

The Netherlands has a smoking ban in all public places, including bars, cafés, restaurants and hotels for smoking tobacco. Some clubs and cafés do turn a blind eye, especially in coffeeshops, however, new laws are being introduced to stop tourists

from entering and buying cannabis. Only Dutch residents with valid ID will be allowed entry.

Admission Prices

Many of the art museums in Amsterdam are free or offer discounts to those under the age of 18. They do not offer discounts for international students or seniors *(see p254)*. Nemo, a favourite family-orientated museum, charges the same price for all visitors above the age of three. The three main discount cards are the I amsterdam City Card, the Museum Card (Museumkaart) and the CJP *(see p254)*. The I amsterdam City Card offers free travel on all public transport, a free canal tour, free access to most museums

Taking a break outside Café 't Smalle *(see p160)*

I amsterdam City Card

and 20 free and 65 discounted offers. The card is available from all tourist offices and online, and is valid for either 24 (€49), 48 (€59) or 72 (€69) hours.

The Museum Card costs €54.95 for adults and €27.50 for under 25s (plus a €4.95 administration fee) and provides admission to almost 400 museums throughout the Netherlands. This includes 33 museums in Amsterdam, but excludes special exhibitions. The card is valid for a year, and you will recoup the cost after three or four visits. The card can be bought from all tourist offices, online and at museums.

Opening Hours

Opening times in Amsterdam vary enormously, but each shop has its hours of business posted on the door. In the city centre, shops are generally open 9am–6pm Monday to Wednesday and Friday; 9am–9pm Thursday, until 5pm Saturday and noon–5pm Sunday. Most of the larger

museums are open daily, usually from 10am to 5pm. Some museums are closed on Monday and have different opening hours at the weekend. A few museums also open on Friday evenings to 10pm and adopt Sunday hours on national holidays. Bank and post office hours in the city tend to be weekdays only, between 9am and 4 or 5pm, although some big-city banks are also open Saturday morning. ATM machines operate 24 hours.

Public Conveniences

For such a practical nation, Amsterdam is short on public conveniences, and visitors more often use department stores, hotels, museums and cafés. In clubs, cafés and concert venues with attendants you will pay a minimum of 50c, with large stores charging 30c upwards and a similar fee for using baby-changing rooms.

Taxes and Tipping

Value-added (or sales) tax is 21 per cent in the Netherlands and will usually be included in the price quoted. The exceptions to this are electronic and computer goods. Non-EU residents can shop tax free in two ways: either shop at places affiliated to the Global Blue scheme, or shop anywhere and ask for a tax receipt, then claim the tax back *(see opposite)*.

Service is always included in bars and restaurants. It is usual though to tip taxis, and in bars and cafés it is customary to tip between 5 to 10 per cent to round up the bill.

The Pink Point next to the Homomonument

Travellers with Special Needs

Information and assistance are available for disabled travellers to Amsterdam. One of the most useful websites is run by the **Amsterdam Foundation for People with a Disability** *(Stichting Gehandicapten Overleg Amsterdam)*. The site reviews the accessibility of restaurants, hotels, cafés, public buildings and public toilets.

At Schiphol airport, help is available through **Axxicom Airport Caddy**. The service is free but must be booked at the same time as your flight. The main train stations have also improved the ease of travel for passengers with special needs. Tactile guidance lines assist visually impaired travellers, mobile ramps make it easier for wheelchair users to get on and off trains and those with a functional disability can arrange free travel for a travelling companion. Many trains have wheelchair-access doors, and most double-decker trains have wheelchair-accessible toilets.

All main pedestrian crossings are equipped with sound for the blind. Most foreign Disabled Parking Disks from recognized organizations are valid in the city, but if the parking sign has a licence number on it, it is reserved.

Senior Travellers

Senior travellers will enjoy the relatively easy pace of Amsterdam. Those wishing to avoid loud, drunken crowds in the evenings should choose a hotel either in the canal district or the Museum Quarter, and avoid areas with high concentrations of bars and clubs (such as the Leidseplein or Rembrandtplein). New Year's Eve can be a problem for anyone who cannot move quickly or easily, as locals tend to go crazy with fireworks on the streets, especially around the Nieuwmarkt area.

There are discounts on public transport (trams, buses, metro) for seniors. To be eligible for travel discounts, take your passport to a GVB office *(see p269)* when purchasing your ticket. There are no senior discounts on offer for either the Museum Card or the I amsterdam City Card *(see p253)*.

Gay and Lesbian Travellers

Few other cities are better oriented towards gay and lesbian tourism than Amsterdam. Most listings magazines include a special section for gay and/or lesbian events *(see p261)*, and the **Pink Point**, next to the unique Homomonument at the Westerkerk, is a great place to pick up tourist information. Although not aimed at tourists, the **COC** (the national gay and lesbian organization) hosts social and sports events in the city. Details are given on the website.

GAYtic is another tourist information service specifically oriented to gay and lesbian visitors. They offer an information kit that can be ordered in advance of your journey and collected when you arrive. The kit contains maps, magazines, discounts and information on parties and events. They also sell tickets to special events, and the I amsterdam Card.

Travelling on a Budget

Amsterdam is not a drastically expensive city to visit, but keep in mind that eating out and entertainment can be more costly than in other European countries.

The I amsterdam website and some magazines list free events and festivals in the city. In summer you can enjoy a picnic in the Vondelpark, or free evening entertainment on the VondelCS outdoor terrace.

The I amsterdam Ciy Card and the Museum Card do not offer discounts for kids. There is a discounted 24-hour ticket on public transport for children aged 4–11, accompanied by an adult. Children under four travel free.

For students, the ISIC (International Student Card) offers discounts in youth hostels, theatres, restaurants, some museums, shops and a few travel agencies, but not on local transport. The European Youth Card (CJP) is a good alternative for travellers under the age of 30 who are not students. It offers similar discounts in 38 countries in Europe.

Responsible Travel

The Dutch take environmental issues very seriously and are constantly striving to improve sustainability on a variety of levels. Amsterdam has a growing awareness of ecotourism, with a few companies offering ecotours, like Wetlands Safari, which provides canoe tours through the reed lands north of Amsterdam *(see p267)*.

There is a steadily increasing number of choices for the environmentally aware visitor. The Conscious Hotel group has two eco-friendly hotels near the Vondelpark *(see p217)*. There is an excellent organic farmers'

De Kas restaurant *(see p231)*

market on Saturdays at the Noordermarket in the Jordaan, where a dazzling array of local organic produce, bakery goods, meat, fish, cheese and other dairy products are beautifully displayed. This market is a favourite with locals and often crowded. Be sure to explore the array of farmers' cheeses to discover what Dutch cheese should taste like.

Another organic market is held on the Haarlemmerplein on Wednesday afternoons, although it is very small.

Amsterdam's most famous organic restaurant, **De Kas**, is housed in a beautiful old greenhouse saved from demolition by its chef, Gert Jan Hageman. Here, they serve the fruits of their own labours, using herbs and vegetables from the greenhouse, combined with locally sourced organic meat and fish. **Brouwerij 't IJ**, housed in an old windmill, is a small microbrewery producing organic beer. For an unusual local souvenir, visit the shop **La Savonnerie**, with soaps made from organic products.

Time

The Netherlands is on Central European Time, which means Amsterdam is 1 hour ahead of Greenwich Mean Time. From late March to late October clocks are set forward 1 hour. Australia is 10 hours ahead in winter (8 in summer); while New York is 6 hours behind Central European Time.

Electricity

The voltage in the Netherlands is 220, 50-cycle AC, and compatible with British equipment, but since the Dutch use two-pin continental plugs you will need an adaptor.

American visitors need to convert their equipment or buy a transformer. Dutch wall sockets require a larger plug than those used in the USA.

DIRECTORY

Embassies and Consulates

Ireland
Scheveningseweg 112,
2584 AE Den Haag.
Tel (070) 363 0993.
w embassyofireland.nl

UK Consulate
Koningslaan 44.
Map 3 B4. General
enquiries: **Tel** 676 4343.
w britain.nl

UK Embassy Den Haag
Lange Voorhout 10,
2514 ED Den Haag.
Tel (070) 427 0427.
w britain.nl

US Consulate
Museumplein 19.
Map 4 E3. **Tel** 575 5330.
w amsterdam.usconsulate.gov

US Embassy Den Haag
Lange Voorhout 102,
2514 EJ Den Haag.
Tel (070) 310 2209.
w netherlands.usembassy.gov

Customs Information

Tel 0800 0143 (free-phone).
w belastingdienst.nl
w vatfree.nl (online refund service)
w global-blue.com

Tourist Information

AUB Uitburo
Leisdeplein 26.
Map 4 E2.
w amsterdams uitburo.nl

I amsterdam Visitor Centres
Schiphol Airport
Arrivals Hall 2.
Tel 702 6000.
w iamsterdam.com

Stationsplein 10.
Map 8 D1.
Tel 702 6000.

Netherlands Board of Tourism and Conventions (NBTC)
PO Box 458,
Leidschendam,
2260 MG.
Tel (070) 3705 705.
w nbtc.nl
w holland.com

UK
Portland House,
Bressenden Pl,
London, SW1E 5RS.

USA
215 Park Ave South,
Suite 2005,
New York,
NY 10003.

Travellers with Special Needs

Amsterdam Foundation for People with a Disability
w toegankelijk amsterdam.nl

Axxicom Airport Caddy
Skyport, Kantoor 1167,
Schiphol Airport.
Tel 406 9806.
Email assistentie@ airportcaddy.nl.
w airportcaddy.nl

Beach Wheelchairs at Zandvoort
Paviljoen Take Five.
Tel (023) 571 6119.

NS Bureau Assistentieverlening Gehandicapten (NS Disabled Assistance Office)
Tel (030) 235 7822.
w ns.nl

Gay and Lesbian Travellers

COC
w cocamsterdam.nl

GAYtic
Spuistraat 44.
Map 7 B1.
Tel 330 1461.
w gaytic.nl

Pink Point

Westermarkt 4.
Map 1 B4.
Tel 428 1070.
w pinkpoint.org

Responsible Travel

Brouwerij 't IJ
Funenkade 7.
Map 6 F2.
Tel 528 6237.
w brouwerijhetij.nl

De Kas
Kamerlingh Onneslaan 3.
Tel 462 4562.
w restaurantdekas.nl

La Savonnerie
Prinsengracht 294.
Tel 428 1139.
w savonnerie.nl

Personal Security and Health

Amsterdam is one of the safest cities in Europe – there are few "no go" areas, and violent crime is rare. However, petty theft is rife, and pickpockets do haunt tourist areas and public transport. Sadly, there has also been a change in attitude towards "tolerance", most noticeably in that there have been attacks on gay clubs. For the most part, this should not impact tourists, but for those who do find themselves in trouble, the city has efficient emergency services and facilities, including a Tourist Assistance service.

Members of the armed Dutch police force

Police

If you have been the victim of a serious crime, call **112**. If the crime is petty theft or of a less serious nature, use the general number listed in the Directory box, or simply go to the nearest police station. Almost all police officers will speak some English. If your property has been stolen, or you have been in an incident that has required medical treatment, you will need to file a police report for insurance purposes. It is important to have all information regarding the incident with you when you go to the police station. If you require any help you can contact the **Bureau Slachtofferhulp** (Victim Support), or ask the police to contact them on your behalf.

Fire engine

Police cars

Ambulance

What to Be Aware Of

Theft is the main problem for visitors to Amsterdam, *(see Lost and Stolen Property)*, but you should also be aware that bar and club areas like Leidseplein and Rembrandtsplein, the Red Light District and city parks can be dangerous for lone tourists in the very early morning hours. In general, wandering at night in most Amsterdam neighbourhoods is safe, and women are fine to walk about on their own.

The Red Light District was once a very busy, bustling area that felt quite safe due to the constant stream of people. Now, after several measures to "clean up" the area, the number of visitors has dropped, and some streets can be very seedy. Keep in mind that you are not allowed to photograph prostitutes in the Red Light District without their permission, and you may be asked to pay a fee to do so.

You are required to have your ID on you at all times, and can be fined if found without it. It is illegal to carry a weapon; consume alcohol in most public places; buy, sell or use hard drugs; buy cannabis outside of coffeeshops; urinate on the street and cycle in pedestrian areas. Uniformed police may perform on-the-spot body searches, or ask for ID.

Attracted by the canals, mosquitoes can be an irritant during summer. Repellent sprays, antihistamine creams, mosquito nets and plug-in devices are available from large pharmacies.

In an Emergency

For serious emergencies, dial 112; this will put you through to a general number for the police, ambulance and the fire brigade. An operator will answer (most speak English) and you will be asked which service you need, and where you are calling from. If the operator decides it is not an emergency that requires immediate intervention, they may direct you to call the **Central Medical Service**, or to report to a hospital with a first-aid department, or in the case of a crime, to report to the nearest police station. If you feel you need extra support, call the Bureau Slachtofferhulp or **Gay & Lesbian Switchboard**, who provide a similar service but for gay and lesbian travellers.

Lost and Stolen Property

While Amsterdam is safer than most American and European cities, theft is still some cause for concern. Pickpockets work crowded tourist areas, trams and the train between the city centre and Schiphol airport, especially in summer. Use your common sense and be alert to your surroundings.

Bicycle and car theft, particularly of foreign vehicles, is also a problem. You must report lost or stolen property in order to claim on your insurance.

Local police stations hold recovered items for a day or so before sending them to the **Central Lost Property** Office. For anything lost on the train, ask at the station. All recovered property is stored at the station for five days, before it is sent to the depot at Utrecht. Call 0900 321 2100 to submit a trace request. Bus and tram drivers check their vehicles after each journey, and any items found are handed in at the depot. From there they are sent to the **GVB Lost Property Office**, who can tell you if your belongings have been found 48 hours after the day you lost them. If you lose your passport, inform your embassy (see p255). Lost credit or debit cards should be reported to the card issuer (see p258).

Hospitals and Pharmacies

Minor problems can be dealt with by a chemist (drogist). For medicine on prescription, go to a pharmacy (apotheek). These are open from 8:30am to 5:30pm Monday to Friday. Details of pharmacies open outside normal hours are posted in all pharmacy windows and in the afternoon newspaper Het Parool. The Central Medical Service (Centrale Doktersdienst) can also direct you to the nearest pharmacy, and can refer you to a duty GP or supply the name of a dentist. Minor accidents can be treated in hospital outpatient clinics, open 24 hours a day; the I amsterdam (see p252) can advise on these. In an emergency, go to a hospital with a casualty unit, or call an ambulance (112).

Pharmacy sign

Travel and Health Insurance

Travel insurance is available through most travel agents and insurance companies, with a wide variety of policy options, and is highly recommended in case of loss, theft or medical emergencies that require repatriation help.

All EU members can receive medical and dental treatment in the Netherlands at a reduced charge. Before travelling, British visitors should obtain the European Health Insurance Card (EHIC) – online at www.ehic.org.uk or at post offices – and seek a refund for any non-private treatment on their return home. You will never be turned away by a doctor even if you do not have an EHIC with you, however, you may have to pay more for treatment.

Drugs

Soft drugs, such as hashish and cannabis, are part of a very Dutch solution: they are decriminalized, but not legal. This allows the government control over the coffeeshops (where cannabis is sold), while it earns money through the businesses. A law banning foreign tourists from entering coffeeshops came into effect in 2013, though Amsterdam police currently turn a blind eye. Smoking on the streets is discouraged, but some coffeeshops now have outside areas to smoke (see p253). Hard drugs are a different matter: anyone caught with them by the police will certainly be prosecuted. Paddos, or magic mushrooms, were banned in 2009. Never try to take drugs out of Amsterdam or the Netherlands: penalties are stiff.

DIRECTORY

Police

Ambulance, Fire and Police
Tel 112 (emergency only).

Bureau Slachtofferhulp (victim support)
Tel 0900 0101.
W slachtofferhulp.nl

Police General Number
Tel 0900 8844.

Main Police Stations
Lijnbaansgracht 219.
Map 4 E2.
Beurstraat 33.
Map 7 C2.
Nieuwezijds Voorburgwal 104.
Map 7 A4.

In an Emergency

Central Medical Service (Centrale Doktersdienst)
Tel 088 003 0600.

Gay & Lesbian Switchboard
Tel 020 623 6565.
W switchboard.coc.nl

Lost Property

Central Lost Property
Korte Leidsedwars-straat 52. **Tel** 251 0222.
Map 4 E2. W verlorenof gevonden.nl

GVB Lost Property Office
Kromme Mijdrechtstraat 25. **Tel** 0900 8011.
W gvb.nl

Lost Property on Trains
Tel 0900 321 2100. W ns.nl

Hospitals

Academisch Medisch Centrum (AMC)
Meibergdreef 9.
Tel 566 9111.

Onze Lieve Vrouwe Gasthuis (casualty unit)
1e Oosterparkstraat 279.
Map 6 D4.
Tel 599 9111.

Sint Lucas Andreas Ziekenhuis
Jan Tooropstraat 164.
Tel 510 89 11.

VU Medisch Centrum
De Boelelaan 1117.
Tel 444 4444.
24-hour first aid:
Tel 444 3636.

Pharmacies

Dam
Damstraat 2.
Map 7 C3.
Tel 624 4331.

Jordaan
Westerstraat 180.
Map 1 B3.
Tel 624 9252.

Koek, Schaeffer & Van Tijen
Vijzelgracht 19.
Map 4 F3.
Tel 623 5949.

Medicijnman
Utrechtsestraat 86.
Map 5 A3.
Tel 624 4333.

Het Witte Kruis
Rozengracht 57.
Map 1 A5.
Tel 623 1051.

Banking and Currency

Amsterdammers are still partial to cash transactions, although the banking system has started encouraging more use of debit cards to pay for all transactions, including small amounts. Surprisingly, credit cards are not as universally accepted in the Netherlands as in many other countries. The larger hotels, shops and most restaurants will take the major cards, but the golden rule is to ask first if in doubt, or check the front door for logos. Amsterdam has an excellent foreign exchange network, and transactions are virtually hassle-free for visitors, particularly English-speakers. There is no limit to the amount of currency you can bring into the country.

GWK exchange counter at Schiphol airport

Banks and Bureaux de Change

You can change currency in offices such as **GWK** (*grenswisselkantoren*). In general, the GWK gives the best overall rates. Their offices are found in the airport, main train stations and some tourist areas. The only bank in the Netherlands that still offers an exchange service for tourists is the **ING** bank found in the city centre; American Express also offers this service. All of the above charge a commission for the service. Independent bureaux de change charge an exorbitant commission and give a poor exchange rate. However, they can be the best option if you are exchanging small amounts, as at the official GWK offices the commission rates go down as the amount exchanged goes up. If you arrive by ferry, don't change any money on the boat and visit the GWK just after disembarkation. This stays open for night arrivals. Avoid changing money in hotels, as their charges can be high.

ATM at a branch of ING

ATMs

Most ATMs will handle cards from the main international banks and many credit cards. Your withdrawal limit may be lower than from your own bank, and there can be an extra service charge. Check on the machine itself if it accepts the same system as your card (for example, **American Express**, **MasterCard**, **Diner's Club**, Cirrus, **Visa** or Maestro). When a foreign card is inserted, most ATMs will offer you a choice of language; after requesting English, it should be simple to follow the directions. This is the easiest method to withdraw cash on a credit card. ATMs are plentiful and can be found outside post offices, banks and GWK offices, and in the main train stations. They can be identified by the small sign above them showing the name of the bank that services them.

Currency Cards and Credit Cards

Most currency or travel money cards are Visa or MasterCard linked. They can be pre-loaded (and topped up) with euros and used in Amsterdam just like a debit card to pay for things and withdraw cash from an ATM. As they are not linked to bank accounts, there is no risk of defrauding main home accounts. This also reduces the risk of identity theft in the event a card is stolen. Traveller's cheques are not widely accepted and can be cashed at GWK offices.

Banks will not advance you cash against credit cards, but most ATMs accept the major cards. Some restaurants require a minimum purchase to use a credit card. Carry some cash just in case.

DIRECTORY

Banks and Bureaux de Change

American Express
Postbus 7319, 1007JH.
Tel 504 8000.

GWK
Tel 316 2097 (general number).
Centraal Station. **Map** 8 D1.
Kalverstraat 150. **Map** 7 B4.
Damrak 86. **Map** 7 C2.
Leidsestraat 103. **Map** 4 E2.
Schiphol Airport Station.
Amstel Station.

ING
Rokin 90.
Map 7 B4.

Lost or Stolen Cards and Cheques

American Express
Tel 1800 528 4800 (US).
Tel (+44) 1273 696 933 (UK).
Tel 020 504 4800.

Diner's Club.
Tel (+44) 244 470 910 (UK).
Tel (1) 514 877 1577 (US).

MasterCard
Contact your bank.

Visa
Tel 0800 022 3110.

The Euro

The Euro (€) is the common currency of the European Union. It went into general circulation on 1 January 2002, initially for 12 participating countries. The Netherlands was one of those 12 countries.

EU members using the Euro as sole official currency are known as the Eurozone. Several EU members have opted out of joining this common currency.

Euro notes are identical throughout the Eurozone countries, each one including designs of fictional architectural structures and monuments. The coins, however, have one side identical (the value side) and one side with an image unique to each country. Both notes and coins are exchangeable in each of the participating Euro countries.

Bank Notes

Euro bank notes have seven denominations. The €5 note (grey in colour) is the smallest, followed by the €10 note (pink), €20 note (blue), €50 note (orange), €100 note (green), €200 note (yellow) and €500 note (purple).

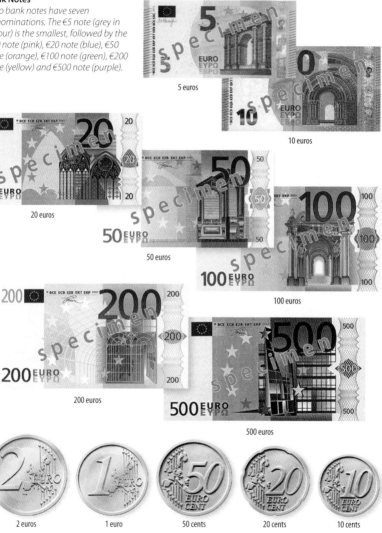

5 euros

10 euros

20 euros

50 euros

100 euros

200 euros

500 euros

2 euros

1 euro

50 cents

20 cents

10 cents

Coins

The euro has eight coin denominations: €1 and €2; 50 cents, 20 cents, 10 cents, 5 cents, 2 cents and 1 cent. The €2 and €1 coins are both silver and gold in colour. The 50-, 20- and 10-cent coins are gold. The 5-, 2- and 1-cent coins are bronze.

5 cents

2 cents

1 cent

Communications and Media

Amsterdam, and its citizens, are plugged in, logged on and wired up, so there are plenty of options for visitors to check their emails or surf the net when visiting the city. For more traditional communication methods, KPN Telecom and Post NL handle telephone and postal services, respectively. Both companies are among the most forward-thinking in Europe. With the exception of children's programmes, most Dutch television stations do not dub programmes or films, and several listings magazines are bilingual or exist in English.

International and Local Telephone Calls

The advent of Skype and VoIP has had a huge effect on the public telephone system. More and more homes are switching over and choosing to save money by relinquishing more traditional land lines, especially for international calls. There are also Internet/telephone businesses that offer such low rates for international calls that it can be cheaper than phoning home from a hotel, or from your mobile.

The Dutch White Pages *(Telefoongids)* and the Yellow Pages *(Gouden Gids)* have a combined website (www.detelefoongids.nl) available in English. Names are listed in alphabetical order. However, if the last name begins with a *de*, *van*, *van der*, etc you must look under the name that follows these articles. IJ is read as a "y" and comes at the end of the alphabet, not in the "i" section. 0800 numbers are free, 0900 numbers are charged a per-minute or per-call rate.

Mobile Phones

There are four main GSM (Global System for Mobile Communications) frequencies in use, so if you want to ensure your phone will work while you are away you should have a quad-band phone. Tri-band phones from the EU will usually work in the Netherlands, but US mobile phones may not. Contact your service provider.

To use your mobile phone abroad, you may need to enable the "roaming" function on your device. It is also more expensive

to make and receive calls while abroad, despite efforts to decrease roaming charges.

A cheaper option is often to purchase a local SIM card to use in your phone. You can only do this if your handset is "sim free" or unlocked. Some of the local/international networks are **Hi (KPN)**, **T-Mobile**, **Vodafone**, **Telfort**, **Orange** and **Ben**. KPN Hotspots gives you Internet access for smart phones; simply send an SMS to: HOTSPOTS, number 4222, and you can log on for 15 minutes for a small fee, which is charged to your phone.

Colourful Dutch pictorial phonecard

Public Telephones

Public telephones can be found on main streets out of the city centre and at train stations and post offices, but they are starting to disappear in cafés and bars. The city's payphones take phonecards, and some take credit cards, but there can be heavy charges for this form of payment. Phonecards can be bought at post offices, supermarkets, newsagents and train stations. Instructions for using the telephones are in English and Dutch. When you phone popular numbers such as airports, you may be offered a choice of languages, or

Reaching the Right Number

- National directory inquiries, dial 1888 or visit www.detelefoongids.com
- Local operator, dial 1888. International operator, dial 0900 8418 Mon–Fri.
- To phone the USA or Canada, dial 001 followed by the number.
- To phone the UK, dial 0044 followed by the number, omitting the 0 from the area code.
- To phone Australia, dial 0061 followed by the number.
- To phone New Zealand, dial 0064 followed by the number.
- To phone the Irish Republic, dial 00353 followed by the number.

encounter an electronic voice that announces how many people are in the queue before you. Most hotels have IDD (International Direct Dialling) units, but be aware that the telephone costs are likely to be inflated.

Internet

Amsterdam is the first major European city to offer Wi-Fi access through a network that covers the whole city. KPN provides the hotspots Wi-Fi system (for a fee), while free public Wi-Fi is available, on request, outdoors. Other free Wi-Fi areas include some cafés, within many hotels, the library and out in the parks.

With the increase in the use of smartphones and tablets, Internet cafés in Amsterdam are disappearing. If you need a computer to access the Internet, the best option is to go to the **OBA (Amsterdam Public Library)**. The main branch of the OBA, near Centraal Station, is Holland's largest library and offers Internet access for a small fee at its 600 computer terminals. Some telephone shops beyond the centre, such as **Sayed Brothers** also offer Internet access.

Internet access at OBA (Amsterdam Public Library)

The **Coffee Company**, a coffee shop chain found on main streets in the city centre, offers free Wi-Fi. Some hotels do not charge extra for Wi-Fi, while others have a closed circuit system where you have to pay a fee, or log on through a modem in your room.

Postal Services

Amsterdam's post offices are distinguished by the **Post NL** logo. In all neighbourhoods, there are sub post offices *(postagentschap)* inside shops, newsagents or tobacconists. Stamps *(postzegels)* can be bought in all of the above places, and in larger supermarkets and souvenir shops. If you send mail outside the Netherlands you will have a choice of Priority or Standard Post. Letters up to 20 g can be sent anywhere abroad for a universal flat rate. It is worth sending important documents by registered mail.

Postboxes are scattered throughout the city. On the postbox there are two slots *(see illustration below)*. A sign on the post box indicates when the next collection will take place.

Slot for all other destinations

Slot for local destinations

Dutch postbox

Newspapers and Magazines

Most foreign newspapers reach the city centre by lunchtime on publication day. The *Het Parool* is the Amsterdam paper that is read throughout the Netherlands, and the *de Volkskrant* and *NRC Handelsblad* are the most respected national newspapers.

Listings can be found in all of the above Dutch newspapers, but posters and listings in the city's bars and cafés may be a quicker, easier guide to entertainment in Amsterdam. *NL 20* and the *Uitkrant* (published by the AUB Uitburo, *see p255*) are free, easily available and have excellent listings, but both are in Dutch. The I amsterdam Visitor Centre also produces a number of free English-language leaflets providing details of festivals and cultural highlights *(see p240)*. Amsterdam gay and lesbian magazines *Gay&Night* and *Gay News* (bilingual English/Dutch) can be bought from most newsagents.

Television and Radio

The main TV channels serve standard European and US fare, but all hotels and homes have cable TV, with 30 or so channels available, including British, French, German, Belgian and Italian stations. British and American shows are subtitled on the Dutch and Belgian channels but are dubbed on the French, Italian and German channels.

English-language stations include BBC1, BBC2, BBC World, Discovery Channel, CNN and CNBC. Comedy Central and MTV both have some Dutch programming. News is broadcast on Dutch Radio 1 (98.9 MHz), pop music on Radio 3 (96.8 MHz) and classical music on Radio 4 (94.3 MHz). It is also possible to pick up BBC Radio 4 on 198 kHzAM and the World Service on 648 kHzAM.

GETTING TO AMSTERDAM

Amsterdam is one of Europe's most popular destinations. As you would expect of a cosmopolitan city of this size, it is easily accessible by plane, coach, car, ferry and train. In addition, travellers from the UK are able to reach Amsterdam via the Channel Tunnel, although passengers must change train at Brussels. Each method of travel has its own benefits and disadvantages, and the choice will largely depend on whether time, money or comfort is the main priority. Whichever method of transport you choose, it is always worth making a few inquiries to find the best deal. Not only is there an ever-increasing selection of "packages" and special-interest holidays on offer, but also prices can fluctuate widely depending on the time of year you travel (new operators and ventures will emerge all the time).

Entrance to Amsterdam's Schiphol airport

Airports

Amsterdam's **Schiphol** airport, the fourth largest in Europe, is a major international transport hub and one of the world's most modern, efficient, clean and user-friendly airports. Schiphol has one terminal hub consisting of three departure halls and four arrival halls, which stream into Schiphol Plaza. In the Plaza you will find a tourist information desk, two bureaux de change desks, a bank, the national rail service NS office and left-luggage facilities. All signs are posted in both Dutch and in English. Also in the Plaza are dozens of high street shops, fast-food restaurants, bars, cafés, newsagents and a fully stocked grocery store. For passengers leaving Amsterdam, the facilities after passport control contain one of the largest tax-free shopping centres in Europe, a museum, a casino, a masseuse, and dozens of restaurants and bars, not to forget a wedding service called "Say Yes and Go",

www.schiphol weddings.nl. For business people and those in transit, there is an amazing range of facilities available, from phone, post and fax services, to business centres and conference rooms. Wireless LAN gives you Internet access throughout the airport.

Tickets and Fares

There is an immense choice of flights to Amsterdam from the UK and the Republic of Ireland, with at least eight carriers operating direct flights. These include the airlines **Aer Lingus**, **British Airways** and **KLM**. Cheap flights are advertised in national newspapers, listings magazines and on the Internet, and are also available through discount agencies. Smaller operators, such as **easyJet**, **Transavia**, **Cityjet** and **Jet2**, can be less expensive than the national airlines. Watch out for flight prices that do not include airport and security taxes and associated surcharges, such as checked-in luggage, as these

can be expensive. Dozens of inclusive package deals are available, and if organized through a reliable agency, they can be far cheaper than booking a flight or ferry and separate accommodation.

Amsterdam is also a popular staging post for overseas visitors to Europe. You can fly from many US cities to Schiphol, and operators running non-stop services on scheduled flights include **US Airways**, **Delta/KLM**, **United Airlines** and **American Airlines**. Other operators fly via the major European capital cities, such as Paris and Rome, but London is probably the cheapest transatlantic destination, with uniquely varied connections. Fare prices vary according to season, but APEX (which must be bought at least 2 weeks in advance) is the cheapest year-round option. The leader in the field of charter flights from the USA is Martinair, which offers mid-range prices on non-stop flights from a number of cities. Cheaper still are the fares of the "seat consolidators" and "last minute" websites, which buy

Self-service check-in at Schiphol airport

up unsold seats from the major carriers and sell them off at a huge reduction. For bargain flights, check out the free weeklies and travel sections of newspapers. Several companies offer excellent-value package tours. KLM has the widest range of options, but can be expensive, so it's well worth shopping around.

The cheapest route for visitors from Australia and New Zealand will also usually require a London stopover, as scheduled flights direct to Amsterdam are expensive. **STA Travel** and Flight Centre, which has offices in Australia, New Zealand and the USA, is a source of expert advice for independent travellers and can arrange all connections.

On Arrival

Arrival and Exit signs will direct passengers arriving from Schengen countries: to baggage carousels and Customs. All other passengers will be streamed into the huge, central shopping and amenities area of the "Schiphol World Avenue", and should follow the Arrivals and Passport Control signs to the ground floor. After passport control is a hall with baggage carousels and Customs. If you have nothing to declare, simply walk through the doors marked Exit to enter Schiphol Plaza. There are sometimes spot checks at Customs, and this can take some time. Bringing food produce, such as raw meats, cheeses and other dairy products into the country is banned. Additionally, you must declare any of the following: merchandise imports, protected animal and plant species, works of art and antiques, narcotics, arms and ammunition you may be bringing with you. Failure to do so may result in heavy fines, and in some cases, arrest.

A KLM flight departing from Schiphol airport

Transport from the Airport to the City

There are several ways of getting into the centre of Amsterdam, 18 km (11 miles) to the northeast. These include car rental (although driving in Amsterdam is not recommended), taxis, buses and trains. Car rental firms are arranged around the edge of Schiphol Plaza, by the exits. Once you have arranged the rental, there are courtesy buses to the parking lots. There are two forms of taxi available: the TCA (see p267) and private taxis at the rank just outside the Plaza. A taxi to the city centre will cost anywhere from €40 to €60, depending on where you

Sign showing departure gates

are going. You also have the option of the Schiphol Travel Taxi, which must be reserved in advance and can be booked online as either a private taxi or, for a lower fare, shared. A shared fare starts at around €20 for a single trip, and €35 for a return, and private rates start at €40 for a single and €75 for a return. Keep in mind that a shared taxi may take a longer time than expected, as it may make several stops before your destination.

One bus travels into the centre of Amsterdam from just outside of Schiphol Plaza: the 197. It stops at Leidseplein, from where you can transfer to the tram system, in about 30 minutes. Single tickets cost €4 and can be bought on the bus, or you can also use the OV-chipkaart (see p269). The most popular way to get to the

city centre, however, is by train, and it costs about the same price. The Schiphol NS station is located directly below the airport, and tickets for the airport train as well as other domestic train travel are available from the yellow ticket machines in Schiphol Plaza. Some of the machines take change, and some will also take credit cards (with an extra fee for use).

Trolleys, which are free of charge, can be taken right on to the platform via the lifts. Trains run four to seven times an hour between 6am and midnight, after which they run once an hour. The journey takes about 20 minutes, and the fare is €3.90, regardless of whether you take the slower Sprinter or intercity train or the faster Intercity Direct, which takes 15 minutes to reach Centraal Station. There are also rail connections from Schiphol airport to most stations in the Netherlands. Rail services are clearly signposted. Tickets for international travel can also be purchased from the ticket offices at one end of the Plaza. A small handling fee of 50c is charged.

Railway platform at Schiphol Plaza, destination Amsterdam

A high-speed Thalys train

Arriving by Train

All trains arrive at Amsterdam Centraal Station, including those from Schiphol airport. The **Eurostar** runs between London and Brussels via the Channel Tunnel. Passengers for Amsterdam must change at Brussels. The journey time is about 7 hours, and there are a range of comfort classes, discounts for seniors and children, special tickets for bicycles and combination packages which includes the cost of a hotel and/or car rentals.

Thalys runs a high-speed service between Paris, Brussels and Amsterdam, ten times a day, with a variety of special offers, package deals and half-price last-minute deals. The FYRA high-speed train, www.nshispeed.nl, is scheduled to run between Brussels and Amsterdam in the future; the train currently runs between Breda and Amsterdam.

Students and those under 26 can benefit from discount rail travel both to and within the Netherlands. The Interrail Global pass allows travel for up to 22 days within one month, and the Interrail One Country pass allows three–eight days of unlimited travel in the Netherlands. For more information, contact **Rail Europe**; you don't even have to be a student to qualify for some deals.

Amsterdam Centraal Station has all the amenities of a big terminus, but can be very crowded with commuters during peak hours and is a magnet for pickpockets. Most tram and bus routes start here *(see pp268–9)*; head for Stationsplein by the main entrance, following signs to the I amsterdam Visitor Centre. The tram stops are only a few metres from the entrance, and the bus stops are across the bridge, in front of the station. The I amsterdam Visitor Centre and the GVB municipal transport authority office are located in the white pavilion building found on the water in front of the station.

Centraal Station is being extensively reorganized until 2017. Parts of the station may be closed and stops moved.

Arriving by Ferry

The Dutch railways, Nederlands Spoorwegen (NS), in conjunction with **Stena Line** and Greater Anglia, operate a boat-train service called the **Dutchflyer** which runs from London to Amsterdam via Harwich and the Hook of Holland. The total journey time is about 12 hours, and a variety of deals are offered, including combined packages that include hotels and day trips and short stays. **P&O Ferries** operates an overnight service from Hull to Zeebrugge or Rotterdam, which is a 10-hour journey. **DFDS Seaways** run an overnight service from Newcastle to IJmuiden (note that the ticket price does not include the journey from IJmuiden to Amsterdam, which is a bus ticket that must be booked separately), and ferry trips can also be booked as a three-day minicruise.

Arriving by Car

An ever-expanding motorway system makes it easy to reach the Netherlands from most countries in western, central and southern Europe.

A valid driving licence is sufficient for driving in the Netherlands, although many car-hire firms and the motoring organization **ANWB (Royal Dutch Touring Club)** favour an international driving licence. To take your own car into the Netherlands, you will need proof of registration, valid insurance documents, a road safety certificate from the vehicle's country of origin and an international identification disc. Major roads (marked N) are well maintained, but Dutch motorways (labelled A) have narrow lanes, traffic lights and sometimes no hard shoulder. European routes are labelled E. There are four levels of speed limit: 100 km/h (60 mph) or

Stena Line's Dutch Flyer on the London–Amsterdam route

120 km/h (75 mph) on motorways, 80 km/h (50 mph) outside cities and 50 km/h (30 mph) in urban areas. From the A10 ring road, the S-routes (marked by blue signs) will take you to the centre of Amsterdam.

The ANWB provides a breakdown service for members of foreign motoring organizations. A non-member can pay for the ANWB's services, or become a temporary ANWB member for the duration of your stay.

If you break down on a major road or motorway, use the yellow telephone pillars. Once in the city, be careful of cyclists and trams (see p266). Trams take precedence and cyclists need ample space. Take care when turning, and allow cyclists priority. Much of the city centre is one-way, and when driving in the canal area, remember that the water should be to your left. Pavements in centre are usually

very narrow, so keep an eye out for people walking in the streets. Main roads, with priority, are marked by a white diamond with a yellow centre; otherwise assume priority is from the right.

ANWB logo

Arriving by Bus and Coach

Long-distance bus or coach travel can be a cheap, if sometimes tiresome, option for those visiting Amsterdam. The **Eurolines** bus service offers routes either through the Channel Tunnel or by ferry from Dover to Calais. There are three daily services in summer from London Victoria station to Duivendrecht Station (from where there is a Metro connection to Centraal Station), and at least one service a day in winter. Eurolines also offers cheap deals the further in advance you book, and some package deals. Fares can start

for as little as £19 one way. There are also discounts for students, children and seniors. One advantage of coach travel is that you are allowed to take two medium suitcases in the hold. Folding bikes are accepted only on the Eurolines coach service to Amsterdam.

Coaches travelling to Europe offer comfortable services, such as reclining seats, air conditioning, toilet facilities and DVD entertainment. The super-long coaches also offer increased legroom.

A Eurolines bus

DIRECTORY

Schiphol Airport

Information Service
Tel 0900 0141.
w schiphol.com

Arriving by Air

Aer Lingus
Dublin. **Tel:** 1890 800600.
Tel 0333 004 5000 (UK).
Tel 0900 265 8207 (NL).
w aerlingus.com

American Airlines
Tel 800 433 7300 (USA).
Tel 0900 040 1666 (NL).
w aa.com

British Airways
Tel 0844 493 0787 (UK).
Tel 020 346 9559 (NL).
Tel 800 Airways (USA).
w britishairways.com

Cityjet
Tel 0871 405 2020 (UK).
Tel 0900 901 9020 (NL).
w cityjet.com

Delta
Tel 800 241 4141 (USA).
Tel 020 721 9128 (NL).
w delta.com

easyJet
w easyjet.com

Jet2
Tel 0800 408 1350 (UK).
Tel (+44) 203 059 8336 (NL and other countries).
w jet2.com

KLM
Tel 020 7660 0293 (UK).
Tel 020 474 7747 (NL).
Tel 1 866 434 0320 (USA).
w klm.com

Transavia
Tel (+352) 2700 2728 (UK).
Tel 0900 0737 (NL).
w transavia.com

United Airlines
Tel 800 UNITED-1 (USA).
Tel 020 346 9381 (NL).
w united.com

US Airways
Tel 800 428 4322 (USA).
w usairways.com

Arriving by Train

Eurostar
Tel 03432 186 186 (UK).
w eurostar.com

NS International
w nsinternational.nl

Rail Europe
Tel 800 622 8600 (USA).
Tel 800 361 7245 (Canada).
Tel 0844 848 5848 (UK).
w voyages-sncf.com (UK).
w raileurope.com (USA/ Canada).

Thalys
w thalys.com

Arriving by Ferry

DFDS Seaways
Tel 0871 522 9955 (UK).
w dfds.co.uk
w dfdsseaways.nl

Dutchflyer
Tel 08445 762 762 (UK).
Tel 0900 8123 (NL).
w stenaline.co.uk

P&O Ferries
Tel 08716 646 464 (UK).
Tel 0107 145 464 (NL).
w poferries.com

Stena Line
Tel 0844 770 7070 (UK).
Tel 0900 8123 (NL).
w stenaline.co.uk

Arriving by Car

ANWB (Royal Dutch Touring Club)
24-hour emergency service
Tel 088 269 2888.

Arriving by Bus and Coach

Eurolines
Tel 0871 781 8178 (UK).
Tel 088 076 1700 (NL).
w eurolines.co.uk

Booking Services

STA Travel
Tel 134-STA (134-782) (Australia).
Tel 0800 474 400 (New Zealand).
Tel 0333 321 0099 (UK).
Tel 1800 781 4040 (USA).
w statravel.com

GETTING AROUND AMSTERDAM

The best way to see Amsterdam is on foot or bicycle. Almost everything of interest is within comfortable walking distance or a short cycle away. The city's layout is quite simple, with its concentric canals *(grachten)* and interlocking roads, but it can seem confusing at first. Remember that starting from the innermost canal, the Singel, the main canals after that are arranged in the alphabetical sequence of Herengracht, Keizersgracht and Prinsengracht (on the outside). If walking or cycling are not your style, there is a range of other options: an excellent public transport system, scooters, water taxis, canal boats – but don't drive. Amsterdam can be a nightmare for even the most experienced local drivers, and there are very limited parking facilities.

Green Travel

The Dutch are experts at "greening" their travel options: trams are electric, families are more likely to travel by bicycle or use a local car-share scheme rather than own a car and buses are fitted with special exhaust filters. The city's infrastructure is oriented to bicycle traffic, and public transport is frequent.

Amsterbike offers electric scooters as a quiet, clean way to explore, and **Wielertaxis** are electrically assisted bike taxis. They can carry up to two people and cost less than conventional taxis. **Mokumboot** and **Canal Motorboats** offer ecofriendly electric boats to rent and **Wetlands Safari** offer canoe tours (April–September).

Walking

Make sure that you are wearing sensible shoes – the brick-cobbled streets can be tiring, as well as hazardous. One main drawback to a stroll around town used to be dog mess, but this has improved a lot since the late 1990s. Local traffic remains a hazard to tourists – trams have their own path in the middle of the road; buses and taxis zip about, sometimes moving between tram lanes; and traffic lanes and bicycles are everywhere, often going in every direction. It is important that pedestrians look both ways when crossing tram routes (trams can be almost silent), and keep off the cycle paths. Cars should stop at pedestrian crossings without lights, but it is always better to cross with care.

Guided Tours

Organized group tours offer many options to learn more about the city, and are led by a number of operators.

Amsterdam City Walks organizes guided walks in English that focus on the history and archaeology of Amsterdam and also take in the Red Light District. Guided tours from **Mee in Mokum** take you around the historic parts of the city and have some of the best informed and most entertaining guides. If you want to go beyond the Canal Ring, the guides from Museum Het Schip offer walking tours in the Westerpark and Pijp areas, past some gems from the 19th–early 20th-century social housing estates designed by Amsterdam School architects *(see p99 & p153)*. With **Amsterdam City Tours** you can explore the city either by boat, bike or on foot. They also offer bus tours to the neighbouring towns north of the city. **Sandeman's New Amsterdam Tours** offers daily guided walking and bike tours of the city. Walking tours leave from the Dam, bike tours from Centraal Station. Other possibilities include a Red Light District tour and coffeeshop tour.

Green Wheels car-sharing hire cars

Driving in Amsterdam

The small inner city streets and canals, the plethora of all sorts of traffic, not to mention the serious parking shortages and high charges, all make Amsterdam unsuited to driving. However, if you do choose to drive, be careful of cyclists and trams in the city. Trams take precedence; take care when turning; and allow cyclists priority. Much of the city centre is one way, and when driving in the canal area, remember that the water should be to your left. The **ANWB** provides a breakdown service for members of foreign motoring organizations *(see pp264–5)*. The car-sharing scheme **Green Wheels** offers a "pay-as-you-go" plan, cheaper than owning your own vehicle. Rentals are charged by the hour. To sign up you need to have an international licence.

Pedestrian crossing, Dam square

Parking

Although the city is ill-suited to motor traffic, provision is made for drivers. However, parking is difficult, and theft rife, so if you're staying in a hotel, it's better to book with a secure parking facility and leave your car there while in the city. If you are visiting the city from outside, park on the outskirts in a "P&R" (park and ride) and use public transport into the centre. In town use a car park rather than a meter or roadside space. If you do park in a public place, remove your car radio and all other valuables.

Parking space is at a premium in the city, especially on-street parking in the centre, and many outlying neighbourhoods. In the city centre, meters are limited to 2 hours and are in use until midnight. In the areas outside

A pay-and-display parking sign

the Canal Ring/centre, all-day passes can be bought. Meters take PIN or credit cards; you need to type in the car's registration number and parking time. The registration is digital and there is no printed ticket. Avoid out-of-order meters as you could get fined; Cition will put a sticker on your car if you have a fine. You can pay it through their website (www.parkingfine.cition. nl). If you use a car park, obtain a ticket by putting money in the ticket machine, which can be some way from the parking place. Illegally parked cars will be fined, but you won't get clamped until you have five unpaid parking fines. There are several 24-hour covered car parks, such as **Q-Park** and Byzantium. All car parks within the city are denoted by a white P on a square blue background.

Taxis

There have been a lot of problems in Amsterdam with small, unregulated taxi firms and dishonest or aggressive drivers, especially around Centraal Station. As a result, the municipality has introduced regulated taxi stands (*kwaliteitstaxisstandplaatsen*) that can only be used by taxis with a seal of approval, known as *kwaliteitstaxi's* (quality taxis), with their registration number displayed on the windscreen. The rules are posted at Centraal Station and most large taxi ranks. The best ways to find a cab are to pick one up at a main taxi rank or phone **TCA Taxicentrale**, which runs a 24-hour service. You will find that the response is fast, apart from Friday and Saturday nights. Rates are quite high, so give only a small tip, unless your driver has been particularly helpful. Other firms include **Sneltaxi** or **Amsterdam Online Taxi**.

DIRECTORY

Green Travel

Amsterbike
Piet Heinkade 11A.
Tel 419 9063.
W amsterbike.eu

Canal Motorboats
Zandhoek 10a.
Tel 422 7007.
W canalmotorboats.com

Mokumboot
Stadionkade 73b/
Nassaukade 351.
Tel 06 1468 3277.
W mokum
bootverhuur.nl

Wetlands Safari
Tel 06 5355 2669.
W wetlandssafari.nl

Wielertaxi (bike taxis)
Tel 06 282 47550 or
06 1859 5153.
W wielertaxi.nl

Guided Tours

Amsterdam City Tours
Tel 0299 411 111.
W amsterdamcity
tours.com

Amsterdam City Walks
Tel 06 1825 7014.
W amsterdamcity
walks.com

Mee in Mokum
Tel: 625 1390.
W gildeamsterdam.nl

Sandeman's New Amsterdam Tours
Meeting points: Nationaal Monument, Dam (walking tours); Centraal Station (bike tours).
W newamsterdam
tours.com

Parking

Parking Amsterdam Centraal
Prins Hendrikkade 20a.
Map 2 D3.

Q-Park
Tesselschadestraat 1g.
Map 4 D2.
Marnixstraat 250.
Map 4 D1.
Nieuwezijds Kolk 18.
Map 7 C1.
Van Baerlesraat 33B.

Map 4 D3.
Tel 0900 446 6880.

Breakdown

ANWB Contact Center
Tel (088) 269 22 22.
ANWB Alarm Center
Tel 088 269 28 88.

Parking Pass

Service Centres
Oranje Vrijstaatplein 2
President Kennedylaan
923. Amstel 1. **Map** 8 D4.
W cition.nl

Stadstoezicht
Tel 14020.
W stadstoezicht.
amsterdam.nl

Car Rental

Adams Rent-a-Car
Nassaukade 346.
Map 4 D1.
Tel 685 0111.

Avis
Nassaukade 380.
Map 4 D1.
Tel 088 284 7020.

Green Wheels
Tel 088 210 0100.
W greenwheels.nl

Hertz
Overtoom 333.
Map 3 A3.
Tel 612 2441.

Taxis

Amsterdam Online Taxi
Tel 06 1963 2963.
W amsterdamtaxi-
online.com

Schiphol Travel Taxi
Tel 0900 8876.
W schipholtraveltaxi.nl

Sneltaxi
Tel 036 536 3200.
W sneltaxi.nl

TCA Taxicentrale
Tel 777 7777.
W tcataxi.nl

Using Public Transport

Amsterdam's integrated public transport system (GVB), for which Centraal Station is the central hub, is very efficient. The only way to travel on the Metro, trams and buses is with an OV-chipkaart, a smartcard that is reusable and can be topped up electronically. The 9292, the national public transport information office, provides information via phone or its website on all public transport within the city and the rest of the Netherlands, but does not make reservations.

One of Amsterdam's modern blue-and-white trams

Trams

Amsterdam's trams are the most common form of public transport in the city. Routes are shown on a free transport map obtainable from the **GVB** office. The most useful routes go south from Centraal Station along Damrak or NZ Voorburgwal (Nos 1, 2, 4, 5, 7, 9 and 16), diverging after the Singel. Lines 13, 14 and 17 are also useful if you need to travel west into Jordaan. Trams start operating at 6am on weekdays and 7am at weekends. They finish just after midnight, when night buses take over. Blue boards above the tram and bus stops give the name of the stop and the route numbers it serves. Information inside the shelters shows the stops and approximate times. Many, but not all, are wheelchair accessible.

To enter, choose either the front door, or the door two-thirds of the way towards the back, where the conductor sits. On entering the tram you will need to hold your OV-chipkaart in front of the grey machine to calculate your fare, or buy a disposable OV-chipkaart

(see p269), good for 1 or 2 hours. If you have a young child or heavy suitcase, you may need to keep one foot on the entrance strip when you board to make sure the door stays open until you have boarded safely.

Tram stops will generally be announced, but if you're not sure where to get off, don't be afraid to ask for guidance. Press a button inside the tram to open the doors. You may leave through any but the conductor's or driver's door. Remember that many stops are in the middle of the road, so take care when you get off. You will need to swipe your OV-chipkaart on leaving the tram so that the correct fare can be deducted from your card automatically, or – with the disposable ones – so that you can transfer to

another tram and continue to use it for the full time period.

Buses

Like the trams, the majority of Amsterdam's buses set out from Centraal Station, but they soon branch out from the city centre and largely complement the tram network. They have the same stops and OV-chipkaart ticketing system as the trams, but you must board by the front door. Local buses depart from in front of the station building; regional buses heading north of the city have their own bus terminal, which is located at the back of Centraal Station, facing the IJ. Bus 22 has a useful route, connecting the eastern and western parts of the city via Centraal Station. Take this bus to visit the Scheepvaartmuseum *(see pp148–9)*, Artis *(see pp144–5)*, or as an alternative to tram 13 or 17 to visit the Jordaan and Western Islands.

Night-bus stops have a black square with the number on it; night buses are numbered from 348 to 392. Night buses run all night, but the service is every hour (every half-hour from Friday to Sunday), so be prepared for a wait, or else fork out a little more to

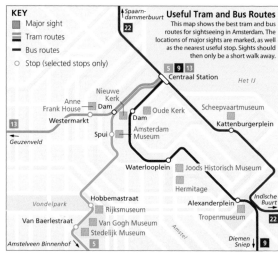

KEY

■ Major sight
≡ Tram routes
▬ Bus routes
○ Stop (selected stops only)

Useful Tram and Bus Routes

This map shows the best tram and bus routes for sightseeing in Amsterdam. The locations of major sights are marked, as well as the nearest useful stop. Sights should then only be a short walk away.

Spaarn-dammerbuurt — 22
Centraal Station — 5 9 13
Het IJ
Nieuwe Kerk
Anne Frank House — Dam
Westermarkt
Oude Kerk
Dam
Scheepvaartmuseum
Kattenburgerplein
13
Geuzenveld
Spui
Amsterdam Museum
Waterlooplein — Joods Historisch Museum
Hermitage
Hobbemastraat
Vondelpark
Rijksmuseum
Van Baerlestraat
Van Gogh Museum
Stedelijk Museum
Alexanderplein
Tropenmuseum — 22
Indische Buurt
Amstel
Amstelveen Binnenhof — 5
Diemen Sniep — 9

A bus serving the north of the city from Centraal Station

take a taxi *(see p267)*. Also note that night buses are more expensive than everyday trams or buses, with fares starting at €4.50 per ride.

Metro

Amsterdam's underground system comprises only four lines, three of which start from and terminate at Centraal Station. Mainly used by commuters, the Metro is not particularly useful for tourists as it only covers four stations in the centre, all on the eastern side – Amsterdam CS, Nieuwmarkt, Waterlooplein and Weesperplein.

The Metro runs for around half an hour longer than trams on weekdays, and uses the same OV-chipkaart ticketing system as trams and buses. Take care late at night, when some inner-city stations may have drug dealers.

The North–South line, the fourth Metro line, is currently being constructed to link the area of the city north of the river IJ with the city centre on the southern shore, and will eventually run all the way to Schiphol airport. The project is impressive, digging through an unstable substratum directly under the historic centre of Amsterdam, although this has caused subsidence of up to 23 cm (9 inches) deep in some houses. It is planned to open in 2017, with a cost of €1.4 billion.

Distinctive sign for a Metro station

Trains

The Dutch national railway company, **Nederlandse Spoorwegen**, or simply **NS**, runs a busy network which is considered one of the best in the world. It is reliable, clean and reasonably priced. Both the **9292** office, and the NS Service Centre, located in the western hall of Centraal Station, can provide information on rail trips. The NS offers a range of day trips around the country. These include train fare, reduced entry to museums and sights, and often a lunch coupon. Day trips are listed on www.spoordeelwinkel.nl. 9292 does not sell tickets, but the NS Service Centre and national ticket offices do. Tickets can also be bought from the yellow machines which can be found at the front and back entrances of Centraal Station. There is a button to press for English instructions, and machines take credit cards (some also accept cash). Information and bookings for rail travel abroad is available from the NS Service Centre.

Tram, Bus, Metro and Train Tickets

You can buy an OV-chipkaart from the GVB, Tourist Board offices and newsagents, as well as disposable cards on the trams, buses or Metro. The size of a credit card, this smartcard works much like a rechargeable telephone card, with each trip being deducted from the credit available. There are two kinds: a disposable, one-time use card for durations of either 1 (€2.90) hour or one to seven days (€7.50–€32), and a reloadable pass (€7.50), usable for five years), which allows users to top up the balance (up to €30).

OV-chipkaarts can be topped up at any of the ticket vending machines and "add value" machines located at all Metro stations and stops, Centraal Station and some supermarkets. In order to validate a journey, users need to hold the OV-chipkaart in front of the grey card readers on entering and leaving a Metro or train station, or when getting on and off trams and buses. On all forms of transport, you will be charged a distance fee, so there are no differences in terms of one form of transport being cheaper. Children under 4 travel free, and seniors and 4–11 year olds have to purchase their discounted cards in advance at a GVB office. The Amsterdam Travel Ticket includes a return train ticket to Schiphol airport and a 24/48/72-hour pass (including night buses) that can be bought at the GVB or at Schiphol airport Tourist Information. The Amsterdam Travel Ticket includes all forms of public transport and museums. Tickets for the Concertgebouw, Stadsschouwburg or Nieuwe De La Mar Theatre include public transport to and from the venue (not valid on the metro).

Always swipe your OV-chipkaart to validate your journey

DIRECTORY

9292 (Openbaar Vervoer Reisinformatie)
Tel 0900 9292.
[w] **9292.nl**

GVB (Gemeente Vervoer Bedrijf)
Stationsplein 14. **Map** 2 E3.
Tel 0900 8011 (GVB info).
[w] **gvb.nl/english**

NS (Nederlandse Spoorwegen)
Centraal Station. **Map** 2 E3.
Tel 0900 9292 (national).
Tel 0900 9296 (international).
[w] **ns.nl** (national)
[w] **nsinternational.nl** (international)

Getting Around by Bicycle

The bicycle is the ideal form of transport in Amsterdam. More than half a million people cycle to school or work, and use a bicycle to do the shopping or go out in the evening. The city's traffic system is biased in favour of bicycles, with an excellent network of integrated cycle lanes *(fietspaden)*, dedicated traffic lights and road signs, and special routes linking different parts of the city. More and more tourists, too, are adopting this way of exploring Amsterdam and its environs.

A row of bicycles for hire

Amsterdam is the ideal place to explore by bicycle

Rules of the Road

Amsterdam's traffic is composed of a chaotic mix of trams, buses, taxis, cars and bicycles, often split into their own lanes. Remember to always ride on the right and that other road users will not necessarily recognize you as an inexperienced tourist and may assume you know how to avoid them. If you are unsure or unsteady, it is worth heading to one of the inner city parks for a bit of practice first.

Motorists and other cyclists have priority when entering the road from the right, unless otherwise stated. Trams have priority, so stay well clear. Many novices dismount at busy junctions and cross on foot; if you choose to do this, be sure to switch to the pedestrian section of the crossing. Do not walk with your bike in a bike lane. You will need to be aware of pedestrians who are clearly tourists and tend to wander into the bike paths. Dutch cyclists often ride through red lights and zigzag through traffic, but don't follow their example. Don't use the part of the road with tramlines, but if you have to move inside the tracks to pass a stationary vehicle, do so at an angle, otherwise your front wheel may get stuck in the tramlines. Also watch out for taxis, people emerging from parked cars and foreign coaches whose drivers may be unsympathetic to cyclists. Don't carry passengers on your bike, or ride on footpaths or pavements, or you could be fined. Be aware that you are legally obliged to have or wear a clear light on the front, and a red, reflective light on the back and could be fined if you don't.

Although the locals don't bother, it is a wise precaution to wear a helmet.

Hiring a Bicycle

Bicycle hire shops abound in Amsterdam. Rental costs start at around €10 per day for a basic, back-pedal brake bike, with costs decreasing per day for longer rental periods and increasing for bikes with gears and/or hand brakes. Tandems are more expensive and may be difficult to manoeuvre on some narrow streets.

Deposits are handled in one of two ways: either a cash deposit, varying from €50 to €150, with a valid, original passport (or in the case of EU citizens, a valid driver's licence), which must be left behind for the duration of the rental, or a credit card imprint.

As well as a range of bicycles and brake systems, **MacBike** and **Orange Bike** also offer extras such as children's seats, saddlebags and even rain gear for those classic Dutch grey and wet days. For those wanting someone or something else to provide the pedal power, many of the bicycle hire firms also rent scooters (some will require a driving licence), or for the more green oriented, check information on bike taxis and electric scooter rentals *(see pp266–7)*.

Traffic lights for bicycles

Bicycles allowed

No entry except to bicycles and mopeds

Taking your own Bicycle

The easiest way to take your own bicycle to the Netherlands is strapped to a bike rack on your car. Your bike travels for free if you are a walk-on passenger on the ferry to the Netherlands; when you book your ticket, simply inform the clerk. On your arrival in the Netherlands, if you want the cycle to go with you by train you are required to buy a ticket for it and enter the train at the doors marked for bicycles.

To take your bicycle by air, you must make a cargo booking with the airline at least a week in advance. It will have to be included in your 20 kg (44 lb) luggage allowance, and you must pay any excess baggage or handling costs.

Buying a Bicycle

Be careful when buying a bicycle that it is not listed as stolen, as you will be held responsible for buying stolen goods and will have a hard time selling it at the end of your holiday. A cheap bike for sale on the street will almost certainly have been stolen, and an expensive one from a specialist shop will probably end up being stolen too. It is worth buying a second-hand bargain if you are staying for a few weeks. There are a number of reputable second-hand dealers that will also buy back used

bikes. Some of the hire companies also buy and sell used bikes.

Bicycle Security

Bicycle theft is rife, so it's essential to secure your bike even when parking for just a few minutes. Fasten both front wheel and frame to a post or railings with a metal U-shaped lock or chain. Locals recommend a lock on the back wheel as well. Hire shops are happy to advise on security matters, and will normally provide a lock in the rental price.

Bicycle Tours

Guided bicycle tours are a popular way to discover the city and its environs at a sedate pace. The price of the tours usually includes bicycle hire, and they tend to run from March through November. **Mike's Bike Tours** City tour includes canals and houseboats, the Red Light District, Vondelpark and the Jordaan, while their Countryside tour visits a windmill and a cheese farm or clog factory. **Yellowbike**'s City tour includes all of the above, as well

as the Museum district and the harbour. The Countryside tour is a 35-km (22-mile) route through the Waterland district north of Amsterdam, and almost exclusively uses paths through a nature reserve, passing small brooks and waterways and tiny, old villages along the way. Orange Bike offers the most extensive range of inner city tours. **Cycletours Holland** only offers countryside trips.

If you want to go it alone, both the Tourist Board and NS Bureau (see p255) provide maps with routes, cycle lanes and refreshment stops. The Arena Hotel (see p247) produces information with suggestions and maps for cycle trips around and outside the city. City tours can take 3 hours, and country trips around 7 hours. For an alternative scenic route, take the tram to the Amsterdamse Bos (Amsterdam Woods) and hire a bicycle or scooter there (Apr–Sep only).

Cycle tours a popular way to see the city

DIRECTORY

Bicycle Hire

Amsterdamse Bos Fietsverhuur
Bosbaanweg.
Tel 644 5473.
Open Apr–Oct: daily;
Nov–Mar: Wed–Sun.
W amsterdam
sebosfietsverhuur.nl

Bike City
Bloemgracht 70.
Map 1 A4. Tel 626 3721.
W bikecity.nl

Damstraat Rent-a-Bike
Damstraat 20-22.
Map 7 C3.
Tel 625 5029.
W rentabike.nl

Frederic Rent A Bike
Brouwersgracht 78.
Map 1 B2. Tel 624 5509.

Holland Rent-a-Bike
Damrak 247. Map 7 C2.
Tel 622 3207.
W holland-rentabike.nl

MacBike
Centraal Station Oost,
Stationsplein 5. Map 8 D1.
Tel 528 7688.
Waterlooplein 199.
Map 8 D5.
Weteringschans 2.
Map 4 E2. W macbike.nl

Orange Bike
Oudezijds Voorburgwal
147. Map 7 C3. Tel 354
1781. W orange-bike.nl

Star Bikes Rental
De Ruyterkade 127.
Map 8 F1.
Tel 620 3215.
W starbikesrental.com

Bicycle Tours

Cycletours Holland
Buiksloterweg 7A.
Map 2 F2.
Tel 521 8490.
W cycletours.com

Mike's Bike Tours
Kerkstraat 134.
Map 4 F2.
Tel 622 7970.
W mikesbiketoursam
sterdam.com

Yellowbike
Nieuwzijds Kolk 29.
Map 7 C1.
Oudezijds Armsteeg 2.
Map 8 D1.
Tel 620 6940.
W yellowbike.nl

Second-Hand Bicycles

Groeno
2e H de Grootstraat 12.
Map 1 A4. Tel 684 4270.
W groeno.nl

MacBike
Nieuwe Uilenburger-
straat 30.
Map 8 E3.
Tel 214 1000.
W macbike.nl

Getting Around on the Canal

The name Amsterdam evolved from the 13th-century dam on the Amstel that was built to allow the city to grow and develop into a working system of 165 canals and 1,300 bridges, earning it the name the "Venice of the North". Today, the inner canals are used more for pleasure boating and living than transport or trading, but firms like courier company DHL are rediscovering the ease and speed of using the canals. Canal boats offer a variety of tours, and boat trips are particularly well suited to those without the time to explore on foot or by tram, or to the elderly and families with children.

Embarkation point for P. Kooij

Canal Tours

There are many operators in Amsterdam offering canal tours with foreign-language commentaries. Boats depart from a number of embarkation points, mainly from opposite Centraal Station along Prins Hendrikkade, the Damrak and along the Rokin. Many *rondvaartboten* (tour boats) have glass tops, some of which can be opened in fine weather. It is not always necessary to book seats for tours, but it is wise to do so for lunchtime, evening and dinner cruises, especially during the peak tourist season.

Night cruises can feature cheese-and-wine refreshments, a stop at a pub or a romantic candlelit dinner. **Lovers** offers a comprehensive selection of such cruises in addition to its daytime trips. Besides city-centre tours, Lovers also operates special services from Centraal Station to Artis (*see pp144–5*), and a hop-on-hop-off Museum Line, stopping near Amsterdam's major museums. On hot days, try

P. Kooij, as it has the most open-topped boats. Instead of just the stag do or hen party, you can now take the plunge and get married while you cruise. **Blue Boat Company** offers to arrange everything, from the tour and reception to the actual wedding. If you are looking for a sailing trip out of the city, try **De Muider Compagnie**.

Canalbus

The **Canalbus** service runs every 30 minutes along three routes, with 11 stops located near the major museums, shopping areas and other attractions. You can embark or alight at any of the stops along the routes, and it is claimed that the Canalbus is the first boat of its kind in Europe to run on gas.

Tickets for a one-, two- or three-day pass can be purchased, and the Canalbus operates a pizza cruise on Monday, Wednesday, Friday and Saturday evenings, from April to November starting from the Holland International Pier at Prins Hendrikkade 33 (across from Centraal Station) at 7pm. It is generally advisable to reserve

a place beforehand at a Canalbus kiosk or online, as they are very popular and can get fully booked very quickly, especially in summer. Other evening tours include a romantic 2-hour candlelight evening tour, floating past the illuminated canal houses while enjoying some fine wines and cheeses. Or you can head out on the IJ to the Amsterdam Harbour area on a harbour cruise.

Other combination tickets include entrance to one of the main museums with a day ticket: the Rijksmuseum (€32), Van Gogh Museum (€29) and the Hermitage on the Amstel (€29). The same company also runs Canal Hopper (a sloop hire), and **Canal Bike** services (*see opposite*).

Museum Boat

Amsterdam's **Museum Line** is less of a tour and more of a way to get around easily and in style to all the major city sights and shopping areas. Boats run every 20 minutes daily, between 10am and 5pm, from opposite Centraal Station. You can buy a day ticket, which allows unlimited use for one day, or buy a Museum Combination Cruise ticket, which includes entry to a museum. Tickets can be bought at the Centraal Station embarkation stage or any landing points. An adult day ticket costs €21, and a child's day ticket is €10.50. Details of landing stages are on the transport map on this guide's inside back cover. It takes about 2 hours of cruising to complete a full circuit.

Canal tour on the Oude Schans, the Montelbaanstoren in the background

A pleasant canal-side café

Water Taxis

Water taxis are more convenient than canal boats for sightseeing as they work just like a land taxi; they take you exactly where you want to go and charge per minute. They are also expensive – for an eight-seater, the tariff is €120 for 30 minutes and €20 is the boarding cost. They also offer tours as part of their "VIP Experience", including food, drink and a guide, which must be booked in advance. Among the itineraries offered are an "Architecture" cruise, a "Hidden City" cruise, a "Candlelight Pub" cruise, and a tailor-made "After Dinner" cruise. If you want to use one of these boats you will need to book in advance from **Water Taxi**. VIP cruises range in price from €35 per person (pub cruise) up to €99 per person (dinner cruise, for a group of eight, more for a smaller group). If you want a more romantic experience, book a private "Honeymoon" cruise for €149.50 for half an hour.

Boat Hire and Water Rules

If you fancy being captain, both Amsterdam Boat Guide and Canal Motorboats offer a variety of ecofriendly electric boats to rent, with no navigation licence required *(see p267)*, or you can use your legs for pedal power *(see Canal Bikes)* or rent a sloop. Either way, there are some basic rules. In general, you may cruise on the canals and in the harbour, with some exceptions.

Port control and police patrol boats can give both warnings and fines if you stray into a zone not accessible for pleasure or pedal boats. Keep to the right (starboard) side. Maximum speed is 18 km (11 miles) per hour; cruise ships and vessels longer than 20 m (65 ft) always have right of way. Pedal boats must not enter the harbour and are banned from the western port.

Sightseeing by canal bike

Canal Bikes

Canal bikes are two- or four-seater pedalboats. Propelling them requires considerable energy, but when you've had enough, you can stop for a drink. You can pick up or leave a pedalboat at any of the canal-bike moorings in the city: Prinsengracht at the Westerkerk, Keizersgracht near Leidsestraat, Leidseplein between the Marriott and American hotels, and along the Singelgracht just outside the Rijksmuseum. There is a €20 deposit and costs €8 per person, per hour. Between November and March, only the Singelgracht, Prinsengracht and Leidseplein moorings are open.

DIRECTORY

Canal Tours

Amsterdam Canal Cruises
Stadhouderskade 78.
Map 4 F3.
Tel 679 1370.
🌐 amsterdamcanalcruises.nl

Blue Boat Company
Stadhouderskade 30.
Map 4 E2.
Tel 679 1370.
🌐 blueboat.nl

Canalbus & Canal Bike
Weteringschans 24.
Map 4 E2.
Tel 217 0501.
🌐 canal.nl

Lindbergh
Damrak 26.
Map 8 D1.
Tel 622 2766.
🌐 lindbergh.nl

Lovers
Opposite Prins Hendrikkade 25–27.
Map 8 D1.
Tel 530 1090.
🌐 lovers.nl

De Muider Compagnie
Krijn Taconiskade 432.
Tel 0294 262 413.
🌐 muidercompagnie.nl

Museum Line
Stationsplein 8.
Map 8 D1.
Tel 530 1090.
🌐 lovers.nl

P. Kooij
Opposite Rokin 125.
Map 7 B4.
Tel 623 3810.
🌐 rederijkooij.nl

Rederij Plas
Jetty 1–3, Damrak.
Map 8 D1.
Tel 624 5406.
🌐 rederijplas.nl

Tours and Tickets
Tel 420 4000.
🌐 tours-tickets.com

Water Taxi
Stationsplein 8.
Map 8 D1.
Tel 535 6363.
🌐 water-taxi.nl

STREET FINDER

The page grid superimposed on the *Area by Area* map below shows which parts of Amsterdam are covered in this *Street Finder*. The map references given for all sights, hotels, restaurants, shopping and entertainment venues described in this guide refer to the maps in this section. A complete index of the street names and places of interest marked on the maps follows on pages 284–7. The key, set out below, indicates the scales of the maps and shows what other features are marked on them, including transport terminals, emergency services and information centres. All the major sights are clearly marked so they are easy to locate.

0 metres	500
0 yards	500

1

Western Canal R.

NASSAUKADE

ROZENGRACHT

Central Canal Ring

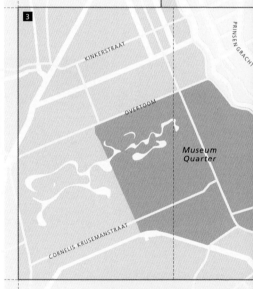

PRINSENGRACHT

3

KINKERSTRAAT

OVERTOOM

Museum Quarter

CORNELIS KRUSEMANSTRAAT

Key to Street Finder

Major sight
Place of interest
Other building
M Metro station
Train station
Tram route
Bus route
Tour boat boarding point
Canalbus boarding point
Museum boat boarding point
P Parking
i Tourist information office
Hospital with casualty unit
Police station
Church
Synagogue
C Mosque
Railway line
Pedestrianized street

Scale of Maps 1–6

0 metres	200	
		1:11,250
0 yards	200	

Scale of Maps 7–8

0 metres	150	
		1:7,500
0 yards	150	

Fresh fruit for sale in the
Noordermarkt *(see p94)*

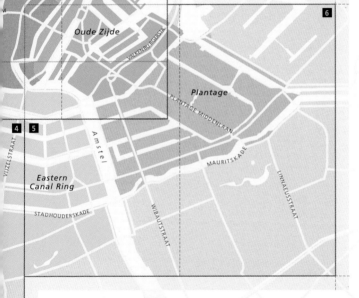

House with an elevated neck gable *(see p99)* on the Geldersekade

Magere Brug, the city's most famous bridge *(see p121)*

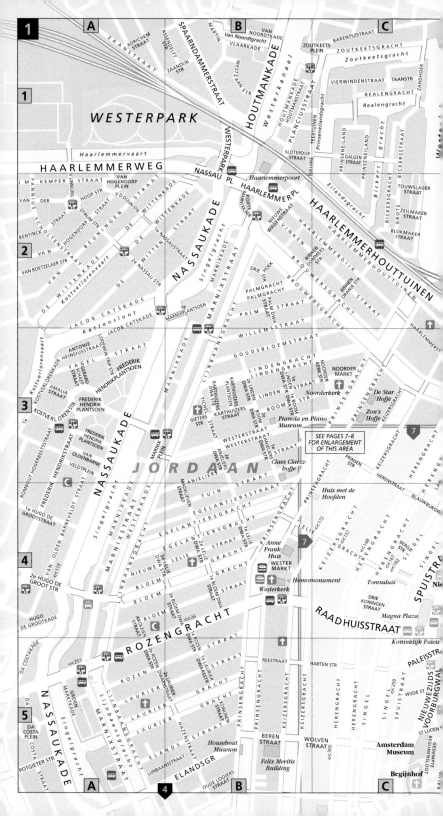

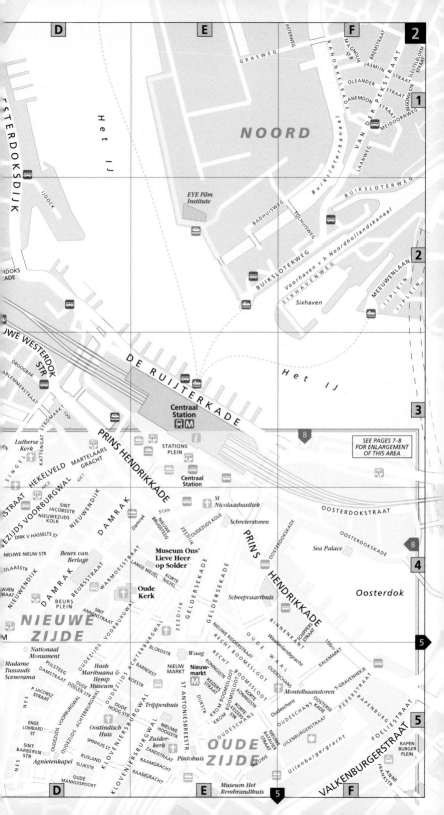

D **E** **F**

2

GRASWEG

ASTERWEG

RANONKELKADE

MAGNOLIA STR

JASMIJN STRAAT

BREEMSTRAAT

BEGONIASTR

SLEUTELBLOEM STRAAT

OLEANDER

ANEMOON STRAAT

VAN DER PEKSTRAAT

MEIDOORNWEG

1

ET IJ

Het IJ

STERDOKSDIJK

IJDOCK

NOORD

BUIKSLOTERKANAAL

LAANWEG

EYE Film
Institute

BADHUISWEG

TOLHUISWEG

BUIKSLOTERWEG

BUIKSLOTERWEG

Voorhaven v h Noordhollandskanaal

SIXHAVENWEG

Sixhaven

MEEUWENLAAN

IJPLEIN

IJPLEIN

2

RDOKS
ADE

JWE WESTERDOK
STR

DROOGBAK

ARLEMMERSTRAAT

DE RUIJTERKADE

Het IJ

3

Centraal
Station

SEE PAGES 7–8
FOR ENLARGEMENT
OF THIS AREA

Lutherse
Kerk

SINGEL

KATTENGAT STROMARKT

PRINS HENDRIKKADE

STATIONS
PLEIN

8

HEKELVELD

MARTELAARS
GRACHT

Centraal
Station

EN

VOORBURGWAL

SINT
JACOBSSTR

DAMRAK

St Nicolaasbasiliek

OOSTERDOKSTRAAT

STRAAT

EZIJDS

NIEUWEZIJDS
KOLK

NIEUWENDIJK

NIEUWE
BRUGSTEEG

ZEEDIJK

OUDEZIJDS KOLK

Schreierstoren

OOSTERDOKSKADE

PRINS

OOSTERDOKSKADE

8

DIRK V HASSELTS ST

NIEUWE NIEUW STR

Beurs van
Berlage

WARMOESSTRAAT

Museum Ons'
Lieve Heer
op Solder

LANGE NIEZEL

KORTE
NIEZEL

OUDEZIJDS

GELDERSEKADE

HENDRIKKADE

Sea Palace

OOSTERDOKSKADE

Oosterdok

4

NICOLAASSTR

DAMRAK

BEURSSTRAAT

Oude
Kerk

VOORBURGWAL

GELDERSEKADE

Scheepvaarthuis

BINNENKANT

SCHIPPERSSTRAAT

5

AVEN
RAAT

NIEUWENDIJK

DAMRAK

BEURS
PLEIN

SINT
ANNENSTRAAT

ZEEDIJK

NIEUWE RIDDERSTRAAT

RECHT BOOMSSLOOT

OUDE

WAAL

Waalseilandsgracht

KALKMARKT

M

**NIEUWE
ZIJDE**

Nationaal
Monument

OUDEZIJDS ACHTERBURGWAL

BLOEDSTR

Waag

KONINGSSTR

RECHT BOOMSSLOOT

'S-GRAVENHEKJE

Madame
Tussauds
Scenerama

DAMSTRAAT

PULSTEEG

Hasb
Maribuana &
Hemp
Museum

BARNDEST

NIEUWMARKT

KORTE BOOMSSLOOT

KEIZERS
BOOMSSLOOT

OUDESCHANS

Montelbaanstoren

OOSTERSE
KADE

RAPENBURG

PEPERSTRAAT

P JACOBSZ
STRAAT

DOELEN STR

OUDE
HOOG STR

Nieuw-
markt

DIJKSTR

KROM BOOMSSLOOT

KORTE
KEIZERSSTR

Oudeschans

UILENBURGERSTRAAT

RAPENBURG

FOELIESTRAAT

ENGE
LOMBARD
ST

OUDEZIJDS VOORBURGWAL

OUDEZIJDS ACHTERBURGWAL

SPINHUISSTEEG

KLOVENIERSBURGWAL

Trippenhuis

NIEUWE
HOOGSTR

ST ANTONIESBREESTR.

KROM BOOMSSLOOT

NIEUWE
BATAVIER
STRAAT

NIEUWE

UILENBURGERSTRAAT

VALKENBURGERSTRAAT

SINT
BARBEREN
STR

Oostindisch
Huis

RUSLAND

Zuider-
kerk

ZANDSTRAAT

Pintohuis

Uilenburgergracht

RAPEN
BURGER
PLEIN

5

Agnietenkapel

SLIJKSTR

RAAMGRACHT

RAAMGRACHT

**OUDE
ZIJDE**

ANNE
FRANKSTR

OUDE
MANHUISPOORT

D **E** Museum Het
Rembrandthuis **F**

5

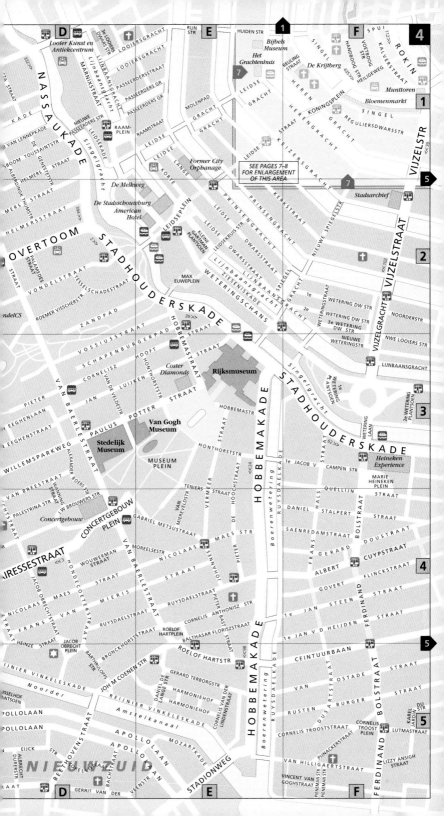

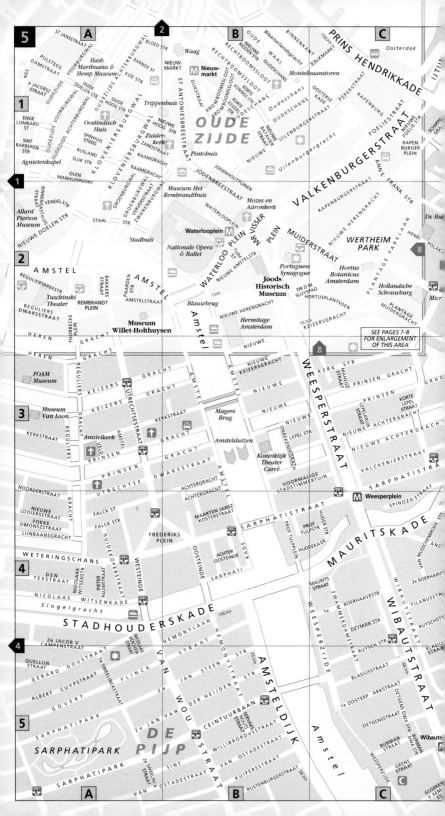

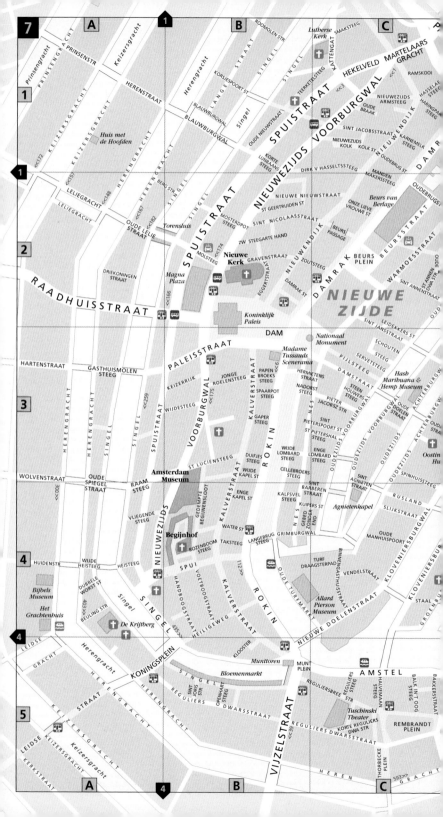

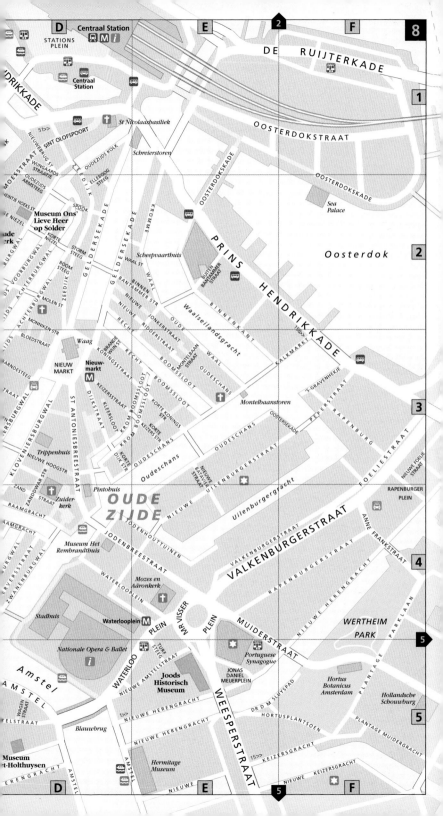

Street Finder Index

General Index

B

Acknowledgments

Dorling Kindersley would like to thank the following people whose help and assistance contributed to the preparation of this book.

Main Contributor
Robin Pascoe has lived in Amsterdam since the 1980s. She is a freelance journalist and writes for various Dutch newspapers. She also works for the Dutch national news agency ANP, the international development news agency IPS, and the BBC.

Christopher Catling has been visiting the Netherlands for two decades, since writing his first guide for business travellers in 1984. He has since written a further four guides to Amsterdam and the Netherlands. Besides this guide, he has contributed to four *Dorling Kindersley Travel Guides*: Florence and Tuscany, Venice and the Veneto, Great Britain and Italy.

Additional Photography
Steve Gorton, Ian O'Leary, Neil Lukas, Rough Guides/Neil Setchfield, Rough Guides/Natascha Sturny, Rough Guides/Mark Thomas 50tr, Tony Souter, Clive Streeter, Gerard van Vuuren

Additional Illustrations
Arcana (Graham Bell), Richard Bonson, Stephen Conlin, Roy Flooks, Mick Gillah, Kevin Goold, Stephen Gyapay, Chris Orr, Ian Henderson, Philip Winton, John Woodcock

Editorial and Design
Managing Editors Vivien Crump, Helen Partington
Managing Art Editor Steve Knowlden
Senior Editor Peter Casterton
Deputy Editorial Director Douglas Amrine
Deputy Art Director Gaye Allen
Production David Proffit
Picture Research Lorna Ainger
DTP Designer Siri Lowe
Ashwin Raju Adimari, Emma Anacootee, Parnika Bagla, Claire Baranowski, Hilary Bird, Willem de Blaauw, Johan Blom, Susan Churchill, Lucinda Cooke, Seán O'Connell, Martin Cropper, Karlien van Dam, Alyse Dar, Russell Davies, Simon Davis, Gadi Farfour, Emer Fitzgerald, Anthea Forlee, Fay Franklin, Anna Freiberger, Robin Gauldie, Vicky Hampton, Annette Jacobs, Gail Jones, Nancy Jones, Maite Lantaron, David Lindsey, Carly Madden, Iris Maher, Hayley Maher, Sam Merrell, Rebecca Milner, Sonal Modha, Claire Naylor, Marianne Petrou, Rada Radojicic, Caroline Radula-Scott, Mindy Ran, Ankita Sharma, Sands Publishing Solutions, Simon Ryder, Debbie Scholes, Sadie Smith, Gerard van Vuuren
Hotel listings: Kim Renfrew
Restaurant listings: Pip Farquharson

Cartography
Jane Hanson, Phil Rose, Jennifer Skelley (Lovell Johns Limited)
Map Co-ordinators Michael Ellis, David Pugh

Special Assistance
Greet Tuinman, Charlotte van Beurden

Photography Permissions
Dorling Kindersley would like to thank the following for their kind permission to photograph at their establishments:
Airborne Museum, Arnhem; Allard Pierson Museum; Ons' Lieve Heer op Solder Museum; Amsterdams Historisch Museum/Willet-Holthuysen Museum; Artis Zoo; Aviodrome; Beurs van Berlage; Boerhaave Museum, Leiden; Carré Theater; Concertgebouw; Coster Diamonds; Domkerk, Utrecht; Electrische Museumtramlijn; Europoort, Rotterdam; Filmmuseum; Frankendael; Anne Frankhuis; Grote Kerk, Alkmaar; Grote Kerk, Edam; Hash Marihuana & Hemp Museum; Heineken Museum; Hollandsche Schouwburg; Hortus Botanicus, Leiden; Joods Historisch Museum; Justitie Hall; Koninklijk Paleis; Krijtberg; Kröller-Müller Museum and National Park, Otterlo; Nederlands Scheepvaart Museum; Madurodam, Den Haag; Maritime Museum, Rotterdam; Monnickendam;
Nieuwe Kerk; Nieuwe Kerk and Oude Kerk, Delft; Oude Kerk; Paleis Het Loo, Apeldoorn; Peace Palace, Den Haag; Portugese Synagoge; Prince William V Gallery, Den Haag; Prinsenhof, Leiden; Prison Gate Museum, Den Haag; RAI International Exhibition Centre; Rijksmuseum; Rijksmuseum, Utrecht; Rijksmuseum van Oudheden, Leiden; Rijksmuseum van SpeelklokTot Pierement, Utrecht; St Bavo, Haarlem; St Nicolaaskerk; SAS Hotel; Scheveningen Sea Life Centre; Sint Janskerk, Gouda; Stadhuis-Nationale Opera & Ballet; Stedelijk Museum; Stedelijk Molenmuseum, Leiden; Technologie Museum; Teylers Museum, Haarlem; Theater Museum; Tropenmuseum; Vakbonds Museum; Van Gogh Museum; Van Loon Museum; Verzetsmuseum; Werf 't Kromhout Museum; Westerkerk; Westfries Museum, Hoorn; Zuiderzee Museum.

Picture Credits
Key: a-above; b-below/bottom; c-centre; f-far; l-left; r-right; t-top.

Works of art have been reproduced with the permission of the following copyright holders: © ABC/Mondriaan Estate/Holtzman Trust, licensed by ILP 1995: 138br; © ADAGP, Paris and DACS, London 2011: 138tr, 206cb; © DACS, London 2011: 42bl, 138bl; © Jasper Johns/DACS London 2011/VAGA New York: 139cb.

The Publishers are grateful to the following museums, photographers and picture libraries for permission to reproduce their photographs:

Ambassade Hotel: 218tr; **AKG, London**: 24clb, 26clb, 27ca, 28cl, 30br, 31tl, 103tr, 130cra, 187tr, Niklaus Strauss 139br; **Alamy Images**: Arttext 140; Bertrand Collet 223tl; eye35.pix 88; Udo Frank 209-10; David R. Frazier Photolibrary, Inc 266bl; Warren Kovach 10br; Frans Lemmens 256tr; marinuse 258bl; Sergio Pitamitz 18cla; Stuwdamdorp 266cr, 267cla; Dan Tucker 158; **Amsterdam Museum**: 20, 25bc, 26–7c, 27tl, 27crb, 27bl, 28–9c, 29clb, 32clb, 33tl, 33cb, 34cl, 35cr, 42cla, 83tl, 83cra, 83cr, 83br, 84cra, 84bl, 85tl, 85crb, 92b, 122c, 122c, 122bl, 123crb; **Amsterdam Toerisme & Congres Bureau**: 53b, 53cra, 91br, 252cla, 253c, 269cr, 271cr; **ANP Photo**: 38br, 39crb; **ANWB (Royal Dutch Touring Club)**: 265tc; **Azzurro**: 235tr. **Cafe Barco**: 225br; **Blawe Theehuis**: Maaike Ankum 48clb; **B&U International Picture Service**: 39cla, 55bl, 103bl, 107br, 182cla, 205tl; **BGB – The travel and PR representation specialists**: 264br; **Brandweer NL**: 256cl; **Bridgeman Art Library**: Christie's London *The Groote Market Haarlem with the Church of St Bavo* Gerrit Berckheyde c.1668 178cla; Giraudon/Musée Crozatier Le Puy-en-Velay France *King Louis XIV* 31br; Kremlin Museums Moscow 32bl; Private Collection *Self-Portrait Kazimir Malevich* 139crb; **Bureau Monumenten & Archeologie** (BMA): 119cra. **Canal House Amsterdam**: 212tl, 216br; **Jean-Loup Charmet**: Musée de l'Armée 32bc; **Ciel Cleu Restaurant**: 231tl; **The College Hotel Amsterdam**: 230br; **Colorsport**: 38cla; **Corbis**: Dave Bartruff 222cla; Demotix/Richard Wareham 53clb; Owen Franken 223c; Hulton-Deutsch Collection 10-11; Frans Lemmens 55-6; Jean-Pierre Lescourret 65br. **Cafe De Jaren**: 224br; **De Kas Restaurant**: 254br, 221tr, 231br; **De Waaghals Restaurant**: 229br; **Jan Derwig**: 101tr; **Double Tree Amsterdam**: 213t, 216bl; **Dreamstime.com**: Antonfrolov 58; Inavanhateren 135bl; Jeremyreds 96; Dariusz Kopestynsky 262cl;

Jan Kranendonk 157br; Lunamarina 1c; David Pereiras Villagrá 62bl; Vitaly Titov & Maria Sidelnikova 249-50; **Drents Museum, Assen**: 22bl; **Hotel Droog**: 217tc; **Mary Evans Picture Library**: 23cra, 23bc, 25bl, 27br, 28bl, 29br, 31bl, 33bc, 34cb, 34bc, 35bl, 35br, 37crb; Louis Raemaehois 36bc; Jean Veber 35br; **EYE Film Institute**: Iwan Baan 153tl. **Foto Natura**: Fred Hazelhoff 207cb. **Gemeentearchief, Amsterdam**: 23tl, 25ca, 25cb, 26cla, 33crb, 101tl, 101cl, 103br, 104bl, 105tr, 105cr, 106tr, 107tr, 107cr; **Gemeentearchief, Kampen**: 25tl; **Getty Images**: 139cra; Jon Arnold 108; Darrell Gulin 164-5; Hulton Archive/Anne Frank Fonds - Basel/Anne Frank House 92tr; Images Etc Ltd; Lonely Planet 134bl; Michel Porro 39tc; Mark R. Thomas 72; Abderazak Tissoukai 2-3; George Tsafos 40; **GVB Amsterdam**: 268cla; 269tl; **GWK Travelex**: 258tr; **GVB Amsterdam**: 268tl. **Frans Hals Museum, Haarlem**: 29tc, 32–3c, 180cl; 180tr, 180bl; 180cl,181tl, 181cra, 181bl, 181br; **Vanessa Hamilton**: 99tl, 103cr, 106c; **Robert Harding Picture Library**: 60tr; Peter Scholey 118cla; **Hermitage Amsterdam**: 147br; **Hilton Amsterdam**: 215cr; **Hollandse Hoogte**: Adrie Mouthaan 152tl; Co de Kruijf 11br; Emile Luider 10cla; Peter Hilz 11tr; **Hulton-Deutsch Collection**: 42tc. **Iconografisch Bureau**: 105tl; **The Image Bank**: Bernard van Berg 54cra; Fotoworld 52b; **ING Group**: 39cra; **International Flower Bulb Centre**: 28bc, 182br, 183tl, 183cla, 183cl, 183clb, 183clb, 183bl; **International Institute of Social History**: 36cla; **iStockphoto.com**: Rob Bouwman 263br; **Collection Jewish Historical Museum, Amsterdam**: 65br; *Mahzor*, Illuminated Manuscript on Parchment, Cologne area, c.1250 66clb; Liselore Kamping 66cla; *Hanukah Lamp* Peter Robol II, silver, Amsterdam (1753) on loan from NIHS, Amsterdam 67tl. **Kapitein Zeppos Restaurant**: 226tr; **KLM Royal Dutch Airlines**: 262br, 263tr; **KPN**: 260c; **Kröller-Müller Museum**: 206cla; **Marriott**: 214t; **Mauritshuis, Den Haag**: 190tr, 190c, 190bl, 191tc, 191cr, 191br, 191bc, 195tl; **MGM Cinemas BV**: 37cra; **Municipal Museum de Lakenhal, Leiden**: 186bl; **Museum Boijmans Van Beuningen, Rotterdam**: 202–3 except 202tr, studio Hans Wilschut 202tr; Designer J.J.P Oud / Production Metz & Co 202br; **Museum Van Loon**: 124tr; **Museum Het Schip**: 153br; **Museum Huis Lambert van Meerten, Collection RBK**: 197tr; **Museum On's Lieve Heer Op Solder**: 86br, 87crb, 87bl, Co de Kruif 87cr; **Museum Willet Holthuysen**: 123tl, 123cra, 123bc; Richard de Bruijn 118clb; **National Express Ltd**: 265cra; **National Fietsmuseum Velorama, Nijmegen**: 35tl; **Natura Artis Magistra**: Ronald Van Weeren: 143tl, 145tc; **Netherlands Architecture Institute Archive**: Isaac Gosschalk 107cl; De Klerk 37tl, 100cla; **NEMO Science and Technology Center**: 152b; **Nomads Restaurant**: 220bl, 228tl. **Olijfje Restaurant**: 225tl; **Orange bike**: 270cla; **Openbare Bibliotheek Amsterdam**: Annetje van Praag Sigaar 261tl; **Pink Point**: 254tl;

Politie Amsterdam-Amstelland: Nick Hoegeveen 256clb; **Prentenkabinet der Rijksuniversiteit, Leiden**: 34br; **Puri Mas Restaurant**: 227tr; **Museum Het Rembrandthuis**: 61br; **Retrograph Archive Ltd**: Martin Breese 34cla; **Rijksmuseum-foundation, Amsterdam**: 28cla, 32cla, 42c, 44bl, 130cl, 130bc, 131tl, 131c, 131crb, 132cra, 132bl, 133tr, 133br; **Rijksmuseum Paleis Het Loo, Apeldoorn**: E Boeijinga 208tr, 209tl, R Mulder 208cl; AAW Meine Jansen 208bc; **Rotterdam Image Bank**: Ossip-van-Duivenbode 200bl; **Royal Palace, Amsterdam**: Erik Hemsmerg 29tr, 41cr, 78cla; **Royal Tropical Institute** 155br; **Scheepvartmuseum**: 21b, 30cl, 31ca, 148bl, 148cla, 148cb, 149tc, 149tl, 149b; **Schiphol Airport**: 263clb; **The Seafood Bar**: 230tl; **Spaarnestad Fotoarchief**: 37ca, 99tr, 101cb; **Srikandi Restaurant**: 220tr; **Stedelijk Museum, Alkmaar**: 36cb; **Stedelijk Museum, Amsterdam**: 138tr, 138cla, 138b, 138br, 139tl, 139tc; © ABC/Mondriaan Estate/Holtzmann Trust, licenced by ILP 1995 *Composition in Red, Black, Blue, Yellow and Grey* Piet Mondriaan 1920 138br; © ADAGP Paris and DACS London 2011 *Portrait of Artist with Seven Fingers* Marc Chagall 1912–13 138tr; © DACS London 2011 *Red Blue Chair* Gerrit Rietveld 1918 138bl; © DACS London 2011 *Stelman Chair* Gerrit Rietveld 1963 42bl; © Jasper Johns/DACS London/VAGA New York 2011 *Untitled* Jasper Johns 1965 139cb; **Stedelijk Museum de Lakenhal, Leiden**: 106br; Stoop en Stoop Restaurant: 227bc; **SuperStock**: age fotostock 150; Bridgeman Art Library 8–9; imagebroker.net 116, 126; Photosindia.com 193tc; **Swissôtel Hotels & Resorts**: 212br; **Thalys International SCRL/CVBA**: 264tl; **Tony Stone Images**: 76br, 175cla; Kim Blaxland 183tr; Rohan 102tr. **Tnt Post**: 261bl; **Tropenmuseum**: 154cr, 154ca, 155tc, 155cl; **Hans Tulleners**: 101cr, 102cr, 104c. **Universiteitsbibliotheek Van Amsterdam**: 98tr; **Vincent van Gogh (Foundation), Van Gogh Museum, Amsterdam**: 42br, 136cla, 136cb, 136bl, 137tc, 137cra, 137cr; **VZA Ambulance Service Amsterdam**: 256bl. **Western Australian Maritime Museum**: 30ca; **World Pictures**: 97bl; **Yellowbike**: 270tr. **ZEFA**: CPA 54bl; Steenmans 55cra. **Zuider-zeemuseum**: 173bl; The Blue Fishvendor 2008 (stencils and spraypaint) ©Hugo Kaagman see www.kaagman.nl, photo Petra Stavast 173tl.

Front Endpaper: Alamy Images: Arttext Rbr; eye35.pix Ltl; **Dreamstime.com**: Antonfrolov Rtr; **Getty Images**: Jon Arnold Lc; Mark R. Thomas Rtc; **Superstock**: imagebroker.net Rbc, Rbr.

Map Cover: 4Corners: SIME/Maurizio Rellini.

Jacket Front and Spine: 4Corners: SIME/Maurizio Rellini.

All other images © Dorling Kindersley. For further information see: www.dkimages.com

Phrase Book

In Emergency

Help!	**Help!**	*Help*
Stop!	**Stop!**	*Stop*
Call a doctor	**Haal een dokter**	*Haal uhn dok-tur*
Call an ambulance	**Bel een ambulance**	*Bell uhn ahm-bew-luhns-uh*
Call the police	**Roep de politie**	*Roop duh poe-leet-see*
Call the fire brigade	**Roep de brandweer**	*Roop duh brahnt-vheer*
Where is the nearest telephone?	**Waar is de dichtstbijzijnde telefoon?**	*Vhaar iss duh dikhst-baiy-zaiyn-duh tay-luh-foan*
Where is the nearest hospital?	**Waar is het dichtstbijzijnde ziekenhuis?**	*Vhaar iss het dikhst-baiy-zaiyn-duh zee-kuh-houws*

Communication Essentials

Yes	**Ja**	*Yaa*
No	**Nee**	*Nay*
Please	**Alstublieft**	*Ahls-tew-bleeft*
Thank you	**Dank u**	*Dahnk-ew*
Excuse me	**Pardon**	*Pahr-don*
Hello	**Hallo**	*Hallo*
Goodbye	**Dag**	*Dahgh*
Good night	**Slaap lekker**	*Slaap lek-kah*
morning	**Morgen**	*Mor-ghuh*
afternoon	**Middag**	*Mid-dahgh*
evening	**Avond**	*Ah-vohnd*
yesterday	**Gisteren**	*Ghis-tern*
today	**Vandaag**	*Vahn-daagh*
tomorrow	**Morgen**	*Mor-ghuh*
here	**Hier**	*Heer*
there	**Daar**	*Daar*
What?	**Wat?**	*Vhat*
When?	**Wanneer?**	*Vhan-eer*
Why?	**Waarom?**	*Vhaar-om*
Where?	**Waar?**	*Vhaar*
How?	**Hoe?**	*Hoo*

Useful Phrases

How are you?	**Hoe gaat het ermee?**	*Hoo ghaat het er-may*
Very well, thank you	**Heel goed, dank u**	*Hayl ghoot, dahnk ew*
How do you do?	**Hoe maakt u het?**	*Hoo maakt ew het*
See you soon	**Tot ziens**	*Tot zeens*
That's fine	**Prima**	*Pree-mah*
Where is/are?	**Waar is/zijn?**	*Vhaar iss/zayn…*
How far is it to…?	**Hoe ver is het naar…?**	*Hoo vehr iss het naar…*
How do I get to …?	**Hoe kom ik naar…?**	*Hoo kom ik naar…*
Do you speak English?	**Spreekt u engels?**	*Spraykt ew eng-uhls*
I don't understand	**Ik snap het niet**	*Ik snahp het neet*
Could you speak slowly?	**Kunt u langzamer praten?**	*Kuhnt ew lahng-zahmer praa-tuh*
I'm sorry	**Sorry**	*Sorry*

Useful Words

big	**groot**	*ghroaht*
small	**klein**	*klaiyn*
hot	**warm**	*vharm*
cold	**koud**	*khowt*
good	**goed**	*ghoot*
bad	**slecht**	*slekht*
enough	**genoeg**	*ghuh-noohkh*
well	**goed**	*ghoot*
open	**open**	*open*
closed	**gesloten**	*ghuh-slow-tuh*
left	**links**	*links*
right	**rechts**	*rekhts*
straight on	**rechtdoor**	*rehkht dohr*
near	**dichtbij**	*dikht baiy*
far	**ver weg**	*vehr vhekh*
up	**omhoog**	*om-hoakh*
down	**naar beneden**	*naar buh-nay-duh*
early	**vroeg**	*vroohkh*
late	**laat**	*laat*
entrance	**ingang**	*in-ghahng*
exit	**uitgang**	*ouht-ghang*
toilet	**wc**	*vhay say*
occupied	**bezet**	*buh-zett*
free (unoccupied)	**vrij**	*vraiy*
free (no charge)	**gratis**	*ghraah-tiss*

Making a Telephone Call

I'd like to place a long-distance call	**Ik wil graag interlokaal telefoneren**	*Ik vhil ghraakh inter-loh-kaahl tay-luh-foe-neh-ruh*
I'd like to call collect	**Ik wil 'collect call' bellen**	*Ik vhil 'collect call' bel-luh*
I'll try again later	**Ik probeer het later nog wel eens**	*Ik pro-beer het later nokh vhel ayns*
Can I leave a message?	**Kunt u een boodschap doorgeven?**	*Kuhnt ew uhn boat-skhahp dohr-ghay-vuh*
Could you speak a little louder please?	**Wilt u wat harder praten?**	*Vhilt ew vhat hahr-der praah-tuh*
Local call	**Lokaal gesprek**	*Low-kaahl ghuh-sprek*

Shopping

How much does this cost?	**Hoeveel kost dit?**	*Hoo-vayl kost dit*
I would like	**Ik wil graag**	*Ik vhil ghraakh*
Do you have…?	**Heeft u…?**	*Hayft ew…*
I'm just looking	**Ik kijk alleen even**	*Ik kaiyk alleyn ay-vuh*
Do you take credit cards?	**Neemt u credit cards aan?**	*Naymt ew credit cards aan*
Do you take traveller's cheques?	**Neemt u reischeques aan?**	*Naymt ew raiys-sheks aan*
What time do you open?	**Hoe laat gaat u open?**	*Hoo laat ghaat ew opuh*
What time do you close?	**Hoe laat gaat u dicht?**	*Hoo laat ghaat ew dikht*
This one	**Deze**	*Day-zuh*
That one	**Die**	*Dee*
expensive	**duur**	*dewr*
cheap	**goedkoop**	*ghoot-koap*
size	**maat**	*maat*
white	**wit**	*vhit*
black	**zwart**	*zvhahrt*
red	**rood**	*roat*
yellow	**geel**	*ghayl*
green	**groen**	*ghroon*
blue	**blauw**	*blah-ew*

Types of Shops

antique shop	**antiekwinkel**	*ahn-teek-vhin-kul*
bakery	**bakker**	*bah-ker*
bank	**bank**	*bahnk*
bookshop	**boekwinkel**	*book-vhin-kul*
butcher	**slager**	*slaakh-er*
cake shop	**banketbakkerij**	*bahnk-et-bahk-er-aiy*
cheese shop	**kaaswinkel**	*kaas-vhin-kul*
chip shop	**patatzaak**	*pah-taht-zaak*
chemist (dispensing)	**apotheek**	*ah-poe-taiyk*
delicatessen	**delicatessen**	*daylee-kah-tes-suh*
department store	**warenhuis**	*vhaar-uh-houws*
fishmonger	**viswinkel**	*viss-vhin-kul*
greengrocer	**groenteboer**	*ghroon-tuh-boor*
hairdresser	**kapper**	*kah-per*
market	**markt**	*mahrkt*
newsagent	**krantenwinkel**	*krahn-tuh-vhin-kul*
post office	**postkantoor**	*pohst-kahn-tor*
shoe shop	**schoenenwinkel**	*sghoo-nuh-vhin-kul*
supermarket	**supermarkt**	*sew-per-mahrkt*
tobacconist	**sigarenwinkel**	*see-ghaa-ruh-vhin-kul*
travel agent	**reisburo**	*raiys-bew-roa*

Sightseeing

art gallery	**galerie**	*ghaller-ee*
bus station	**busstation**	*buhs-stah-shown*
cathedral	**kathedraal**	*kah-tuh-draal*
church	**kerk**	*kehrk*
closed on public holidays	**op feestdagen gesloten**	*op fayst-daa-ghuh ghuh-slow-tuh*
day return	**dagretour**	*dahgh-ruh-tour*
garden	**tuin**	*touwn*
library	**bibliotheek**	*bee-bee-yo-tayk*
museum	**museum**	*mew-zay-uhm*
railway station	**station**	*stah-shown*
return ticket	**retourtje**	*ruh-tour-tyuh*
single journey	**enkeltje**	*eng-kuhl-tyuh*
tourist information	**VVV**	*fay fay fay*
town hall	**stadhuis**	*staht-houws*
train	**trein**	*traiyn*
travel pass	**Ov-chipkaart**	*oh-vay-chip-kaahrt*

Staying in a Hotel

Do you have a vacant room?	**Zijn er nog kamers vrij?**	Zaiyn er nokh kaa-mers vray
double room with bed	**een twee persoonskamer met een twee persoonsbed**	uhn tvhay-per double soans-kaa-mer met uhn tvhay-per soans beht
twin room	**een kamer met een lits-jumeaux**	uhn kaa-mer met uhn lee-zjoo-moh
single room	**eenpersoons-kamer**	ayn-per-soans-kaa-mer
room with a bath	**kamer met bad**	kaa-mer met baht
shower	**douche**	doosh
porter	**kruier**	krouw-yuh
I have a reservation	**Ik heb gereserveerd**	Ik hehp ghuh-ray-sehr-veert

Eating Out

Have you got a table?	**Is er een tafel vrij?**	Iss ehr uhn tah-fuhl vraiy
I want to reserve a table	**Ik wil een tafel reserveren**	Ik vhil uhn tah-fuhl ray-sehr-veer-uh
The bill, please	**Mag ik afrekenen**	Mukh ik ahf-ray-kuh-nuh
I am a vegetarian	**Ik ben vegetariër**	Ik ben fay-ghuh-taahr-ee-er
waitress/waiter	**serveerster/ober**	Sehr-veer-ster/oh-ber
menu	**de kaart**	duh kaahrt
cover charge	**het couvert**	het koo-vehr
wine list	**de wijnkaart**	duh vhaiyn-kaart
glass	**het glas**	het ghlahss
bottle	**de fles**	duh fless
knife	**het mes**	het mess
fork	**de vork**	duh fork
spoon	**de lepel**	duh lay-pul
breakfast	**het ontbijt**	het ont-baiyt
lunch	**de lunch**	duh lernsh
dinner	**het diner**	het dee-nay
main course	**het hoofdgerecht**	het hoaft-ghuh-rekht
starter, first course	**het voorgerecht**	het vohr-ghuh-rekht
dessert	**het nagerecht**	het naa-ghuh-rekht
dish of the day	**het dagmenu**	het dahgh-munh-ew
bar	**het cafe**	het kaa-fay
café	**het eetcafe**	het ayt-kaa-fay
rare	**rare**	'rare'
medium	**medium**	'medium'
well done	**doorbakken**	dohr-bah-kuh

Menu Decoder

aardappels	aard-uppuhls	potatoes
azijn	aah-zaiyn	vinegar
biefstuk	beef-stuhk	steak
bier, pils	beer, pilss	beer
boter	boater	butter
brood/broodje	broat/broat-yuh	bread/roll
cake, taart, gebak	'cake', taahrt, ghuh-bahk	cake, pastry
carbonade	kahr-bow-naa-duh	pork chop
chocola	show-coa-laa	chocolate
citroen	see-troon	lemon
cocktail	cocktail	cocktail
droog	droakh	dry
eend	aynt	duck
ei	aiy	egg
garnalen	ghahr-naah-luh	prawns
gebakken	ghuh-bah-ken	fried
gegrild	ghuh-ghrillt	grilled
gekookt	ghuh-koakt	boiled
gepocheerd	ghuh-posh-eert	poached
gerookt	ghuh-roakt	smoked
geroosterd brood	ghuh-roas-tert broat	toast
groenten	ghroon-tuh	vegetables
ham	hahm	ham
haring	haa-ring	herring
hutspot	huht-spot	hot pot
ijs	aiyss	ice, ice cream
jenever	yuh-nay-vhur	gin
kaas	kaas	cheese
kabeljauw	kah-buhl-youw	cod
kip	kip	chicken
knoflook	knoff-loak	garlic
koffie	coffee	coffee
kool, rode de witte	coal, roe-duh off vhit-uh	cabbage, red or white
kreeft	krayft	lobster
kroket	crow-ket	ragout in bread-crumbs, deep fried
lamsvlees	lahms-flayss	lamb
lekkerbekje	lek-kah-bek-yuh	fried fillet of haddock
mineraalwater	meener-aahl-vhaater	mineral water
mosterd	moss-tehrt	mustard
niet scherp	neet skehrp	mild
olie	oh-lee	oil
paling	paa-ling	eel
pannenkoek	pah-nuh-kook	pancake
patat frites	pah-taht freet	chips
peper	pay-per	pepper
poffertjes	poffer-tyuhs	tiny buckwheat pancakes
rijst	raiyst	rice
rijsttafel	raiys-tah-ful	Indonesian meal
rode wijn	roe-duh vhaiyn	red wine
rookworst	roak-vhorst	smoked sausage
rundvlees	ruhnt-flayss	beef
saus	souwss	sauce
schaaldieren	skaahl-deeh-ruh	shellfish
scherp	skehrp	hot (spicy)
schol	sghol	plaice
soep	soup	soup
stamppot	stahm-pot	sausage stew
suiker	souw-ker	sugar
thee	tay	tea
tosti	toss-tee	cheese on toast
uien	ouw-yuh	onions
uitsmijter	ouht-smaiy-ter	fried egg on bread with ham
varkensvlees	vahr-kuhns-flayss	pork
vers fruit	fehrss frouwt	fresh fruit
verse jus	vehr-suh zjhew	fresh orange juice
vis	fiss	fish/seafood
vlees	flayss	meat
water	vhaa-ter	water
witte wijn	vhih-tuh vhaiyn	white wine
worst	vhorst	sausage
zout	zouwt	salt

Numbers

1	**een**	ayn
2	**twee**	tvhay
3	**drie**	dree
4	**vier**	feer
5	**vijf**	faiyf
6	**zes**	zess
7	**zeven**	zay-vuh
8	**acht**	ahkht
9	**negen**	nay-guh
10	**tien**	teen
11	**elf**	elf
12	**twaalf**	tvhaalf
13	**dertien**	dehr-teen
14	**veertien**	feer-teen
15	**vijftien**	faiyf-teen
16	**zestien**	zess-teen
17	**zeventien**	zayvuh-teen
18	**achttien**	ahkh-teen
19	**negentien**	nay-ghuh-teen
20	**twintig**	tvhin-tukh
21	**eenentwintig**	aynuh-tvhin-tukh
30	**dertig**	dehr-tukh
40	**veertig**	feer-tukh
50	**vijftig**	faiyf-tukh
60	**zestig**	zess-tukh
70	**zeventig**	zay-vuh-tukh
80	**tachtig**	tahkh-tukh
90	**negentig**	nayguh-tukh
100	**honderd**	hohn-durt
1000	**duizend**	douw-zuhnt
1,000,000	**miljoen**	mill-yoon

Time

one minute	**een minuut**	uhn meen-ewt
one hour	**een uur**	uhn ewr
half an hour	**een half uur**	uhn hahlf ewr
half past one	**half twee**	hahlf tvhay
a day	**een dag**	uhn dahgh
a week	**een week**	uhn vhayk
a month	**een maand**	uhn maant
a year	**een jaar**	uhn jaar
Monday	**maandag**	maan-dahgh
Tuesday	**dinsdag**	dins-dahgh
Wednesday	**woensdag**	vhoons-dahgh
Thursday	**donderdag**	donder-dahgh
Friday	**vrijdag**	vraiy-dahgh
Saturday	**zaterdag**	zaater-dahgh
Sunday	**zondag**	zon-dahgh

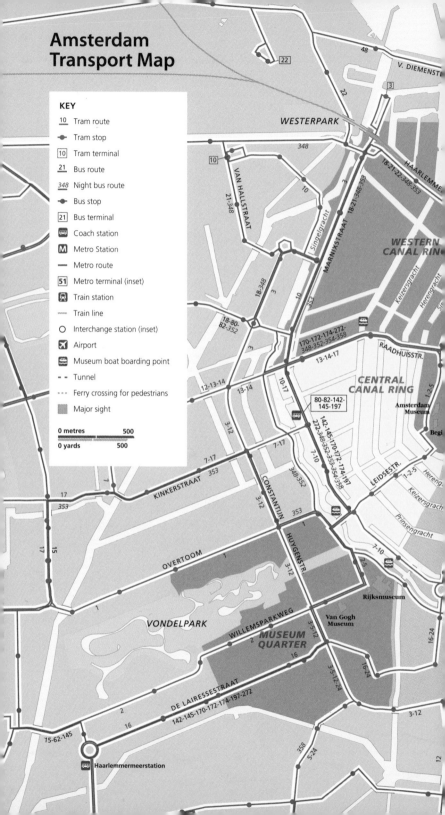